D1359678

The Loving Subject

The Loving Subject

Desire, Eloquence, and Power
in Romanesque France

Gerald A. Bond

University of Pennsylvania Press
Philadelphia

University of Pennsylvania Press
MIDDLE AGES SERIES
Edited by

Ruth Mazo Karras,
Temple University

Edward Peters,
University of Pennsylvania

A listing of the available books in the series appears at the back of this volume

Copyright © 1995 by the University of Pennsylvania Press
All rights reserved
Printed in the United States of America
Library of Congress Cataloging-in-Publication Data

Bond, Gerald A.
  The loving subject : desire, eloquence and power in Romanesque France / Gerald A. Bond.
    p.   cm. — (Middle Ages series)
  Includes bibliographical references and index.
  ISBN 0-8122-3322-0 (alk. paper)
    1. France—Civilization—1000–1328.   2. Personality.   3. Secularism—France.   4. Love in literature.   5. Bayeux tapestry—Themes, motives.   I. Title.   II. Series.
  DC33.2.B58   1995
  944'.02—dc20   95-17882
                                                                                      CIP

Frontispiece: The enigmatic scene 15, "Where a clerk and Ælfgyva . . . ," from the Bayeux Tapestry (ca. 1066–82); discussion in Chapter 1. Bayeux, Centre Guillaume le Conquérant. Reproduced by special permission of the City of Bayeux from a slide prepared by the Caisse Nationale des Monuments Historiques et des Sites, Paris.

Contents

Acknowledgments   vii

Introduction   1

1 Arresting Subjects: Ælfgyva and the Coloring of History   18

2 The Play of Desire: Baudri of Bourgueil and the Formation of the Ovidian Subculture   42

3 Natural Poetics: Marbod at Angers and the Promotion of Eloquence   70

4 Craft and Power: William of Poitiers, Courtesy, and the Impersonation of Wit   99

5 The Makeup of the Lady: Adela of Blois and the Subject of Praise   129

Conclusion   158

Appendix   166

Notes   207

Select Bibliography   263

Index   269

Acknowledgments

This book represents an interaction between my research and a long line of critical readers going back to 1983–84, when I was associated with the Centre for Mediaeval Studies at the University of Toronto. Many of those readers may still disagree with what I have done with—or done to—this historical material, but their encouragement, suggestions, and critiques have been nonetheless of enormous aid to me in my attempt to make sense of this material. I would like particularly to thank my wife Martha, Mieke Bal, Christelle Baskins, Ali Behdad, Ben Bond, Giles Constable, Roberta Krueger, Amy Lindamood, Kimberly LoPrete, William D. Paden, Brian Stock, Winthrop Wetherbee, and the anonymous readers of the manuscript for the press. Also, I have profited enormously from the readings, lectures, and discussions associated with two ongoing interdisciplinary seminars at the University of Rochester: the Cluster for Interpretation and the Susan B. Anthony Center for Women's Studies. Finally, my departmental colleagues have challenged me implicitly and explicitly over the last decade to reflect upon some of my basic assumptions, and this book has benefitted in countless ways from that challenge.

Technical aspects of the book have also received help from others. Harry Butler and Douglas Cooke assisted with the preparation and checking of the Latin texts, Rachel Bond with that of the Index, Dianne Ferriss with that of the Bibliography. The American Philosophical Society supported basic research with a Travel Grant, and my chairmen repeatedly found ways to allow me to write at crucial moments. Finally, I am grateful to the city of Bayeux for permission to reproduce images from the Bayeux Tapestry, and to Sébastien Sébal at the Caisse Nationale des Monuments Historiques et des Sites in Paris for help in obtaining them.

Portions of Orderic Vitalis, *The Ecclesiastical History*, ed. Marjorie Chibnall (Oxford: Oxford University Press, 1969–80), are quoted by permission of Oxford University Press.

amatis amissis

Introduction

In this book I seek to complicate the subject of the High Middle Ages by analyzing the changes in the conception of the private secular self that took place in French elite culture around the turn of the twelfth century. Those changes only become visible when the focus of inquiry is shifted from its traditional targets, images and texts in epic or hagiographic mode, to others in lyric or epistolary mode. Though widely cultivated and preserved at the same time, these latter modes as well as the voices in them remain essentially unexamined and uninterpreted. Specialists continue to face enormous problems in establishing reliable texts, and non-specialists often face equivalent problems in finding and understanding what has been published. I want to collect and analyze some of this extraordinary material in order to show the necessity of redrawing the current picture of French Romanesque culture and its role in the history of Western representation of the self.

My analysis develops four theses. First, in late eleventh-century France one finds theories, artifacts, representations, and practices which attest to wide-spread interest in an elite, secular, and private self. Second, cultural products of a "personal" nature could only proliferate within a social nexus which itself assigned particular value to the construct of "person," and they would only interest agents of the dominant institutions as that construct began to affect structures of power. Third, such a nexus correlates to a hybrid subculture which had developed from the increased employment of clerics, the extended education of children from wealthy and powerful families, and the expansion of a "household" directly dependent on seigneurial favor. Finally, the novel images of the self which begin to appear are neither uniform nor coherent; they represent instead contested positions within an arena of ideological controversy over the privileged issues of desire and eloquence.

The rise of a new secular culture in France during the half century or so around 1100—a period now widely recognized as pivotal—has attracted remarkably little attention. Recent studies of the period, despite the success of their revisionism, continue to be devoted primarily to the struggles between and among those who prayed and those who fought. Few even take note of the success at court and school of private and secular persons whose primary interests lay in doing something very different.

Such new persons abounded nonetheless in Romanesque images, documents, groups, and signsystems on the margins of the dominant martial and religious cultures, margins enlarged by the breakdown of the central organizational structures inherited from the Carolingian era. Many regional courts had become reasonably independent from the weak and limited king, many schools had moved far from the traditional Christian curriculum; force contested authority, knowledge contested faith. The relatively small number of interconnected families who dominated these institutions found themselves increasingly split between the demands of the military and religious professions, while the professions saw their hegemony challenged by itinerant preachers, wandering knights, and strong noblewomen. Finally, the entire cultural superstructure was being undermined by a growth in population and a redistribution of wealth which threatened its very base.[1]

In this troubled and troubling world, a new and distinctly secular group began to form, primarily between the courts of the counts and the schools of the bishops. That increasingly lettered and leisured group contested normative markers and values, and had created distinct patterns and codes of dress, manners, talk, play, and pleasure by the end of the eleventh century. At the powerful and sophisticated courts of Blois and Poitiers, for instance, new theories and practices of desire and eloquence arose which, as I attempt to make clear in the final chapters of this study, exploited the popularity of court forms of language and love for hegemonic purposes. Adela of Blois was promoting the praise of ladies in Latin lyric by the 1090s, William of Poitiers the praise of knights in Romance lyric by a decade later. Modes of ideology as well as markers of literacy, these competing models constituted two of the most successful forms of that "French elegance"[2] which would dominate European elite culture for centuries.

In the schools, the contrast between Angers and Orléans, located at opposite ends of the intellectually fertile Loire Valley, can serve to highlight the radical changes which were taking place in this period and which I will explore in detail in two middle chapters. Angers centered its interests on a new science of the material world, developing along with that a sophisticated theory of eloquence that one sees in the fascinating work of its schoolmaster, Marbod of Rennes. Orléans specialized in literary concerns, and its teachers and students such as Baudri of Bourgueil appreciated, imitated, and adapted the Classical authors. The two schools defined different positions on the forefront of an explicitly humanistic agenda around 1100 whose very existence has long been overlooked by medieval cultural critics. The common concern with nature and language accompanied radically revised practices and attitudes toward desire and its objects—both male and female—which defied the censure of ecclesiastic officials. Along with other late eleventh-century French schools at cathedrals and abbeys, they set the initial parameters for the "twelfth-century renaissance."

The great popular religious movements that swept France at this same time cannot be completely ignored. While their spiritual goals lie outside the scope of this study, their social agendas profoundly affected and were affected by the idealistic image of the individual within the new secular culture. Those movements received decisive impetus from the campaign for secular reform launched by Pope Urban II during his lengthy stay in central France in 1095–96. Pilgrims, hermits, recluses, itinerant preachers—such new figures of natural religion began to proliferate, all working in one way or another toward the apostolic goal of bringing salvation into individual lives. They particularly attracted those who felt excluded from the Church: the poor, the ignoble, and women of every class and status—in fact, these figures played an early and effective role in the struggle against misogynist practices. Such popular movements supplied voice and power to the argument for the importance and worth of individual existence which in many ways marks the twelfth century.[3]

These extraordinary developments tightly engage what I have called "the secular culture of Romanesque France." The rest of this book serves to define and defend the term in some depth, so that here I merely wish to demarcate the field. To begin with, the new culture must be distinguished (but cannot be separated) from the official and traditional ones associated with the dominant ecclesiastic and lay institutions of power. Treating "secular" as a term of orientation rather than origin, I use the word to describe those practices, discourses, images, and texts which represent an affirmative view of the social, physical, and emotional life of individuals. Like all concepts, that of "the secular" has fuzzy edges—perhaps even more than usual in Romanesque France. Yet it finds a reasonably clear center in the importance of the word and topic in contemporary discussions. In Medieval Latin the use of *seculum* pointed to the general material world and its adherents, as well as to the worldly studies or occupations pursued by clerics. In the French vernaculars the use of *mon(de)* indicated the significance of the court from the perspective not of moral depth but of social height, the locus of honor as both means and end of status. The interconnections between the Latin and vernacular terms made by their speakers define the rich domain of "the secular," whose contested development I want to study here.

By "Romanesque" I designate first the chronological limits of the study, here restricted to the pivotal half-century or so around the turn of the twelfth century when elite art itself was rapidly expanding its engagement with and representation of the secular world, and when that world's Romance languages so closely tied to the modern concept of the Romanesque definitively entered the written culture.[4] But the term's implication that things Roman—literature, philosophy, and science as well as art—particularly intrigued this period will become a more central topic as the study progresses. I will argue finally for a different notion of Romanesque than that seen through the eyes of many art historians and critics. Viewed through its conservative artifacts, Romanesque texts and images appear to lack modern notions of subjectivity.[5] Yet when viewed through its more innovative artifacts, that same culture can be seen to have developed methods of interpreting and imitating Antiquity precisely in order to fabricate new forms and means of subjectivity.

My concentration falls on France, especially that cluster of courts and schools in and around the Loire Valley which led Europe in reconceiving and representing human nature. In that region, various problems of secular identity seem to have condensed quickly onto *amor*, a word with a great range of meaning: desire, love, friendship, favor, peace, etc. This deceptive range has often hampered modern interpretive efforts. Medieval French epic is often said to ignore "love," for instance, yet the word *amor* occurs frequently even in the earliest texts. The evident slippage between Romanesque and modern usage needs to be addressed if we hope to understand how and why *amor* became such a central topic. And that understanding matters, since the ventures made into this domain established new paradigms of male and female desire that were imitated, debated, and ridiculed throughout the High Medieval period.[6]

The French exploration of *amor* necessarily proceeded hand in hand with the *inventio* of its voice within the censorious written culture. In fact, I shall argue that the representation of desire in Romanesque France was widely viewed as inextricably bound with that of eloquence—and that both were widely judged dangerous. The homology between the two is already evident in the earliest documents, as I demonstrate in the first chapter, and continues to function throughout the High Medieval period in many Latin and vernacular discussions. The linkage, caused finally by the need for a material script which lay at the heart of the new secular culture, will bounce us back and forth between language and sexuality in our examination of the Romanesque person.[7]

Because it joins desire and eloquence, finally, secular lyric occupies a central position in this study. But I understand that word to designate a mode of discourse[8] as well as a genre of literature, and include therefore other sorts of texts and images which also represent the representing self, occupy a relatively short amount of time or space, possess a certain autonomy from their context, and foreground matters of style. Such "lyric" clearly underwent a wide-ranging cultural reevaluation in Romanesque France. It is difficult to know whether more Latin poetry (especially "personal poetry") was being composed, for instance, but easy to see that much more was being preserved, often in book form by its own author. Furthermore, "personal letters" and anecdotes were recorded much more frequently in permanent form, and I repeatedly bring in such second-person and third-person modes of "lyric," though their analysis and history remain peripheral to my interests. Finally, visual "secular lyric" began to be inserted into Romanesque art, and I examine in Chapter One a stunning example from the Bayeux Tapestry not only in order to ask what and how it means, but also to raise unavoidable theoretical questions about the relations among signs, subjects, and power that govern the presentation and representation of the self.

I do not believe that one can somehow avoid theory when examining past representations of the self any more than one can avoid the particular interests and investments of the self which examines them. If there is any hope of not begging the question, therefore, it seems to me that two different theoretical discourses are required to analyze the new Romanesque person. One comes from a branch of Roman rhetoric which sought to understand the relationship between individuals and the fictive selves they promote to try to control institutions, the other from a branch of contemporary criticism which seeks to understand the relationship between institutions and the fictive selves they promote to try to control individuals.

Under the term *persona*, French Romanesque writers themselves knew a theory of a public self constructed in language which they inherited from Antiquity. Uniting and blurring English derivatives like person, personality, impersonation, personage, and persona, *persona* occupied a privileged position in Roman thought, a position derived ultimately from efforts to build around the concept of "(individual) person" the civic structures which still inform what as well as how one now names Western Civilization.[9] Apparently derived from *personare*, "to sound through," and thus implying originally a mask of the voice (and not, like Greek *prosopon*, a mask of the face), the word acquired an enormous range of often contradictory meanings.[10] In the middle of that range lay the central conception which I shall be rendering with "impersonation," understanding this term to mean something like "a character/role staged in public primarily through discourse" and to apply equally well to the sound of individual social existence as to the individual voice of rhetorical invention. This irresolvably ambiguous concept thus floats between "a being with speech" and "a speech with being," sincerity and deception, society and art. Much criticism of the Western concept of person in reality overlooks the significant and disturbing fact that it itself derives from a "device of transformation and concealment," as Robert Elliott has put it.[11] Its fundamental duplicity implies a deep instability inside this key notion, despite the fact that it and its history have been used since Antiquity to stabilize the interpretation of actions as well as texts.

It is hardly an accident that Cicero, the great Roman theoretician of rhetoric and ethics, became the authoritative source of the modern philosophic and social sense of "person" within Western culture, for he frequently speaks about (and, in the dialogues, through) *persona*, though not always consistently. One of the most succinct and influential discussions occurs in the treatise for statesmen know as *De Officiis*, where Cicero specifies that nature "dresses" us in two *personae*: a universal self defined by reason, and a particular self defined by individual traits.[12] His striking choice of the word *persona* to designate both human nature and human being exploits the centrality of discourse in the word's basic sense of "dramatic character." Merging Platonic philosophy with Aristotelian rhetoric, he produced a program of ethics to adjudicate between the conflicting demands of the two persons and their goals: virtue and utility. Because of the repeated success of educational programs based on his ideas of *humanitas*, no ancient author played a greater role in the transformation of "person" into one of the most important concepts of the dominant Western culture.

Greek dramatic technique found another and very different influential Roman interpreter a generation later in Horace. He recognized that the power of *personae (dramatis)* or "characters" comes from the fact that well-crafted words can produce in the listener the sense of the "presence" of a real person, and that they have the same capacity to stir up emotional response—a capacity which had led Plato to condemn theater at the end of the *Republic*. Horace combined dramatic technique with rhetorical (and therefore civic) discipline in his *Epistula ad Pisones* or *Ars poetica*, that prescription for composition that has influenced countless Western writers. Within the dialectic of rational prescribed technique (*ars, studium*) and natural inventive ability (*natura, ingenium*), he argued, the successful poet needs to portray characters well (154–57): "If you want [the audience] to sit and wait till the curtain comes down And the cantor intones 'vos plaudite . . . now is the time,' Make careful note of the way each age group behaves, And apply the right tone to their changeable natures and years."[13] Well-drawn characters are both technically and ethically appropriate, and the ideal poet must be an ideal citizen (309–22).

Horace's originality, both in the *Ars* and in his poems, lay in using the device while he described it, "slipping into many opposed attitudes," as C. O. Brink has argued.[14] He thus expanded and privileged the rhetorical figure of "impersonation" (*prosopopeia*) by adopting a slippery authorial voice within a lyric context. It will be useful to distinguish this invention of voices for the self from the general invention of voices for characters (*fictiones personarum*) by calling it "self-impersonation." Like Plato and his Socrates, Horace's self-impersonations destabilize the speaking subject of the text as they destabilize the truth spoken in the text.[15] Horace's irony separated him clearly from Cicero, then, because he treated "the author" as another character for which a voice must be crafted; by contrast, Cicero created his dialogic self-impersonations (Laelius, Scipio, etc.) as honest and sincere spokesmen. With support from the practices of the other Roman satirists and love-poets—about whom a contemporary historian, the obscure Velleius Paterculus, complained that "they declaim nothing in their own person"—Horace's duplicitous *persona* stands at the core of the rhetorical poetics which played such a prominent role in the medieval lyric tradition.[16]

The theories of *persona* that elided individual being and individual discourse entered the medieval period with the Christian absorbtion of the schools and curricula based on Cicero and Horace which had dominated Roman liberal education in Late Antiquity.[17] But that entry came at high cost. On the one hand, the word became entangled in discussions about the "person" of Christ; Boethius, for instance, located it at the heart of a Neoplatonist philosophy (as in *Eutyches*, 4.8: *persona vero substantia indiuidua rationalis naturae*) as well as a Neoplatonist poetics (as in *Consolatio*

Philosophiae).[18] On the other hand, influential Christian philosophers such as Augustine of Hippo separated the public self and its public language from a private self and a private language discovered through and in writing.[19] These separations and reinterpretations of the word *persona* and the concept "person" so successfully dominate our view of the medieval period today that its rhetorical and poetic usages have become invisible; even Hans Rheinfelder's extensive catalogue makes no mention of them.[20]

There do exist, of course, many studies of self-impersonation in medieval literary texts, especially those under the influence of Jean de Meun's epochal *Roman de la Rose* (ca. 1275). Leo Spitzer's 1946 study of the "poetic I" has been followed and supplemented by many others; but however well they may describe fourteenth-century narrative texts, they do not apply well to all medieval literature. Valuable studies exist of the technique of voice in twelfth- and thirteenth-century literature, especially lyric, but are rarely cited outside their own fields. And almost no attempt has been made to study Romanesque theory or practice, despite the fact that it presumably would tell us something about later techniques as well.[21]

Is there any concrete reason to think that Roman theories of self-impersonation were studied and practiced by French Romanesque writers? To begin with, as we shall see in Chapter Three, the greatest literary theoretician of the age, Marbod of Rennes, considered the invention of "characters" to distinguish the best poets, at least while he was still teaching at Angers (ca. 1067–1096). Furthermore, many of his poems display a complex practice of voice without equal in the period. Self-impersonation was an explicit concern for his contemporary Baudri of Bourgueil as well, as the following apologetic passage written probably about 1096 shows:

When I write about things as if they were real
And when I put words to many self-impersonations [*personis*]
And describe myself one time as happy, another as sad,
Or youthfully say "I love" or "I hate" something or other,
Believe me: I do not speak the truth but make it all up:
No desire has attached any covenant at all to me.
But this way of composition grew on me more
And thus I composed what corresponds to much in me;
Thus nothing more than the material seed is mine
And the fact that I thought this manner to be more clever.
Therefore, please let the verbal significance be mine,
But the material intention be its own, not mine.[22]

The distinction between *sententia* and *intentio*, the apologia for imagination, the relation between author and speaker—all this attests to a conscious practice of self-impersonation which I explore in Chapter Two. For now, I merely want to signal both the importance of the medieval *persona* for the interpretation of his poetry, and the importance of his poetry for understanding the medieval *persona*.

Having established the presence of self-impersonation in French Romanesque culture, we now need to ask how exactly it works in a text and on a reader if we want to be able to employ it later. Unlike self-reference in general, it first of all requires an explicit framework of fictionality: an assumption of honesty and sincerity precludes the perception of *persona*.[23] First-person discourse becomes self-impersonation only when the referent for the word "I" is seen to vacillate between one who makes the text and one who speaks the text—and their respective intentions. And the concept of intention, however troublesome today, is routinely invoked when self-impersonation is present. It seems to have been particularly handy to explain/excuse aberrant texts so that topic and voice could avoid censure.[24]

This vacillation in the assignment of personal reference directly affects the semantic structure of any first-person discourse. At one extreme, the "I" is explicitly indicated to be both speaker and maker; no textual marker suggests distinguishing them. At the other extreme, the "I" is explicitly indicated to belong to a fictive speaker; their distinction is so manifest that no connection can be made between them. These two extremes correspond to discrete empirical states (or at least the presumption of such states) which are usually but not always established by names indicating "this 'I' is author," or "this 'I' is non-author."

These categories of kind display great variation in degree. Speaker-is-not-author drifts increasingly toward speaker-is-author as the first-person discourse of a fictive character is perceived to increasingly undergo authorial irruptions; and there is a corresponding drift in a counter direction as the first-person discourse of the demonstrable or presumed author is perceived to increasingly undergo fictive eruptions. The more one perceives shifts from the semantic ground (either "author" or "non-author") set by the initial indices, the more one recognizes the presence of *persona*. Modern usage of the term favors the authorial ground for reasons that probably derive from the desire to retain the special features of authenticity guaranteed in everyday discourse by the use of the first person.[25]

Finally, in contrast to a figure of speech such as metaphor whose utility and pleasure comes from obscuring the determination of meaning, self-impersonation relies upon obscuring the ascription of meaning. When *persona* dominates a text, the reader has little trouble seeing meaning, because denotations remain intact; determining significance, however, is difficult, because connotations depend largely upon cultural codes which frame individual discourse. Both the desire for closure and its continual frustration establish a force with great potential to move the reader emotionally and intellectually, as well as to exploit the reader for poetic and political purposes.[26]

In treating self-impersonation thus as a textual device, I do not want to play down its equal importance as a social device. In Roman as in modern theory, *persona* also designates "the presentation of self in everyday life," as the title of Erving Goffman's influential study (1956) named it. Such models of identity have found widespread acceptance in the twentieth century among psychologists and sociologists, on the one hand, and dramatists and filmmakers on the other.[27] Within such a model, *persona* retains its full force as a willful and functional fiction of selfhood; language may never refer directly or exactly to the material world, but Roman rhetoricians and philosophers knew that there it finally had to work. Even if we no longer hear the voice which spoke Romanesque lyric nor see the body from which it came nor know the life it lived, understanding the "person" it mediated supplies us with both a method and a purpose for not severing the speaker from the spoken.

For all its power to elucidate the presence, mechanism, and significance of Romanesque impersonation, the Roman theory of *persona* seems to me unable by itself to analyze the developments I want to investigate. It remains blind, often intentionally so, to the constraining forces which must be examined if one is to explain the sudden appearance and ultimate success of the new secular person. Medieval theory of the political subject provides no aid, since without exception it serves secular and religious authority by defending the necessity of faith/troth and obedience.[28] To my mind, therefore, the most helpful critique of *persona* is found in insights about the "subject" of cultural discourse which have emerged since the 1960s. I want to take the time to explore (and modify) some of those insights because I shall argue that the concepts of *persona* and subject have much more in common than is currently acknowledged, sharing important traits in their grasp of the public self such as the centrality of language, the power of artifice, and the necessity of contradiction.

Theorists of the subject, like those of *persona*, debate many particulars. Yet they share the perception that conceptions of persons, even those held by a particular person about his or her own self, are not the natural, voluntary, expressive, and coherent vehicles of individuality, authority, or identity that they are routinely said to be. Their existence and use is, rather, largely determined by various forces which precede in time and exceed in power any particular act or agent of personal conception, and which are at best only partially perceived in everyday life. It is convenient to divide such forces into practices of institutions, features of discourse and image, or operations of the mind; yet they constantly interact, and their relative importance and effect on individuals is disputed.[29]

These inescapable forces upon conceptions of the self can be traced to dominant groups and practices which attempt to control behavior in order to maintain existing social formations. Viewed through such groups and practices, so-called "individuals" are better understood as "subjects," a term whose ambiguity stems from its earliest theorists. In a seminal discussion to which I shall return, Louis Althusser defines it as both "a free subjectivity" and "a subjected being;" since he argues that the free subject is deluded, his subject is "always already" dominated and deceived.[30] The word's ambiguity has expanded to the point that the phrase "the subject of . . ." can be completed with a large number of abstract nouns.

Althusser's insights into the tautology between ideology and subject, and into the practices that connect them, have proved critical for my investigation of the secular culture of Romanesque France, primarily because of their ability to illuminate the historical appearance and success of what we call "the individual" within official culture.[31] In a central thesis which has been widely quoted, Althusser claims that "ideology interpellates individuals as subjects" ("Ideology," p. 162), redefining the classic Marxist notion of ideology to designate an ahistoric structure, "a 'representation' of the imaginary relationship of individuals to their real conditions of existence," whose function lies in constituting subjects, as theirs lies in affirming its truth and power.[32] Forms of "interpellation" (hailing from a position of authority), the "hey, you there!" which recalls individuals to order, constitute the common and concrete practices of ideology understood in this way.

Many problems remain with Althusser's fragmentary theory (he subtitled it "notes toward an investigation"), but it has the primary advantage that it begins and ends with everyday, real-world phenomena, offering the means of particular interpretation of ideological work within historical societies.[33] Yet it is too idealist and structuralist, i.e., too restricted by a belief in a unique and all-powerful system; as Diane Macdonell comments, "ideology (singular and general) is out of place in the history of class societies. And so is 'the subject'."[34] A useful heuristic model would need to relinquish the notion of a single overwhelming ideological structure, multiply the means and media of interpellation, distinguish between the attempt and the result of the act of hailing, and reduce absolutes and necessities to generalities and probabilities, since actual human interaction like actual human language is inconsistent, fuzzy, contradictory, and downright messy.

The three terms of his central thesis, in fact, need to be adjusted without becoming lost in a detailed theoretical debate. To begin with, ideology is singular and impersonal only as a idealistic construct; in practice, one finds competing ideologies whose agents hail—sometimes simultaneously—a given individual to subjecthood. Each ideology claims its subjects to be natural, unique, coherent, and so forth, claims which conflict with those of other ideologies competing to implement the same individual. This competition among ideological systems carries important consequences, It allows, for example, an individual to elude one subject by opting for another, an form of relative subjectivity which we will find repeatedly in Romanesque documents. Althusser himself should have recognized such ideological pluralism. It lies behind the first half of the article whose second half I have been citing, Macdonell notes; and Susan James has demonstrated that in other writings "[Althusser] argues that not only do the manifestations of subjecthood change from society to society, but also the concept of subjecthood itself changes."[35]

Althusser's middle term, "interpellate," also needs modification, for his claim that individuals are "subjected" by the simple act of being hailed is too simplistic. All such hailing attempts subjection, but subjection itself can be measured finally only by the individual's playing the subject for reasons which seem to me to range from informed choice to imposed force.[36] Also, the interpellating "Hey, you!" which Althusser analyzes is always followed by the interrogating "What do you think you're doing?" which he ignores. This everyday coupling of the two acts implies that ideological agents must address performance as well as subject in order to control, as Berthold Brecht knew well, and that their immediate goal is confession, as Michel Foucault argued repeatedly.[37] Performance introduces interpretive time into subject theory, and that temporal dimension allows a wide variety of particular responses which constitute the "individual subject." Because Althusser collapsed the ideololgical drama into a single momentary act, he had little chance to imagine much less address the crucial possibility of individual agency. For him, as the social theorist Anthony Giddens famously pointed out, individuals are always "dopes." [38]

Finally, I do not see how to avoid limiting the conceptual ambiguity of the word "subject" itself. As pleasurable and significant as that may be, it seems to me that unless agent and subject remain finally distinct, subject theory will be limited to what Paul Smith has called "a purely *theoretical* subject, removed almost entirely from the political and ethical realities in which human agents actually live." [39] In this regard, Althusser's initial proposition that "ideology interpellates individuals as subjects" seems to me more accurate than his subsequent examples and explanations. One can accept that individuals act as subjects—they also act as persons—but the difference between the actor and the role cannot just be silently elided if subject theory hopes to conceive of a past or a future different from the present. For these reasons, I limit the term "subject" to public representations of the self, those common, material, and authorized images of individuals which implicitly or explicitly carry out ideological functions within a dominant discourse. [40]

Having sketched out these modifications of the three central terms of Althusser's central thesis, I want to examine the subject and its relation to the individual in more detail. Public subjects can be conceived as forming a kind of language which, like other cultural signifying systems, circulates between normative systems of storage and particular acts of usage. [41] The most obvious storage system consists of forms of naming which exist within a given language and whose significance derives from specific usages by members of groups and institutions. These forms have to begin with proper and given names which subject newborns to the history, status, conflicts, and plans of the family long before the individual is born, much less self-conscious ("What's Montague? . . . Romeo, doff thy name . . . which is no part of thee"). Nouns which designate roles, types, characters, origins, and traits perceived to be important within a given ideological program also function as subjects by assigning the individual a predetermined position and value. During the Romanesque period, for instance, certain nouns such as "lady," "knight," and "clerk" designated privileged and disputed subjects. Finally, even pronouns can carry out the work of ideology, though to my mind not actually by the widely cited structural features explicated by Emile Benveniste but by the irreversible power relations between the nominal subjects they inescapably stand in for. Not only "you," but also "them," "he/she," and "us" can serve as subjects. [42]

Important work over the last two decades has demonstrated that subjects are specified less obviously by the representations of persons displayed within, and the corresponding subject position constructed by, a large variety of cultural media.[43] Even a partial list would contain those rituals, modes of discourse, rules, norms of dress, manners, entertainment forms, architecture, and images which project a fixed position and worth for individuals and groups. Presented under the guise of some absolute such as revelation, truth, history, science, tradition, or convention, this kind of subject hides unusually well author and agent behind authority. The cults of saint and warrior which form the two main pillars of high medieval ideology supply obvious examples. Because such cultural forms are crafted from signifying practices which ideologies constantly attempt to regulate and utilize, they can never escape complicity with the structure of power; but at the same time, neither the particular production nor the particular consumption of such subjects conforms exactly, always, or everywhere to ideological design.

Understanding subjects in this way makes it easier to theorize about subjectivity without losing the agency of a conscious and concrete individual, and to historicize the implications of Althusser's theoretical insights. If ideological systems, agents, and subjects are multiple, artificial, and often competitive, each individual must build up during development a complex repertoire of self-respresentations from interactions with the subjects which have been projected effectively on him or her. The nature of such a repertory prevents me from accepting Jacques Lacan's influential argument that the child becomes a subject at a single moment in its development by "recognizing" its image in the symbolic order.[44] I see little utility for the study of concrete persons and material practices in presupposing a primal entry into subjecthood—except for analyzing documents, such as monastic confessional texts and their derivatives, which themselves presuppose such an entry. What seems to me crucial about an adult's sense of subjectivity is that it derives from multiple subjects whose ennumeration and description is valid only at the level of specific lives.

But we have to be careful here. The response of an individual hailed as a particular subject by one or more ideological agents—that is, individual subjectivity—is undeniably complex and opaque. Much of that response we cannot understand: there is no science of particulars, and it is difficult to control the interference of the observer's own sense of subjectivity. Furthermore, theorists from Ovid and Augustine to Marx and Freud have demonstrated conclusively that much of that response is not understood even by the responding individual. The individual unconscious, created by the particular collection and hierarchy of subjects into which a person has been called, constantly and covertly interacts with public presentations and common representations of the self. We can only hope to see a portion of this interaction by analyzing first-person discourse as medium and record of the "play" of particular interpellations and interrogations with particular responses and resistances: the "drama" of the subject. And this drama, I argue, forms the main impulse for and content of Romanesque secular lyric.

Subject and *persona* thus have much to say to each other. The particular virtue of the the latter lies in its ability to highlight the individual's awareness of and freedom with constructions of the public self, while that of the former lies in its ability to highlight the inevitable but routinely suppressed constraints exerted by any ideology. Through its subjects, an ideology restricts, shapes, and hierarchizes impersonations in order to limit the power of individuals; while through its self-impersonations, an individual reshapes and reinterprets subjects in order to limit the power of ideology. Subjects are thus a kind of impersonation prescribed and validated by an ideology; individuals speak and act their parts, but ideologies direct the scene. Self-impersonations, on the other hand, are always staged in the presence of subjects, but only some of them engage at any given moment the privileged subjects or plots of a particular ideology. Taken together, the two concepts provide useful and appropriate tools for the analysis of the French Romanesque secular culture precisely because they reveal its startling awareness of the link between fictions of voice, necessity of desire, and means of power in the constructions and utilizations of the new loving subject.

Let me conclude with some words about the plan and structure of this book which, despite the preceding theoretical sections, targets general readers interested in medieval culture rather than specialists in the various disciplines or methodologies it engages along the way. General access for most readers is already blocked by great difficulties with primary and secondary sources. The deep "cultural diglossia" produced by the split between oral and written cultures means that, since writing belonged primarily to a Church controlled by men, extant documents show a great bias toward the institutional, the religious, and the male.[45] Probably because of the ubiquity of official disapproval if not censure, moreover, many marginal texts have not been preserved. What has been published lies in scattered and rare sources which often lack all but the most basic forms of commentary. In fact, I take as one of my main objectives the retrieval, translation, and annotation of at least some of the main documents concerning the new Romanesque subject and the secular culture associated with it.

Coupled with my general distrust of histories derived from a single origin, tradition, or outcome, such documentary limitations have led me to adopt certain structural and methodological strategies. As a first principle, it seems to me crucial that we not view Romanesque French culture, any more than its subjects, as uniform or even coherent. In fact, it often seems best characterized (and to have characterized itself) by juxtaposition without demand for synthesis, tolerating and even encouraging the coexistence of competing forms of thinking and behavior. Dialectic enjoyed paradigmatic status in the schools, and many cultural arenas show a surprising interest in and patience with contradiction. Coherent visions, whether constructed then or now, generally portray less truth than utility.

For these reason, I have conceived this work as a composition in the literal sense, a well-formed group of studies about individual agents and documents variously interconnected. To borrow as metaphor and subvert as pun a bit of scientific terminology, the chapters of this book resemble more the "data points" than the "graph" eventually drawn around them. Pushing the analogy further, I think of the subject as the "field" upon which I "plot" the points, the signifying space within which I locate my analyses. With such a structure I hope to reduce the distortion of my own guiding thesis on the one hand, and to increase the presence of the past on the other.

The book does not attempt to write a history, although it does attempt to make an historical and theoretical argument about the significance of the dialectic between *persona* and self-impersonation. It samples the uneven and hesitant process of reconceiving the private secular person in Romanesque France by looking through the eyes of particular agents in particular institutions. Simultaneously witness and participant, actor and author, these agents produced visions and versions of the emergent culture. They are linked in diverse ways (for instance, Baudri was a vassal of William and a flatterer of Adela), but those linkages may reveal more about the results of social stasis than the causes of cultural change.

Finally, each chapter begins with a specific text (or group of texts) which differs from our current understanding of the Romanesque norm in its conception of person and attitude toward voice. These texts all resist clear and coherent analysis in one way or another, triggering thereby a set of questions which initiate an examination of their various interpretive codes. Although I repeatedly draw comparisons and contrasts among the chapters, I primarily want to elucidate the texts with relation to their own particular system(s) of meaning. Such a composite approach has the virtue of returning the reader repeatedly to the raw material of history: previous and particular interpretations of experience within previous and particular frameworks of analysis. By keeping the beginnings complicated, I hope to recover enough neglected artifacts and neglected ideas to entice others to look, or look again, at this intriguing moment in Western European culture.

1. Arresting Subjects: Ælfgyva and the Coloring of History

Any study of the dialectic between *persona* and subject that characterizes the Romanesque secular "loving subject" must begin with the representation of the subjection of desire and eloquence which the martial aristocracy wanted to have displayed.[1] One of the most intriguing examples occurs within the famous Bayeux Tapestry, arguably the greatest extant work of secular art in the eleventh century. In the midst of a carefully planned narrative designed to legitimate the invasion of England, a curious and disruptive scene (see Frontispiece) arrests the spectator's look. The Latin caption, "Where a clerk and Ælfgyva . . ." (*Ubi unus clericus et Ælfgyva*), draws attention because it displays both a unique ellipsis of the verb and a vernacular use of the indefinite article, hinting in this way at cultural struggles which informed the production and interpretation of the image.[2]

The couple stands behind what has always been taken to represent a doorway, although every other doorway in the Tapestry has a rounded ("Romanesque") arch, and this might better be seen as another of the many cut-away views of buildings. Formed of two unusual striped columns with animal head finials connected by a carved lintel, it represents by conventional synecdoche a great house apparently located in Rouen, William's Norman capital.[3] The upper border contains directly overhead a small stylized plant separating a pair of animals and a pair of birds, items that repeat throughout most of the Tapestry; the lower border contains another such plant situated between a male nude and a pair of dragons.[4] Both borders may comment upon the scene, although their relevance has been disputed.

Identified by her name as English and by the name's very inscription as noble, Ælfgyva is the only full-sized female figure in the Tapestry.[5] She is dressed in traditional garb, wearing an ample, floor-length, green outer garment with extremely full sleeves and a border at the bottom; her head and shoulders are covered by a red kerchief. One can see, especially on her left arm, the sleeves of a red shirt she wears underneath. She stands centered within the architectural frame, three-quarters turned toward the observer, arms parallel and bent, hands open, looking to her left at the tonsured *clericus* or "clerk." He wears the clothes of a noble at leisure: brown shoes, red hose, a knee-length tan tunic bordered at the bottom, belted at the waist, and laced at the wrist, and a voluminous blue cape gathered at the throat by an unusually large rectangular brooch. He stands in a frontal pose with legs spread, leaning and looking to his right toward Ælfgyva. With his left hand upon his hip, he extends his right out behind the near column to contact her left cheek.

Much has been said—and much more not said—about the act depicted in this most puzzling scene. Despite visual parallels, even recent critics still deny that image meant to imply actual sexual intercourse.[6] Given the lower border, I have no doubts about the scene's general content; given the clerk's pose, however, I do have doubts about specific intent. Does the scene portray "lover and lady," "rapist and victim," or something in between? Ironically, the question of sexual violence (much less that of the gendered subject) never seems even to have been asked. Taste and propriety always betray as much as they reveal of the past, and in this case they have actually obscured what I would like to call the heart of the matter.

The Bayeux Tapestry treats otherwise but of politics and war: why, then, is this image of desire included, and why here? It is the most enigmatic episode in the tapestry's narrative, but its allusion obviously made some kind of sense to at least some viewers. It would be nice to know who Ælfgyva and the clerk were, and to know for sure what happened, but I do not intend to contribute to the long list of commentators attempting factual identification.[7] In the first place, my interest (and that, I shall argue, of the Tapestry's creators) starts with a different problem: the contrast between the eye's attraction to and the mind's neglect of features such as texture, color, and volume. Exploring their struggle for and with meaning will point in the direction of a very different hermeneutic than the one usually identified with the Romanesque image.[8] Furthermore, I do not believe that the scene's significance depends upon the particular story it hoped to recall. Its work proceeded with indifference to the distinction between event or story, present or past, rape or love, and I want to argue that that indifference itself forms the latent content. Finally, because embroidery was tightly associated with the very construct of the feminine, the panel helps recover some of the history of secular medieval women, particularly important in a period where little other information is available.[9] In these ways it reveals more about cultural history than political, and the struggles it portrays can teach us much about the suppressing and suppressed traits of the feudo-heroic culture.

The work of interpreting an artifact, like that of creating it, proceeds within particular contexts. Only by examining with care these contexts, whether medieval or modern, can we hope to get "outside" them. In this case, it is particularly important to review the research on the political frame of the Tapestry's message on the one hand, and the material frame of its production on the other.

This "tapestry" is not, in fact, a tapestry at all, but an unusually narrow (about 50 centimeters, or 20 inches) and unusually long (about 70 meters, or 230 feet) piece of embroidery consisting primarily of figures created with wool on a bleached linen background in a style known as "laid and couched work." It has been called a "hanging" in more recent discussions, but its strong linearity has also suggested "strip-cartoon," "frieze," and even "film."[10] It showed up in the documentary record for the first time in 1476 as "a very long and narrow stretch of fabric embroidered with images and captions representing the conquest of England which is stretched around the nave of the church during the feast and octave of the relics" in the cathedral at Bayeux; few now believe that was its original site.[11]

Strong circumstantial evidence supports the conclusion that it was commissioned sometime between 1066 and 1082 by Odo, half-brother to William the Conqueror and Bishop of Bayeux from 1049/50 to 1097.[12] Portrayed a generation after his death by Orderic Vitalis as eloquent, generous, courtly, ambitious, and "a slave to worldly trivialities," Odo became after the Conquest the second wealthiest man in the Anglo-Norman realm after the king himself.[13] He was acutely aware of the power of patronage, and spent lavish sums of money on churches and monasteries as well as on the education and training of clerks for secular and religious positions. His attraction to "the secular," a word Orderic repeatedly links with him, included all the typical activities of a noble male: eating, drinking, fighting, and loving—a son, John, is attested.[14] He counted among his protégés not only some of the most significant churchmen of the age, but also some of its most significant poets: Serlo of Bayeux, Hildebert of Le Mans, and probably Marbod of Rennes. All three paid their debts with obsequious encomia during the 1080s, when Odo's arrest for attempting to buy the papacy (1082) and his banishment for revolting against William Rufus (1088) had badly damaged his power and reputation. He ended his days as a participant in the First Crusade, dying in Sicily early in 1097 on his way to Jerusalem.

The Tapestry he commissioned constructs a version of the Conquest justifying the Norman invasion and takeover of England and emphasizing the importance of Bayeux, its relics, and its bishop. It aims thus not simply to recall and please, but to interpret and persuade, its function as much political and rhetorical as mnemonic and aesthetic. These traits permit us to identify it as "official culture," actively shaped by figures of central power, and therefore as a deeply ideological artifact.[15] Like contemporary Norman historians, it argues that the assumption of the English crown by Harold, earl of Wessex, upon the death of his brother-in-law Edward the Confessor in January of 1066 constituted a betrayal of the latter's promise to make William of Normandy his successor; and that Harold, as Edward's primary supporter, had personally provided surety for this promise. To render that interpretation visible, the embroidery unites two tales: Harold's Voyage to Normandy, and William's Conquest of England.

The story of the Voyage, which probably occurred in 1064, contains in turn two clearly separated narrative units: "Harold's Journey" to William's court (Plates 1–17a in the superb complete facsimile by David Wilson) and "William's Expedition" to Brittany (Plates 18–28). English sources seem correct in stating that Harold undertook the journey to free a brother and a nephew held hostage by William since 1052, when he had helped Edward come to the throne; the most coherent interpretations of the culminating scene at Rouen see in it Harold's plea for the release of his nephew. Norman sources recount simply that Harold went to renew his earlier promise to William.[16] The "Expedition" documents the various types of troth established between the two men, including those of comrade, host, and ally. Seen from subsequent events, these narratives illustrated to a Norman audience William's "faith" and Harold's "treason," justifying the eventual seizure of the English crown. The location of the Ælfgyva panel on the seam between these narrative units of a tale of English betrayal supplies a first indication of its significance in Norman eyes.

Finally, the only account of the activities at Rouen is a single sentence in the official history of William of Poitiers: "[The duke] then led Harold with all due honor into Rouen, the capital city of his principality, where various kinds of courteous hospitality refreshed in a most entertaining manner those who had suffered through the effort of the journey."[17] Little attention has been paid to this unique source by interpreters of the Ælfgyva scene. Since William's history, while independent in origin, generally correlates closely to that of the Tapestry, the Ælfgyva scene might somehow be seen as the designer's attempt to represent abstract concepts such as courtesy, hospitality, and entertainment, in order to establish an important aspect of Duke William's image as secular ruler.[18] Locating the historicity of the panel in such performative terms provides very different answers to the problems it poses than those proposed until now.

The material and cultural implications of the medium will also aid the interpretation of the Ælfgyva panel. By what process did such an object come into being, and what role did it usually play in its own society? Fortunately, a surprising amount of contemporary testimony exists on these topics.[19] To begin with, English embroidery stood in high regard throughout the Anglo-Saxon period, and was the most common form of "art" (although to call it so is to deform it) patronized and enjoyed by the preconquest nobility. The extant record only hints at the staggering loss of embroidery and weaving similar to the Tapestry, which, if preserved in any quantity at all, would revolutionize our conception of medieval art. This medium praised the power of fighting men and provided a daily "text" (woven artifact) of aristocratic life celebrating prowess and fame. The late eleventh-century court was literally surrounded by these storied images, positioning its collective self within a social and ethical space whose significance lay displayed on the material means of its closure.

The technique of embroidery, like that of painting, plays a significant role in establishing its expressive register, as George Digby's description makes clear:

> In laid and couched work, first the threads are laid over a given area, packed tightly together to give a massed effect which fills the contours of the figure from edge to edge; secondly, another series of threads, usually but not necessarily of the same colour, is laid at right angles to these, this time at short intervals one from another, usually about ⅛ of an inch apart; lastly, these are couched down with the same thread which secures each of them and so holds the whole complex firmly in position. . . . The outline of the contours of the figures is worked in stem or outline stitch, as are all of the thin lines.[20]

The bold masses of color and the outline stitch add the detail and precision which carry the primary responsibility for the hanging's overall "legibility," a particularly striking feature of this work.[21]

Digby demonstrates as well that the Tapestry required three discrete artistic functions: historian, designer, embroiderer.[22] Of these the first and second—often combined in a single person—were generally executed by men. A passage in a version of the *Life of Saint Dunstan* written around 1070 by Osbern, precantor at Christchurch in Canterbury, furnishes a good example of the ambient understanding of the relationships among these functions/persons. As a young man at the royal court, "[Dunstan] was compelled by the repeated and religious request of a certain lady to sketch out (*praepingeret*) a priestly stole with artistic technique which then she adorned with figures (*figuravit*) for sacred ritual by copying that in gold-work."[23] With the double authority of historian and designer, Dunstan functioned as the image's "prefigurer," setting the parameters for rational interpretation by carefully selecting the determining signifiers (costume, gesture, word, position) from the various codes available to him.

Such a view of a harmonic synthesis between the two artistic functions is, of course, idealistic. Since line and figure carry the weight of denotative semantics, no designer can escape historical intention, but in practice other intentions enter and often interfere. Those of the Tapestry's designer are perhaps seen most clearly when one examines a black-and-white photograph of the back side of the panel (see p. 24), where the embroiderers' work least distracts the eye. Formal intention generally faces the technical challenge to represent in a still and visual medium a story of deeds characterized by motion and emotion. In the Tapestry, the physical, discursive, and causal motions typical for the heroic main story raise most of the technical difficulty, but in this "lyric insert" about Ælfgyva the problem is one of emotion. The use of the "pregnant moment" (the traditional phrase seems particularly apt) as a pictorial device represents a classic solution, with classic problems for the historical intention, as we shall see.[24]

In addition to a formal intention, the designer also shows a material intention through his obvious pleasure in play, especially noticeable at horizontal and vertical margins. The towers and trees that divide the larger syntagmatic units of meaning are literally para-graphic; their syntactic status releases form from meaning, and they become fantastic.[25] The upper and lower borders, carefully distinguished from the main text, also routinely escape historical intention. Until the Battle of Hastings overwhelms them, these Other Worlds are dedicated primarily to vegetable and animal nature, drawn in a ludic and fabulous manner, only occasionally yielding to the hegemony of the linear discourse.

Finally, the designer actually appears to have had separate historical intentions. Good evidence has been accumulated that he was an Anglo-Saxon, likely a monk at Saint Augustine's in Canterbury who had access not only to English images but also to English histories.[26] Most striking

The reverse side of scene 15 (see Frontispiece) from the Bayeux Tapestry (ca. 1066–82). Bayeux, Centre Guillaume le Conquérant. Reproduced by special permission of the City of Bayeux from a slide prepared by the Caisse Nationale des Monuments Historiques et des Sites, Paris.

is his interpretation of "Harold's Voyage" from an English point of view, as only English texts report that Harold undertook the journey for his family's sake (perhaps without Edward's permission). As recent historians have argued, "The Tapestry, then, seems to have one message for its Norman audience, but also to hint at a version known to the Canterbury writer, Eadmer."[27] That such a struggle would exist and would be represented in the representation advises caution as we proceed.

The third artistic role, that of the embroiderers, belonged without exception in this period to women, as the passage about Dunstan suggests. Until the commercial success of thirteenth-century English embroidery (the *opus Anglicanum* praised throughout Europe), such work—simultaneously handwork and hard work—lay beneath male genius and its value structure. Osbern's contrast between his saint's creation (*operatio*) and the lady's imitation (*imitatio*) neatly expresses the gendering of artistic process which would become standard in Western discourse. The labor of embroidery proceeded in a variety of locations, according to eleventh-century evidence, from aristocratic sewing circles to the private work of peasant women. Content and style have suggested to most observers that the Tapestry was embroidered by noblewomen, but whether in a secular or religious context remains unsure; both are attested. The interrelated hierarchies of labor, gender, and cultural value complicate interpretation, as we shall see when we return to the problem of texture and color.[28]

These multiple creators finally raise the issue of mnemonic agency within the feudo-heroic society. An often quoted entry in a cartulary from the monastery at Ely records a donation from a noblewoman named Ælflæd of "a hanging woven and embroidered with the deeds of her husband designed in memory of his prowess." That husband was Byrhtnoth of Essex, one of the most powerful military men in England, about whose glorious death in 991 a very different and, as it turned out, more permanent record was also constructed: the Old English epic known as *The Battle of Maldon*.[29] The picture of the service rendered to the chivalric culture by these two "documents" and their agents, the lady and the clerk, is useful. The similarity of their nearly invisible labor to glorify and preserve that right memory so fundamental to the martial aristocracy signals a common frame whose further exploration will advance our interpretation of the panel.

Both lady and clerk were positioned in many ways outside, beneath, and even against the culture and discourse which produced the Tapestry and which it both reflects and reflects upon. In order to demonstrate this position and simultaneously to begin to tease out the text's various strands, we need to examine the two "intentions," both narrative and aesthetic, which struggle over the reading of the Ælfgyva panel. I shall argue that the former is a product of institutions of "masculine" power, the latter of mechanisms of "feminine" pleasure. Power has its pleasure, of course, and pleasure its power, and neither is essentially gender-marked; we will have to use caution in employing such a simple and simple-minded binary structure. Its utility here relies upon the generalism that the official discourses of neither the feudo-heroic nor the ecclesiastic culture of the late eleventh century condoned the pursuit of pleasure. To reduce anachronism, we might better consider such discourse as "high story," a kind of well-crafted narrative, part "story" and part "history," whose existence and preservation cannot be separated from the power of the "high" or dominant group. Heroes and saints in such high story fled the seductions of the feminine world with exemplary success, and the increasingly intense promotion of their composite, known to crusading pilgrims as the *miles Dei*, could only reinforce that position.

Looking first at the panel's narrative intention, oriented along the warp and weft of the linen background, one notes immediately that it aims to condemn. Although straightforward enough in content, the mechanism of that condemnation rewards detailed examination. The Tapestry's horizontal axis determines the linear sequence of captions and figures (the syntagm) and, even missing specifics, we must concur with the argument that the Ælfgyva panel relates somehow to the concern with illegitimate coupling and illegitimate succession. Only conceived as an act of "English bad faith" could it appear here within the embroidery if contiguity, syntagm's glue, were to be conserved. Only as a marker of status and a vessel of lineage would a woman, even a noblewoman, fit into such a story. The privacy of the sexual subject is itself denied on this axis by the location and publication of the image. Whether Ælfgyva yields or resists, she as woman will carry the blame—for that reason and to that end she is named. Either act would be treated by the law as a crime against male property: she threatens status by bringing shame and subverts lineage by introducing bastards. In all the senses of the word, Ælfgyva is "framed" by the house at whose exact center she stands. The horizontal condemnation thus aligns with aristocratic history itself which, as William Brandt has shown in persuasive detail, structured time, space, and causality (not to mention gender) along dynastic lines.[30]

The vertical axis, on the other hand, establishes an ecclesiastic world-view through the figures in the lower border. Their general function has been discussed to a certain extent, yet it seems to me that semiotic theory offers a very precise term which aids their interpretation: external focalizor. Mieke Bal defines the term with respect to both images and texts as an element outside the narrative which mediates between the agent of seeing and the object of view.[31] In this panel, one focalizor is designated by the dominant diagonal from the upper right to the lower left which leads the eye from the urbane clerk to his alter ego, the libidinous male nude in the border. Except for the hair and the detailed genitalia, filled in conspicuously with light brown thread, the figure is rendered in a simple outline stitch that always lends an element of caricature, as Digby has commented.[32] Literally and figuratively emptying the sign of urbanity by reducing a master of culture to a slave of nature, the diagonal establishes a satirical force on the clerk by stripping him of ornament. The objective of such ecclesiastic "humor" is to guarantee moral reading, to which the clerk himself points the way. His left hand and arm establish what I take to be a gesture of *superbia*, which otherwise only the equally reprehensible Guy, Count of Ponthieu (Pl. 10b), and Harold (Pl. 31a) use, both at the moment of breaking faith. The right hand, probably denoting motion, connotes transgression and possession by crossing a physical barrier which, as image, represents by metonymy the social and moral limits associated with the kind of family which would own such a house. Furthermore, visual analogues make clear that "face-fondling" was an established gesture of sexual interest as well as sexual aggression.[33] Thus the vertical axis first attacks the clerk as he violates his minor orders.

The impulse for symmetry argues implicitly for a second focalizor, for the alternate diagonal from upper left to lower right leads to another accusing figure in the lower border. The focalizor indicated by this diagonal under-stands Ælfgyva as a bipedal dragon of bidirectional flame known in her language as a "firedrake" (*fyrdraca*). Firedrakes appear elsewhere in the borders, but remain primarily ornamental until placed below this highly charged space where latent meanings are quickly activated.[34] Educated spectators (originally, Odo and his entourage) recall now that the Anglo-Saxon name of that dragon consists of elements that carried within ecclesiastic ideology the universal connotations of "desire" and "evil." This *omen* rejects from an ecclesiastic orientation the very specificity of her *nomen* in the caption. Glossing over her identity, the commentator can only see her as Woman, the favorite tool of the devil. Where the horizontal axis denies privacy through specificity, then, the vertical denies historicity through typology. Allegorized into an image of worldly temptation, the whole incident finally reveals itself as but a local form of the ancient commerce between Luxuria and Superbia.[35] Thus the ecclesiastic commentator attempts to "cancel" the image with a chiasmic gloss which imposes morality through satire and allegory. Rejecting whore and lecher, he joins forces with the feudo-heroic commentator in attacking unauthorized desire.

These two axes of symbolic power signal a new concern with social control, for with the Conquest came both a reformed state through the imposition of a tight feudal society and a reformed church through the imposition of the Gregorian program. With the possible exception of Norman Sicily, no other medieval state was in a better position to tax, discipline, and punish its subjects—no more efficient bureaucracy would be created before the Renaissance.[36] These beginnings of a rational and rationalized system of control which could reach down to the level of individual private life—a process reified in England by the Domesday Book a decade later—will eventually produce the ubiquitous system of subjects exposed by Michel Foucault's analyses of eighteenth-century France. The attack on Ælfgyva and the clerk seems to me to herald this new age, and to justify our seeing it as a first glimpse of a modern ideological apparatus. In its concern to extend and strengthen its grasp, the Anglo-Norman union of ideologies unwittingly shows its hand, betrayed by its desire to craft subjects whose "love," fidelity, and service it can control for its own needs.

Despite there being some consolation in the fact that the designer's desire to arrest sexual subjects in the act permits us to arrest a new ideology in the act, we have nevertheless allowed the image's discursiveness to overwhelm our thinking—in fact, to force us to think with what its historian would define as rationality by preferring the (visual) gloss to the (visual) text. In order to escape that trap, we need to read and judge the image while ignoring external condemnation, as desire itself ignores societal injunction, in order to turn to the question of aesthetic intention. If we block out narrative intention through close and closed reading, we gain sufficient time to allow the image to provoke alternate readings, since its craft can maintain a defense against the textual forces besieging it. That defense relies on an intention to engender desire, which relies in turn on the female embroiderers whose mediating presence, like that of the stitches before our eyes, has been looked through more than looked at.

Gender has, in fact, received even less attention than sex in discussions of the Tapestry's meaning. The Ælfgyva panel acutely raises the question, however, for its embroiderers may be presumed without undue anachronism to have been particularly invested in "filling in the details" of the prefigurer's sketch. A beautiful young noblewoman and a handsome, young, urbane clerk—this is the stuff of romance, and they could hardly have avoided experiencing a powerful reaction, whether positive or negative, to the embroidered subject. I need not rely simply on the tacit assumption of a putative psychological continuity across ages or genders, since the settings of certain Old French lyric genres such as the *chansons de toile* or *chansons d'histoire* prove that noblewomen indulged in erotic revery while stitching—or at least in the fantasy of such revery, if one takes the setting to be wholly fictional. Modern ethnography, moreover, has documented the close associations among handwork circles, singing, and communal female fantasy in a variety of world cultures.[37] Thus we can conclude with some confidence that, for the first and only time in the Tapestry, the embroiderers saw themselves reflected in their work, although what "self" they saw and how they could "see" it at all are topics that cannot be passed over lightly. For now, it is sufficient to conclude that these embroiderers could hardly avoid being "hailed" or "interpellated" as subjects by the arresting scene they set out to lay and couch.

How exactly did this occur? Throughout most of the Tapestry, the embroiderers work invisibly. Relying primarily on color and texture, their craft produces a beauty that usually aligns itself with ideology; filling out designs of aggression beneath texts of hegemony, it serves by intriguing, pleasing, clarifying, and persuading. But these functions change with the subject(s) projected by the Ælfgyva panel. Its suggestive appeal retards the look, distracting and relieving it from the pressure of narrative intention. The laudatory beauty of the figures and garments it creates in the medium counters the condemnation in the high story prefigured for it. Here, for a single moment, aesthetics contests ideology for control of interpretation.

In embroidery, beauty primarily consists of color, texture, and volume, but what and how can these traits signify when they notoriously resist interpretation? No code translates such features in the Tapestry; the color blue, for example, does not *mean* anything here. Moreover, the three interact and interfere easily in embroidery: volume establishes ground as well as figure does, one color constrains the choice of the next, and texture affects the perception of both.[38] If anything, they only give witness to the medium's technical limitations. Only a few colors lay at the embroiderers' disposal; five are employed for most of the Tapestry, with another three added occasionally. A single embroidery technique (itself required by the enormous surface to be covered) determines a texture whose only variation comes from the different alignments of the threads. These factors can be said thus to constitute a syntax without a semantics, a code without a message. They signal at most their own presence, but, almost blessedly, signify nothing. In fact the pleasure of beauty has to include—in this case, at least—the relief from the pressures of reason and power.

Yet lack of meaning cannot be equated with lack of significance. In the first place, by calling attention to themselves, these features entice the spectator's look to the image's surface, and induce it to remain there through the pleasure it mediates. This pleasure in surface and material characterizes the entire medium; in fact, it lies at the heart of the traditional categorization of embroidery as craft and not art. But for its creators, "superficiality" constitutes a virtue rather than a fault, for it locates genius in the act of shaping, not escaping, material.

Significance also arises from the inevitable relation of signifying practices to ideologies and their subjects, a relation that exists because the centers of power supply the final signified (the connotation of connotation) of signs in its domain, irrespective of the signifier or its initial signified. Dramatic characters, social types, and subjects are signs (or sign clusters), and as such can be produced, projected, modified, and imposed by official institutions with an authority that silently pressures individuals into "choosing freely" scripted identities. Such "symbolic power" (control over the production, use, and interpretation of signs) was little contested at the start of the Romanesque period in France: power lay largely in the regional, personal, and irrational force of specific agents rather than in the ubiquitous, impersonalized, and rational power of a general discourse that has been found in the modern age.[39]

There is another significance to the lack of meaning for color, volume, and texture in embroidery. "Palpable" signs like few others, they mark in the aesthetic metacode the dominance of the "poetic" function, as Roman Jakobson used the term, in the image conceived as message.[40] That function's prominence points to embroidery's cult of the visible signifier, not the latent signified. Embroiderers (along with other "craftsmen") make no pretense about illusion, no claim for truth. Reworking Ovid's famous comment about Pygmalion (*Metamorphoses* 10.252), we can say that "ars adeo *patet* arte sua," their art lies in fact *exposed* in its technique.[41] The embroiderers' pleasure and power lie in making visible the means of representation, in loudly declaring through texture that the work is artifice. This attitude also marks rhetoric, the persuasive art of verbal decoration, and it is hardly an accident that ornaments of language were called *colores* (*rhetorici*). In Romanesque France the popular treatise by Marbod of Rennes (himself a flatterer of Odo of Bayeux) had reestablished the means and goals of such decoration, as we shall see in Chapter Three. Rhetoric and embroidery share the ambiguous task of pleasing and persuading, but they also tend to interfere with mechanisms of meaning as they ornament, diverting attention and subverting intention by coloring the history they relate.[42]

In this manner, these features of embroidery mark the spatial and temporal "presence" of those working it, the embroiderers, like the deictic function of language that announces the presence and interest of the speaker. In other words, these apparently empty signifiers point outside the work to the context of its production, because only there can one find the female labor that they trace and the social formation exploiting it. Essentially excluded from positive representation within the signified, the female embroiderer appropriates the signifiers and their interplay for her self-representation.[43] Her position right in front of this panel, over whose subjecting construction she literally pre-sides, must be taken to establish a position of close reading—in this medium, at least, an act which is strongly gender marked—since only from that site can craft's pleasure be felt.[44]

The self-referential technique of embroidery thus serves here to arrest *the look*, in Norman Bryson's sense, at a subject of power by provoking what we might call *the stare* at its surface.[45] As it binds that subject to a text of beauty and craft, it evokes the momentary projection of another subject. The result is that the panel becomes the locus of a struggle between the poetic and the referential, desire and duty, pleasure and power. The story told in and of this struggle allows us to explore more deeply the nature of the disruption caused by the appearance of these unruly subjects within dominant Romanesque discourse.

But our hope to recreate meaning, to make sense, still faces significant obstacles. The panel itself lacks the necessary visual and narrative detail—as one sees well with the modern questions about whether the Clerk is striking or stroking Ælfgyva—to transmit sufficient information about character or plot. As with any underdetermined text, the observer is caught between knowing too little and guessing too much. Without sufficient visual information, neither we nor the Norman audience can "see" the panel's significance, a dangerous blindness in an artifact where significance and power interlock. How, then, does it work? How could it hope to work?

It has always been assumed that the historical incident was well known, an intuitive position I took at the beginning of this discussion. This is also the theoretical position of the "pregnant moment" device, as Wendy Steiner's comment (about painting) makes clear: "More generally, the temporal limits of painting could be overcome by isolating a moment in the action that revealed all that had led up to it and all that would follow . . . [it] is obviously associated with historical and iconographic art, since it usually cannot function with full effect unless we already know the story captured in the moment of the painting."[46] But the split in subject induced by this lyric insert changes both "us" and "our" knowledge. It urges us—but now my phatic use of this pronoun suddenly seems less innocent—to reconsider the actual process of understanding which is undergone by a complex and disparate group of viewers, including ourselves. This one panel fractures the observing group and its "knowledge" along lines of nationality, profession, power, class, and gender, and in that fracturing lies much of its value. The sudden presence of multiple and competing interpretive codes and subjects warns us against the kind of iconographic determinism where formal analogy can seem to certify unique and coherent origin, content, or significance.[47]

For these reasons, it does not matter whether the panel displays event, high story, or even fiction. If it was an event, presumably only Ælfgyva and the clerk witnessed (as they participated in) this particular scene, and its representation here is consequently already an imaginative construct. Hence even the Tapestry's earliest viewers could only have understood the panel through the fiction it cues. Furthermore, within a very short time any particular knowledge about it—or at least the particular significance of such knowledge—must have been lost, for otherwise it is difficult to explain its absence in all contemporary written sources. We do not have a window upon historical reality, in other words; its significance is not "out there." The image has been highly interpreted not only through existing structures of language and image, of course, but also through paradigm (especially "stock characters"), syntagm (story), and setting.

The high story of Ælfgyva and the clerk was grasped within its own culture, then, rather through the history of its representations than through its representation of history. In the leading role, Ælfgyva stands for the conventionally noble, beautiful, and educated young ladies of the Anglo-Saxon court. Whoever she was, whatever her exact role in the event, and whatever its outcome, that figure served as a privileged site of both fear and pleasure. As feminist criticism and theory has amply demonstrated, the female body provides the best currency in any patriarchal economy. Moreover, precisely because female sexuality figured so prominently in the dominant secular ideology of the Romanesque period, at whose center lay the "conjugal bed," as Georges Duby puts it, it supplied the readiest marker of both service and revolt. Thus even the bare outline of Ælfgyva's act and story serves to elicit for medieval even more than for modern viewers an image of the power of the female body to "disturb" readers of high story.[48]

From the perspective of the feudo-heroic institution, a noblewoman's significance lay in her ability to promote the dominance and permanence of the male hierarchy. Her relationship to husband, brother, father, or lover acquired representational status by virtue of their implications for that ideological program. Only her role in that highest of high stories mattered, and official forms of Romanesque secular culture such as the Tapestry remained completely indifferent to "the rest" of her actions or emotions. Whether Ælfgyva was worshiped or violated by the clerk, her effect on the status and lineage of the house that frames her would be destructive, and she would be condemned. The image, in other words, did not need to specify the act in any more detail, for no more "facts" were required of the Tapestry's designer within the social formation he sought to represent.

In Romanesque secular culture, both official and general, stories circulated about the subjection of female sexuality to male power, and about women who sought to escape that subjection. Many of those stories, as Kathryn Gravdal has pointed out, are rape stories of one form or another. The standard medieval vernacular term for "to rape" (from the Latin "to seize") was "to force (a woman)" (*esforcier* [*une femme*] in Old French), and in a certain sense the female body was always "forced" by feudo-heroic practice, as by its representations.[49] For a relevant example one could hardly do better than to turn to the Norman historian, William of Poitiers, whose high story so closely matches that of the Tapestry itself. After a Poitevin education, he served the Duke of Normandy for more than a decade before becoming (ca. 1065) archdeacon at Lisieux, apparently until his death. The extant portion of his encomiastic history, like the Tapestry, tells only of one woman at any length; she enters just after the conclusion of the victorious campaign in Brittany:

> The Prudent Victor, Dutiful Parent, wanted also to have provided for all time and in the best way for his children. For this reason he decreed [in 1064] that the sister of Herbert [count of Maine] would be brought to him from Teuton lands with very great expenditure of his munificence and marry his

> son [Robert Curthose], in order that through her he and his progeny would possess Herbert's inheritance by right, as his sister's husband and nephews, so that no dispute would weaken it or tear it away. And since the boy was not yet advanced enough in age for marriage, [William] had the nearly nubile girl kept under guard with great honor, entrusting her to the care of noble and wise men and ladies.
>
> This highborn virgin, named Margarita, was more worthy for her famous beauty than any pearl (*margarita*). But not long before the day she was to be joined to her mortal husband, the Son of the Virgin, Husband of Virgins, and Heavenly Emperor took her away from men; the dutiful girl burned for him with a healing fire, she yearned for his desire with prayer, abstinence, pity, humility—in sum with every goodness, vehemently wishing to not know any wedlock but his.[50]

This tale would have been neither significant nor recordable without the twin ideological values of right succession on the one hand and divine justice on the other. For the first, a son was obligatory, and he had to be of age and worthy in order to be able to resist challenge from neighbors, vassals, overlords, or relatives. Since the second-born Robert Curthose was but a ten-year-old, his claim to power required strong measures indeed if the permanence of his father's dominance were to be guaranteed. In such cases, the best plan always called for the seizure and forcing of whatever woman happened to function as agent and sign of right succession—in this case, the daughter of the captured count Walter and his wife, whose subsequent poisoning the historian neglects to tell. Margarita's will and desire are irrelevant to the dynastic story the duke wants told, and she exists only as "Herbert's sister." The historian names her in the second half, but only for the purpose of appropriating the virgin's desire with which he plays for the story of Christ. With her body hailed as the historical subject and her heart as the hagiographical, Margarita's person—like Ælfgyva's— is exhausted by the dominant ideological programs that conspire to arrest her.[51]

This example from the Tapestry's immediate cultural milieu reveals clearly the perpetual genetic subplot that served to figure noblewomen within official culture predominantly in their capacity to engender "lines" of heredity and power, known to the secular world as lineage. Margarita is further subjected by discourse as well as by deed, for only the subjugation of the female body made for history. The ubiquitous violent acts and terrible stories of "forcing a woman" are perhaps finally inseparable from the self-conception of every martial aristocracy. If we had access to more popular cultural artifacts from the period, moreover, we would no doubt find that both male fantasies of sexual possession and male histories of sexual ownership circulated in Romanesque culture, since they show up in the twelfth century all over Europe as oral boast and written poetry.[52]

What about the secular lady's own view of her sexuality? It would be nice hear the voice of an historical lady in the secular world from this time and space, but it does not exist so far as I know, although there is a small amount of contemporary testimony from female religious of aristocratic origin.[53] For the Romanesque period, the best evidence comes indirectly from literary evidence which, despite the importance of imagination, is remarkably consistent. Judging from later examples, one concludes that eleventh-century lyric gave voice to a feminine subject, caught between structures of class and gender, who laments the engagement of her desire with masculine ambitions and its institutions. This material apparently ranged from the complaint of the young woman married badly (*malmariee*), to the complaint of the young woman who has been abandoned (*delaissiee*), to the complaint of the young woman who has been raped (*esforciee*). I cannot prove that such complaints circulated in Anglo-Norman England at the time of the Tapestry, but their wide dispersal in the twelfth century strongly suggests it. This marginal discourse of aristocratic feminine desire ultimately served to maintain the social formation by allowing the ritual staging of consolation to supplant and deflect any impulse for real change.[54]

We can prove, however, that the voice of female desire was directly accessible to the Tapestry's designer. The fascinating lyric anthology now known as *The Cambridge Songs* was copied in England sometime after 1060, apparently at St. Augustine's in Canterbury, which owned it by the twelfth century. The last quarter of the anthology—perhaps close to a third of the original, since a folio has been lost or, more likely, removed—contains exclusively songs of French origin, many of which are love songs of one form or another.[55] In one notable case, for instance, a woman speaks in the first-person recounting and regretting the signs of the spring:

A gentle breeze arises from the west,
and a warming sun comes forth,
now the earth bares her bosom
and flows out with her sweetness.
    Spring has come forth in royal crimson,
donned his best clothes,
scattering the earth with flowers,

the boughs of the trees with blossoms.
    Animals build lairs,
and sweet birds nests,
among flowering trees
they sing out their joys.
    While I see this with my eyes
and hear this with my ears,
alas, instead of those great joys
I am filled with these great sighs.
    As I sit alone by myself
and turn pale thinking about these things,
if by chance I lift my head,
I neither hear nor see.
    You, at least, by the grace of spring,
listen and ponder
the leaves, flowers and meadows;
for my soul is ailing.[56]

Nearly maddened by the simultaneous presence of the subject of desire and absence of its object, the woman's only recourse is to turn inward. With her ambiguous closing address to an unknown listener, she transfers the image and discourse of desire to an alter ego and retreats to silence and sorrow. Along with that of other languishing women in the anthology, this voice reveals a stock female character of a "natural" desire and eloquence which circulated in the written culture of late eleventh-century England. The poem thus helps us understand the ideas of the historian and designer of the Tapestry, who were working in the same place and at the same time that the manuscript was copied.

    The clerk was equally well known as a stock character of desire and eloquence. Here he has been lovingly portrayed, especially his face and cloak, as if we might miss the youth and beauty, on the one hand, and the wealth if not nobility on the other.[57] The angle of the body and the gestures of the arms transmit a certain urgency as well. Whether we should see sexual aggression or aggressive sexuality, however, is indeterminate; the confusion of the two, in any case, occurred surely as often in the past as it does in the present.[58] His features and figure seem to point to an investment on the part of a designer perhaps attracted to a scene of illicit pleasure in spite of himself. He, too, was a *clericus*, although probably in a monastic setting, and must have had strong feelings toward his worldly double.

In such a context and in such dress, the word *clericus* designates not "official of the Church" but "official of the world" (*servus mundi*), a young product of the schools who had taken lower orders and was trained in letters (in the widest sense). Contemporary Norman historians note that sometimes even laymen were nicknamed "Clericus" if they were highly *litteratus*.[59] This *clericus* is one of the many who found employment as "chaplains," secretaries, scribes, *notarii* ("note-takers"), advisers, and lawyers. They ranged from bishops and abbots serving in the great courts of princes, as C. Stephen Jaeger has shown, to young and lowly functionaries serving in the courts of minor lords. The "clerks" in particular (the translation I have used throughout to distinguish them, imperfectly, from "clerics" by their lower age and office) qualified for positions by literate education, but actually acquired them through a combination of influence and favor. In many cases, finally, such court service eventually led to or accompanied ecclesiastic promotion, a method of advancement that came under increasing fire as the Investiture Controversy heated up in the 1070s.[60]

As clerks infiltrated every level of the secular aristocratic court, they became increasingly involved in it, especially since their functions were rather administrative than spiritual, agents of writing more than religion. Abelard, for instance, confessed that when he was *clericus* in Brittany he pursued fame and money with little regard for spiritual matters, and Marbod of Rennes wrote a short poetic letter to a young friend warning him that the profit and pleasure of court service would ruin him (PL 171.1717). Guibert of Nogent confesses openly the gain from versifying he sought as a young clerk in Normandy:

> My friends were clearly my enemies [during the study of composition], for although they gave me good advice, yet they often plied me with talk of fame and literary distinction and through these things the winning of high status and wealth.[61]

Not enough attention has been paid to the role of such compositions within the economy of favor which drove both secular and ecclesiastic employment. By the time of the Tapestry, clerks employed at court had become known simply as "curials" (*curiales*), and their mobility, dress, and behavior scandalized conservative observers.[62]

Lettered, leisured, young, attractive, and often poor, the clerk became a stock character of sexual aggression and aggressive sexuality, both

as subject and author of amatory texts comic as well as serious. Unlike
knights and ladies of the Romanesque court, who had no approved self-
impersonation as lover within official culture of the 1070s, clerks adopted
that *persona* and publicly staged it all the time. If nothing else, their explicit sexual neutrality by profession—in principle, at least—procured for
their self-staging an appearance of fictionality which allowed them to speak
about topics otherwise taboo in court discourse. As we shall see later, they
also used the concept of "game" to protect them from censure. There is
ample evidence, moreover, that they were reading publicly and sending pri-
vately such poems, and that their audience included ecclesiastic and secular
princes, fellow clerks, and ladies in both convent and court.[63]

   One example from a group of late eleventh-century poems now known
as *Carmina Leodiensia* supplies us with a good impression of this well-
studied character at the time of the Tapestry, and its early date and high wit
rewards a close look. Following the dedication to Marbod of Rennes of a
scientific text I will examine in the third chapter, the poem was written and
sent by an unknown Walter as a patent *captatio benevolentiae* and, it seems
to me, as a disguised defense of the nakedness of his treatise:

Aeolus, strong king, guardian of the windy band,
If you make right the wrong done to me by a wind
I will give you incense and spice, I will sacrifice a calf.
I will tell you why I am complaining: I was already embracing my
      woman-friend,
When suddenly an angry wind which no young person could like
Hits the doors with repeated bangs while we are in our hideaway;
We thought that blowhard was some jealous person
Who wanted to catch us in loving embrace:
Things were in hand, the deed was nearly done.
We get up not slowly, everything is changed quickly:
Kisses are sundered, things covered that had been bare.
So lock up this wind for a hundred centuries,
Lock him in prison lest he get outside
And practice similar tricks in other places.[64]

Witty, risque, urbane, self-conscious, and facile, this "Goliardic" voice reappears with many variants in the *Cambridge Songs* and throughout Medieval Latin lyric of all kinds.[65] Eleventh-century poetic "trifles" (*nugae*) at-

test to its high visibility within general Latin culture at the time of the Tapestry's execution.

Such analogues permit the conclusion that even a fragmentary depiction of setting, character, and plot could abundantly activate the recreation of a narrative of desire with enough detail to determine meaning and significance. The painful irony of Ælfgyva's story is that—like all such stories, whether of passion or violation—it could only be told and understood as cliché despite its individual and experiential origin. That status as cliché, moreover, confirms that the panel must be finally seen as high story to be encoded by imaginative interpretation, rather than as history to be decoded by factual documentation.

In making a very close reading of the Ælfgyva panel, I wanted to restore in part the historical interpretative codes which attended it, and to attempt to articulate the defense of the arrested subjects elicited by the material and the labor which informed their representation. It remains now to reopen the reading by restoring the panel to the Tapestry, and asking how and why such characters could have attained the status implied by their inclusion in a "founding charter" of this new official culture.[66]

We can start by recognizing that ladies and clerks resembled each other as subjects to a degree which is difficult for a modern observer to comprehend. Although not central figures in feudo-heroic ideology, both wielded substantial symbolic power on its margin, dominating Romanesque court literacy. Furthermore, they inscribed men of power beyond death itself, as one sees clearly in *The Battle of Maldon* and Ælflæd's embroidery, both designed to praise the deeds of Byrhthnoth. Lady and clerk promised to mediate a permanence essential to family authority. Yet both also menaced its power structure, since the production of the best means of permanence, children and books (*lib(e)ri*), ultimately escaped its ability and control.[67]

As power relations changed across the eleventh century, the sexually charged plot of "the Lady and the Clerk" rose in paradigmatic status for a martial aristocracy trying to re-establish authority through genealogy. For such a readership, it portrayed the dynastic implications of "free speech and free love" or, in Romanesque terms, "eloquence and desire." Ælfgyva's hand gesture, which I have ignored until now, supplies the most important index of this function. Only three figures make this gesture in the Tapestry, all in the process of speaking before a figure of power.[68] Ælfgyva, then, figured generally as the subject of desire, is represented in the Tapestry as a subject of eloquence; while the clerk, figured generally as the subject of eloquence, is represented as a subject of desire. Their interchangeability points to the ancient association and condemnation of pleasure and ornament which found new currency in the late eleventh century.

This new paradigmatic status of what R. Howard Bloch has termed "the imbrication of signification and generation" seems to me sufficient to account for the inherent meaning of the lyric insert for the Romanesque audience, but not for its significance at this location in the Tapestry.[69] The most likely explanation relies on the passage in the history of William of Poitiers which I mentioned at the beginning of this chapter. Within its specific narrative and political context, the Ælfgyva panel can be viewed as an attempt to render visible the "hospitality, courtesy, and witty refreshment" at Rouen by evoking a story and story-type very familiar to the aristocratic court. The weary English were entertained, and perhaps mildly threatened, by this clever tale of a (Norman?) clerk's conquest of an English lady.[70] The wit of the story and its telling would mark well the cultivated taste and aggressive diplomacy of the ducal court.

Yet the story had another kind of refreshment to offer as well, since the transgressions it related implicitly undermined the orders which governed the context within which it was told. Ælfgyva and the clerk are not only unruly, in that they refuse restraint, but also disorderly, in that they cross the boundaries of their "natural" orders.[71] In the Tapestry, as in the other documents of the age, this threat to order is isolated and finally overwhelmed by the sheer magnitude of the text. But the beauty and appeal of the intruding episode, highlighted by the failure of language, point to the strength of subversive subjects and a seductive plot which pushed against the limits imposed by political and discursive control. The union of generation and literacy, the desire of subjects, the transgression of norms—by incorporating these collective fears as fiction into court discourse, the story entertains by recreating and releasing class anxieties widely visible in Romanesque secular culture. "Good listeners" could be pleased by a class-closing story of the censure of the crime, the subjection of the individual, and the restoration of order.

For this reason, the panel also carries an historicized theoretical value by providing a privileged view into the Romanesque drama of the subject. The narrative intentions project a downward subjection (here and throughout the Tapestry) on the part of the feudo-heroic and ascetic-monastic alliance which King William and Archbishop Lanfranc had forged. The aesthetic intention, on the other hand, projects an upward subjectivity on the part of marginalized groups appropriating language and desire for power. In the charged space between these two intentions, a "loving subject" was emerging by the 1070s through the very means of coloring the high story which sought to remind all spectators of their rightful place.

Formed by the contest between the interpellations of new alliances of authority and the performances of new "persons" of power, the loving subject was neither stable, uniform, nor coherent. In the first place, as we shall see by the end of this study, many changes occur during the crucial generations around the turn of the twelfth century due to the constant shifting of social and ideological alliances. Furthermore, at any given moment loving subjects can be found in many variants, because power itself varied greatly from region to region, agent to agent, institution to institution. Finally, as this semiotic "window on the past" makes particularly clear, both subjection and impersonation of desire and eloquence are constrained by constructs of gender. If we are to understand both the unity and the diversity of the emergent secular culture in Romanesque France, it seems to me, we cannot forget the sight of these troubling but inherent traits of the loving subject represented almost by oversight in this Anglo-Norman artifact.

2. The Play of Desire: Baudri of Bourgueil and the Formation of the Ovidian Subculture

The analysis of the Ælfgyva panel of the Bayeux Tapestry revealed the ambiguous role of desire and eloquence in the formation of new subjects within the aggressive court culture of the 1070s. Represented as necessary but dangerous because of their powers, "lady" and "clerk" were explicitly condemned for their desires by the ruling hierarchy and its legitimating structures of dominance. Yet mechanisms of resistance and subversion, primarily play with ornament, were found even in such official texts. These mechanisms mediated the construction of multiple subjectivities—founded on sexuality, eloquence and gender—in response to the monotonous discourse of subjection. The possibility of such response would be increased by a revolution in Romanesque secular culture which found a new orthodoxy for self-impersonation.

A significant factor in this revolution can be traced to the revalorization of nature and art which occurred in the great humanistic movement commonly designated as the "Loire School," a loose association of Latin writers who laid the foundation during the final decades of the eleventh century for the poetic renaissance of the twelfth. In the next two chapters, I want to examine two of them: Baudri of Bourgueil, abbot of Bourgueil ca. 1078–1107, and Marbod of Rennes, schoolmaster and chancellor at Angers ca. 1067–96. Very different writers at the margin and the center of the Angevin diocese, respectively, they represent two different solutions to the suppression within the dominant Romanesque discourse of a subject of eloquence and desire.

As is also the case with Marbod, Baudri remains largely unknown outside of a small circle of specialists.[1] Yet his voluminous poetic production, most of which was completed by 1100, should be particularly attractive for all students of High Medieval culture. Not only his practice of voice, but also his idea of the self, his decriminalization of desire, his treatment of friendship, his allegorization of myth, his theory of game, his plea for unre-strained reading, his defense of poetry—all these are especially significant at such an early date.[2]

Perhaps the most intriguing feature of this poet, however, is his thor-ough familiarity with Ovid. In fact, his poetry offers rich and nearly unique testimony to the earliest "generation" of what Ludwig Traube labeled a bit expansively the *aetas Ovidiana*.[3] Since no other extant Romanesque poet displays such Ovidianism, analyzing Baudri's texts promises to provide important insights into the complex interaction between the amatory and poetic curiosity of his generation. Clearly, the forbidden subjects projected by the "personal" portions of the Ovidian corpus powerfully appealed to poets and readers attracted to the problem of constructing a new identity. They constitute a kind of Ovidian subculture, a true subculture which takes shape around the distinctive activities and focal concerns of a well-defined group, on the one hand, and both separates itself from and shares much with its dominant culture on the other.[4] This subculture's profile will pro-vide an idea of the politics of Ovidianism on the threshhold of the High Middle Ages.

Baudri's extant writings fall roughly into two groups: the poems he wrote primarily while abbot, which exist in a unique manuscript, and the religious and historical works he wrote while bishop, which are scattered among various sources.[5] Spread over more than a half-century, these works give credence to his own claim that "learned writing (*littera*) is a great part of my life" (197/CCXXXV.12). Although the second group has great inter-est for Romanesque religious history, I am concerned here primarily with the "secular" and "personal" texts from his abbacy. One is immediately struck by their quantity and diversity. The poems in the most recent edition number 256, although two of these were written to and not by Baudri.[6] They range from single-line exercises (on the moon, for example) playing with figures of thought and word, to the complex piece written to and for Adela, Countess of Blois, which celebrates something like the Bayeux Tap-estry within its 1368 lines. One finds riddles, epitaphs and other inscription poems, pseudo-Ovidian letters, hymns, satires, didactic pieces, and even a dream-poem. In generic preference (epitaph, epistle) as in script it remains fundamentally Carolingian, even if its deeper concerns—including voice—presage the twelfth century.

Two groups dominate: epitaphs and epistolary poems.[7] Anyone ac-quainted with the medieval Church is in a position to appreciate the pur-pose and nature of the epitaphs, for they are paralleled by the religious use of other media of the same period: fresco, statuary, book illustration, chant, hymn. But when we turn our attention to the seventy or so epistolary poems Baudri wrote while abbot, we are introduced to texts whose audience is less extensive than that of the epitaphs and whose fascination with what must be called the "play of desire" (*iocus amoris*) does not match preconceptions of monastic poetry.[8] It might be most practical to begin with a random example, although Baudri's epistolary poems vary so in length, tone, and status of the addressee that it is difficult as well as hazardous to select a "typical" poem. The shortest are but a few lines, the longest over two hundred; some are amorous invitations to young boys, others formal appeals to eminent personages. Somewhere in between lie poems such as the following, written to an unspecified Odo:

To Someone Who Had Promised Him a Letter

A brother monk has reported to me news of you,
Which I welcome, and I plead for a meeting.
He reported that you do not forget me
And quickly gave me your words of greeting.
He reported that you love me ardently   5
And that having seen me once, you carry me in your heart.
He reported to me that if you had a reliable
Carrier, you would send me a letter.
I received with joy whatever he reported to me about you,
And now I repay you with a contract of friendship: 10
See, I will return a word of greeting to you who are greeting me,
But only if you yourself will answer me in verse.
I have joined words to verse, verse to words,
So that I might be pleasing in some way at least.
And I plead that another meeting place be given   15
So that you might put yourself right before my eyes.
Therefore send me, please, the letter through this (brother)
        of mine;
Send me one which is suitable so it will please me more.
But if you ask to whom I am actually sending this song,
The conclusion indicates that by what it says: Goodbye, Odo.[9]   20

Two messages are juxtaposed—though not necessarily integrated—in this strange poem. Odo's message concerns *amor*. Putting the indirect discourse back into direct, one hears the power of Odo's declarations: I do not forget you (3); I love you ardently (5); having seen you once, I carry you in my heart (6); I would send you a (private) letter if I had someone trustworthy to carry it (7–8). Such language intentionally evokes the talk of lovers, and the text itself does not permit the determination of Odo's precise meaning. In his own message, Baudri offers a *fedus amicitie* (10), inviting Odo to play with his verses in the hope that their form or content will please. When one juxtaposes the requests of Odo and Baudri, the poem can be interpreted tentatively as emblematic of the entire book, for the two voices speak to conflicting demands of desire and poetics. Striking in contrast to those of most contemporary monks is the text's highly personal tone and its lack of Christian thought, Classical reference, or rhetorical ornamentation. These traits, which occur throughout his poetry, combine to establish the primary aspects of what he repeatedly calls his *rusticitas* or *simplicitas*, words which describe both his love of the country life and his use of a simple style.[10]

Such a text may disappoint; as Jean Leclercq has observed, documents of this kind are hardly masterpieces.[11] Baudri himself commented to a fellow poet sometime between 1084 and 1089 that "I confess that my songs are worth nothing in themselves" (99/CLXI.181), and continually referred to them as "children's toys" or "trifles" (*nugae*), a Horatian derogatory term for artless poetry in widespread use at this time. The poem to Odo tends at first sight merely to confirm Otto Schumann's dismissal of Baudri as unimportant.[12] Yet such a public formula of humility is not only standard in monastic discourse, but the "confession" cannot be separated from its apologetic context.[13] Baudri's careful collection of a "book" of his poems is sufficient to demonstrate that he held his own poetry in high regard. This fact alone recommends critical exploration irrespective of any aesthetic judgment one might eventually make.

What are these texts exactly? Following their editors, I have called them "poems" (*carmina*) up until now, but the word barely fits the object. Certainly the form is poetic, for the elegiac couplet has literary roots deep into Antiquity. Furthermore, Baudri has decorated the text with rhetorical flourishes such as *conduplicatio* (1, 3, 5, 7, 9: *rettulit*) and *adnominatio* (11; 13–14).[14] Little else, however, confirms that we are looking at a "poem." It would seem, in fact, to be a letter, as the structure indicates. The fully articulated art of letter-writing (*ars dictaminis*) is traditionally thought not to have reached France from Italy until the middle of the twelfth century, yet many of its constitutive elements had been developed much earlier. This text already displays the four-fold division so characteristic of its method:

exordium (1–2), *narratio* (3–8, 9–14), *petitio* (15–18) and *conclusio* (19–20).[15]
Because such texts are both poems and letters, they are commonly called
Briefgedichte in German criticism, a term I will translate with "letter-poems"
for the remainder of this discussion.

Providing a glimpse of a generating thought structure more complex
and more important than one might expect from these self-proclaimed
"trifles," this text has suggested the parameters of a more detailed investigation. What exactly does the poet mean by *amor/amicitia*, and why does
he speak of a "contract?" What is the nature and purpose of this poetic
interchange, which he usually calls *iocus*? What *persona* did he make speak
in his compositions, and where did it come from? And who practiced such
literary trifling, and why?

We must step back for a moment to consider the cultural context
of the poems, since their interpretation cannot be separated from their
late eleventh-century framework, which consisted first and foremost of the
world of Benedictine monasticism. Founded and richly endowed in 990 by
Emma, sister of Odo of Blois and wife of William of Aquitaine, Bourgueil
was similar to many religious houses in central France of the period which
had become increasingly wealthy as the eleventh century and its economic
boom progressed. Benefiting on the one hand from growing lay interest
in reformed monasteries, and on the other from able and zealous administration by the abbots, many such establishments were at the peak of their
power and wealth at this time. It was precisely such material success, however, which rendered these houses susceptible to attacks from both insiders
and outsiders; as Jean Leclercq has pointed out, the crisis of monasticism
around 1100 was a crisis of prosperity.[16]

Baudri's house was wealthy, and his literary world depended upon this
wealth. Not only did it remove him from daily necessity and create a sense
of a privileged elite in amenable surroundings, but it also supplied *cuncta
studentibus apta* (77/CXXXIX.159) of which he made such constant use:
parchment, pen, tablets, stylus; scribes, illuminators, messengers; community and personal books; travel, colloquies, and banquets. In addition, it
provided leisure, for Baudri's poetry was first and foremost a product of
his free time: "while there is time and inclination, let us write satires and
songs" (121/CLXXXIII.6). Monastic life was conceived and summed up as
a sacred *otium*, determined by a solitude with God.[17] But the idea of being
inactive seems to have been as unacceptable to his private person as it was
(in the form of *acedia*) to his public role, and he turned to versifying as a

healthy pastime. "Tell them he did not want to live an idle life," he instructs his own book as a defense for writing poetry, a position he repeats to the poet Godfrey of Reims: "I prefer to devote myself to books and verses than to pass time idle like a packhorse."[18] Such a choice was possible for him because of the great importance attached to reading and writing throughout the history of Benedictine monasticism. Yet by the second half of the eleventh century, monastic instruction of letters had been challenged by that of the rapidly expanding cathedral schools. This was especially true in central and northern France, which by all accounts was at the forefront of the contemporary school world in the collection, study, and imitation of the *auctores*.

Baudri consciously combines both literary traditions, reacting in a complex manner to the success of the secular schools in the field of *grammatica* as his fellow abbot Anselm of Bec did to that of *dialectica*. He attacks (as in 112/CLXXIV) or attempts to convert those who teach in the world for money; to one Gerald of Loudun, for instance, a student of the famous Manegold of Lautenbach, he offers the peaceful library at Bourgueil (77/CXXXIX). At the same time, it is obvious to every reader of Baudri's verse that the abbot-poet was attracted to those humanistic schools, studying their writings and corresponding with their inhabitants. Like many of his contemporaries, he both feared and sought the criticism of schoolmen, disliking their worldly investments yet admiring their learning and ingenuity.[20]

This increased attention to humanistic concerns in Romanesque central France accelerated the development of the letter, the most active literary form in the Latin culture at this time. Baudri's generation and region were instrumental in ushering in the great age of medieval letter-writing, and many large and important collections exist from his own milieu.[21] Variously designated by *epistola*, *littera* (*litterae*), *libellus*, *carta* or *cartula*, *opus* or *opusculum*, and even *tabulae*, the letter's variety was extreme.[22] Ivo of Chartres's letters are often lengthy epistles about larger matters of the Church; Geoffrey of Vendôme writes in the main about the particular business affairs of his own abbey. The great generic breadth of the *epistola* poses problems for theorists of genre, as Ernstpeter Ruhe has observed, because the medieval application of the term conflicts with modern notions of the normative function of generic designations.[23]

Particularly relevant for an understanding of Baudri's poetry is the subgenre consisting of monastic letters of friendship. As Jean Leclercq has commented a bit disingenuously, "for every stage of monastic life there are letters of friendship in abundance whose sole purpose was to give pleasure to the recipient."[24] Friendship letters in poetic form were vastly less common, however. They had been cultivated for a short time by Carolingian writers, especially Alcuin and Theodulf, both of whom were intimately connected to the Loire Valley, where they both died. At the end of the eleventh century, poetic letters besides those of Baudri were again being written, the extant examples pointing to figures associated with the so-called Loire School: Marbod of Rennes, Hildebert of Le Mans, Godfrey of Rheims, Rodolf Tortarius, etc.

Whether poetry or prose, medieval letters were much more public than their modern equivalents. Baudri sometimes sent them by private messenger (*legatus*, as in poem 255/XXXIV), but more often by a fellow monk or traveling stranger who routinely read them to various audiences before they reached their destination. The self-referential conclusions of Baudri's poems, which at times are so distinct that they were probably written on the outside of the original letter, evoke eloquently the semi-public nature of the medieval letter by addressing the reader with formulas of humility.[25] Their significance for us concerns context as well as text. Facing a double audience—the known and private (*cui proprie legatur epistola*, 5/XL.23), and the unknown and public—epistolary authors resorted to double systems of meaning. As one slightly later writer expressed it: "I direct (my) words to others, (my) intention to you."[26] The former grants access to all readers, the latter only intimate friends. Like the *tornada* of the troubadours and the *envoy* of the later French poets, such a *clausula* (105/CLXVII.20) simultaneously invites and restricts the decipherment of the text. This inherent "duplicity" constitutes a central trait of the medieval letter.

Baudri's letter-poems form an exception within the monastic epistolary repertory.[27] They display the presence and suppression of powerful Freudian mechanisms on both psychological and institutional levels in their particular fusion of private practices and public poetics—both illicit activities for a monk. But they also testify to the nascent consciousness of a new secular writing elite defined precisely by its unprecedented cultivation of *amor* and *iocus*, two terms whose deep ambiguity escapes the simple translations of "desire" and "play" I used in the title of this chapter.

Baudri never wrote an explicit and coherent treatise on *amor* and, as abbot of a Benedictine monastery, could not have done so in the atmosphere of reform which characterized late eleventh-century France. But considered in its entirety, this collection of letter-poems could justifiably be entitled *De Amore*, for it covers about the same range of *amor* with its Romanesque organization that a more scholastically oriented Andreas Capellanus will with his legalistic text a century later. When the scattered statements are gathered from the individual poems and analyzed, they provide a detailed picture of Baudri's fundamental concept of the amatory impulse in his modern age.

Its foundation lay in a variety of theories and practices of Christian friendship that evolved with Western ecclesiastic culture itself. Two streams of thought had emerged from Antiquity: a mystical or Platonic view of friendship as the highest form of human love, and a political or Ciceronian view of it as the essential relationship in the maintenance of the state.[28] Although the two were united by Augustine, for whom friendship was essential to the city of God, the subsequent monastic tradition favored the mystical interpretation of friendship, especially in its poetry and letters. The Ciceronian notion of political friendship dominated the secular world of the courts and the schools, while monastic writers concentrated upon an internal friendship and, increasingly, the means of its expression. By the twelfth century the art of epistolary writing and the doctrine of friendship had become completely intertwined with monastic thinking, and would remain so throughout the High Middle Ages.[29]

Certain of Baudri's favorite expressions and images of friendship seem to have been the common property of the age, even though they appear with particular density in his letter-poems. He routinely indicates the quality of his friendships through the adjective *specialis*, for instance, a significant term throughout the Middle Ages.[30] Also, he continually refers to the fusion of the hearts and minds of true friends (as in 103/CLXV.5–8). Baudri and his contemporaries expressed this identity through the concept of "another self" (*alter ego* or *alter idem*). Writing to a monk and good friend Ralph, for instance, Baudri makes the following plea: "(my) other self or (my own) self, let (our) two spirits be one, and let (our) two bodies become the same body."[31] Anselm used the same term in his letters, and Marbod in his poetry. The idea, adapted from Cicero's influential treatise on friendship, was nearly proverbial.[32]

The centrality of Cicero's text in the discussions of friendship in Romanesque schools is indicated by an anonymous poem of the period which begins with the following: "Asked what a friend is, a certain philosopher thought a few minutes before answering: another self."[33] Marbod made explicit and careful use of Ciceronian concepts and language in the eighth

chapter ("De Vera Amicitia") of his *Liber decem capitulorum*. Rodolf Tortarius's tale of friendship of Amicus and Amelius makes use of the same
concepts within a court setting where "true friendship" (*verus amor*) constitutes the final good of knighthood.[34] The widespread interest in central
France in such a Ciceronian concept has not been examined in detail, and
it holds great potential for exploring the variety and utility of Romanesque
humanism. Furthermore, its relationship to a secular and vernacular concept of "true love" (*bon'amor, fin'amor*) which will soon appear in the same
region merits careful consideration.

Despite Baudri's undeniable debt to monastic and Ciceronian traditions of friendship, his own treatment of friendship remains essentially
—and surprisingly—unique. Loving friendship is not explicitly a means
toward union with Christ, as it was for so many of his monastic contemporaries, even though Baudri argues in his poems to secular teachers (as in
77/CXXXIX) that the monastic literary life permits its fullest expression. In
fact, the life of the soul is generally excluded from these texts of the heart.
At the same time, despite the ultimate source of the notion of *alter ego* mentioned above, Baudri does not share the Ciceronian notion of friendship
which already intrigued the schoolmen of his own day. The questions of
uirtus and *utilitas* so important to Cicero are completely absent from his
texts.

A key to understanding Baudri's particular notion of friendship is provided by his routine substitution of *amor* for *amicitia*. The two had been
linked since Antiquity and could function as synonyms in controlled contexts.[35] The former ranged broadly from "sexual desire" to "friendship,"
"love" to "peaceful relations." Because of this inherent ambiguity of the
word *amor*, Baudri is able to flirt simultaneously with codes of friendship between monks and codes of desire between males.[36] One must be
careful in making such a statement, for monastic friendship was characterized by its use of ecstatic and flowery language which, when removed
from its Christian context, can deceive the modern ear with its talk of love.
Nevertheless, no matter how cautiously one proceeds one cannot escape
the conclusion that Baudri intentionally evoked homosexual relationships
in many of his poems by discussing *amor* between males in a context devoid
of explicit Christian values.

Both practice and discourse are well attested in Baudri's milieu.
Homosexuality, especially pedophilia, had been a target of invective and
satire already in the mid-eleventh century when the reforming ascetic Peter
Damian attacked it in a pamphleteering treatise.[37] But it was the cult of

"Ganymedes" which particularly attracted many of Baudri's contemporaries. Nearly unthinkable in Western society today, love between adult and adolescent males formed a laudable object of practice and poetry in some circles during the early High Middle Ages, as in Antiquity. Both praise and satire of such a love are common in the Latin texts of the late eleventh century. Often marked by a frank eroticism, pedophilic verse was the most radical genre of contemporary poetry.[38] Baudri may not have collected all the poems he says he wrote to boys and young men, yet at least eighteen of his letter-poems are specifically addressed to them.[39] In a piece whose location at the beginning of the first booklet suggests an early date of composition, for example, Baudri spends almost twenty lines describing the beauty of a young boy, only to retreat at the last moment with a final "I praise you for refusing to be Jove's Ganymede" (3/XXXVIII.24).

Such language spills over into the other poems not sent to boys. Writing to Galo (a poet of obscure fame), for instance, Baudri concludes a long adulatory passage with the declaration: "I am living for myself if I live for you; my greatest delight (*uoluptas*) is to do something which might please you."[40] By using *uoluptas*, which can indicate either sensual (as in 8/XLIII.355) or spiritual (as in 202/CCXL.27) delight, Baudri toys with double meaning, especially since he has already stated in the same poem that "I love you more ardently than I indicate" (*plus quam significo te uehementer amo*, 16). Homosexual love is always a potential meaning in these texts, a fact highlighted by Baudri's cautious qualification of friendship in an unusually specific letter to a "long-desired John" arguing that "It is also that kind of holy friendship which is unmarked by any taint" (11/XLVI.13–14). The force of Baudri's letter-poems, like that of the troubadour lyric, lies precisely in their hazardous play with the taboo, their display of the dialectic between the public language of restraint and the private thought of release embedded in a generic framework whose inherent duplicity reinforces the reader's inability to resolve the ambiguities.

Nevertheless, it seems to me that Baudri's correspondents are often not just objects of desire, but actually subjects of desire. This is especially true of the *pueri*, most of whom belonged to the religious community. Given the abbot's authority within the ecclesiastic hierarchy and especially within his own monastery, his pedophilic gaze cannot avoid creating a sort of secondary subjection *ex officio*. He exploits his position, whether consciously or not, when he courts adolescents under his power. No matter how much he wants to speak in his own person, and no matter how innocent he thinks his game to be, his letter-poems interpellate such correspondents as subjects. From this perspective, we have a first indication of the capacity of a *persona* to camouflage a subject. In later chapters, I shall argue that this capacity accounts in an important manner for the initial access and ultimate success of Romanesque lyric at the French secular court.

Behind Baudri's complex treatment of *amor* lies the kind of deeper cultural development one perceives through other marginal texts of the period—such as Marbod's much darker lyric which I examine in the next chapter—the emerging conviction that *amor* is an integral part of nature to which all humans were subjected. In its most optimistic and idealistic form, this dominion of nature derived directly from God. There are hints at an acceptance of the divine origin of *amor* in many passages in Baudri's poems. When Baudri laments a nineteen-year-old canon from Tours named Alexander, for instance, he admits that beauty and youth had brought stains upon that soul but requests indulgence because both traits had been given by God (40/CII.9–10). The most blatant statement of the position occurs in a fictive letter written to the exiled Ovid by an imaginary friend named Florus, where the following apologetic passage occurs:

> God filled our nature with love;
>> Nature teaches us what he taught her.
> If love is to be blamed, the agent of love is to be blamed;
>> For the agent of love will be the agent of the crime.
> That we exist is a crime if it is a crime that we love;
>> God who gave me being, granted me loving.
> And yet God himself did not make evil, when he made love;
>> for what is evil is born from vice.
> You were the reciter, not the author of love;
>> No flame was ignited by your teaching.[41]

The implications of this extraordinary passage for our understanding of the rise of a new poetry of desire at the turn of the twelfth century cannot be overlooked. This syllogistic defense by Baudri of both Ovid and—as every reader quickly recognizes—himself contains two important arguments. The first states that *amor* is "natural," that is, it supplies by God's design the motor force of *natura* (from *nascere*, "to give birth"), the ongoing re-creation of the world.[42] Furthermore, since Nature is instructed by God, that is, since natural law imitates divine law, it follows that *amor* is not inherently reprehensible but virtuous (*honestus*). Both of these arguments are implicit in the designation of God as *actor*, for as such he is identified both with the First Cause of Aristotelian physics and with the *daimon* of Neoplatonic creation. By using a fictive and pagan speaker and thus avoiding the necessity to erect an elaborate theological apparatus, Baudri is able to give direct voice to an opinion that one otherwise only glimpses between the lines of eleventh-century texts: that desire is a legitimate part of internal and external nature, of the microcosmic and macrocosmic orders. When speaking in his own person, Baudri restricts his defense to poetry and skirts any hint of the divine origin of *amor*. But the perception voiced so unequivocally by the fictive Florus merges with Baudri's treatment of monastic friendship to form the continual subtext of the letter-poems.

Finally, it is surprising and significant that the culminating act of *amor* for Baudri is the meeting and discourse of friends (*colloquium*). It can be presented as a quasi-erotic encounter, such as the one offered in a Virgilian mode to the young boy Avitus (129/CXCI). It can be a chaste and joyful meeting between loving friends, where writing can finally be replaced with intimacy: "now let stylus, tablets, and messenger be gone; let us be for each other what these things used to be for us."[43] And it can even be a literary dinner party, a *convivium*, such as the one described at length by Baudri in his anticipation of good food, good company, and good reading (208/ CCXLIX + XXXLIV.1–30). In fact, many of the poets he writes have read in his presence: the nun Muriel (137/CXCIX.7–10), an Ovidian poet named Stephen (90/CLII.21–22), even Godfrey of Reims (99/CLXI.15–16). Literary exchange has become the ultimate object of all drives, sexual as well as religious.

Baudri's letter-poems reflect in their variety his generation's new acceptance of all forms and aspects of the natural and ultimately divine force of *amor*. Incorporating elements from the rich tradition of monastic friendship and from Late Carolingian theories of natural desire, Baudri reclaims and defends *amor/amicitia* at the individual level as the mediating and unifying force of human existence. Yet as we have just seen, his concept remains inseparable from the poetic medium which gives it voice, and to this medium we now must turn.

Although Baudri's poetry has deep roots in the cult of *amor* and its privileged medium in the monastic tradition, his use of the distich announces an equally consistent preoccupation with Ovid, the *auctor* least compatible with a monastic interpretation of Christian values. Fundamental here is his idiosyncratic notion of game (*iocus*) which strikes every reader. It begins with a literary practice that he repeatedly describes with considerable detail. No other writer of his generation, and perhaps not in the entire medieval period, writes so much about the physical act of writing. One result is a palpable thematic poverty, but another is a cumulative wealth of detail about the material process of producing poetry, from which one gains a good view of the labor of Romanesque versification.

Baudri gives ample support to the important recent proposal that "the Middle Ages was a wax-tablet culture," since he speaks repeatedly of his instruments for composition: wax tablets (*tabulae, tabellae*) and stylus (*graphium, stylus*).[44] The tablets normally consisted of two frames of wood held together by straps (*corrigiae*), although the poet describes lovingly one special set of eight tiny tablets (12/XLVII). The size of the tablets varied widely. Baudri estimates that each surface of his dwarf tablets, scarcely three inches on a side, could hold eight hexameters (12.XLVII.9–10); the *pagina* of a regular tablet was three to four times that. The usual pair of tablets could thus contain fifty or sixty verses, and it is probably no accident that the vast majority of Baudri's poems fall within that limit. Into these frames was poured hot wax which, when cool, provided two writing surfaces (*paginae*), easy to write on if the wax was freshly prepared. Although usually black, a special green wax is twice mentioned by the poet (12/XLVII.33 and 196/CCXXXIV.37–38) as being easy on the eyes. One wrote with a stylus, pointed at one end and blunt at the other.[45] The wax could be corrected easily with the blunt end or with a file (*lima*), after which a correcting wax (*litura*) was poured into the resulting holes. It was also recyclable and, compared to parchment, cheap.

Using these tools, Baudri composed his poems in private, as the following passage makes clear: "One morning I had prepared my tablets and stylus and was about to begin my poems, as was my habit. I was alone therefore, and I usually spend my free time alone."[46] He never speaks of dictating to a scribe, although his tablets were usually tranfered to parchment by scribes. The choice to send the tablets themselves was likely motivated out of a desire for greater privacy, as the letter-poem to Odo with which I began indicates.[47] In a manner typical for Baudri, however, his wish for privacy could reflect concern for improprieties of form (as in 86/CXLVIII.36–38) as well as of content (as in 200/CCXXXVIII.5–6, where he stresses the unusual fact that he wrote the *carta* himself).

As all students of Baudri have realized, the exchange among friends of tablets or parchment containing verses constitutes the essence of his notion of *iocus*—if one excludes for the moment the amatory implications of the word. Ludic terminology abounds in his poems, often in unusual forms and unlikely contexts that confuse the unaccustomed reader. One finds not only *iocus*, the Classical word for play or game of the mind, but also *ludus*, the word designating primarily physical (including erotic) games.[48] Baudri asks Marbod *ut mecum ludas*, prudently specifying *in carmine*; he has "alluded" with many in verse, he often "eludes" sounds, he hopes to "collude" with Odo, he wishes his nephew could have "preluded" for him, and he urges the Bishop of Ostia to "illude" with him.[49] A good "game of poetry," or *iocus*, is offered to anyone who will listen: a young boy, a bishop, a nun, clerics and monks, and even a Duke Roger, probably Roger II of Sicily.[50] The adjective *iocosus* bestows the poet's highest approval, and can qualify not only various persons but also a great range of objects and actions from *uita* to *uerba*.

Though not exhaustive, even such a listing establishes beyond doubt that "game, play" was a dominant concept for Baudri and that it was indissolubly linked to making verses. But he applied it to the entire gamut of poetic activity. When a friend named Letaudus is announced, Baudri puns on the essential meaning (*omen*) of the name (*nomen*), finding it in "happy" (*letus*). This common etymological device derives ultimately from Isidore of Seville, where it was employed as a very serious philosophic/philologic technique located at the heart of grammar itself.[51] It arrests our attention here because of its ludic characterization (101/CLXIII.16): "I am playing on the sounds and I often play with sounds" (*Vocibus alludo soleoque eludere uoces*). In labeling such a gnomic procedure a "play with sounds" while himself playing with sounds (*alludo . . . eludere*), Baudri reveals that "play" is a key element of style—especially of his favorite rhetorical ornaments, *repetitio* and *adnominatio*. A playful style must be *leuis, iocosus* (250/XXIX.10). Any genre, moreover, including epitaph (see 179–84/CCXVII–CCXXII) and lament (see 92/CLIV), is subject to such delusory play. Implicitly gamelike, too, is the necessity to write within established metrical limitations, and even the relationship between literal and allegorical senses is described in one of his late poems as a *iocus misticus* (220/CCLIII.6). Finally, as I noted in the Introduction, Baudri enjoyed playing with self-impersonation as well. Apparently adopting the arguments and techniques of Marbod we shall see in the next chapter, he took on various personalities in his letter-poems whose fictive nature he carefully (and deceptively) describes in a number of apologetic passages.[52] Substituting the illusive voice of an unreliable speaker for the authorial voice of the poet-abbot, Baudri rejects serious style, content, and function with a radical claim to a pure ludic function.

Thus every aspect of versifying, from the interplay of sounds to the interlude of poets, is subsumed explicitly by Baudri under the absorbing and dominating concept of *iocus*, one of the most fully developed in the Western tradition.[53] For perhaps the first time since Late Antiquity one sees in these poems by Baudri the production of texts written in the first person and in the official language which intentionally mock the possibility of an authoritative reading which their documentary nature (as letters) invites. We would be wrong, however, to interpret the poetic act as "merely" a game in Baudri's eyes, despite his own statements in that direction. Endowed with, in fact claiming all the alterity and seriousness ascribed to all games by Johan Huizinga and others,[54] this "game" of Baudri's is simultaneously both trivial and essential. Its very promise lies in the hope that it can bridge the gap between the pleasure of the material world and the goodness of the spiritual through the virtue of the ingenious. All that the human heart, the locus of both imagination and desire, can create is but a child's toy, but that toy simultaneously expresses and reifies the best of the human condition.

This ludic poetics comes from the works of Ovid. No investigation of the abbot's poetry has overlooked his Ovidianism, yet his particular and subtle treatment has only recently begun to attract detailed attention. Studies of "Ovid in the Middle Ages," moreover, routinely ignore the significant evidence provided by Baudri's texts of what he himself (see 90/CLII.22: *Naso nouus*) would probably have called a "Neo-Nasonian" revival.

There is no point in trying to rehearse the complicated and important story of Ovid's literary afterlife. Not only has a complete study never been carried out, but the Roman poet's conflicting images (amatory, ethical, scientific, literary) complicate the picture.[55] For my purposes, two crucial moments can be identified. The first arrived in Late Antiquity with the efforts to unite the imagination and eloquence of the *Metamorphoses* with the truth of Christianity. Many of its stories of imagination and desire were explicated through Neoplatonic critical strategies during the fifth century, and from the Carolingian Renaissance onward the interpretation of that natural model gradually produced a coherent theory of reading and writing *fabula* (story, myth, lie, fiction) that blossomed in the hands of twelfth-century poets and thinkers.[56]

To teach Ovid's poems inside the schools meant to elaborate simultaneously a theory of "right reading" of a literature of *amor*. A variety of old and new devices were employed to adapt them to the Christian schoolroom, including gloss, commentary, *accessus*, and allegory. Suited by content and style to the demands of adolescent education, his works were exploited by student and teacher alike throughout the High Middle Ages, especially at Orléans, just a few kilometers from Baudri's place of birth and education.[57] Ovid was copied for distichs, mined for *sententiae*, robbed for hexameters, cited for *praecepta amoris*, and imitated shamelessly. Furthermore, pseudo-Ovidiana from the twelfth and thirteenth centuries abound, ranging from strict imitation to interpretive recreation.[58]

For some reason, Baudri's assimilation of the literary implications of *fabula* is easily demonstrated but universally ignored. Ernst Robert Curtius pointed out long ago that the abbot-poet furnishes the first systematic discussion of the allegorizing of exempla in a letter-poem to lady Constance, carmen 200/CCXXXVIII.95–134.[59] The remark has not occasioned interest among those researching the evolution of medieval *fabula*, nor has it been noticed that the poem actually makes a long defense of his mythological poem 154/CCXVI+CCLV, as the constant cross-references prove. I translate the former text in the Appendix and will analyze it later, but one passage is worth quoting here at length:

Just as there are stories of bad people in the books of the ancients,
    So are placed in them good things which you should do.
Diana is praised for her characteristic virginity,
    Perseus represents the conquerer of the monster;
The virtue of Hercules is displayed in many deeds;
    All such things are allegorical if you understand . . .
In our books not one tip (of the letter), not one stroke is
    Missing which could teach us to avidly desire the heavens.
But I wanted to put forward the Greek trifles as proof
    That every literature of the world teaches us
That the whole world speaks as with one tongue
    And that each and every man educates us . . .
Let the Latin tongue be enriched by enemy booty;
    Let the vanquished Greek and Hebrew serve.
May neither of us lack reading's lesson;
    Let everything that is, be book and text for us.[60]

The ultimate source of the apology lies in a widely cited passage in Augustine's *De Doctrina Christiana* (2.60–61), but that notion is applied here in an interesting and significant moment of secularization to the reading of the *auctores* for personal development.

Curtius could have found literary embodiments of such principles in Baudri's only long poems, 154/CCXVI+CCLV and 134/CXCVI, composed about the same time. The former, now missing beginning (62 verses) and end (a few hundred verses), follows in its extant 1242 lines the fifth-century *Mithologiae* of Fulgentius, elaborating some of the myths to great length while reducing others to a single distich.[61] In his reworking, Baudri makes repeated comments about the relationship of *fabula* to moral truths, mostly concerning *amor*. These theoretical statements are not found in Fulgentius, but stem (as far as one can tell) from Baudri himself. They serve as a humanistic rejection of Fulgentius, who had repeatedly denounced "Grecia mendax."[62] But they also reveal Baudri's familiarity with a sophisticated theory of *fabula* some decades before William of Conches and the other early twelfth-century authors normally cited in this regard. A careful separation of material and significance also defends, to be sure, his own literary and erotic imaginings, as the letter-poem 200/CCXXXVIII to Constance makes evident.

The heart of his second long poem (134/CXCVI.169–234, 561–1342) consists of a digest of Martianus Capella's highly influential *Marriage of Philology and Mercury*, presenting the reader with a Neoplatonic vision of the intermediary realms. To this material Baudri adds the Biblical story of Creation (99–168), as well as the *gesta* of William the Conquerer (235–560). The result is an amalgam of *historias ueteres* (98) of varying surface authority but, by implication, of equal figural value. Yet the described stories are actually tapestries (*uela*, *aurea*), textiles hanging in the chamber of Adela of Blois which included something similar to the Bayeux Tapestry, as we saw in the first chapter. It is their secondary artifice that Baudri actually lauds. Finally, the tertiary artifice of Baudri's own poem must be included, since it is that fabulous composition—a dream vision—which the poet is selling to the Countess for a cape. Thus three ingeniously symbolic devices (*fabula*, *uelum*, *carmen*) mediate simultaneously in space and time between the spiritual world and the material world, between the past and the present, between the pagan and the Christian. The poem becomes in the final analysis a paeon to the power of human inventiveness (*ingenium*) through representation and interpretation to provide access to the metaphysical universe.[63]

One of Baudri's most intriguing little poems, and one of the few which is not epistolary, demonstrates with particular skill his command of the texts and interpretations of *fabula*:

The Storm

A storm is rising; clouds cover the sky;
    the thickened air has thundered a bit.
Nimble ants run back to their fortified homes,
    the heavens gleam with slanted paths.
And yet this storm is not to be feared very much: 5
    after a bit of rain the bright day will be here.
I know what the storm and signs signify to me:
    Jupiter and Juno now are entering the bedroom.
If (pagan) people reject this storm in terror,
    I embrace it in welcome, let it be mine!   10
To me this storm is not at all grievous, not at all odious,
    to me it portends difficult access.
So come, oh favorable storm, hasten;
    now I shall not ignore the storm's warnings.
From your coming I shall learn indeed the gods' secrets   15
    and from your withdrawing I shall read what I need;
For after the cloud's retreat and the lightning's withdrawal,
    I hope to enjoy even you in tranquil peace.[64]

The opening naturalism quickly fades as *natura* is glossed by *fabula*. But his explanation that Jupiter and Juno are entering the bedroom (8) obscures as it clarifies: does Baudri want us to understand thunder, lightning, and rain literally as divine fornication? His obscurity forces us into a stance toward an allegedly vatic text that mirrors the one he has taken toward an allegedly comprehensible nature. Nor are we aided by his concern for personal signification (*quid michi significet*; *michi portendet*; *michi quid sit opus*), since it renders truth personal and suggests that *fabula* must find its meaning through a biography accessible to neither medieval nor modern readers. We seem to have reached a dead end, since individual, private interpretation escapes both science and religion.

Are there any alternatives? The text links the storm to death by the word "threats," to sexuality by "bedroom." One might be tempted to understand it therefore as an emblem for the forces of nature itself; and since nature's interpretation forms the actual content of the poem, it must find its symbolic function in the dramatization of the interaction between nature and reason. Between the two is stretched the fabric of imaginary discourse, *fabula*, which both explains and conceals. In this way, the storm can be further interpreted as the threat posed by Ovid's *Metamorphoses* (and Classical letters more generally), whose pagan picture of violence and sexuality at the heart of nature demanded an altered mode of interpretation, what Baudri calls here *difficiles aditus*. Both "dense" texts, *natura* and *fabula*, could be resolved if signs were linked directly to significance—but Baudri never actually reveals what he knows or hopes to know. His Virgilian promise of prophetic knowledge is emptied by his Ovidian display of rhetorical technique; meaning remains personal and textual, so that the poem offers the process of interpretation but denies the product. Yet his striking optimism about the final legibility of these texts and about the final reliability of individual *ingenium* serves to help us appreciate the excitement and hope of the earliest generations of the *aetas Ovidiana* about the epistemological possiblities of imaginative discourse.

The more innovative aspect of Baudri's Ovidianism, however, lies not in the theory of *fabula* based on the *Metamorphoses* but in the practice of *persona* based upon the other works which entered the curriculum, especially in central and northern France, during the second half of the eleventh century. The magnitude of the shock caused by their introduction into Romanesque secular culture can be measured by the imitations, adaptations, and commentaries that began to spring up. We perhaps should speak of the appearance of a "New Ovid" (by analogy to the "New Aristotle") whose foremost trait was its interest in impersonation, as that in interpretation had marked the "Old." Where the fabulous mode of the Old Ovid tended to annihilate the literal text by denying the very possibility of its truth, the personal mode of the New Ovid tended to redeem it by denying the possibility of its falsehood. A term such as "New Ovid" would be useful to label the discontinuity in grammarian discourse caused by the introduction of these subversive but authoritative texts (and their consequent interpretative structures) into the discipline.

I have argued elsewhere in detail that the arrival of this grammarian discontinuity shows up clearly by comparing the three pairs of long letter-poems which Baudri wrote at Bourgueil.[65] They provide an especially useful set of documents for viewing the emergence of the new *persona* since, as we have seen, the folial order of the letters in his authorized copy is also chronological. In other words, the sequence in the manuscript can be read as Baudri's—and to some extent, I would like to argue, his generation's—successive attempts to face the formal and intellectual challenge of Ovid's radical texts.

In the earliest pair (7–8/XLII–III), which purports to have been sent between Paris and Helen, Baudri confines himself to an exploration of *persona* as "character." It is modeled upon a direct Classical source, namely the opening letters (16 and 17) of the second section of Ovid's *Heroides*.[66] Both characters have been sharply redrawn. Paris speaks with a double voice: that of a man of battle and that of a judge of beauty, both of which pull him toward Helen. She, too, speaks two roles, the one driven by her rational will, the other by the obligations of her person. Both are finally strong, intelligent, and moral characters.

Because Paris and Helen were already well-known literary figures, their characters in these texts are so specific, and they speak with a clear voice (marked by arrogance and resignation, respectively) of their own while Baudri remains silent (that is, he does not use "I" in the text to refer to himself), there is no question of self-impersonation here. Character and author appear to be clearly distinguishable by the audience along a number of lines: Paris is a warrior, a leader, and a lover; Helen is a woman, a queen, and a wife; Baudri is none of these. Yet Baudri does not totally absent himself. It would be difficult to discern his presence in Helen's letter, despite the Ovidian precedent;[67] but he intrudes at least three times into Paris's letter, thereby establishing semantic shifters which activate alternate readings. The first intrusion occurs with the gratuitous and long (110–38) excursus about pedophilia and *fabula* in Greece, the second with the sudden appearance of references to the Loire region (Orléans, Bourgueil) within Paris's description of the Trojan realm (193–98, 207–9), and the last with the lengthy and highly self-reflexive *conclusio* (273–300) so characteristic of Baudri's letter-poems.

At least some portion of the readership must, therefore, have perceived that Baudri was hiding behind his Paris, as Ovid hid behind his and as Ovid's Paris hid behind his own fictional lover (cf. *Heroides*, 16.245–46).[68] Clearly Paris and Baudri are somehow one; as *augur*, *iudex*, and *uersificator*, both establish with divine approbation the aesthetic norms to be applied to lovers and/or poetry. But Paris remains a distinct character. Despite the sporadic irruption of Baudri's voice, his letter does not lead the reader to question the authorial self by establishing a dialogue between its maker and speaker. Until writing, desire, and self begin to merge, Baudri will neither wish nor be able to construct a literary *persona*.

When Baudri returned to the double letter form sometime later (97–98/CLIX–X), he altered his approach considerably. First, he gave up the imitation of a direct Classical model, inventing his own content, themes, and voices. Baudri turned now to the "senilia," the *Tristia* and the *De Ponto*, inserting citations and reminiscences from the works of the embattled and embittered exile rather than those of the adulated court favorite of the *Heroides*.[69] If his first pair of letters had shown particular interest in treating the character (especially Paris) as author, this second concentrates upon treating the author as character, moving us closer to a full self-impersonation.

The exchange is initiated by an intimate friend of Ovid's named Florus, who defends the poet by demonstrating that his life was pure and his poetry morally irrelevant. The heart of the argument comes with the revolutionary syllogizing about the divine origin of nature and love that I quoted earlier, which permits him to conclude that Ovid was just the *recitator*, not the *inuentor*, of desire (59). Florus finishes with a passionate declaration of their spiritual unity and announces his decision to join him in exile and death. Ovid's reply elaborates his own defense. Innocent by nature, his imagination and poetry, not his person, are responsible for his exile. Lovers of both sexes like his teachings, but his verses do not teach them to love, rather what and how they should love. He finishes with a lament, wish, and prayer, leaving the reader with the vivid portrait of the misery of the poet.

As in the first letter pair, tyrannical power remains a central issue, but now *amor* has been brought inside the textual framework. Not the destructive force whose Virgilian dramatization provided the implicit background for the earlier letters, this *amor* is a creative and complex natural force expressed in the sweetness of lovers' intimacy. If Baudri's earlier characters prided themselves on restraint, these revel in release; from a rhetoric primarily forensic he has moved to a rhetoric primarily ornamental. His technique of impersonation has also altered considerably. Although not *by* Ovid, the texts are explicitly *about* Ovid, and Baudri is careful to eliminate the blatant irruptions which loudly announced the artifice of the earlier letters. The switch to affective language increases the verisimilitude of the voice, for its effect of creating a virtual image of the poet ("Ovid") retards one's search for extratextual reference by eliciting a sympathy that binds the reader more tightly to the fiction through emotive association.

A different process, however, leads in the opposite direction as strong resemblances surface between Baudri and "Ovid." The late eleventh-century reader could hardly ignore the agency of a living Neo-Ovidian author who himself was the target of jealous anger through the confusion of poetry with mores, an older and exiled[70] poet whose works are read and admired by young people, and a passionate friend of younger men (cf. 98/CLX.37–42 and 157–58). This biographical subtext probably could thus be extended to further and more intimate levels, but the text is never reduced to such private meaning, for if "Ovid" cannot escape Baudri, neither can "Baudri" escape Ovid. From the interaction of the works of the Classical poet and the reading and writing of the late eleventh-century poet-abbot, a "Baudri" begins to appear who, though as yet unnamed, will provide the foundation for the full self-impersonation still to come.

In a final pair of letters (200–201/CCXXXVIII–IX) which I translate in the Appendix, Baudri and a "Lady Constance" exchange letters of identical length (178 lines). Suddenly, the game is reversed: the reader now must locate the author *outside* the poem if self-impersonation is to be established. To my mind this "Constance" is the same noble nun named Constance who appears in a few other poems, so I shall restrict my analysis to Baudri's letter here, postponing hers until the later discussion of the new feminine voice.[71]

Baudri opens by announcing that although his letter is about love and is a love poem, it contains no "poison." Constance means more to him than the ladies of *fabula Greca* meant to their men, a pronouncement which leads him into a theoretical excursus which, I noted earlier, appears to be the earliest comprehensive theory of what Macrobius (*Commentary on the Dream of Scipio*, I.2) called *narratio fabulosa*. Stressing that he is a *iuuenis*, the fifty-year-old makes an eloquent plea for a "true love" (*uerus amor*, 200.27) in which he might simultaneously love her passionately and share her chastity. Her literary abilities and her beauty move him deeply, but only with a "special love" which ignores the desires of the flesh. He admits to his pleasure in happy literary games of amatory content (*ioci, nugae*), defending them against attack, and concludes by praying for her merciful response.

Like a polyphonic ("many-voiced") composition, or *simphonia*, the personal voice composed by Baudri extracts its fundamental tone from his institutional role as *preceptor* (that "person," as Cicero said of himself repeatedly, which administration imposed upon him).[72] To this, as his constant concern about external judgment reveals (compare 2: *maligna lingua* and 178: *timor*), he adds an apologetic overtone by claiming the sincerity and authority of the role/voice of *uates*, a title explicitly awarded by Constance (201.19–26), through his combination of chastity and allegory. But he undercuts that first overtone with a second established by Ovid's limping meter, playful rhetoric, and *persona* as lover-poet. The combination of the three voices indicates an effort to establish and authorize a new poetic voice for the composition of and about a new private "self" which embraced nature, poetry, and their intertwined productive powers.

But this intellectually ambitious and judiciously orthodox text does not "explain" most of Baudri's other letter-poems, where he never claims the vatic voice with its requirement for unambiguous readings of love and poetry within the frame of the poem. Such texts constitute the final step in the collapse of character and author associated with the emergence of the complete literary *persona*. A delicate expression of this mixture can be found in a wishful piece (108/CLXX) where skin and parchment, reading and loving, and desire and imagination are indistinguishable:

To a Friend to Whom He Was Sending a Letter

> O would that I had been my own messenger
>   Or the letter which your hand stroked,
> And that I had had then the same consciousness I have now
>   And that you would not have recognized me until I desired.
> Then I would have explored your face and mind as you read,
>   but only if I could have contained myself long enough.
> The rest we would have left to the propitious gods and to fortune,
>   For God comes sooner to grace than man.[73]

In addition to employing complex and ambiguous notions of both *amor* and *iocus*, this poignant letter-poem provides an image of their fundamental identity. Shorn of all specific reference, it has been reduced to a disembodied voice of creative desire (*ingenium*) speaking in an irreal mood. Without stable subject or predicate, the utterances remain illegible in a profound manner. Only the act of reading, confounded with that of loving and mediated like it by the moving hand, has meaning, since both the reader and the read have been excluded from this pure game.

As this last poem shows, my academic separation of *iocus* and *amor* must now be abandoned, for true poetry and true love are inseparable here. The true lover-friend is the poet, and the poem is the true medium of loving friendship. The one who is loved is conceived as a text; the text is approached as one to be loved. Classical letters "desire" the reader; the malevolent critic is a "pimp." Baudri's very literary success—as Winfried Offermanns notes—resides in his striking ability to suspend his creations between truth and lie, to leave the reader unsure of the nature of the relationship between Baudri and his correspondant, as Ovid had done with his mysterious Corinna.[74]

At the heart of this fusion lies the *f(o)edus* ("contract, treaty"). Like so many others the poet employs, the word is fundamentally ambiguous. Related to *fides* and *fidus* and common in political discourse, the word was also used from Ovid onward to imply sexual union, and had become a standard term in monastic and feudal discourse as well.[75] Aware of and playing with the these connotations, Baudri denies on the one hand that his love poems are real, since no *amor* has tied him with any *foedus*; yet he pleads with the poet Galo, "Would that the same *foedus amoris* might join you to me as the love I have requested joins you to me."[76] The security or pledge (*pignus*) for this contract is the letter-poem itself (148/CCX.9–10), a bittersweet "love-token" which instills joy through its verbal contact yet leaves its recipient yearning for what Baudri, like the troubadours to follow, calls "other things" or "the rest" (*cetera, reliqua*).

Such ambiguity explains why Baudri was attacked early and often. If his spirited responses are strung together in a single discourse, they supply what appears to be the most explicit Romanesque defense of making poetry about love. Writing poetry, he says, is first a way to spend free time, and it helps me dispell tedium; I prefer to spend time that way than to lie idle like a packhorse; and being active keeps the temptations of evil at bay; besides, writing poetry exercises my imagination, which I like; it is also the only way I know to greet my friends; I know the poems are a bit undernourished and unadorned, but a recherché style is boring; yet I am stirred to ardent zeal, I confess, by an obsessive desire for praise as a poet; you should know that writing poetry is a form of refreshment (*recreatio*) which can alleviate your cares and make you more productive when you return to work; besides, I don't think making verses ever will or ever did infect my behavior; and it doesn't hurt anyone else, because I don't tell people that they should love, just how to love; you can't blame me anyway, because the material is not mine, only the meaning; futhermore, I write what pleases boys and girls because I want my poems to be read; so read it right and don't pimp my words.[77] And with that final jab, Baudri rests his cafeteria-style defense of the *iocus amoris*, declaring it neither counter to Christian teaching (because the texts are not serious) nor commensurate with it (because the texts are not allegorized).

Finally, what kind of audience was interested in the precious imaginary games he wanted to play, and for what reasons? One of the great advantages of studying the late eleventh century through this particular set of literary documents, a sort of poetic cartulary, lies in its social as well as its personal coherency. In the kind of analysis often undertaken for similar poetry of this period, where individual texts are chosen—whether consciously or not—for their formal or thematic anticipation of the twelfth (or nineteenth) century, one must forgo not only biography but also sociology. Such a procedure is necessarily anachronistic, and produces, moreover, a false impression of the autonomy of poetry. But Baudri's letter-poems (and, to a limited extent, the epitaphs) provide us with explicit and implicit data about the names, locations, and professions of his addressees, revealing the profile of the group which shared his values.

Only a few of the correspondents belonged to the upper ecclesiastic or secular ranks.[78] The vast majority belongs to the lower ranks of the monastic and cathedral schools, although most of these cannot be located with any specificity.[79] There remain persons identifiable at best by name only or, failing even that, by some generic qualifier (*amicus, poeta*). Most if not all of the latter can be safely situated, however, if one makes the reasonable assumptions that all those who are qualified as "learned," "richly endowed by *littera*," or who write and read Latin verse, belong to the schools in one way or another. This profile identifies the lower schools as the primary locus of the resurgence of Ovidian poetry before 1100, a conclusion supported by Ralph Hexter's study, and as the locus of any putative Ovidian influence on the secular aristocracy (through students such as the rich, young nobleman satirized in 4–5/XXXIX–XL).[80]

Baudri's audience, then, was composed mostly of the teachers and especially the students and pupils of the cathedral and monastic schools; it was also predominantly male and, like that of the other poets of the age, strongly regional.[81] Yet the few exceptions to these general traits are important, for they reveal that the audience was defined through the literary culture of the schools, rather than by the schools themselves. Adela of Blois, whose role we will examine in depth in Chapter 5, leads a small but important group of noblewomen (all nuns except herself) who participated in the poetic games of Baudri and his contemporaries. Duke Roger (of Sicily) and John the Poitevin architect can also be invited to participate by virtue of their ability and interest in ingenious artifacts. Representing the secularization of traditionally clerical literary values on the one hand, and of a vulgarization (through *rusticitas*) of content, grammar, and rhetoric on the other, these exceptions in Baudri's audience reveal that an important transition was in progress. Personal poetry employing simple style and Ovidian content, already well established in the lower schools, was being sent in search of patronage outside the institutional confines to educated members of the secular world.

Viewed through the letter-poems, this socially heterogeneous group forms an Ovidian subculture, the earliest known from the high medieval period. Moreover, to make use of a notion introduced by Brian Stock, it is a "textual community" whose members "may not have shared profound doctrinal similarities or common social origins, but they demonstrated a parallel use of texts, both to structure the internal behavior of the group's members and to provide solidarity against the outside world."[82] In this case, one is dealing not with a religious community reading the Bible, but with a literary community reading Ovid. Poem replaces commentary; poet, priest. This secular, textual subculture arose with the spread of literacy in the eleventh century which Stock analyzes; like the religious communities, it accepted the distinction between the living text and the dead letter, and distinguished between ritualistic repetition and individualized interpretation. In fact, this Neo-Ovidian community hovering outside the border of official ecclesiastic culture constitutes a striking marker for the spread, secularization, and fetishization of literacy, since it locates the act of reading and writing itself at the center of its cult.

The members of this community could be called clerks, if the word were understood in the broad and noninstutitional sense as Baudri himself uses it: "Learned writing shapes your character; your character is as it should be for a clerk: namely witty, light-hearted, playful (or: poetry loving), amicable . . . ."[83] By defining *clericus* as an internal characteristic rather than an external station, Baudri opens membership to outsiders who share these traits. His group becomes by its own definition an elite capable of transcending normal boundaries of estate and profession, since worth is established by heart, mind, and imagination. Derived from, but no longer restricted to, the "clerk" we saw satirized in the Bayeux Tapestry, this widespread figure constitutes an important version of the polymorphic loving subject emerging in France toward the end of the eleventh century. Through his letter-poems and other secular writings, Baudri seems to be reconstructing and recombining subjects from the particular ideological systems operating upon him, especially that of the Reformists, whom I take to be those black-hooded enemies of all *leuitas* threatening him and his book in the opening poem (1/XXXVI). He relied for this defense primarily upon self-impersonation in order to "elude" interpellation as abbot and monk by withdrawing into an immune world of letters which denied stable nomination (that is, subjection through naming) of any kind.

A similar shift has been traced by Georges Duby for the word "noble" in the eleventh century; as older definitions of nobility lost their unique value in the face of the increasing power and wealth outside the Carolingian aristocracy, the word ceased to designate solely the class but increasingly the quality of character.[84] This strong parallel suggests not only that Baudri's poetry can indeed bear upon—and perhaps modify conceptions of—investigations of the eleventh century more generally, but it also proposes an explanation for the attraction of his "games." Baudri himself marketed the *iocus amoris* straightforwardly as an exemplary pastime; to Duke Roger, for example, he invokes the theme of what he calls *refrigerium* or *recreatio*: "intersperse such poetic games among your manifold concerns; the state will find you more productive because of it."[85] The fact that people have pastimes is not particularly intriguing; the selection of a particular form by a group within a strong class structure constitutes, however, a socio-historic phenomenon which carries information about that group's conscious and unconscious values. When countesses and dukes begin cultivating and composing poetry about love (first in Latin, then in the vernacular) as a pastime, a significant shift in the concept of aristocracy has occurred.

For all its unique qualities, then, Baudri's poetry evokes and responds to some of the most pressing concerns of its time. If the striking absence of indication of noble status in the majority of the letter-poems reflects in fact the ignoble status of their recipients or authors—as as has been asserted for Baudri himself—then we can begin to understand the acceptance of his proposal for an internal aristocracy of the heart established through participation in the subtleties of poetic and amatory gaming. Those excluded by birth from nobility must have been strongly attracted to a redefinition of superiority based upon the internal capabilties of the individual, rather than upon external accident of family. At the same time, Adela of Blois and Roger of Sicily belonged to a nobility which was witnessing the acquisition of traditional traits of aristocratic status (power, wealth) by outsiders; they could see in this new cult of the *lector amicus* (86/CXLVIII.38)—and both words are significant—important support for defending superior social status. Once true poetry and true love have been established as markers of an internal and true excellence, both the haves and the have-nots see the utility. Such an understanding of the social function of these amorous games permits us to regard them and their reception as products of the tensions within Late Carolingian culture in the last half of the eleventh century. Freed by self-definition (as games) from the concerns of the external world, Baudri's letter-poems could appeal to a variety of individuals and groups as a new and special token of excellence.

We are able, moreover, to view through this poetry the crucial formative stage of a new secular culture with a new attitude toward the impersonation of desire and eloquence.[86] Its humanistic credo included a cult of the *auctores*, an optimistic depiction of a man-centered world, a faith in the virtue of human *amor*, a cult of individual genius, and a passionate belief in the value of literary activity. As Baudri succinctly expressed it: "None of the poets attained heaven through poetry, yet learned writing (*littera*) often led them to heaven" (91/CLIII.8–9). By 1100, the way was opened for the formation of a new elite of the heart where cleric and lay alike could construct a voice of subjectivity—all while maintaining an echo of subjection which promised not to disturb the existing social formation.

*   *   *

This chapter constitutes a shortened and much revised version of my "*Iocus amoris*: The Poetry of Baudri of Bourgueil and the Formation of the Ovidian Subculture," *Traditio* 42 (1986): 143–93. Portions have been added from a subsequent article, "Composing Yourself: Ovid's *Heroides*, Baudri of Bourgueil and the Problem of Persona," *Mediaevalia* 13, "Ovid in Medieval Culture," ed. Marilynn R. Desmond (1989 for 1987): 83–117.

3. Natural Poetics: Marbod at Angers and the Promotion of Eloquence

The letter-poems of Baudri of Bourgueil demonstrate that new secular perspectives on poetry, desire, and *persona* could be found by the last quarter of the eleventh century even within Benedictine monastic culture. The surface innocence of his cult of the *iocus amoris* contradicts the powerful psychological and ideological investments which underlie his loving subject. In that sense, his lyric practice serves, in spite of its ideosyncratic nature and lack of discernible influence, to describe wider concerns of the Romanesque secular culture, particularly with respect to the new strategies for contesting subjection through self-impersonation. If we want to look at the contemporary theory on these topics, we need to turn to the upper schools associated with the cathedrals where theory itself was practiced.

The richest eleventh-century source I know of lies in the *carmina varia* and other secular compositions of Marbod of Rennes, surely the most unjustly ignored theorist and poet of the entire Latin Middle Ages. They were written for the most part while he functioned as archdeacon, chancellor, and schoolmaster at Angers from around 1067 until 1096 before becoming bishop of the city whose name, somewhat misleadingly, he now bears. Much of his obscurity no doubt stems from the fact that, like Baudri of Bourgueil, he matches poorly the Gregorian ideal of the age; moreover, a number of his most innovative texts were suppressed in 1708 by a Jesuit editor, and only republished in 1950. Since little work of any kind has been done on Marbod, the recovery of those texts provides an opportunity to examine his secular work more generally.[1]

Marbod's career divides into periods of about three decades apiece. Traditionally assumed to have been born around 1035 into a well-to-do Angevin mercantile family, he appears as a young man in the documents of the Benedictine abbey of Saint-Aubin, which was closely allied with the count of Anjou and his policies. At an early age he entered the episcopal school of Saint-Maurice, which at that time (ca. 1045–55) was directed by students of Fulbert of Chartres, whose epochal reforms permeated

eleventh-century Angevin culture.[2] Marbod's early literary training can be
appreciated from the powerful picture he paints in his *Liber decem capitulorum* (2.52–60), written when he was sixty-seven, where one can see
the torment which (Ovidian) texts of desire and imagination held for the
young clerk.[3] The "trifles" he retracts in that confessional text likely came
from this first period and probably include many of those suppressed in the
eighteenth century, such as the poetic love-letters sent by a young woman
"To a Boy-Friend Promising Money" or by a young man "To a Jealous
Girl-Friend."[4]

Marbod must have risen quickly in the system, since by his early
thirties he had been placed in charge of the school and the scriptorium, an
office variously called *cancellarius, scholasticus,* or *magister scholae,* to which
he brought "learning and imagination," as a later bishop of Angers comments (PL 171.1463). This promotion had doubtless much to do with his
own merits and his family's money, but it also may have been influenced
by Odo of Bayeux, whose patronage he apparently enjoyed in the 1060s.[5]
In 1076/77, Marbod acquired the office of archdeacon, one of three in the
diocese, not relinquishing it until 1102. In this important office he worked
for the first few years alongside the famous Berengar of Tours, another
student of Fulbert of Chartres, and functioned as the bishop's substitute,
performing as the everyday figure of justice in matters of church government and spiritual justice.[6] During these middle years of his life, he wrote
a good number of his extant works, secular as well as religious, including
saints' lives, epistolary poems, and the very successful lapidary and rhetoric.
It is intriguing to note that, as with his contemporary Baudri, only the in-
come, leisure, and immunity conferred by higher office permitted Marbod
to "publish" beyond his immediate circle of friends.

At the Council of Tours in 1096, Marbod was promoted to bishop of
Rennes, an election which suited Angevin strategies for containing Anglo-
Norman aggression and Papal strategy for reforming the French church.[7]
Coupled with that of Hildebert of Le Mans, his promotion put a damper
on regional poetry; Baudri laments to Emma the loss of Marbod, "the
bright star of poets," whose departure has left the world to beastly men
(ed. Hilbert, 153.51–62). Despite the difficulties presented by a new office
which he did not want, Marbod continued to write prolifically, especially
hagiography. Intellectually and poetically he seems to have accommodated
himself to his new position, as one sees in his admonitory letters to the nun
Agnes and the itinerant preacher Robert of Arbrissel. Also, his *Liber decem
capitulorum* (ca. 1102) presents a coherent statement of Christian Human-

ism, probably reflecting as well the influence (political more than literary) of Hildebert, presumably the *presul doctissimus* (1.64) to whom he sends the work for judgment.[8] Near the end of his life, Marbod came full circle, retiring to Saint-Aubin to die as a monk in 1123.

Marbod's secular achievements can be appreciated readily through the complex and intriguing lament entitled "Troubled Recreation" (*De Molesta Recreatione*). I know no better means prior to 1100 of understanding the relations between *persona* and subject which lie at the heart of the lyric renaissance of the twelfth century.[9] Like many of its companion pieces among the suppressed texts, it cannot be assimilated easily to Marbod's oeuvre, so I will use it as a "side door" into his practice of self-impersonation.

Troubled Recreation

I usually take my recreation to the sound of the harp,
banishing as often as I want the ennuis of a carefilled life.
My citharist is not the Cytherean boy himself,
But this boy is not far from that Cytherean god
Whose sweet melody surpasses the heavens in its subtlety.   5
This one sings a song about a certain hapless knight
Whose lover mourns because fate has snatched him from her.
As she mourns, her every word wounds my mind;
The sounds played on the harp fill the whole hall with laments,
To the harp's complaint my heart becomes sad, sorrowful.   10
The girl prepares to raise the limbs of him lying on the ground,
now pale, now without breath, pierced with a wide-tipped lance.
With arms stretched out about to embrace the body, she falls
in the midst of her effort and becomes senseless, sightless;
reviving almost instantly, she scratches her face with bloody
          fingernails.   15
She pines away on the ground, saying things I do not want to
          relate.
It is terrible to recount the causes of her grievous lament:
mouth, eyes, face, buried now in icy death;
she commits each to memory (they are not as she knew them),
giving him an outpour of kisses (but not as she did recently).   20
Recollect what she says as she dries the blood from his wounds!
Recollect what she recalls as she gazes at his face!

These things the boy portrays (so that) it becomes reality,
    not a song;
as he plays, the intertwining of lute and voice
imitates more than passably the girl's embraces.   25
My changing heart moves through various emotions
And I seem to undergo whatever I hear from the harpist.
Thus care replaces play for me.
As it pains me, everything changes around,
for the welcome recreation becomes unwelcome torment.[10]   30

Even reading this poem nine hundred years later and in translation, one perceives Marbod's great interest in portraying human nature with all its complications. Moreover, he seems as concerned with reproducing emotions as with describing them; if sympathy can be said to drive the content, empathy drives the form. The internal song and singer, finally, invite reflection on lyric itself, particularly its concern with affect and style.

We appear to have immediate "access" (*aditus*) to the poem, as Marbod's first readers would have said, yet one slowly realizes that it engages us less through its noise than its silence, less through what it shows than what it hides and ignores. We feel intrigued, pleased, and somehow even obligated by the poem's "blanks," to use Wolfgang Iser's term, which remains useful despite its original restriction to cognitive aspects.[11] In fact, two different kinds of blanks, narrative and discursive, forestall closure: actions elude observation, intentions elude words. The listener/reader must pick up the cues in order to restage mentally four dramas: the knight's aggression, the girl's love, the boy's sympathy, and the speaker's recreation. Moreover, this "four-fold" play could take place only inside referential frames which have now largely disappeared along with their respective power groups. The modern audience, thus, experiences a double need to recreate—to retell, to replay—these stories, one elicited by the presence of textual silences and the other imposed by the absence of contextual sounds.

To begin, the characters are, in fact, subjects, a status indicated by the generic labels they carry. The word "knight" (*miles*), for instance, designates the most important subject of feudal ideology. We recognize him from the Bayeux Tapestry, where we saw him in a context of dynastic aggression whose "high story," as I wanted to name it, served to legitimate the profession of arms.[12] But here his subjecthood is different, since the representation of a nameless corpse by a Romanesque French cleric could hardly avoid engaging the discussion of violence itself which had fueled the Peace and Truce of God. Also, since idealizing discourse will soon replace this traditional epic scene of mourning with a lover's passion and a lady's joy, Marbod's dead knight seems to carry almost epochal significance, as if with him were passing the "heroic" culture itself.[13]

Unlike the *miles*, the *amica* who holds him rarely appeared in official representation during the Romanesque period. As we shall see in Chapter 4, her subject position derives from the discourse of the chevalric profession, rather than that of the aristocratic order.[14] Neither wife nor relative, the Girl-Friend stood in no legal relation to the knight from any institutional perspective despite her putative ubiquity in the everyday chivalric society. "Outlawed" by her desire, she was excluded from social structures and their power to grant stability. She comes into the picture here as mourner; her grief marks his excellence, her words his memory.[15] But the deterministic effect of that traditional subject position is constrained by the signs of her subjectivity: she now must be interpreted, no longer simply decoded. With such a portrait Marbod creates a voice with which to reconsider nature itself. He deflects the usual clerical attack against desire by binding the reader through sympathy—a strategy we also found in the Ælfgyva panel—and thereby presents a humanizing if not indeed humanistic view of both woman and nature that we will want to explore in detail later.[16]

The Girl-Friend functions also as a figure of memory. Her attempt to defeat time (death, change, nature) is underscored by the terrible plea: *Collige, quid dicat, dum vulnera sanguine siccat! Collige, quid memoret, dum vultibus eius inheret!* (21–22). Governed by a rhetorical figure known as reduplication (*conduplicatio*) designed specifically to arouse pity, this couplet's emotional appeal drives the Speaker back toward the safety of the frame as if threatened by the "material" of nature inside.[17] As a consequence, we are unable to tell exactly who utters that command or to whom it is addressed: the Speaker to the Boy, the Boy to the Speaker, or Marbod to the reader. Without that information, we cannot determine for which speaker and in what form memory—the only consolation for death available within this poem—will fulfill its function with the aid of language.

If we move outward another level, we find the Boy gazing with his inner eye at the Girl-Friend while she gazes at the Knight. Because of his limited interests we see but two moments of the action. The first, of course, is the point when she *grasps* (in the most physical sense of that word) the death of her lover, an act which almost kills her as well. But a second moment which threatens to revise even this most private history interests him as much as the first. The Boy's asides (19, 20) display his fascination with the irony that she makes now the same movements (embracing, stroking, kissing) in grief that she had earlier in joy. These two foci of the singer's gaze suggest that this prepubescent voyeur of human sexuality has selected generic traits (what else could he know, what else could he say?) to relate a story he finally cannot comprehend.[18]

The Boy's art lies primarily in the reproduction of affect. To this end he crafts and joins *verba* and *melos*, manifesting his ingenious powers. The figure of that joining, named in the text as embrace (*amplexus*), evokes the interweave or interlace found throughout much of Romanesque art. Significantly, neither word nor concept appears in rhetorical treatises, ancient or medieval; its origins appear to lie in Germanic ornamentation, its source more popular than learned. Thus it shows up in twelfth-century vernacular aesthetic as *lassar/laisser* ("to lace") and its derivatives such as *laisse*, the Old French term for the basic structural element of epic narrative. Here this figure has become a complete trope of the secular: Girl-Friend and Knight embrace (13) without union, an act imitated by music and text (25), as the poem's voices intertwine without unison. It also figures epistemology, since it allows even what cannot be understood to be enclosed: the Girl-Friend embraces Death; the Boy, Pleasure; the Speaker, Genius. Not one of these abstracts surfaces in the text, as if to imply that not one can be uttered in its domain. But they can be enveloped within poetic figure and, though nameless and senseless, enter into a culture which would otherwise reject them.

One more frame back, the Speaker listens and, finally, laments; like the Girl-Friend, his "game" turns to sorrow (cf. 15–16 and 29–30). The picture of her grief and despair, so realistically depicted by the Boy, evokes a reaction in him similar to that of Aeneas at Carthage: his pity leads him to lament her specifically as well as to shed more general *lacrimas rerum* for the constancy of change. In his voice, moreover, we begin to hear didactic overtones absent from the others. The residue of the song's performance, or the poem's reading, is a "picture of grief" which initiates a sequence of interpretation and judgment. Yet because it leads him to empathize with the Girl and refuse to represent her as a traditional (ecclesiastic) subject of female desire, the Speaker's pity forces readers to redirect their condemnation toward the source of grief, the rule of nature through *cupiditas*.[19]

Yet readers cannot escape what they condemn. Although the Speaker gazes at the Girl-Friend, he seems to be staring at the Boy; the object of his lament and final agent of his torment are not identical, as the suggestive figure of *adnominatio* or paronomasia in the opening lines hints broadly: *Est citharista meus non ipse puer Cithereus/Sed puer ipse deo paulominus a Cithereo* (3–4). The reader expects by context some praise of musical ability, the talent which presumably brought the Boy to his post, but Amor was known for his beauty, not his music.[20] His allegorical significance (*omen*) derives from his name (*nomen*): he embodied desire and particularly, for the Greeks at least, the desire for young men (a connotation implied here by the label *Cithereus*, or "male Venus"). When the Speaker stresses how the Boy harpist resembles Amor, then, he buries beneath a deceptive (if not fallacious) simile two possible translations. The first obliquely praises the adolescent's beauty, the second intimates the Speaker's physical attraction to him. The latter extends into an obvious allegory so that motion ("the boy plays") translates quickly into emotion ("Desire arouses").[21]

The Speaker's distress now appears to have two sources: one explicitly incited by his gaze through the Boy (and his art) at the represented Girl-Friend, and another implicitly aroused by his stare through the Girl-Friend (and her desire) at the representing Boy. As we thus return the Speaker's desire to interpretation, we recuperate a register of pedophilia which increases the poem's recreative potential. In social terms, moreover, we now see that the desirous Speaker subjects the younger and subservient Boy with and to his stare. Mediated by true mimesis (desire, representation, reproduction), the song which began for him as recreation from care ends by recreating the very care from which it arose by arousing his desire and its frustration. The text's authoritative examples invite the friendly interpreter to adopt a radical position, agreeing to observe *and* refusing to condemn the consequences of being subject to nature.[22]

Multiple speakers, multiple narratives, and multiple intents now pose a new question: is the poem's maker identical to its speaker? Emile Benveniste's influential description of the production in the act of speaking of a split subject—that of the said and of the saying, of the *énoncé* and of the enunciation—suggests from a theoretical perspective that the two must differ.[23] The question is only one of the extent and nature of the difference between the empirical Marbod and his "spokesman" constructed within language. Does the former reflect (upon) himself in the text, or does he simply lurk outside as an eavesdropping voyeur? For anyone unfamiliar with the poet's other writings (and this includes most modern readers) or for anyone suspicious of arguments of authorial intention or coherence, he will remain outside. Yet this is a dangerous text for a man in Marbod's position to refuse to enter, for even friendly readers, it seems to me, would have found the voicing technique disturbing. With Death and Desire on the scene, the Author's absence radically opens interpretation.

The Speaker certainly sounds like Marbod. A cleric of some obvious institutional importance, burdened with business (*negotium*, implied by *sollicite . . . tedia uite* 2), he seeks in his free time (*otium*) relaxation or refreshment (*recreatio*) through a private performance of a "popular song." But the Speaker says not a word about writing a poem, stands out for his changing heart rather than his constant mind, and reveals a pedophilia which escapes criticism.[24] Nor does style indicate Marbod's presence, as it can be ascribed to the Boy or the Speaker, including the only two major rhetorical figures (*adnominatio* in 2–3, *conduplicatio* in 21–22). Finally, one finds no "signposts" pointing outside which might force an external search for irony, judgment, or significance: no moralizing, no significant citations or reminiscences from the *auctores*, no biblical or patristic echoes, no hint from the rubric.[25]

This "side door" seems to have led to a dead end. On the one hand, the resemblance of the Speaker to Marbod's official person is so strong that there is little incentive to listen outside the poem. On the other hand, the babel of the internal voices is so loud that there is little possibility of hearing outside the poem. If we cannot get to Marbod from this text, perhaps we can get to this text through Marbod. But the question of nomenclature becomes important again: what do we mean, exactly, what *can* we mean exactly with this name "Marbod?" He was an "author" (ultimately from Greek *autos*, "self"), generating by himself images of his self within a written culture. He studied and taught Roman self-representation, he *wrote* and he wrote *texts* (both closely associated with a deeper sense of the interior self), and he employed the first person.[26] To the distant reader, whether removed by space, time, profession, or class, the name "Marbod" cannot function as a simple nametag for an empirical person with whom there has been no concrete relation of any sort.

It is clear that rejecting the author's complete presence in a text differs greatly from accepting his complete absence from it, replacing him as Michel Foucault would do with an "author function" existing within discourse alone. Both the Roman theory of *persona* and the Romanesque practice of reading, even "silent" reading, constrain us to examine the agent along with the discourse, the actor along with the role.[27] By the use, therefore, of the name "Marbod" in such a context (that is, when refering to the maker of a text carrying that name), I mean to designate the mental

and social construct of the "prescribed author" held by an historically determined group of readers. An author is "prescribed" in two senses. First,
the construct results from hearing or reading texts prescribed with the
same name: e.g., *Marbodus, De Ornamentis Verborum*. Like Hume's famous
notion of selfhood, the "prescribed author" can be viewed as the memory
of associations of the name with texts, an economical semiotic vehicle with
affective and cognitive content which is readily reactivated in the mind before or during the reading of another text carrying the same name. Second,
this construct expands the range of significance of a particular reading as
it reduces the range of meaning. As an extrapolation and personification
of sense, the "prescribed author" functions as the locus of a collection of
interests, means, and goals which the reader (medieval as well as modern)
identifies with intention. When granted "authority," it becomes the first
conceptual framework activated for all kinds of interpretive decisions.

Despite the variety of his publications and offices which we surveyed
earlier, Marbod kept a consistent prescribed *persona*, one perhaps best seen
from the introduction to his death roll in 1123:

> We announce to you the death of the venerable lord bishop Marbod, always
> to be remembered with praise, eloquent in speech, outstanding in religion,
> famous for moral virtue, extremely well studied in the field of letters; his dis-
> course was always flavored with salt, from his mouth flowed an eloquence
> sweeter than any honey. And although at that time all of France hummed
> with various centers of learning, yet he as king of orators held the citadel of
> French eloquence.[28]

Through its repetition of the trait, this eulogy nearly equates Marbod
with Eloquence itself, the trait which first rendered his existence historical
as he spontaneously composed a hexameter at a dinner party with Odo
of Bayeux and William the Conquerer. To French Romanesque readers of
Latin poetry, then, the primary connotation of the name "Marbod" was
"the model of eloquence," and it mattered more than the subjects designated with "son of a merchant," "schoolmaster of Angers," or "bishop of
Rennes."

The variety of Marbod's writings, however, obstructs easy conclusions. "Doctrinal" texts ranging from saints' lives to hymns form one
group; "official" texts designed to please, damn, or lament secular and
ecclesiastic figures of power, another. Neither contributes directly to our
enquiry, since the "De Molesta" is neither doctrinal (although it might reflect a moral view) nor political (although it might present a class critique).
Three other groups remain: his "naturalist," "poetic," and "amatory" writ-

ings. The first includes all texts about nature, no matter what the genre; the second, all those which treat language as material means; the third, all poems about friendship and desire. The last group, I want to argue, can best be read against the background of the unique Angevin contributions to the study of nature and language.

Of all the writers in France during the last third of the eleventh century, Marbod alone displays a continual and deep interest in nature. Much "scientific" work was being done by him and his contemporaries in western central France during his tenure at Angers,[29] but this material remains generally unknown, unappreciated, and misinterpreted. Since the question of natural science sits alongside that of language at the center of most forms of Humanism, whether in twelfth-century France or fifteenth-century Italy, its investigation here will open up new interpretations of the period's significance for larger questions concerning the High Middle Ages.[30] In fact, this movement fostered an intense and important production of those "books of Nature" upon which the next century's grand syntheses would rest.

Marbod's most influential work, the "Book of Gems" (*Liber Lapidum*/ *Liber De Lapidibus*), gives a good idea of the extent and significance of Angevin naturalism. In it he sets out to recount in hexameters the secrets of sixty "stones"; 125 manuscripts and many translations attest to his success.[31] By pretending to write for the special few, he constructs an elite subject for naturalist discourse: "I was moved to compose a short little book suitable for carrying about which would be comprehensible primarily to me and to a few of my friends; for whoever vulgarizes mysteries reduces majesty, and things known to the crowd do not remain secret."[32] For each stone he lists origin and description, and catalogues physical and psychological powers. His unsuccessful investigation of a precious stone known as chrysoprase, for instance, provides a good example of his method, content, and subject:

But India, the home of gems, sends chrysoprase.
Carrying the juice of leeks and mixed in color,
It gleams with golden drops as if with a purple dye.
What virtues it might have I have not yet been able to discover;
But I believe they exist, and it is not a crime not to know everything.[33]

We should compare the gem's treatment in the short prose mystical interpretation of uncertain authorship which accompanies the lapidary in some manuscripts:

Chrysoprase is purple with little gold specks on it.
It signifies those who spend their life always in
hardships and in labor of suffering by always remaining in charity.[34]

The contrast is striking. In the former there speaks a new voice of reason in whom the unknown in nature and in himself incites curiosity; in the latter, the old voice of faith who asserts the truth by and of transcending nature. In the new self-impersonation, Marbod investigates the pagan world— both its objects and its books—for its "power" (*vires, virtutes*), that strength of a man (*vir*) acquired through discipline. Thus the fact that he took much from Alexandrian sources, despoiling the Egyptians differently than Augustine had in mind, reinforces rather than diminishes the cultural importance of his book; further, it attests to the important break from their predecessors being made by these "naturalists" in the Loire Valley schools. With his practical and positive search for the secret powers of nature and its texts, underscored by the complete absence of Christian doctrine, Marbod announces in the lapidary both a new object and a new subject of knowledge.[35]

Alongside it in a number of the manuscripts one finds the "Book of Herbs" (*De Viribus Herbarum*), a second and much longer natural treatise in hexameters traditionally dated to the mid-eleventh century.[36] This equally successful text is usually ascribed to a certain Odo of Meung on the basis of a single manuscript, although it has also been argued that Marbod himself authored it. Whether he wrote it or not—and I do not think it likely—he certainly conceived of the herbal and the lapidary as companion paradigms, since he mentions them together (PL 171.1566, 1687–8). The herbal's science relies upon a vaguely Aristotelian theory of four *gradus* or states (hot, cold, wet, dry) and four degrees of potency. The discussion of the rose, for instance, begins thus:

The rose seems to be called rightly the flower of flowers
because it outstrips the other flowers in beauty and odor.
Yet it is not only able to help us with beauty and odor,
but also helps us with various powers.
In the first degree its force is dry and cold:
It soothes holy [=Saint Anthony's] fire if applied in crushed form,
And also calms the stomach and intestines if they heat up.[37]

The herbal's practical medicine, based upon the extractable *vis* of 77 (later 97) plants, supplies evidence of a naturalism very similar in attitude and purpose to that of Marbod's lapidary. And they share the same speaking self, that naturalist who subjects nature through discipline for the benefit of society.

Both treatises differ strikingly from the model of monastic science set by the *Physiologus (latinus)*, the Alexandrian bestiary of which at least two versions were in circulation in France at this time. This well-known, ultimately Neoplatonic text written in the early Christian era proposed to demonstrate the correspondences between the natural order on the one hand, and the moral and religious orders on the other. Furthermore, the great success of the eleventh-century versified version by one Theobaldus, probably an Italian, had established a powerful mediating role for the grammarian artist which must have been very attractive.[38] In a short and possibly fragmentary version ascribed to Hildebert of Le Mans, for instance (PL 171.1218–24), Christian intention and poetic invention signal a strong divergence from the kind of naturalism practiced by Marbod and his circle. The latter looked away from such a poetico-moral impulse, establishing a new science founded upon nature's material power to enable humans to remain in this world, rather than its mystical power to enable them to escape it.

One final text from this group illustrates this point well. A student and friend of Marbod's named Walter dedicated and sent to him a prose treatise, the *Physiognomonia*, which explicated the science of reading facial and bodily signs. Walter's book is the oldest extant version of a Latin compilation and translation from ca. 250–375 of three Greek treatises on physiognomy. This new science requires a full and explicit theory of signification:

> Whoever studies physiognomy ought first to commit to memory the signification of signs, second to remember their values, and third to unite whatever signs he has found and relate them to each other, just as he might arrange it in the case of language.

If the syntax of the science derives from language, its semantics often relies upon established animalian values:

> Thin and narrow and depressed sides argue for timidity, and those stuffed with flesh and hard indicate wild men. But those which are round as if swollen announce one who is talkative and vain: for it points to frogs.[39]

With its lengthy and detailed exposition, its use of an explicit theory of language and signs, and its lack of magic or religion, this treatise (and the impulse for its recovery) points in many ways toward the rediscovery of Aristotle and the High Medieval science which followed.

Such investigation in Marbod's immediate group both stemmed from and reinforced an affirmative image of nature as an ordered and virtuous realm of mysterious power to which humans can find access through the trained intellect. An equally affirmative but somewhat different image can be found in another lyric.

Description of Vernal Beauty

Spring's grace forbids me to be in a bestial mood,
And I borrow my mindset from the elements:
I rejoice in nature itself—rightly, I think.
A thousand different colors adorn the flowers,
The ground cloaks itself in a fleece of grass.   5
I see the orchard turn green with leaves and set fruit.
Orioles, blackbirds, jackdaws, woodpeckers, nightingales
compete with equal praise in singing their various songs.
There is not a nest in a tree without chicks
And a new generation, featherless, hides in the bushes.   10
With roses emerging, the gardens are beautiful.
Add in with these the field which gleams with grain;
Add in the vines, the grapes as well, and later the nuts.
You could count in the dances of the young wives and mothers,
And young men's games, and a joyful and cloudless day.   15
Whoever sees so much beauty and neither softens nor smiles
Is unyielding, and has strife in his heart.
Whoever does not want to describe the earth's splendor with
      praise
Begrudges her Maker, whose glory is served
By numbing winter, summer, autumn, spring's virtue.[40]   20

This programmatic song of joy begins with the problem posed by death, since the speaker sets out to abandon a "bestial mood" implicitly induced by the gloom of winter. Spring's *gratia* (a word invitingly ambiguous) overwhelms him, and he devises a laudatory catalogue of nature's virtue which arises from its final cause, procreation, as the inclusion of out-of-season fruits (grapes, nuts) emphasizes. Faced with the glorious renewal of the world, he concludes in the final lines that death (implied by *bruma rigens*) and desire (implied by *veris honestas*) both honor the Lord.

By genre (*descriptio*) and discourse, this text recalls a poetic genre which had both ancient and contemporary analogues.[41] It describes and praises nature's beauty as it would a woman's, enumerating her traits, establishing her *honestas*, defining her lineage, and displaying her effect (the speaker's good mood) upon the male observer. When nature is grasped through this technique as a woman, atomistic symbolism is replaced with an organic functionalism; we see *natura naturans* rather than *natura naturata*, to make use of the well-known terms of the Carolingian philosopher John Scotus. The vernal phenomena of (female) beauty and (male) desire—symbolized by the flowers and the birds, respectively—initiate a reproductive sequence to be embraced as the natural antidote to death. Reversing the metaphor, woman is redeemed through the order of nature when she incites desire toward the "authorized" end of legitimate procreation, thus entering the divine order as *genetrix*.[42]

But nature is also a book, as *gramineum vellus* (5) and *auctor* (19) imply.[43] With the prefix *ad-* in *adjungas* and *adnumerare* (12–13), the speaker indicates the exceptional inclusion of the social and textual orders within nature's beauty. Marbod implies thus that this poem (for which the word "game," as in 15, was routinely used) and its maker/speaker must likewise function as indices of the virtue of nature. The poetic praise of beauty and the desire it elicits become legitimate when they serve their designed purpose. This song of youth and joy thus bases both content and poetics on the natural order, thereby redeeming the troubled male speaker in the process. A man of dark feeling in the opening lines and of right reading and writing in the closing, the *auctor* of the poem matches his creation with that of the *auctor* of the world, restoring the harmony between them.

Clearly this poem of procreation forms a kind of counterpiece to that of recreation with which I started. Strikingly linked by an imperative *conduplicatio* (there, *colligas . . . colligas*; here, *adjungas . . . adjungas*), the two differ in nearly all respects. "Troubled" treats of human nature, "Description" of mother nature—the former describes a movement from play to melancholy which the latter reverses; the former shows illicit desire and death, the latter natural mating and rebirth; the former opens the text by divorcing speaker from maker, while the latter closes it by identifying them; the former, finally, represents the art of humans, the latter that of nature and her *artifex*. Taken in conjunction with the naturalist writings, the pair permits a deep insight into Marbod's views. Their evident contrast uses the power of the thoroughly humanist mode of dialectic to establish a kind of *Sic et Non* on the virtue of the creative urges of nature.[44] In the view of "Troubled," humans are subjected by nature, driven by desire and aggression to self-destruction; in that of the treatises, it is rather humans who subject nature to their self-preservation by exercising reason; in "Description," finally, the two merge their intentions in the harmonious dance of creation.

Texts such as these attest to lively Angevin interests in the investigation of nature and its subject. In optimistic form, they proposed a theory of nature and its reading which promised to reveal the *abdita rerum* to those with the proper approach. At the same time, Marbod in particular questioned the final ability of even his own human nature to resist being overwhelmed by the very forces they sought to release. Eclipsed on one side by the simplistic earlier symbolism ridiculed by M. D. Chenu, on the other by the search for causes and models lauded by historians of science and literature, respectively, this Angevin program has escaped the attention of scholars.[45] It concentrated upon *effect* and, because of its concern with "virtue," one might thus describe it as a "virtual naturalism," to distinguish it from other strains. From it comes the background as well as the impetus for a revived interest in poetics and eloquence, with whose discipline it was intimately linked in Marbod's thought.

As a grammarian who paid close attention to questions of language in both theory and practice, Marbod's interest in science seems curious. Still, his friend Walter argued that writing provides the semiotic system for nature, and the poem we just examined demonstrates that nature provides the value system for writing. Might, then, their "virtues" be consonant? In fact, Marbod takes exactly such a position in his popular and influential writing guide, "The Figures of Speech" (*De Ornamentis Verborum*). This *libellus* unfortunately has been totally ignored, despite its surprising popularity and influence throughout the twelfth century, as Edmond Faral first documented and Rosario Leotta has recently confirmed with his provisional count of some thirty-five manuscripts.[46] Since rhetoric and humanism (in the narrow sense) are inseparable, Marbod's successful booklet merits a closer look.

In a short prologue the speaker urges his student, a would-be writer of poetry and prose, to consider rhetorical colors "as gems or herbs." With them, he continues, "the work becomes splendid like a garden of delights where gently blows the fragrance of various odors, and the fruit from the flowers' seeds will not be lacking, the listener's mind persuaded by the ornament's beauty." This natural simile, interwoven with reminiscences from the *Rhetorica ad Herennium*, positions rhetoric as a branch of virtual naturalism.[47] One thinks also of the image of the fruit orchard planted in a maximizing pattern which Quintilian calls *quincunx* (*Institutiones*, VIII.3), citing it as an example of the virtuous interaction of art and nature. Persuasion remains the goal of rhetorical training but its benefits have been shifted from the public rhetorician to the private writer, "the one who wants to adorn himself with praise through writing" (*qui laudem sibi vult scribendo parare*), as Marbod puts it at the end of the treatise.

In the second section Marbod provides names and definitions (*nomina cum glosis*) for thirty figures, all but one of which are taken from the fourth book of the *Rhetorica ad Herennium*, now known to be a pseudo-Ciceronian text.[48] In addition, for each he supplies examples which are twice "modern": their content derives from his own culture, and they are cast in hexameters which make ample use of external and internal (Leonine) rhymes, the latter (*similiter desinens*) being one of Marbod's favorite "colors."[49]

If I consider this booklet a crafted text of its own age rather than a degenerate rhetoric from Antiquity, its significance becomes clearer. It is the first high medieval rhetoric for poets, and displays a strong interest in "translating" the study into the terms of its own age—an intriguing mark of a wish for identity with and an awareness of difference from Roman culture. Perhaps the most interesting moment comes with Marbod's surprising addition of a new figure. Between *similiter desinens* ("homoeoteleuton") and *adnominatio* ("paronomasia"), two other colors he used often, he inserts the following: "*commistum* is where two superimposed [words] come together" (*commistum est, in quo duo superposita conveniunt*). Since he invented this term, separating the concept from the source's discussion of the preceding figures, we might be able to gain better access to the subtext of the treatise by examining the examples supplied to explain the new figure:

It is wrong to make up beauty, to neglect reputation,
To pursue a whore, to be called "marvelass."
This man who wants to seem strong and high-spirited,
Fears with the heart of a rabbit terrified by the lion's mouth:
He flees like a deer, bellows at his wounds like a cow.[50]

The figure finds its clearest use here in the penultimate verse, where one easily hears the play of *corde . . . leporis* and *ore leonis*; other examples include *formam componere/famam spernere*, *dama fugit/vulnera mugit*, and apparently the hapax *miracunnum*. Geoffrey of Vinsauf seemed to understand the figure thus in the examples (*potuit quod profuit, carne sine carie, simplex et supplex*) he offered a century later in his *Poetria nova*.[51]

Marbod's very act of invention suggests that he thought of himself as a modern "author," albeit in a hesitant fashion. But more significantly, his new figure ("something mixed up," from *commiscere*) seems different from the others. It repeatedly figures and refigures itself: it "mixes up" the two figures that surround it in the metatext; it "mixes up" words in the text; and it refers to the "mixing up" of natural categories (male and female, noble and base, human and animal) in the secular culture. As an anonymous, reworked version of Marbod's treatise in a thirteenth-century manuscript put it, the figure means "to pursue depravity, to speak perversity, to threaten torture."[52] By demonstrating such deep symmetries, this new figure emblematizes the dangerous link between art and nature created within language, doing exactly what it says.

I will return to this figure in a moment. For now let us note that this deep symmetry reappears explicitly in the conclusion, where Marbod admonishes his young hopefuls with the following adaptation from Horace's *Ars poetica*:

In the meantime, you who want to write should regard
The nature of things as the poet's mirror and model.
Like one who learns to paint, whoever yearns to craft well
Should first adapt his own work to her exemplar.
Having emerged from Nature when aroused by Reason,
Art works to preserve the model of its own origin.
Thus whoever wants to adorn himself with praise by writing
Should strive to reproduce gender, age, emotion
And social status as they are distinct in reality.[53]

Marbod here asserts the existence of a full and finally Horatian humanistic theory which culminates in the verisimilar composition of *personae*.[54] The orders of nature and reason are mediated by, and are homologous with, the order of discourse: "colors" are to language as gems to stones, herbs to plants. This homology points to a coherent pedagogic program based upon the belief that the material world (including discourse) contains powers which can be extracted for human use through *studium*. The mutual reinforcement between *ars* ("training") and *natura* ("native ability") in the theories of Pseudo-Cicero and Horace—directed toward the rhetorician and the poet, respectively—reaches here a new level of abstraction. The passage's implication that the Horatian invention of character/voice (*persona*) marks the mastery of the Ciceronian ornamentation of discourse reveals that Marbod sought finally a synthesis rather than a simple digest, of rhetorical theories and the educational systems built around them. Despite their many differences, Cicero and Horace held in common the well-known idealization of the civic self in the figure of the orator, which found its most permanent form in the complex articulation of an elite educational system founded on the *ars rhetorica*.[55]

Marbod's basic interest in combining these two theories of eloquence derived ultimately from an education based on the new curriculum that had been introduced by the reforms of Fulbert of Chartres in the early eleventh century. His knowledge of its principles can be seen, as Curtius pointed out, from the extended argument in the *Liber decem capitulorum* that procreation leads us to believe in Providence: "the artist seems foolish and reprehensible whose work passes like a vessel of clay. Thus the ignorant craftsman is blamed for the inept work and faltering craft condemns its creator."[56] But by uniting a virtual naturalism with a grammarian rhetoric, he appears to have taken another step by founding (or at least developing) at Angers a full doctrine of natural poetics. Embracing the beauty and utility of nature and language, his doctrine marks the first form of a synthesis whose imitations and transformations will mark the repeated success of literary humanism and its subject in Western Europe.

But I have had to push aside some disturbing problems in order to make this attractive and, finally, familiar synthesis, and I want to recuperate them. To begin with, this well-articulated and impressive theory of natural poetics poorly describes its author's own practices. Its premise of elite access to arcane powers, which it shared with the lapidary, contradicted the commitment to facility and utility that runs as a leitmotif through Marbod's other writings. He did compose some highly figured lyric pieces such as the COMMENDATIO VIRTUTUM PER COMPARATIONEM or the DE LAPSU ET REPARATIONE HOMINIS (PL 171.1653 and 171.1731), the latter composed entirely in one of Hildebert's favorite ornaments, *articulus* ("phrase"). But Marbod usually avoided the high style and its figured *dignitas*. In fact, he seems to have preached at Angers, sometimes verbatim, Pseudo-Cicero's directive that "all *narratio* should have three qualities: brevity, clarity, and plausibility."[57]

Moreover, his deep concern as a pedagogue for universal access (*aditus facilis*)—perhaps from an awareness of the relationship between power and knowledge through his own experience as an inside outsider—constantly urged him toward the direct and the practical in his secular texts.[58] "Separating things out, I have written with an easy brevity," he writes in the epilogue to the *De Ornamentis Verborum*, "because I thought that those things which were plain would be more pleasing"; "these [poems of mine]," he writes to Hildebert, "lie open with easy access to ignorant and learned alike"; and in the *Vita Sancti Roberti* he warns that "since the Deeds of the Saints are committed to writing so that the will of every reader or listener might be incited to imitation, the writer must carefully see that he not exceed anyone's capacity, that he look to the utility of all." Marbod's praise of the figured style, then, is in bad faith, since, as he makes clear in many other texts, he is "content to proceed on the direct path."[59]

This bad faith exists in more than one dimension. In poems to Hildebert (PL 171.1653) and Walter (PL 171.1724–26), both praised by him as true *uates* and authors of "marvelous poems," Marbod stresses that his own compositions, devoid of figures, lack any sophistication—a claim which he undercuts with rhetoric. The line to Hildebert I just cited, for instance, concludes with what appears to be a straightforward admission of inferiority: "I am content to proceed the direct way, and to weave words with this technique, however rude" (*Nobis directo satis est procedere calle, Quamlibet et crassa contexere verba Minerva*, PL 171.1653). But Marbod is playing a complex game here. On the one hand, the "confession" of *rusticitas* makes a mostly social, not stylistic statement. Known since Alcuin, as recent work has shown, its message depends upon the performative context.[60] In addition, the obvious intertextual allusion of the phrase *crassa Minerva* produces a strong paradoxical effect. Its source lies in Cicero and Horace, as the schooled reader (or one with a good dictionary) understands, and in both passages it defines that enemy of all sophistication, the *rusticus*. Marbod's clever use of such a reminiscence patently certifies that he precisely not such a person, thus masking/marking the *urbanus* and his pride with a feint of humility.

Similar deceptions lie at the heart of the new figure he introduced into the center of the rhetorical treatise, a figure which is both disfigured and disfiguring. On the discursive level, it degenerates before our eyes, as it were, into a kind of barbarism whose form denies function; as the manuscript variants reveal, the example finally fails to clarify the new figure. On the ideological level, the unmanly lechers and cowards evoked here constitute subjects disfigured by the very process (*formam componere*) whose virtue rhetoric recommends and systematizes. The power of artful language finds a troubling example in this bastard figure, then, which finally stages the self-destructive potential of eloquence when devoid of virile virtue. As he did in considering the forces of nature, Marbod seems to have envisioned two simultaneous subjects of eloquence: one who subjects it through discipline to his own benefit, another who is subjected by its through the pleasures of the material. In the second chapter of his *Liber Decem Capitulorum*, Marbod followed Augustine (at least when writing as bishop) in dating this double subject to the moment when the onslaught of the new oppositional forces of reason and desire irrevocably and irresistibly split the construction of self-consciousness and self-expression within language.

The "disturbing" poem composed of embraced discourses which I used as a side door into Marbod's lyric led to the exploration of Marbod's understanding of nature and language and their ability to exceed the capacity of any given explanatory discourse. The portrayal inside the text of both as characters whose attempts to make sense are compromised by emotions warns against finding a firm reading position outside the text from which to judge unambiguously. As readers of readers, we cannot escape the disturbing embrace of natural discourse. In other words, not only does this text force us along with the Speaker back into nature through empathy, it forces interpretation itself back into nature through the materiality of language.

This is the power and threat of Marbod's deep interest in and long practice of self-impersonation, powers an eighteenth-century Jesuit would have known well. Marbod consciously adapted Horace's theories and practices of the fluidity of the speaking subject and, like Horace, created "persons" to point reflexively to his imagination and eloquence. In other words, the various self-impersonations, even in their most radical shapes, find their stability in the extra-textual impersonator who hovers over the creation and destruction of textual subjects as he works with the ductile matter of human nature.

I would like to return to his suppressed lyric in closing this chapter in order to demonstrate the way in which such an historical understanding of the split self can inform our reading. Again and again Marbod returned to the power and seduction of *persona*, using the technique in almost a third of his one hundred or so extant lyrics, especially those in which a speaker addresses the problem of desire, for which lyric was the privileged vehicle. A certain taxonomy suggests itself when one reads his poems, for the *personae* tend to fall into four broad categories: biographical, amatory, satirical, and penitential.

Satire was widely practiced and widely approved in Romanesque

France and England, its putative moral content supplying an apologetic shield for invention which protected both the individual and the institution. In fact, it could be called the most legitimate secular genre of the period. The list of late eleventh-century satirists is long, and includes Peter the Painter, Serlo of Bayeux, and Geoffrey of Winchester; Udo Kindermann has convincingly demonstrated that theoretical discussions were also common. The astounding extent of Romanesque satire had a good deal to do with its ability to earn approval as well as positions for humanistic versifiers through its moral content, but it also had to do with the pleasure and power of manipulating language itself.[61]

As we have seen, Marbod was praised—and doubtless feared—for his satiric quips or "salty words" (*sales*) which, like those of his Classical models, challenged linguistic as much as societal norms. His problematic voice is perhaps best heard in another supressed poem:

Against a Boy Given Over to a Sordid Desire

He is too filthy and foul and stinks like a young goat,
Whose touch you love, who has made you his dirty mattress.
Every time you dare to purge him with your fingers, you are
    happy,
And you consider it a reward when his stain blemishes you.
When you take to the river with him to let the water
    wash off the pitch,   5
You do not clean yourself with the water, you pollute the water.
You will not act unpunished, for you will stick to his filth,
Yet fear not your back because I am aiming my threats elsewhere.
Since you are beardless, I will use words instead of a rod;
Rods will stop, but words will hurt you more: 10
You will become a disgrace in my writing for centuries,
You will be a topic of conversation for as long as day and night
    shall last.[62]

The poem falls clearly into two halves. In the first, the speaker piles up images and words of filth to disgust the boy (along with many readers), in the second he threatens him—reworking Horace's *laus aeternat*—with an undying poetic afterlife. The two halves stick together with "pitch" (*bitumen*), a word whose evident non-literal use attracts immediate attention.

As a dirty and sticky residue, this pitch functions as an insoluble sign of the union of pleasure and disgust—for all who watch—in the boy's act of masturbation. It also carries ambiguous potential for symbolic ("filthy desire") and allegorical ("entrapment") senses from its use in Classical and Christian authors, as good dictionaries reveal. Here, it further symbolizes the poem itself as final residue of the boy's act, for the text carries the same qualities for the reader, especially for the male and clerkly reader, as the boy's act does for the speaker.

The style of the first half and the content of the second establish the speaker's strong presence. He is clearly a poet and a moralist, though one cannot tell whether the speaker is a man of religion. He surprises us in fact with his appropriation of Roman ways of thinking and writing and concomitant avoidance of Christianity. The boy is threatened with eternal damnation, but in Poetry rather than Hell, at the hands of the Poet rather than the Devil. Thus a slight gap between the speaker and the "prescribed author" (Marbod's person *ex officio*) is opened by a gradual awareness of the text's blanks, and is widened by questions about the speaker's motivations. Like all poets he takes pleasure in and profit from language, but here that language is patently "filthy." Will not the pitch stick to him as to the boy (7), even if both are just playing? How can he keep clean? Since the story of the boy's shame becomes the means of the poet's fame, finally, the speaker's moral position seems compromised by his vested interest. Voyeur and tattletale, the speaker succeeds in raising as many questions about his means as about his ends.

Thus the voice of Roman satire appears recreated and problematized at the same time. The satirist himself is satirized, and it seems no longer possible to equate him with the composing agent who, through the technique of *persona*, keeps his hands clean—as I, through a disembodied and academic voice, also have done. By creating a difference between speaker and author, Marbod not only protects his official self, but also forces his reader to consider the problems of eloquence, sexuality, and their inevitable interconnections. As the poem progresses, in fact, there is a shift from a satiric object to a satiric subject, to use the terminology set up by Jill Mann to discuss later Goliardic poetry.[63] Marbod's self-impersonation displaces the poem's final moral locus to the reader's consciousness, where the battle between desire, imagination, art, and discipline must now take place as interpretation is returned to nature.

An amatory *persona* also sounds through Marbod's lyric which could be found elsewhere among his contemporaries and which was closely attached to the figure of the clerk. The speakers in the erotic "trifles" (*nugae*) of the Romanesque period generally fall into two (not completely separated) subtypes, it seems to me, depending upon the agent of the play endemic to the genre. In one case, the speaker is the primary player, manipulating lovers in his fictional world; in the other, it is more the poet manipulating language in texts. Both types supplied the clerk with the important credentials for employment, as we shall see in detail in the next chapter, since they allowed the display of learning, wit, and secular talents which so attracted the Court and so repelled the Church.

As we saw earlier in analyzing his friend Walter's witty poem, "Aeole, rex fortis," Marbod was fully acquainted with trifles featuring speaker-centered play. But in his own eleven amatory poems he tended to be more interested in author-centered play, as the following supressed poem shows:

To the Same [Girl] Recovering

I cry when you cry, suffering comes to me when you suffer,
Nor, God knows, can I bear the wounds from you;
And although I might pretend, my face will tell you,
Clouds of sadness appear over my countenance.
It pains me when you write that you wounded me so unexpectedly   5
Without reason, and that you will not start such things again.
You wet your face with tears, you bring up sighs from the depths,
Asking in a devoted tone that mercy be granted.
At that submissive word my heart cannot be proud,
Jealousy and anger lie prostrate when the fierce tongue falls silent.   10
I grant you mercy now that you have confessed, to have asked is enough
          punishment for you,
Only please do not trick me with deceptions.
Art simulates truth and changes the names of things,
And knows little about loving the one it calls "beloved."
Trained skill especially imitates many things   15
When it moves the imagination toward some kind of endeavor.
This I ask you not to do, nor to become for me a speechifier in this:
Display what you know about imitation some other time!
Love me not from books but from your entire being,
Cherish me in the frame of mind in which I cherish you who are worthy
          of the heavens.[64]   20

This self-reflective text addresses a girl who, as the rubric to the preceding poem indicates, had accused the speaker *iniuste* of some unutterable wrong.[65] Now repenting, she has written begging for mercy, and the speaker responds with a letter structured by five "quatrains." Following an emotional *exordium* (1–4), the two-part *narratio* (5–12) lays out the girl's message and his response, and then constructs a theoretical argument (13–16) to support the *petitio* (17–20) which closes.

The speaker here remains dead serious throughout, though it is interesting to note that his "voice" is not uniform. In place of a formal *exordium* comes in fact the sort of voice found in traditional female laments, as the male speaker explicitly claims to mimic a woman's tears. A very different voice then takes over, that of the angry lover who, like a king or a god, suppresses his pride in order to grant mercy to a humble petition. A third voice follows, that of the philosopher who argues nature over art with the heavy *sententia*, "Ars simulat verum mutatque vocabula rerum" (13). Finally, one hears the voice of the humble suitor asking that this heavenly being love him. This composite voice of a subject of nature has been put together from separate and sometimes contradictory strands of discourse. We experience it as uniform only because of the continuous textual presence of the first-person pronoun, and because of our anticipation of a coherent mental presence behind that.

The (prescribed) author, by contrast, plays. For him, his double's text is ironic, since it opposes the beliefs he holds by profession. As leader of and example for an episcopal school famed for the study of eloquence, Marbod ultimately had to commit his official self to the control of desire and language—in other terms, to continence and rhetoric. The speaker's central *sententia* (13–14) furnished for the author, in fact, the best defense of poetry by arguing for a complete divorce between word and thing, a nominalist poetics. For Marbod's official person, *carum* must be but a word, and we are left with the paradox of sincerity. Only by promoting the very hypocrisy repeatedly denounced by the speaker (3, 13, 15, 18) could the poet avoid censure. Yet such a *rethor* (17, in a pejorative sense) was limited to simulating a love learned from books, as the speaker rightly concludes, and nature herself would have to denounce the author for his art. Faced with the condemnation of both nature and art, the reader must, it seems to me, take a split subject position to avoid total nonsense.

A third and very different kind of voice is the biographic, though its claim to that title ultimately comes into question. A fascinating case of this *persona* emerges in another unusual poem:

The Sapphire Vase

There is a gallery in Rome where I take myself while wandering
    about;
Looking for new things, I found a sapphire vase.
The ignorant vendor was selling incense with the sapphire;
My companion bought the incense for thrice three pennies
And I lavishly bought the vase for three and a half shillings.   5
Since I was concerned about carrying it without jarring it,
I paid the price of an elegant wicker box.
The vase was put in whole, I remember about that,
Brought out cracked: I feel very sad and unhappy about that.
If it had been carried in among court nobles   10
As it had been put in then, it would have been of high value.
But the porter pressed down on it—may no day be prosperous
    for him![66]

The combination of a first-person speaker and a documented trip by Marbod to Rome in 1102 seems to assure the autobiographical status of this
text. In fact, the entire critical commentary on this surprisingly popular
text (extant in 15 mss) consists of a short metrical analysis by Walther Bulst,
who in his appropriate concern for some hard facts concluded that the text
had "eine lebensgeschichtliche Beziehung."[67]

    But is this a biographical poem? Certainly if Marbod wrote and pub-
lished it in 1102 or 1103, as Bulst reasonably proposes, every reader who
knew of his journey would assume that the poem's speaker and maker were
identical—at least at the beginning. But what does a critical reader think
twelve lines later? Anyone reading the poem as an anonymous text (as it is
transmitted in many manuscripts), for instance, could not possibly recognize the schoolmaster at Angers much less the bishop of Rennes. Buying
low and selling high, disparaging clients, lamenting wretchedly the loss of
profit—this speaker can only be a merchant or someone completely imbued
with the "mercantile spirit." Since Marbod's own father was a merchant of
luxury goods, moreover, this speaker takes on added historical and perhaps
even psychological significance.

    As we observed in the Introduction, self-impersonation depends for
its pleasure and effect upon an uncertain relation between speaker and
author and the temporality of the reading process. Both work well in this
poem, where we have to ask not what it means, but what it does. Because

we have insisted on retaining Marbod's social *personae* (bishop, merchant's son, poet) in our analysis, we can be aware of and intrigued by the widening gap between speaker-as-merchant and author-as-bishop. The merchant, though satirized by virtue of profession within an ecclesiastic context, is redeemed by a taste for things that are elegant, old, and valuable. In a similar vein, since the prescribed author (a bishop by office, a poet by deed) never completely breaks the link between the speaker and himself made by the rubric (*Marbodus: De Vase Saphirino*) and the opening line, the bishop is satirized by his greed.

The mix of voices affects the interpretation of the vase itself, whose symbolic potential is signaled by the poem's rubric. For the merchant, the Roman vase signifies new wealth and social superiority; for the poet, Ancient ornament and intellectual superiority; and for the bishop, Christian truth and moral superiority.[68] Marbod's clever manipulation of its symbolism, coupled with his ingenious erasure of the lines between poet, bishop, and merchant, leads me to conclude that urbanity rather than biography attracted his contemporaries. His stunning command of the powers of an open text which is at once simple and complex in meaning shows his preeminent position in secular Latin lyric in Romanesque France.

A final category in which Marbod excelled is the penitential confession in which a male speaker describes, analyzes, and laments his own despicable state. These *personae* have complex and daring thoughts about taboo subjects, as the following lament reveals:

Dissuasion of Unseasonable Desire in an Assumed Voice

My mind is saddened, my power weakened,
My body decays, my heart laments, my strength dissolves,
My skin is changed, my face is wet with weeping,
Nor can I pour out enough of the tears which overflow inside;
When no way is provided by which it might end up where I want,   5
I utterly despair of the thing I want to reach,
But I neither desist nor find alleviation for my grief.
A lame man chasing a hare, I use up my effort in vain,
I follow the stag like a worthless turtle and I play for [or: write to]
        myself.
But neither do I cease in this way nor does my rage grant me
        relief when I am tired.   10

Oh if I knew something with which I could stop,
How happy I would be if what I want, I could not want—
Not want with one will, not two.
For I languish wanting, I demand medicine not wanting it;
On the other hand, I ask for medicine wanting it, I languish not
      wanting it.   15
Thus I want what I do not want, on the other hand I do not
      want what I want.
I stir up laughter in me at myself divided about myself,
Hate-filled laughter, sad, tearful laughter.
Rotting in this decay will I continue to desire?
What end will there be, good Christ, to such ruin?   20
Will I want to turn myself over to the former birdlime
And, as soon as I get out, to take a step back in the net?
As a boy I loved many young girls, as a man adult women,
As a boy I loved many young boys, as a man adult men.
I bent to my will all those I loved with little effort.   25
A matching age, beauty and boyish smile,
A happy face, sweet voice, witty talk—
All this easily won over for itself those women it pursued
And a mutual fire burned in equal wood.
Today a difference in age forces me to put an end to vice;   30
Now neither gender offers me its arms for an embrace,
Nor could I become again, even if I wanted to, what I was then.
What young person will submit to the dictates of someone now
      almost an old man?
Or will I, a white-haired man, chase old maids with grey
      temples?
Old age ought not to have a lusting heart   35
And an old man's sexual drive should be despicable.
Thus it remains but to die: if sick grief disturbs me
So that I am a lecher in spirit only, I do not want to live.[69]

It is astonishing to see the speaker confess to such emotions and deeds in the course of this self-pitying account that recalls at times Ovid's *Tristia*, at other times Augustine's *Confessions*. The lecher had never been found a worthy speaker for a medieval first-person text—and its appearance here suggests strongly that it has now become a privileged subject elevated to textual value by cultural conflicts we can barely see. In this poem, the power of *persona* to "give voice" to marginal societal types—sometimes with exaggerated traits as here for didactic effect—is put to full use. Its slipperiness circumvents censure to allow the portrait and analysis of a person judged deviate, and protects Marbod from censure for having dirtied his hands with such material.

The heart of the self-portrait lies in the speaker's central recognition: *Sic quod nolo volo, rursum quoque quod volo nolo; In me diuisus, de me michi concito risus, Risus exosos, risus tristes lachrimosos* (16–18). Hating, deriding, and lamenting his split self, the speaker sees himself clearly for a moment, and seems to flirt with repentance when he then asks "good Christ" about the end of it all. But the story of his pleasures pricks his imagination and rekindles his desire, and he ends his lament in the depths of despair. The mortal link between imagination and desire constituted the essential fact of human nature for a wide range of thinkers and poets at the turn of the twelfth century, and the vivid sight of its consequences in this character leads readers, and perhaps male and older readers like myself above all, to add pity to disgust.

Given that the poem's title announces the clear division between Marbod and his speaker, one might not even want to consider any possible overlap. Yet even here we should be cautious. For in his autobiographical *Liber decem capitulorum*, apparently written in 1102, Marbod writes about old age as an unhappy old man of 67 in the second book, "De Tempore et Euo." He renders his *confessio* (II.211) all the more forceful by giving it an ambiguous status between biography and typology. The problem of sexual desire dominates man's life already with the readings of the *puer*, and still disrupts the imaginings of the *senex*: "Then the bad habit disturbs old age, And although the ability to have intercourse has been removed Seeing that cold blood inhabits his innards, Yet insatiable desire itches below the heart And seeks in affect what does not occur in act." Furthermore, Marbod confesses, it has always attracted his writing: "Alas, how wretched this Day will be which readies torments for me, I who have always followed the downward paths along my carefree journey And spent my free time with my mind overcome by the charms of the flesh; Its attention quickly ran to every sort of sin, No virtue saves its work from being a crime."[70] Sliding between the *vita hominis* and *vita sua*, on the one hand, and between *nefas actum* and *nefas operum* on the other, Marbod uses the *persona* to protect his person from the confession of his natural self. The parallels between the "Dissuasion" and the "Confession"—which in my mind must have been written about the same time, shortly after Marbod became bishop—compromise both texts by raising questions about the truth of the one, the fiction of the other. The confessional voice loses a bit of its sincerity, the dissuading voice a bit of its mendacity. For the final time, perhaps, Marbod demonstrates his mastery of a device whose essence lies in hypocrisy—at the very moment he renounces its causes and effects.

These four very different impersonated texts give some idea of the range and subtlety of Marbod's experiments with the technique, and argue as well for the interpretive utility of historical and historicized theory. No other poet of the age and few of the succeeding centuries could be cited as his equal, and he deserves in many ways to be considered the architect of the revolution in twelfth-century secular lyric.[71] Furthermore, he seems to have located lyric within a specific social agenda designed to enable a wide audience to reflect upon nature, language and their interaction. Kept short for the sake of interest, clear for the sake of pleasure, and lifelike for the sake of virtue, the new lyric promised extraordinary general access while preserving privileged readings. By the time he left Angers to become bishop of Rennes, he had established the parameters for a complete cultural reevaluation of secular lyric which could appeal to regional power figures. Its humanist subject, manipulating and manipulated by language and desire, would prove remarkably adept at hiding ideological concerns behind the voice of nature and art.

4. Craft and Power: William of Poitiers, Courtesy, and the Impersonation of Wit

If the dangerous practices of Marbod, Baudri, and the many other poets experimenting with sexuality and textuality had been as limited and obscure as the paucity of sources seems to indicate, they probably would have had little impact. But we must remember that in general the ecclesiastic culture increasingly selected against the preservation of their texts, whether for formal, stylistic, or conceptual reasons. Furthermore, perhaps the more significant (and even less understood) influence of such writers was in the vernacular rather than the Latin culture. For by virtue of such existing features of the central French court as the pleasure in texts of desire, the increased presence and influence of clerks, the expansion of full literacy, and the utility of role-playing, members of the elite secular culture found the new material accessible, enjoyable, and useful.

The crossover of the loving subject from school to court which seems to have begun by the 1070s must have been accelerated by the attacks of the Reformers, particularly during the six months that Urban II passed in central France from November 1095 to April 1096. During that time he and his large entourage spent a month in each of the regional cultural centers of Limoges, Poitiers, Angers, and Tours, repeating earlier denunciations of the incontinence and simony of clerics, the warfare and investiture of lords. But for this trip the pope made two epochal additions: he condemned Philip, King of France, for his unholy liaison with Bertrada of Montfort, and he called for an armed pilgrimage, or crusade, to recapture Jerusalem. By consciously expanding the Church's claim to judge the sexual and aggressive behavior of the secular world in order to reform it, Urban initiated a wave of moral censorship through the region with long-lasting repercussions.

The prominence and duration of the conflict between Philip and the Papacy over Bertrada served to centralize the critique of aristocratic practices of sexuality and marriage within official culture. Their struggle fostered the ecclesiastical construction of illicit desire as a new *malitia* of the *militia* at the very moment that the old *malitia*, aggression, was being re-directed and revalorized by such diverse movements as the tournament and the crusade. Despite a cycle of excommunication and repentance, Philip never actually gave up the woman he "seized" from Fulk of Anjou and married in 1092, and the Reformers refused to give up the issue. The result was an obsession with the king's sexuality within French cultural discourse which goes a long way toward explaining how "love" could have come to hold such a prominent and contested position in the French elite secular culture at the start of the twelfth century, as well as why and how vernacular artifacts serving as its vehicle suddenly became worthy of record.[1]

Urban targeted the secular culture of the schools as well, and here his Angevin policies in February 1096 seem to me emblematic. On the one hand, he recruited the popular preacher Robert of Arbrissel for his reform program, while at the same time he promoted Robert's teacher Marbod to bishop of Rennes. These tactics he continued when he moved east, as the censorship of the poetic and sexual practices of the abbot Baudri at Bourgueil, the archdeacon Hildebert at Tours, and the bishop John at Orléans make perfectly clear. Such a thorough invasion of professional, poetic, and sexual lives of the regional clergy placed secularity itself under suspicion. Urban's successes in court and school assured that the new battleground of the Vices and the Virtues would be in the realm of secular culture, hitherto judged more foolish than evil, and that the primary enemy would be the unrestrained desire not just of men and women of religion, but of all Christendom, beginning with its leaders.[2]

It is striking that the loving subject, derived from Roman practices and theories of *persona* and developed within regional school lyric, first attracted serious attention from lay figures of power in the same area where Urban waged his campaign. This parallelism may indicate that it offered particular benefits in the intensified ideological struggles of the region: the cult of the self as a figure of desire made a potent and liberating weapon against the repressive forces in Romanesque France, while the cult of the self as a figure of eloquence served as a strong and wily defense against censure. Moreover, the technique itself seems to have carried increasing cultural value in lay and clerical eyes as a sophisticated marker of elite status; this, at least, is the implication of the expanding range of Baudri's correspondents noted earlier. And this status could only arise within the frame of the increased currency of literacy itself among the regional aristocracy.[3]

In the remainder of this study, I want to look at two very early appropriations of the lyric loving subject by highly visible members of the upper aristocracy: William of Poitiers (1071–1126) and Adela of Blois (ca. 1067–1137). Unlike the latter, the former has received much modern attention from political and literary historians.[4] Born in 1071, he became at the age of fifteen count William VII of Poitiers, simultaneously holding the titles of duke of Aquitaine and duke of Gascony. After a short marriage (or simply betrothal) to Ermengarde of Anjou, he married Philippa-Mathilde of Toulouse, the twenty-two-year-old widow of Alfonso of Aragon, in 1094. The birth of a son William in 1099 freed him to set out with an impressive army on his own "pilgrimage" to Jerusalem in 1101. To the great embarrassment of ecclesiastic historians, the army was decimated soon after crossing the Bosporus, and William was lucky to escape to Antioch with a few men.

After returning home in October 1102, he faced repeated challenges to his power from secular as well as ecclesiastic forces. All sources agree that in that same period the count began to compose and sing "witty" songs; the earliest extant ones probably date from 1106. William's affair with Maubergeonne or Dangerosa, the wife of his own viscount of Châtellerault, apparently began about then as well.[5] By 1112 his attempts to divorce Mathilde and marry Maubergeonne triggered a revolt by (or at least in the name of) his son which lasted for seven years. Excommunicated by the Poitevin bishop, Peter II, who died in 1115 in the count's prison, he was finally forced to renounce the liaison three years later as his wife, whom he had supported as countess at Toulouse since 1113, retired to Fontevrault. For all practical purposes his rule ended with a successful Spanish crusade in 1120, the same year his son came of age and married Maubergeonne's daughter, since little is heard about him until his death six years later.

The size and complexity of William's domain presented significant problems for government which were worsened by his being "quite a young boy" (*satis puer*, he had a scribe write in 1096) at the time of his accession to power. Bounded by the Loire on the north and east, the Garonne on the south, and the Atlantic on the west, Aquitaine contained seven powerful and contentious viscounties. His control relied upon private rights over allodial property, feudal lordship over various benefices, and legal superiority over the remainder. Outside Poitou, the seat of his power and wealth, great and small adversaries repeatedly challenged his hold, especially the viscounts of Limousin in the east and "the treacherous Gascons and Angevins" (Song 11.16) in the west. Inside the county constant problems arose with independent-minded castellans as well as with the "provosts" (*praepositi*) or officials appointed out of his own household. Even in Poitiers, the prosperous capital whose love of the Romanesque could be seen in its new ecclesiastic and domestic architecture, comital control was challenged by the recent success of Reformers.

These problems were aggravated and complicated by William's forceful personality. In the professional realm, sources indicate that he had been well trained to fight as a knight and impressed allies and enemies alike as "bold, valiant, and fierce." Like many other male aristocrats of his generation, he was also "generous in the courting of women," as a later vernacular biography (*vida*) put it laconically, and even monastic chroniclers describe him without compliment as an avid womanizer. His biting wit was legendary, appearing frequently in historical and poetic sources. Finally, indirect evidence indicates that he must have been reasonably well educated in letters, whether by one of the famous schools of Poitiers—one of which, St.-Hilaire, he headed as titular abbot—or by a private teacher (*didasculus*), such as the one engaged for his son.

His education could not relieve the continued antipathy of a Church that saw in him a coherent picture of rebellion against, and punishment by, God. His neglect of ecclesiastic rights, his defense of Philip of France, the failure of his unnumbered crusade, his affair with Maubergeonne, and his shocking imprisonment of Peter of Poitiers produced distorted monastic representations of him. For his own part, William resented and repudiated the interference of Reformers in temporal affairs, beginning with those of his lord, Philip. Sources indicate that William angrily asserted his independence in the profession of knighthood and the office of count—and in sexuality, which by 1100 had become figured as central to both through the debate over love and marriage.

These various conflicts permeate the small but remarkable body of song texts which were recorded in the thirteenth century under his title (*coms de Peiteus*). Because William appears to have radically altered secular court poetry and because he had such a strong sense of himself, as our phrase puts it, his lyric has attracted remarkable attention from critics since the early twelfth century. I shall begin to examine his self-representation by extracting one striking passage from each of the ten extant texts that all editors have ascribed to this troublemaker.

Song 1

Comrades, I shall do a song that's [very] well-made
And in it there will be more folly than sense
And it will be a total mixture of love, joy, and youthfulness.

Song 2

For I never saw any lady with such great fidelity
who would not take her case where she knows she can find clemency
So that, if she is separated from Worthiness, she makes an accord with
      Baseness.

Song 3

But I shall tell you about the cunt, what its nature is,
As a man who has done bad things with it and taken worse from it:
Although any other thing decreases, if someone steals from it, the cunt
      increases.

Song 4

I have a woman-friend, I don't know who she is
For I never saw her, so help me;
She never did anything which I like, or dislike,
And I don't care;
For there was never a Norman or Frenchman
In my lodging.

Song 5

I shall do a song, since I am dozing
And riding and staying in the sun.
There are ladies who are ill-advised,
And I can say which:
Those who turn a knight's love
Into pain.

Song 6

May he live well who raised me,
For he granted me such a good profession

That I have never failed anyone;
For I know how to play on a cushion
At any (game) touched upon;
I know more about it than any of my neighbors,
No matter which one you look at.

Song 7

Obeisance should be rendered
Toward many people by anyone who wants to love;
And it is appropriate that he know how to perform
Pleasing acts,
And that he guard himself from speaking in court
In a boorish way.

Song 9

As you know, I ought not to boast,
Nor do I know how to furnish myself with grand praises;
But if ever any joy could flower,
This one above all should produce seed
And become pure beyond the others,
Just as the dark day always brightens.

Song 10

Our love goes along the same way
As the branch of the hawthorn,
Which stands trembling on the tree
Through the night, in rain and sleet,
Until the next day when the sun spreads
Through the green leaves on the twigs.

Song 11

Everything I used to love I have thrown away:
Knighthood and worldly pride;
And since it pleases God, I accept it all,
And pray Him to retain me with Him.[6]

The sudden emergence of such sophisticated vernacular lyric has raised questions about the origins of its form and content, the time and place of its appearance, and the personal, professional, and political motivation of its composition. Many theories have been proposed, many sources espoused. If we restrict our view to actual secular lyric *practices*, we cannot overlook the presence of two different kinds literally in front of him: clerics writing Latin poetry as a pastime, entertainers composing vernacular songs as a profession—and both seeking reward. Not surprisingly, perhaps, each "influenced" William's songs in genre, form, style, content, and vocabulary. The details of this double influence do not concern directly this investigation, but William appears to have combined in complex fashion the two major eleventh-century lyric practices at court.[7] Why he would want to do that is another question, one that is more socio-historic than poetic.

William had a distinct "voice of his own," a voice which is nothing if not cocky. Yet the selections above clearly show that, at least in his poetry, that voice both contradicts itself and alters its personality; the former perception forces us to doubt its authority, the latter its authenticity. It is of course possible that William held opposing ideas, that he changed his mind over time, that none of the voices was genuine, or that some of the songs belong to other composers. It is also possible that he employed Romanesque school techniques of multiple representations of semi-fictional selves.[8] In any case, the presumptions behind much of the history and criticism of his "personal lyric" quickly prove shaky. Clearly, nineteenth-century concepts such as "individuality" or "self-expression" cannot be invoked here without careful qualification if we wish to avoid hiding the very thing which needs to be explored.

Once truth and sincerity are questioned, how can we avoid concluding that William's texts stage only a "persona" in the twentieth-century literary sense of a disembodied and instable voice? It helps to remember that, like the mask from which its name derives, a *persona* disguises yet cannot avoid signaling the presence of an empirical agent; its game as well as its work, as we have seen, lies in appropriating the reader's desire for stable reference. Here the historical power and authority of this particular agent offer stability for the interpretation of the speaking self. The most compelling documented link between the historical and lyric self-impersonations lies in William's wit, as he seems to have made constant use of it and it seems to have drawn particular attention from contemporary observers. The anecdotes they relate, though widely cited, have not been well analyzed—nor well translated—and reward a closer look within a careful understanding of the argument structure within which they occur. Through them we will be able to see the presence of a subject which grounds self-impersonation and its interpretation within regional and temporal variants of aristocratic ideology.

I shall argue, then, that one needs both the freedom of the Classical *persona* and the constraint of the modern subject in order to interpret the speaking self in William of Poitiers's songs. And one needs to interpret on such a theoretical basis, I shall further argue, in order to understand the historical production of a new breed of loving subject which would prove enormously successful in French elite secular culture.

William was not the first to stage the male subject of "courtesy" in the court culture of Romanesque France, for others can be glimpsed through the dense screen and tight frame through which monastic historians viewed the world.[9] That obscurity can be traced in part to the challenge such subjects posed to the masculine culture of fame-through-prowess, which was entrenched in the secular court and with which French monasticism had found a relatively peaceful coexistence by the end of the eleventh century. Also, monks deplored the new court male who pursued vain goals, ignored religious values, promoted the worth of women, and prized unmanly behavior. These factors sufficed to render courtesy, like heresy, all but unworthy of monastic record, and only its condemnations betray the extent and significance of the altered practices.

Let us start once again with a specific text. When Guibert, abbot of Nogent (1104-ca. 1125), sat down about 1115 to compose his *Memoires* (*Monodiae*), he assigned a prominent role in his conversion to the "example" of his relative and friend Evrard, count of Breteuil (sur-Noye), who had renounced the world in 1073 to take up an itinerant religious life with a few companions. One day this "exile" encountered someone impersonating him so well that he felt as if he were meeting his own self. This aggravating and disturbing incident persuaded him, he later informed Guibert, to enter the Benedictine order at Marmoutier (Tours), where he remained until his death sometime after 1105.

The composite portrait of Evrard and his double provides a detailed and unique view of the courtly male aristocrat in pre-twelfth-century France:

> He was in the age of full flowering, since he was of the most pleasing elegance and particularly since he was rich in family nobility as well as in astonishing beauty . . . One day when he was in some village engaged in some business or other, there suddenly stood before him someone in a scarlet coat and silk pants with puttees damnably cut away, with hair effeminately parted in front and sweeping the tops of his shoulders, looking more like a loverboy than an exile . . . We have been told that this man, while in the world, cared so much for fine clothing in order that he would not be surpassed by those richer than himself; and he was of such a tempestuous character that it was no easy matter for anyone to approach him even with a word. . . . He had a certain very courtly habit of getting anyone he knew to be eminent in letters to write something in prose or verse for his understanding in a little book which he often carried about with him for the purpose, so that while collecting the sayings of those who were famous in these studies, he might weigh the significance of every one of the sayings. And although he could not understand such things by himself, yet from the explanation of those to whom he showed his notes he unfailingly would soon comprehend them, especially concerning who had crafted the most carefully in terms of meaning or metrics.[10]

Since I am more interested here in the secular figure being distorted than in the monastic distortion of that figure, I wish to look through Guibert's text rather than at it. But his fascination with violence, writing, and sexuality threaten the very possibility of interpreting this pivotal *exemplum*.[11]

An analysis of the episode within Guibert's own conservative monastic framework will help limit the effect of its distortion. No longer count and not yet monk, Evrard was dead to the world but not yet alive in Christ at the central moment of the story. He and his companions were "wandering" outside the orders of society and of the stable meaning that they mediate, as Guibert's language emphasizes: *nescio quas externas provincias . . . die quodam . . . nescio quid acturus . . . aliquo vico*. Like the forest of Broceliande, the town is one of those Other Worlds where men who have lost their way, spiritually and physically, confront fabulous beings who put them to the test. Only within the context of such an Other World will Guibert's readers accept—in fact, anticipate—the appearance of Evrard's double, a counterfeit self who, mixing desire and deceit, still circulates in the market of power.[12]

The undisciplined Evrard can only read the literal text of the apparition, and his angry denunciation of the scoundrel's impersonation and arrogance reveals his own unbent pride. Educated and religious readers, on the contrary, know to interpret the corporeal lie as spiritual truth: although a false reflection of the count's body, the diabolic double nonetheless accurately reflects the count's soul.[13] Lack of discipline (*regula*) and attachment to the world have been refigured and personified here as an impudent lover. Through an act of grace Evrard's anger suffices to turn him toward the rule of God and a life of humble service where he grasps, finally, the lesson of disciplined reading: texts, like persons, are doubled, and the material always deceives. His movement from count to exile and then to monk signifies the mental pilgrimage (*iter mentis*) from the suppression of appetite to the rejection of pride and the adoption of reason.

Turning back now to the secular person that Evrard abandoned, we must wonder about the very possibility of literal truth in such a well-crafted story which plays such a central role in the author's own strategies. Yet the close personal ties between Guibert and the count, his careful indications of his source, his concern for realism, and his critical acumen together give confidence not to reject the portrait, even if the stance against itinerant religious corresponds better to the time of Guibert's writing than of Evrard's experience.[14] Evrard's former "social self" (Guibert says *persona*) clearly stages a male version of what the author elsewhere (III.2) names *elegantia francica*. Here we can discern three key elements: a cult of personal beauty, a cult of love and ladies, and a cult of literary morsels. Since Guibert displays the portrait as outstanding in degree but commonplace in kind, it would seem hard to doubt that by the 1070s new court practices had arisen in Romanesque France which were encoded under the term "elegance."[15]

For seventy-five years already monastic observers had railed against "sissified" modes of male appearance and behavior at court, which chroniclers first noted spreading out from southern France at the turn of the millennium. The Cluniac historian Ralph Glaber associates them with "the men from Auvergne and Aquitaine" who accompanied Constance of Arles when she came north to marry Robert the Pious in 1003. Various sources decry their invasion of Germany forty years later at the time of the marriage of Henry III to Agnes of Poitou, and Orderic Vitalis and others note, scornfully, that they became the fashion in England with the reign of the "libidinous" William Rufus in 1087. Appropriate to neither real men nor true clerics, these changes included extravagant new forms of dress, discourse, hair, and ornament which observers explicitly declared deviant.[16]

The passage in Guibert of Nogent, however, provides the first clear indication I have found of a general secular aristocratic adoption of the "person" of lover in the presentation of the public self. The abbot clearly intended the word "loverboy" (*amasius*) to identify for his readership a recognizable and admired figure of court life—otherwise the derogatory term would have little force in this context. Significantly, he also suggests that elegance was a superficial role (the thrust of the term *persona*) adopted in competition for dominance at court by ambitious men, who used its illusions to disguise their aggression.

Orderic Vitalis confirms the dominance of the lover in the cult of elegance in an often-quoted depiction of the Anglo-Norman court a decade later which begins with the following charges:

> At that time effeminates set the fashion in many parts of the world: foul catamites [Ganymedes], doomed to eternal fire, unrestrainedly pursued their revels and shamelessly gave themselves up to the filth of sodomy. They rejected the traditions of honest men, ridiculed the counsel of priests, and persisted in their barbarous way of life and style of dress. . . . Our ancestors . . . used to wear decent clothes, well-adapted to the shape of their bodies; they were skilled horsemen and swift runners, ready for all seemly undertakings. But in these days the old customs have almost wholly given way to new fads. Our wanton youth is sunk in effeminacy, and courtiers, fawning, seek the favors of women with every kind of lewdness.[17]

Such perverted figures of male homosexual and heterosexual desire differ greatly from the clerk-as-lover we saw portrayed in the Bayeux Tapestry, who was represented as an outsider or, at best, "marginal man" whose desires were suppressed by the story the court told to and about itself. The Benedictines Guibert and Orderic condemn the lover precisely because of his new position on center stage, his role now "played" by secular nobles as well as by clerks. Further corroboration comes from the court culture of Adela of Blois, where, as we shall see in detail in the next chapter, humble lovers and elegant style were already being staged and rewarded by the early 1080s. This appearance of the *iocus* ("drama" as well as "game") of love within official culture, rather than of the act of desire outside it, signals the beginning of the construction of the loving subject within secular court culture.

In a cult of elegance centered on the lover, exactly what role belongs to poetry? Significantly, Evrard's nascent literary interests—of which Guibert approves—occasion the only use of the word "courtly" (*curialis*) in the passage.[18] Unfortunately, it is not clear whether the author describes the count's actions in the world or in the monastery; its placement at the end of the example may indicate the latter. In any case, poetry's entanglement with the new culture is clarified by Guibert's description of his own court experiences during the very time of Evrard's flight and conversion:

> In the meantime, after steeping my mind unduly in the study of versifica-
> tion . . . , guided by my folly, I had come to first take up writings of Ovid and
> the pastoral poets and to aim for amorous pleasantries in divisions of types
> and in intertwined letters. . . . my mind was seduced by such enticements of a
> poisonous freedom, considering only whether courtly talk could be brought
> together with some poet or other.[19]

This testimony is precious: although it is supported by other indirect evidence, I have found nothing else quite as specific. At the time Guibert describes, he was a young student "intent on literature alone" (*solis litteris intentus*, I.19) and, through that, "the pursuit of high status and wealth" (*culminum opumque assecutiones*, I.17). The desire to unite contemporary love talk with Roman love poetry was hardly his alone; the "Ovidian subculture" we explored earlier indicates that it was shared by many educated young people of that generation. Yet his particular comments deserve careful attention, since they strongly imply that by the 1070s an intense interaction had begun in courts of every kind between the cult of eloquence and poetry and the cult of elegance and love—and they make it clear that both sides had vested economic, social, and political interests in the results.

Guibert's confession also points to the general importation of models of behavior into the courts, as great and small clerics lured by the hope of reward brought to "worldly service" their own varying practices and ideals from the Latin, ecclesiastic, and written culture of the schools. As we have already seen, one can distinguish (but not totally separate) an ethical humanist model of the upper clergy, which explicitly included Christian values, from a ludic grammatical practice of the lower clergy which implicitly excluded them. If examined from the standpoint of ideology, these two different intentions separate such models into "top-down" and "bottom-up" groups, though the distinctions are not absolute. The former was supported by and supporting the central authority of institutions, the latter the marginal power of individuals; the former argued generally for control and service, the latter for release and freedom. As such models added the extrinsic authority of favor to the intrinsic authority of writing, they founded new subjects within the secular culture whose particular attraction often relied upon the power to manipulate language.[20]

The presence and success of such subjects within eleventh-century narrative sources reflect the pressure exerted upon traditional subjects which were tightly imbricated with feudo-heroic ideology and centrally represented in official culture—such as those in the Bayeux Tapestry with which we began. In eleventh-century central France, as is well known, secular and ecclesiastic authorities had come to view private warfare as the most serious threat to the established structures of power and to the social "order" they projected. Modifications of the traditional subject of aggression began to appear in official as well as in aristo-popular culture; these include the pilgrim-knight, the tournament-knight, and the lover-knight we have just seen, all attempts to stage and resolve the problem of chivalric violence in one manner or another.[21]

A fascinating example of these attempts can be found in the only extant "proto-romance" prior to the twelfth century, the *Ruodlieb*. Written down in Latin about 1070 in southern Germany, it reveals the extent of theorizing and/or propagandizing about ideals for secular male aristocrats, and reflects closely the interests and pleasures of Henry III (1039–56) and his wife, Agnes of Poitou. The portrait of the titular protagonist assembles a number of the male secular subject-positions circulating in eleventh-century court discourse: companion, family member, courtier, feudal lord, lover, husband, and king. Constructing as well as problematizing a new secular ethic between Christian principles and natural desires, the incomplete text is the first extant example of that innovative "mirror for princes," romance, which would gain great success in the coming centuries. Its intriguing contrast between sophisticated thinking and storytelling on the one hand and unsophisticated Latinity and poetics on the other points to a strong participatory role for the brilliant "quasi-literate" imperial court, whose significance for the development of High Medieval culture, C. Stephen Jaeger has been right to insist, has been badly neglected.[22]

A different kind of evidence about the existence and force of such models in France comes from eleventh-century personal names originally taken from oral narrative sources of an epic nature. The character Olivier, for instance, was added to the legend of Roland and Charlemagne during the eleventh century. Since his name means "olive tree," and since that tree "signifies peace and humility," as the earliest Oxford version proclaims prominently (*ço senefiet pais e humilitet*, 73), his character seems associated with the propaganda for the Peace and Truce of God. Furthermore, in the visual arts his long hair ties him to new court fashions. By the middle of the eleventh century, his name starts to precede that of Roland in the order of family name-giving, supplying an interesting case of the replacement of a traditional subject by a modified and updated version.[23]

A more radical variant of the subject of aggression was attached to the name of Gauvain, a frequent target of "character assassination" in later Arthurian romance. His traits included elegance and love along with prowess, and what later texts allow us to conclude about his general portrait points to a strong parallel with that of Evrard. Both show courtesy as a restraint upon violence through a service to ladies which inculcates new norms of social behavior. The popularity of Gauvain's name in the 1090s in central and western France warrants the association of his traits with the ideals of the reign of William of Poitiers, and provides potential extrinsic evidence for evaluating the subject of his songs.[24] The fact that historical agents were being christened in a kind of primal interpellation with new fictional names, whether "Olivier" or "Gauvain," both encourages us to regard those characters as true subjects and supplies an index of their symbolic power.

A third variant of the traditional subject of aggression known to be widespread in central France at this time can be found in the story of two Aquitanian comrades-in-arms, Amis and Amile. It first appears as an example of "true friendship" (*verus amor, pura amicicia*) in a Latin epistle traditionally dated to around 1090 that Rodolf Tortarius, a poet-monk at the royalist abbey of Fleury, sent to a well-placed "friend" named Bernard. A poet as committed to the glory of Roman poetry as to the power of the French aristocracy, Rodolf merges the cult of friendship from school culture with the cult of troth from court culture. At the end of a series of examples of friendship, he recounts in a hundred or so elegiac couplets "a history [which] is believed to be a fiction (*fabula*) composed by serious men, where there seem to be certain truths mixed in with the falsehoods"; it is, he adds, known to everyone in France and Germany. The heroes of this very popular and later heavily Christianized story indicate a new world order where friendship and fidelity between true knights gives purpose to the profession and supplies the greatest secular virtue—greater than justice itself, as Rodolf concludes sententiously (*Maior amicicia denique iusticia*, 324), leaving a fascinating residual ambiguity about authority which, I believe, cannot be resolved.[25]

Like no other event, these modifications of the male subject of aggression supply the surest index of the cultural changes which, despite many continuities, would finally separate the High Medieval court from its Late Carolingian predecessor. Yet while Olivier and Amis, the subjects of efforts by Cluniac monks and Humanistic scholars to reform the knight, were undoubtedly popular, it was Gauvain and his ilk (Baudri's "Jupiters and Marses," ed. Hilbert, carmen 200.97–104) who appear to have won over the hearts of the upper aristocracy in central France, as Guibert's testimony indicates. Men serving the court (*uiri curiales*, as Orderic Vitalis calls them) in central France, more heterogeneous in origin than in function, were deeply involved in constructing a new secular culture in which the cults of elegance and eloquence were combined with that of aggression to project a new male subject. Although attacked by a host of conservative spokesmen, these "courtiers" would eventually overrun Europe with the courtly culture they had constructed.

The best, and certainly the earliest inside view of the interactions between the male Romanesque subjects of aggression and courtesy emerges from (as it helps account for) the speaking self staged by William of Poitiers in his songs. Moreover, because his contemporaries evidently foregrounded his wit almost as much as he did, as Hans Ulrich Gumbrecht has recently stressed, we have a basis for mapping the implications of literary analysis onto social criticism, and vice versa. In this way, we can draw conclusions which, precisely because they avoid universality, reveal some of the particular ideological ramifications of the new identities constructed by and for the Poitevin secular world.[26]

William's ten or eleven extant songs have been analyzed repeatedly and subtly for the last half century, producing fruitful results which await evaluation. I want to promote that evaluation by reversing the usual perspective in order to look at and through the anecdotes constructed around them and their author. Such an approach foregrounds the conception of history as empowered interpretation, confronts the socio-historical work of concepts of person, and focuses upon the consumption of artifacts by groups rather than their production by individuals.

A beginning point is provided by the description of two lost songs written by the Benedictine monk William of Malmesbury around 1125 in his *Deeds of the Kings of England*:

> There lived then William, the Poitevin Count, a foolish and unreliable man who, after returning from Jerusalem . . . , wallowed in every vice as if he believed that everything were governed by chance, not ruled by Providence. Furthermore, seasoning his inanities with a certain false beauty, he claimed them as wit, distending the jaws of his audiences with coarse laughter. Thus

he raved that he would found an abbey for concubines, building some little houses like monastic huts near a certain castle called Niort; and he sang on, naming this one and that one, all well known to be whores, to be appointed as abbess or prioress or other official. Also, when he had expelled his legal wife, he carried off a certain viscount's spouse whom he desired so much that he stuck the slut's image on his shield, saying repeatedly that he wanted to carry her in battle as she bore him in bed.[27]

It is very likely that these songs should be dated to 1107–8, when the count showed his only interest in monastic foundation, when he probably began his relationship with Maubergeonne of Châtellerault, and when Bertrada of Montfort retired to Fontevrault on the death of Philip of France.[28] Bracketed in the *Deeds* between accounts of William's failed crusade and his attacks on Reform bishops, the description of the songs serves as proof of the count's corruption and apostasy. The monk-historian also condemns him for a second and equally important trait which Guibert of Nogent's Evrard did not possess: verbal license. The initial adjective *fatuus* ("foolish [speaker]"), announces this trait even before the detailed description of his inanities. The count's disregard for the orthodox paradigms of marriage and rhetoric provides the chronicler with a prime example of the moral degeneration of the aristocracy to which Reformers traced so much of Christendom's trouble.[29]

The two songs are linked by a common discursive mode and a common construct of aristocratic male sexuality. The first, "Abbey," is primarily satirical, and functions on a number of levels.[30] Reto Bezzola made the likely proposal that its plot and language satirize ladies who entered the Order of Fontevrault, founded by Robert of Arbrissel in 1100 for women seeking a new form of religious practice and a new place in ecclesiastic doctrine.[31] A more general satire aims at the concealed role of private interests in the founding of monasteries by feudal lords—such as William's own military order at Montmorillon, the Maison-Dieu, which he strategically located on the Limousine border at the time of the revolts by ecclesiastic and secular rulers. Finally, travesty (in the etymological sense of "cross-dressing") arises from the disjunction between the clothes of a manifest female subject ("nun") of ecclesiastic ideology and the body of a latent female subject ("concubine") of secular ideology.

Critics seem to have always assumed that the Count was singing about the business of prostitutes, and have translated *pellex* as "whore" and *prosti-bulum* as "brothel."[32] In actuality, that is highly unlikely. In the first place, *pellex* designates in general the female lover of a married man ("mistress, concubine, ladyfriend"), technically distinct from a woman who sells sex to anyone with money. Furthermore, most Romanesque historical references to "whore" (*meretrix, scortum*) designate not professional prostitutes but noblewomen sexually active outside marriage; in fact, a bit later in this very passage, the historian labels William's mistress a "little whore" (*meretricula*). At the turn of the twelfth century, Bertrada was the most prominent *pellex* in France; Philip's attempts to legitimate his marriage to her undoubtedly prefigured as well as preceded those by his vassal William. Finally, William himself never speaks of professional prostitutes in his extant songs nor even of the urban world at all. But he repeatedly names and satirizes hypocritical noblewomen who, like Bertrada, disguise private acts of desire with public declarations of virtue:

In Auvergne, beyond Limousin,
I went along all alone, in pilgrim's guise;
I came across Lord Warren's wife,
And Lord Bernard's;
They greeted me openly
In the name of St. Leonard.

The speaker pretends he cannot speak, is led covertly into the ladies' chamber, and, after being tested with a long-whiskered and long-clawed cat, is found appropriate:

Lady Agnes said to Lady Hermessen:
"He is mute, as is easily seen;
Sister, let us prepare ourselves for dalliance
And pleasure."
A week and even more I stayed
At that tower.

How often I screwed them you will now hear:
One hundred and eighty-eight times!
So that my tackle almost broke
And my harness,
And I cannot tell you what great sickness
Overtook me from all that.[33]

The parallels between this song and the anecdote suggest that the latter is more lkely about noblewomen than prostitutes, and that the former fits into a consistent concept of *cavalier*. Rather than calling such women names, William often called them *by* name in order to interpellate them and their husbands as his subjects.[34]

A portion of the verbal structure of "Shield" can also still be perceived. Its humor evidently pivoted on the verb "carry" as it switched from public metonomy to private metaphor, forcing the listener to juxtapose "to carry (the shield which carries a portrait of) her in battle" with "to carry him in bed (as a horse carries its rider)." Its seriousness, on the other hand, resulted from the noun "shield" as it collected discordant referents in a manner reminiscent of another song:

I own two horses for my saddle in a good and noble manner;
They are good and brave in battle and worthy,
But I cannot keep them both, because the one does not tolerate the other.

If I could tame them to my liking,
I would never want to take my equipment elsewhere,
Because I would be better mounted than any man alive.[35]

Like these horses and the women they represent, the shield indicates by metonymy the knight who carries it, especially since it was becoming "personalized" during this period with early forms of the heraldic device which accompanied the rise of the tournament and which Maubergeonne's image represents. Marking an epochal process of chivalric individuation, the new device here overrules convention by replacing the shield: the count wants "to carry her" (*illam ferre*).

The two lost songs thus resemble each other much more than one might think. Both publicize the identity of a knight's "girlfriend" (*amica/amigua*); both link sexual pleasure and social dominance. Their common speaker combines in himself prowess and desire tested in the traditional manner through the performance and narration of "deeds" (*faitz*, as in Song 3.6). Already William's earliest extant songs declare that true knights prize women as part of "the good equipment" (*lo bon conrei*, Song 2.16) which supplies both means to and signs of power. This "chivalric love" (*amor de cavalier*), as Leo Pollmann has called it, runs explicitly or implicitly throughout many of the extant songs, from Song 1 with its two "horses" to Song 10 with its intertwining of the vocabularies of war and desire.[36] It is worth noting that the inseparable combination of prowess and desire matches the only two facts we know about Marbod's generic *miles*, whose life and death revolved around loving and fighting. But William's *joi* counters Marbod's melancholy as he locates the end of pleasure, fame, and discourse in a profession and class from which the Angevin cleric was excluded and to which the Poitevin count proudly belonged.

We need to be careful not to view this voice as some natural form of self-expression, as if "knight" were somehow a uniform, coherent, and unproblematic notion. William speaks, for instance, neither as a feudal knight serving a lord, nor as a courtly knight serving his lady, nor as a crusading knight serving Christ. He performed these roles at times in his life, and their constructions would become exceedingly important to the High Medieval French image of the *chevalier*, but they cannot be accommodated to his most common representation. Wistfully, perhaps, he speaks near the age of forty with the voice of a young knight serving his girlfriend within the context of a Romanesque practice of knighthood for which, in order to avoid confusion with competing practices and theories, one might do well to retain his own term, *cavalaria*.[37] A devotee of prowess, sexuality, and elegance—at least by the time he renounced "joy and pleasure And squirrel and vair and sable" (Song 11.41–42)—that voice matches the character of Gauvain which became popular in Poitou during his reign and for whose social correlative the term *bacheler* would later be used.[38]

Our desire to celebrate his subjectivity as lover must be tempered, however, by his desire to celebrate his authority as count. One hears that desire distinctly in the concern for "lordship" (*senhoratge*) and "fief" (*honor*) in the dynastic lament of Song 11, where he uses the everyday official voice with which he also speaks in charters.[39] In the remainder of the songs, however, he binds his men to him with appeals to a knight's ethics rather than the count's rights. Like an increasing number of his peers, he recognized in the professional term "knight" an honorific and useful term for the expanded class of martial elite. But the more general the term, the more ideological its content; and there can be little doubt that William would have resisted above all the Cluniac concept of *miles*. By appropriating and augmenting the symbolic power of such artifacts of the aristo-popular culture, he seems to have sought to construct and promulgate a chivalric identity for his domain which stood diametrically opposed to that of the Reformers.[40] Because that identity is a self-impersonation which selects, omits, rearranges, exaggerates, and idealizes traits, it must be considered a *persona*; because it is also an ideological projection designed to unite regional figures of power under his control, it must be considered a subject.

Up to this point I have intentionally limited my discussion to chivalric traits, excluding others from my view. But now I want to turn to those evoked by the revolutionary and unique choice of medium. Many of William's peers, after all, practiced and probably preached sexual freedom for noble males, and he can hardly be considered unique in that area. But he is apparently the first and surely the most important secular ruler of his age known to have composed, performed, and probably collected his own vernacular songs on the topic. We should not overlook the significant change of subject in that performance: Evrard and Gauvain did not "do songs." William not only "did" them, but even impersonated himself as a song-maker in certain songs. This sudden appearance of a new set of traits in the aristocratic male *persona* in central French culture demands careful attention.[41]

We are fortunate to have a description of the count's performance from Orderic Vitalis, particularly since no other troubadour merited such "historical" attention. The brief picture he painted in 1135 is remarkably complete:

> William Duke of the Poitevins was bold and worthy and very funny, outdoing even the witty professional entertainers with his many witticisms. . . . When the duke of Poitou had completed his devotions in Jerusalem he returned home with some of his companions. Once restored to prosperity, being a gay and light-hearted man, he often recited the trials of his captivity in the company of kings and magnates and throngs of Christians, using rhythmic verses with witty modulations.[42]

Though shorter and less detailed than the portrait from William of Malmesbury, this one is much more favorable. Orderic leaves no doubt that William's compositions were songs and not poems, stressing their oral performance, musico-textual identity and public reception. With a triple repetition of the word *facetus* ("witty") he highlights the same trait isolated by William of Malmesbury—but evaluates it positively instead of negatively. Interestingly, both historians were probably influenced by contemporary Latin poets. Orderic's laudatory eye-witness was most likely Baudri of Bourgueil, who knew the count of Poitiers as his feudal lord, then Orderic as his close friend. William of Malmesbury, on the other hand, viewed the count through the eyes of Hildebert of Le Mans, even if he had not been informed by him. Hildebert was his favorite contemporary author, and supplied the two laments for Peter of Poitiers which close the historian's account. The two poets could hardly have been further apart, as we saw Marbod himself commenting in the last chapter, and their divergent evaluations of the count's performances originate in the split subject of eloquence in school culture.[43]

It has been pointed out that the performances described by Orderic resemble the salacious Song 5 which I quoted above and which concerns a pleasurably painful week spent with two dissembling ladies. Because that song is formally the least sophisticated of those extant, it may also be the earliest. Its satire, moreover, extends to the impersonation of a pilgrim/crusader (*pelerin*) with a striking resemblance to Bohemond I of Antioch, whose pilgrimage in March 1106 to honor the Limousine saint Leonard captivated all of France. A month or so later Bohemond married the king's daughter Constance of France at Chartres in what can only have been a spectacular wedding celebration put on by Adela of Blois. By June Bohemond was in Poitiers to help recruit for the Holy Land at a papal council. There he surely would have been William's guest, since he had entertained the count of Poitiers for six months at Antioch after the defeat of his army. The great courts at Chartres and Poitiers in the spring of 1106, Bohemond's two most visible and prestigious moments in France, supply the most likely settings where William could have sung such a song before audiences of the size and quality described by Orderic.[44]

What a fascinating moment of cultural intersection! Attempts to analyze William's performances always treat them perforce as general phenomena, but here we sense the interpretive implications of a particular performance. Keeping in mind that we can only deal with probabilities, we can nonetheless profit from identifying the prominent and competing groups at this very early moment in William's career as a versifier. One would have to begin with Adela and her court, championing among other things a close relationship between the lady, formal poetry, and a type of true love; Bohemond and Constance, who recalled by contrast everything William had lost five years earlier; Philip and Bertrada, reconciled yet again to the Church and to Fulk of Anjou; and a host of clerical poets and professional entertainers, pitting poems against songs in search of favor and reward. The humor and subtlety revealed in Song 5 over the last few decades thus served "real" and direct political objectives in addition to (and in interaction with) "imaginary" and indirect ideological goals. Through this new medium of self-impersonation, William could play with subject and as subject, calling those below, around, and above him to a new kind of symbolic contest.[45]

Orderic's praise matches well the evidence from the songs, especially the serious love songs where poetics carries a thematic importance. One cannot miss the rhetorical ornamentation of Song 7, the metaphysical metaphors of Song 9, and the stunning imagery of Song 10:

With the sweetness of the new season
The trees put forth leaves, and the birds
Sing, each in their own language,
Following the measure of the new song;
Therefore it is well that a person take possession
Of that which he most desires.

From the place which most pleases and suits me
I see neither messenger nor sealed letter,
So that I neither sleep nor laugh
Nor dare draw forward
Until I know whether the result
Is just as I am asking.[46]

Sophisticated poetic features such as these serve to mark the textual presence of what Dante would eventually call a "regular" poet—one disciplined by the ethical and verbal norms of high Humanism. That audible presence suggests in turn that Orderic's implication that William sought to compete with the "professional singers" (*histriones*) only tells part of the story.

William himself prized and praised above all his formal technique, and twice directly addresses it. In the Neo-Ovidian Song 6, wishing to prove his "sure mastery" in every kind of court game, he cites the song's own complex strophic structure, a fancy new form (*coblas doblas*, "paired stanzas") which he apparently invented, judging from the imitations of Marcabru and later troubadours. The blatant "interlacing" of poetic, social, and sexual domination in that song leaves little room for doubt about the politics of playful crafting. But the ideological implications of such artistry show up even better in Song 7 because of an abrupt change of voice near the end. The song begins with a highly ornamented stanza which combines a popular natural opening (*Natureingang*) with a learned rhetorical figure (*adnominatio*):

Since we see meadows flowering
Again, and orchards becoming green,

Creeks and springs becoming clear (of ice),
Breezes and winds,
Surely each one should enjoy the joy
About which he is joyful.

Four stanzas follow, one of which I quoted at the beginning of this chapter, which lay out a detailed program of "true love" (*fin'amor*) based upon the indisputedly courtly virtues of patience, humility, obeisance, and service. But the reader is surprised and confounded by the concluding boast of the sixth stanza:

About this song I tell you that it is worth more,
If someone understands it well, and it receives more praise;
For the words are made in equal groups,
Each and every one,
And the melody—I myself am proud of it—
[Is] good and worthy.[47]

The sudden presence of a metatextual voice intensifies the split between lover and poet, humility and pride, discourse and intention. The double-dealing speaker harks backward to Ovid and his imitators, and forward to the voice of future courtly lyric which W. T. H. Jackson analyzed in an article which has become classic.[48] Here, however, a strict hierarchy is maintained by the concluding claim of the poetic voice to have crafted the amatory voice. The latter, in other words, is embedded as fiction within the former's ostensibly veridic discourse.

How can we explain the sudden interest and pleasure in craft on the part of a powerful French aristocrat at the beginning of the High Middle Ages? It is one thing to compose lyric poetry within a traditional "discourse" in most of the senses given to that word by Michel Foucault.[49] It is yet another thing to initiate such a discourse by bringing together ambient practices in order to "invent" (*trobar*) a new kind of vernacular lyric which displays a high degree of self-consciousness by juxtaposing speaker and maker within the text. What does the figure of the poet which William thereby claims have to do with the preservation and extension of power, the primary goal officially imposed upon him by office, profession, and family? And to ask that question is to ask whether this *persona* is not, in fact, a subject.

Part of his motivation no doubt came from the general increase of the cultural value accorded to creativity which, Martin Stevens has shown, lies at the heart of the dominant High Medieval notion of the individual.[50] Stevens's position needs to be modified by understanding the linkage of desire and creation in much twelfth-century thinking, and by viewing the doublet within the multifaceted cult of "genius" (*ingenium*) which was beginning to emerge from such diverse twelfth-century French cathedral schools as Chartres and Orléans. Moreover, Latin writers closely associated with those centers of learning had long been composing poems for Adela of Blois, as we shall see, and it is very possible that her success with the medium supplied William with a persuasive example of a profitable collaboration between poetry and power. Appropriating contemporary theories and practices such as those by Marbod and Baudri, the count could erect and defend a "modern" and "rustic" poetics which would rapidly raise the value of secular culture—and of the culture of the secular—south of the Loire.

The impersonation of such a creating self also carried significant ideological value. As an "ingenious craftsman" citing Classical authority, William could lay claim to the prestige of the Romanesque secular poet and of the cult of literacy and letters associated with that figure. The hidden and usually sexual interpretations encouraged by many of his songs, whether established through allegory, biography, or both (for instance, the name "Agnes" in Song 1, which functions both as *nomen*, Agnes of Gimel, and as *omen*, "chastity"), fostered the attractive image of a sophisticated, elite, secular, and aggressively male audience at play in the Poitevin court. That image served to augment the cohesion and authority of his court by adding the "play-group" bond of ingenious craft (such as we found in Baudri's circle) to the professional bond of chivalric loyalty. The prowess, desire, and elegance associated with the figure of the court knight were thus tied to the literacy, love, and eloquence associated with the figure of the court clerk. Offering possibilities for both subjection and subjectivity, this Poitevin hybrid would compete with good success against the host of other chivalric subjects which emerged across the High Middle Ages.

If we want to consider William's speaking self as such a conscious hybrid, we need to ask how he thought to connnect them with each other by situating them more carefully within their larger context: the discourse of wit (*facetia*). I do not see how one could doubt its central importance here, since it appears in almost all song-texts by him and all historical texts about him. In fact, a late twelfth-century historian, Ralph of Dicet, reports that the count was actually nicknamed "the witty/courtly" (*Willelmus comes Pictavie, qui vocatus est facetus*); since Ralph seems to obtained his information from William's granddaughter Eleanor, who herself brought crucial aspects of Poitevin courtesy into England when she married Henry in 1152, the possibility ought to be considered seriously.[51]

Antonio Viscardi, C. Stephen Jaeger, Laura Kendrick, and others have shown that *facetus* routinely characterized the verbal facility of clerks. Yet in the secular court the term denotes not just "doing what one wants in words," as Quintillian's definition (cited by Kendrick) puts it; Orderic found even William's melodies *facetus*, and the word must already carry for him the more general sense of "clever, playful, entertaining, courtly" common in twelfth-century sources. It is all but synonymous with terms such as *lepidus, iocundus, urbanus,* and *curialis,* which ultimately identify a sophisticated manipulation of form associated with elite members of court.[52] William, of course, constructed his idea of "wit" in Romance, and his own terms can probably be found in Song 11, where he characterizes the former courtly self he is renouncing as *cuendes e gai* ("charming and gay," Song 11.29), terms very close in concept to those (*iocundus et lepidus*) used by Orderic to describe him in the passage we examined earlier.

The cultural ramifications of this humorous facility in language will help us to understand its subject. William of Malmesbury follows the description of the inane witticisms (*nugae, facetiae*) "Abbey" and "Shield" with three examples of the "customary wit" (*consuetus lepor*) and "insolent gibe" (*dicacitas insolens*) which the count directed against bishops resisting his attempts to marry Maubergeonne. The second and third deal at length with the martyrdom of Peter of Poitiers; the first incident, on the other hand, has no such hagiographic frame, and promises a clearer view:

> When he was denounced and excommunicated by Girard, the Bishop of Angoulême, and ordered to put aside his illicit lover, he said: "You will curl with a comb the hair pulling back from your forehead before I announce the repudiation of the Viscountess!" a gibe against a man whose very thin hair required no comb.[53]

Despite its brevity (or perhaps because of it, since brevity or economy has long been recognized as a pre-eminent trait of wit), this one-line retort possesses greater subtlety than presumed by all who cite it. We might begin by asking where exactly its humor lies. The monk's explanation that the bishop had very thin hair which needed no comb has satisfied modern observers, but that bald joke—the pun is irresistible—hardly seems remarkably witty. We would do well to remember Freud's insight about the witty joke (*der Witz*) that "we do not know what is giving us enjoyment and what we are laughing at."[54] Here, in fact, we cannot see the subject of William's wit (in all senses of the phrase) until we put it under analysis.

First, a close look at the Latin text reveals that the witticism reported here actually consists of two utterances: one written in Latin covering another performed in Romance. I avoided translating the striking metaphor *refugum capillum* with the common English phrase "receding hair" because the original (literally "hair fleeing backward, retreating hair") is both rare and obscure. The single authoritative attestation comes from Lucan, where, near the end of his godless epic about a godless age (*De Bello Civile* 10.132), he describes some of Cleopatra's attendants as "having curled their head (of hair) and wearing their hair flying back from the forehead" (*pars . . . torta caput refugosque gerens a fronte capillos*). These men evidently have a full head of hair, and a twelfth-century commentator at Orléans interpreted *refugos* simply as "curling back." The reminiscence also reappears in the interesting revision of *The Life of Saint Dunstan* which William of Malmesbury made about the same time, and it has been shown that he used Lucan repeatedly to critique degenerate court life, especially that of William Rufus.[55]

This repetition indicates clearly that the historian wanted to cover the "false beauty" of the count's insipid utterance with true wit featuring learned reference and rhetorical ornament (*adnominatio*: "refugum . . . repudium"). But what, then, did William of Poitiers say, and what was he talking about? Since nothing about the style or context of "to curl with a comb" suggests a written source, and since only William of Poitiers would have used the fashionable cultivation of hair as an attack on the bishop, it would seem that he responded: "You will curl long hair with a comb before I renounce the viscountess." Exactly what humor those words had for him and his companions, however, is another question.

Theorists of wit from Cicero to Freud have always agreed that wit is either primarily referential or primarily linguistic, and that a test of substitution can determine which is present.[56] In this case, substituting neither similar language (for instance, "you will have curly hair") nor similar thought (for instance, "you will become king") retains the original force, although the former seems somehow closer than the latter.

Obviously, the count means to designate an impossible future moment, strengthening "I shall never renounce the viscountess." Yet William adds a counterattack by replacing "never" with an isolated and distorted trait: his enemy's thin/straight hair. The imagined portrait of a Reformed bishop with a carefully cultured head of hair provokes laughter by contrasting his ascetic *persona* with the courtly *persona* cued by the connotations of full and curled hair (young, modern, handsome, urbane, virile).[57]

William's language still eludes us. But the redundant phrase "with a comb" now draws attention, for neither the cleric nor the count needed to specify the object; "you will curl long hair" would have sufficed. The very act of according value to objects figured as valueless ("not worth a comb" was a contemporary locution) tends to be humorous and shows up repeatedly in other witty anecdotes by the count. Moreover, by naming and thereby stressing the instrument, William may have made possible a double entendre, whether directly through some word play on *penche* ("comb") which we can no longer perceive (a diminutive form, *penchenil*, designates the pubic area of a woman in a song of William's younger contemporary Marcabru), or indirectly through the processes of condensation and displacement which Freud found at the heart of wit. Doubled and displaced meanings appear in wit in general, as well as in this extended example from the count's poetry:

But you do not hear me boasting so much
As if I were not forced to retreat the other day,
When I was playing a big game
Which I liked very much at first
Until it was set up on the board;
When I looked, it no longer served me,
It was so changed.

But she said to me in reproach:
"My lord, your dice are small,
And I invite you again at doubled (stakes)."
I answered: "Even if someone gave me Montpellier
This wouldn't be stopped."
And I raised her board a bit
With both my arms.

And when I had raised her board,
I hurtled the dice;
And two of them were well-squared, valid,
But the third was loaded.

And I made them strike hard against the board,
And (the game) was played.[58]

Many parallels like this make it very likely that William's wit resided primarily in the instrumental phrase "with a comb," whether by triggering absurdity, obscenity, or both.[59]

Although I have used the word "wit," more or less translating Latin *facetia*, William himself knew it as *gap*, a word which meant both "satirical gibe" and "boast." Such behavior can be seen throughout Germanic and Romance epic, and often in chronicle and history as well; Raoul Glaber decried its frequency at the court of Dijon in 1017.[60] As anecdote, further, the *gap* provided incentive and form to memory, and thus can be seen as an elemental mode of history or "historeme," as Joel Fineman recently called it.[61] Like twentieth-century "flyting," it displaces physical aggression onto verbal behavior within a highly structured social context where markers of status are severely limited, highly visible, and hotly contested.[62] By belittling and enlarging character traits, its user can assert and defend hierarchy in a bloodless battle which, as Cicero notes at length, had many advantages for its user. It fulfills such a "normal" role in chivalric representation that one must wonder whether it should not be identified with chivalric ideology itself. Not a rustle but a noise, not a trace but a presence, William's wit flaunted its power as it taunted its subjects, loudly proclaiming the authority of its master.[63]

It is intriguing that the vernacular and Latin terms only partially translate each other: *facetia* covers the satirical gibe but misses the boast of the warrior's *gap*, while *gap* covers the satirical humor but misses the play with language of Cicero's *facetia*. In other words, the Latin term intends a claim to eloquence which William of Malmesbury renders palpable with the metaphor of the curl, while the Romance term extends a claim to power which William of Poitiers renders palpable with the metaphor of the comb. Their common element is sufficient for textual translation but insufficient for cultural *translatio*. Like the bastard figure of *commistum* we found at the heart of Marbod's modern rhetoric, this anecdote stages the ambivalent and contending subjects of wit in a struggle for symbolic power that characterized the hybrid culture of the new courtiers which William of Poitiers found so attractive.

The conservative monk-historian's rejection of the count's *facetia* betrays his awareness of the threat posed to traditional orders and institutions by the emerging hybrid culture. It also reveals that William of Poitiers explicitly claimed (*revocabat*) the title of "witty" or "courtly," as Ralph of Dicet later states, suggesting that he sought to use that trait to combine his disjuctive self-impersonations into a new, specifically Poitevin subject. His various constructions of such a knight-courtier, interlocked with that of the *clericus curialis*, gave birth to a subject-position within aristocratic ideology which would long concern the secular court.

"The count of Poitiers was one of the greatest courtiers of the world and one of the greatest deceivers of ladies and a good knight in arms and generous in his courting and he knew well how to compose and sing."[64] The parataxis which governs this early thirteenth-century *vida* indicates one solution to the problem of the many voices in William's songs: count, courtier, lover, knight, noble, and poet simply "add" together to form the speaking self.

Yet the difficulty of placing William's speakers in a single or simple ideological position suggests another solution. For it is one thing to defend human sexuality and ingenuity, another to identify those acts with a social elite, and yet a third to couple them with a claim for territorial control. The first is rather liberal within Romanesque ecclesiastic ideology, the second rather centrist within Romanesque social ideology, the third rather conservative within Romanesque political ideology. Although displayed and perceived as coherent—the primary effect of the credence granted to linguistic continuity and textual presence of the first-person pronoun—the speakers do not add up.

These contradictions provide an excellent argument for abandoning altogether the humanistic illusion of a natural, unique, congruous, and expressible self in William's songs. The voices must be seen rather to "multiply": to cluster, interact, and interfere with each other as oppositional subjects. Paul Smith's modified definition demonstrates how useful the concept of subject is to describe what we have seen: "[Subject is] . . . the term inaccurately used to describe what is actually the series or the conglomeration of *positions*, subject-positions, provisional and not necessarily indefeasible into which a person is called momentarily by the discourses and the world that he/she inhabits."[65] His stress upon the subject as a con-glomeration of subject positions enables us to theorize the multiplicity of William's voices, the conventional nature of their subject-positions, and the unique nature of their colligations.

Yet even Smith's modified concept of the subject remains insufficient, because it fails to account for the roles of craft and power in the production of these particular subjects. Precious little of what we know about William of Poitiers and his songs would support interpreting his use of the first-person to represent the results of having been "called" by his world and its discourses. In fact, both his texts and his behavior have led observers repeatedly to the conclusion that he revolted against some forms of subjec-tion while altering others for his own purposes. In other words, William's activity as "agent" escapes our theories of the subject. Manifesting itself first and foremost in the count's infamous wit, that agency corresponds well to the sort of theories and practices of *persona* which we examined earlier. "Slippery" (*lubricus*) in language as in love, William's facile ways enabled him to slide through a variety of subject-positions, all of which surely "corresponded to something in him," as Baudri of Bourgueil said about himself. Yet William's slipperiness was oriented more toward mas-tery than resistance. By literally impersonating himself, he could lay claim to the highest achievement of poetry, an achievement restored in cultural value by Marbod's renewal of the Horatian ideal.

At the same time, this slippage must not be interpreted as a free play among disembodied voices, a conclusion which led Ezra Pound in 1910 to claim him as a "modern" poet.[66] William grounded his chivalric and witty subjects as well as their creator within a conservative view of the social formation: none escaped the specific ideological drama of his dy-nastic interests. He sought to avoid subjection by other figures of power, whether papal, royal, or comital, and the slippery subjectivity of the speaker in his songs served that goal. Yet with that very subjectivity he asserted power over his own subjects by creating a new Poitevin elite identity based upon the cultural value of self-impersonation. The explicit and implicit correspondences between his poetics and his politics separate him from Medieval Latin poets such as Baudri, for instance, who explicitly claimed "immunity" for his poetry and its voices. William, by contrast, consciously interwove person and *persona* beyond the degree routinely arising from the ties between ideology and language, dictating both the subject and the discourse of his own power.

5. The Makeup of the Lady: Adela of Blois and the Subject of Praise

The pressure on the masculine secular subject we found in compositions by and about William of Poitiers was matched by the equal pressure on the feminine secular subject. The eleventh century seems to have witnessed the medieval highpoint of women's rights in many economic, social, and legal areas, and that status put pressure on their representation within official cultures.[1] In the courts, the induction of aristocratic women to the center along with the cult of elegance and love brought a revised secular feminine subject apparently accompanied by a reduction of real power. In the schools, the increased attention to topics such as beauty, nature, and art forced a reconsideration of the position and configuration of the ecclesiastic feminine subject. The confrontation of these processes, exacerbated by the repeated condemnation and excommunication between 1094 and 1104 of "the concubine" (*pellex*) Bertrada of Montfort, initiated a contest over the "lady" which would reverberate throughout the High Middle Ages.

In order to see the beginnings of that contest in some detail, I want to examine the influential court culture which arose around Adela, Countess of Blois.[2] Born not long after the Conquest to William of England and married at about seventeen to a man twice her age, Adela seems to have shared the government from the moment her husband, Stephen, took power in 1089. She assumed its regency in 1096 when he departed on the First Crusade (whose success he missed by returning home early), and again in 1101 when he undertook the disastrous crusade that claimed his life. She continued to hold power after 1102 for and then alongside her sons, William (ca. 1098—ca. 1105) and Thibaud (after 1107), introducing her own chancellery and generally steering the county toward Norman political and cultural influence. After more than thirty years of rule, she finally retired to the Benedictine convent of Marcigny in 1120, where she died seventeen years later.

It would be hard to quarrel with the judgment of Orderic Vitalis (see below) that "this noble lady governed her husband's county extremely well"; as Kimberly LoPrete has argued forcibly, earlier views of a decline during Adela's reign no longer hold up. Adela faced numerous challenges. Her domain included the counties of Blois, Chartres, and Meaux, and was bounded by the Loire River, Anjou, Maine, Normandy, Capetian "France," and the county of Troyes (controled by her husband's family). In addition to internal pressures caused by social, political, and economic changes similar to those in Poitou and elsewhere, external pressure came from the constant aggression of the Angevins (to whom the all-important Tours had been lost in 1044) and the Capetians (with whom there were repeated conflicts after Thibaud came of age in 1107). Unlike William of Poitou, however, Adela apparently maintained good relations with the local bishop, Ivo of Chartres, whose prestige in canon law she exploited in order to strengthen her authority.[3] Distributing her great wealth to buy favor, using her "gentility" to negotiate alliances, and arranging advantageous marriages for her children and relatives, Adela seems indeed to have maintained the "the glory of the realm," as an anonymous poet noted (see below).

In personal terms, Adela seemed to have it all: status, power, wealth, beauty, grace, brains, education, virtue, and a spirited nature. If Godfrey of Reims's poem is addressed to her, as I shall argue, she had red hair and black eyes, not an unlikely combination to emerge from Norman and Frankish ancestry. No other woman attracted contemporary writers to such a degree and in such a way, and the many laudatory texts written to her describe certain personal details; yet, given the vested interests of their authors, the historicity of the "person" they portray is difficult to determine. Furthermore, her "own" voice is absent from the written record; except for charters (not long after 1102, for instance: "I, Adela, countess of Blois and daughter of the most glorious king William of England and formerly the dearest wife of the count palatine Stephen . . ."), no document exists where she uses the word "I."[4] As a result, we shall find it even more difficult than usual to claim to know this historical figure, for it seems that there is at once too much and too little information. Nonetheless, there is sufficient evidence to conclude that she set a powerful model, and a model for power, for the ladies of France.

Rather than work through the unified vision of one specific (and unavoidably male) observer, thereby accepting both what he says and how he says it as a departure point, I want to begin with a selection of different and differing representations of Adela from the early 1080s to the early 1120s.

All are contemporary except those of Orderic Vitalis, who did not begin writing his history until around 1125. These fleeting images stir up troubling and troublesome questions about Adela's "person" which otherwise escape attention.

1. Orderic Vitalis, monk at Evreux (1085–1142), describing Adela's marriage in the early 1080s in a book of *The History of the English Church* which he wrote in 1127:

> Stephen count palatine of Blois, anxious to strengthen the bonds of friendship [=make an alliance] with King William, sought the hand of his daughter Adela in marriage. By the counsel of his advisers her father gave his consent, and she was united to him with very great celebration. They were betrothed at Breteuil and honorably married at Chartres.[5]

2. Ivo, Bishop of Chartres (1090–1115), writing ca. 1091:

> The royal blood in your excellency descends from both sides and commends the nobility of your family in the eyes of men. But for religious minds that is exceedingly outdone by your upright behavior and your abundantly dispersing hand, as far as I have learned. Hence I am astonished for what reason you would say that you love like your own self your cousin Adalaide whose adulterous embraces with William [of Breteuil] you work with such effort either to defend or to prolong; and you neither watch out for your own safety or theirs very properly nor forsee to any extent what great danger and great disgrace threaten me in this affair.[6]

3. Baudri, abbot of Bourgueil (ca. 1078–1107), apostrophizing his poem to Adela, probably 1087–1096:

> Yet there is one thing in which the daughter surpasses the father:
>> She approves of poetry and knows how to spend free time with books.
> She also knows what her favor is to poets:
>> No one returns empty-handed from her worthiness.
> On the contrary, a flowing supply of generosity [ms, ed: composition] exists
>> inside her
>> And she knows how to prefer (some) poems to (other) poems.
> Thus do not fear: she is very courteous:
>> She herself will grant a time, she herself will grant a place,
> And I judge the Countess will not send you back empty-handed;
>> Even though you are unpolished, she will act in her accustomed
>> manner.

Nor will she bestow upon you the little you deserve,
    She will bestow what is to her praise and honor.
Her munificence is barely known now to the world,
    Yet her gifts call men from remote regions.
I know her, but she does not know me;
    Rustic simplicity has concealed me from her.
Nor would I dare now to send out a poem to her,
    But she sent me a message wanting to have my poem.
Recently she heard something or other of my poem;
    She urged me approvingly to continue.
I am continuing it, not because it can equal her worthiness
    But so that it might thrive from her worthiness.
Great subject matter has ennobled my verses,
    My verses do not ennoble the material.
She is dignified by virtuous manners and chaste feelings,
    She is adorned by a noble offspring and a husband's love.
And yet there are many whose glory and worth
    And beauty can commend them to young women and who
might have tried for her—but what would it help to have tried?
    She holds her marriage agreement to be inviolate.[7]

4. Hildebert, bishop of Le Mans (1096–1125), writing for her an epigram of leonine hexameters sometime after 1096:

Whoever equates you with mortals is a fool and a sinner;
    It is little praise, but you will (always) be for me the foremost of
        goddesses.[8]

. . . and a letter about the same time:

Penury has a impudent face; nothing is shameful when it helps. Penury both pushes people to crime and intercedes for grace. You will pardon me, therefore, if I request something beyond what is merited when I am pushed by penury. You teach me to hope for things beyond merit by continually bestowing things beyond merit. Should you ask what I request and by what presumption: I need a chasuble, you promised me one. I judge that you who hasten to award even things not promised will not neglect what you have promised. Farewell.[9]

5. Stephen, Count of Blois (1089–1102), beginning a letter to Adela a bit after June 20, 1097, at Nicaea:

Count Stephen (sends) to Countess Adela, his sweetest friend, his wife, whatever his mind can think up as very good or very pleasant. May Your Love know that I am pursuing the holy journey to Romania with all honor and all bodily safety. I was careful to send you from Constantinople written news of the chain of events in my life and pilgrimage; but lest something unfortunate happened to that messenger, I am rewriting you this letter. I made it through to Constantinople with enormous rejoicing, by the grace of God. The Emperor indeed received me most worthily, honorably and—almost like his own son—lovingly, and presented me with very ample and very precious gifts; and in the whole army of God there is not one duke or count, nor any other powerful person, whom he trusts or favors more than me. Truly, my love, His Imperial Dignity has urged and urges me often that we commend one of our sons to him; and he has promised that so much and such glorious wealth would be handed over to him that he will not envy me in the slightest. In truth I say to you, there is not such a man living today under the heavens. For he enriches all our leaders very generously, he comforts all the knights with gifts, and he refreshes the poor with food. . . . Your father, my love, gave many great things, but he was hardly anything with respect to this man. These little things I desired to write you about him so that you might know a little bit about who he is.

. . . and adding a note to a second on March 29, 1098, at Antioch:

These are admittedly few things, dearest, which I write you about many things, but [that is] because I cannot express what is on my mind. Dearest, I command you to act well, and to get [the affairs] of your land eminently in order, and to treat your children and your vassals fairly, as behooves you, because you will surely see me as soon as I can. Farewell.[10]

6. Orderic Vitalis, writing in 1135–37 about events of 1100–01:

Also Stephen, count palatine of Blois, was an object of contempt to almost everyone, and was continually reproached because he had fled disgracefully [in August 1098] from the siege of Antioch, deserting his glorious comrades who were sharing in the agonies of Christ. He was continually chided by many people, and was driven to embark on another crusade as much by fear as by shame. His wife Adela also frequently urged him to it, and along with the flattering words of a loving wife used to say, "Far be it from you, my lord, to lower yourself by enduring the scorn of such men as these for long. Remember the courage for which you were famous in your youth, and take up the arms of the glorious crusade for the sake of saving thousands, so that Christians may raise great thanksgiving all over the world, and the lot of the heathen may be terror and the public overthrow of their unholy law." These speeches and many more like them were uttered by the wise and spirited woman to her husband.[11]

7. Anonymous poet, writing 1096–1102:

Since the whole world proclaims the countess of Blois,
    Let us bow over her hand for a short time.
But entering the garden springing forth with different flowers,
    I do not know which of so many flowers I shall pluck first.
So many good qualities run together, when I turn them over in my
        mind one by one,   5
    That it makes me hesitate about which to choose first!
No woman could be found in our age
    To whom so great and so many advantages have been given
        at once:
If you ask about family, she is the sister and daughter of a king;
    About the merit of her life, she is very religious;   10
About glory, she is the mother and wife of a duke;
    About her total wealth, she has great wealth in her house.
Fortune gave ample wealth, Nature beauty,
    But Wealth has not given arrogance nor Beauty disgrace.
The wealthier she is, the less haughtily she acts,   15
    And the more beautiful she is, the more modest;
And possessions have not perverted her conduct nor beauty her
        modesty;
    But it is a rare thing for beauty and modesty to both be
        present.
A woman is a trifling thing; although a woman, this one is
    Not a woman, having no womanly trifles!   20
She is a woman by sex, but a man by acting manfully;
    With her as leader the glory of the realm stands firm and
        continues to be strong:
In this weak sex is the strength and mind of a man [. . .].[12]

8. Orderic writing in 1135 on events of 1106–7:

In the year of our Lord 1106, at the end of February, when a comet with a very long tail was seen in the western regions, the renowned Duke Bohemond came to France after capturing Antioch, and took as his wife Constance, daughter of King Philip of France. The marriage was celebrated magnificently at Chartres, where the Countess Adela made generous provision for it. . . . In the year of our lord [1107] Pope Paschal came into France; he was received with honour by the inhabitants and faithfully carried out his spiritual duties. At that time Ivo, bishop of the town of Chartres, outshone all other distinguished teachers in France by his learning, both spiritual and secular; at his invitation the Pope celebrated the feast of Easter at Chartres. The countess Adela too gave generous sums for the Pope's needs and earned the eternal blessing of the apostolic see for herself and her house. This noble lady governed her husband's county well after his departure on crusade and carefully brought up her young sons to defend the Church.[13]

9. Ivo of Chartres writing in 1107:

Egress, bread, water, and all necessities for this life which are under your power are forbidden by your order, I hear, to my sons the canons at Notre-Dame. What else is it to do this but to send innocent and unarmed men to their death without audience or trial? For hunger and thirst harm just like a sword. What edict could the fierce Turks, persecutors of the Christian name, promulgate more ferociously against the servants of God than to remove their necessities of life? Therefore I advise Your Nobility with a warning, and warn you with advice, to change for the better the incautious severity of your sentence until the hearing, and [not] to condemn the unconvicted, the unjudged, to death with such a severe sentence.[14]

10. Hugh of Sainte-Marie, monk of Fleury (ca. 1100–20), dedicating his so-called *Ecclesiastic History* to Adela in 1109:

I judge, fairest lady, the present work a fitting gift to dedicate with humble affection to Your Graciousness, since you are not only to be preferred to many barons of our age, but also are famous for your family, distinguished for your worthiness, and learned in letters, which is "gentility" or great courtesy. . . . If you will be intent on these things, laziness will not weigh down the splendid and virtuous sharpness of your native intelligence. Moreover, regarding the celebration of your virtues, with which the loftiness of your origin and the joy of your nature have infused me, I blush to speak of them now lest I should seem to use fawning levity. But I will speak at another time when there is the opportunity.[15]

11. Hildebert, writing when Adela retired to Marcigny in 1120:

Every time I hear about the things going on around you my spirit is happy and rejoices; for I hear that you are being led down the path of God's commandments and that you run to the land of the living with unhindered feet. I also hear you have become someone poor in spirit from a rich woman, a humble nun from a most splendid countess crowded by troops of pleasers, and that like a very abject little servant-girl you provide what is necessary to the other daughters of Christ who serve the Lord with you, and that you serve them most dutifully. Surely this change is a change by the right hand of Him on High.[16]

This arbitrary selection of texts raises a number of interesting questions. First, the representations are noticeably disjunctive and even contradictory. Baudri of Bourgueil and his younger friend Orderic Vitalis, for example, obviously praise very different "persons." Did they simply see what they wished, or are the representations merely formulaic; did Adela in fact change over time, or did she manipulate her public image? If we want to understand her role in the cultural changes in Romanesque France, we must be cautious about judging the status and author of the person(s) we see.

Second, Reto Bezzola's authoritative assertion that Adela "did not create a literary court" needs to be refuted. Writing in the 1940s, he seems to have tapped nationalism as much as sexism: he wanted to refute Medieval Latinists in Germany and he wanted to solidify the claim for William of Poitiers as the ingenious and outrageous progenitor of French courtly poetry.[17] Yet, already as a very young woman—a full generation before any other noblewoman known—Adela hired both professional singers (*ioculatores*) and school poets (*uersificatores*) to praise her, and this activity needs to be investigated within the framework of her comital politics.[18] A close look at the extant panegyric will also shed light on the new role of poetry which she introduced into Romanesque secular culture.

This primary material can be located within a nexus of ritual praise, feminine image, and ideology. This nexus I want to call "dominism," a neologism derived from Latin and vernacular terms (*domina, dominus, dominare*; *midons, dompna, domneiare*; *dame*, and so forth) which inform the various cults of the lady as a being of superior goodness and beauty. Interesting work has been carried out on this general topic, of course, for later periods and practices. Here at the turn of the twelfth century, as the praise of ladies for secular qualities beyond those of wife and mother changed and expanded its scope, we can examine the moment when authors and patrons (or "matrons") first wove together separate cultural strands to reform the secular subject of desire.[19]

Finally, the often conflicting representations of Adela constantly raised —and continue to raise—the issue of what we now call gender. There is some evidence, as we shall see, that Romanesque women themselves, lay as well as religious, struggled with the subject of their sex and speculated how it engaged their public person. At the heart of their search, I shall argue, lay a troubling gender essentialism: a belief in a determinate relationship between biological and social roles. The representations of Adela above reflect the struggles between sex, *persona*, and subject with particular clarity. They imply that she (like her contemporaries) sought strategies to negotiate simultaneous interpellation into conflicting positions, especially by the names "woman" and "lady," and that she turned to the power of impersonation to recreate her subjects.

For a variety of reasons, the connotative expansion of the words for "noblewoman, lady" in Romanesque France has been accorded little attention, despite excellent recent historical studies on noblewomen.[20] Yet the concept of "lady" was being contested by the end of the eleventh century in the schools and the courts under the pressure of neo-conservative forces. A powerful sort of name-calling (*femina, mulier, uxor, domina, matrona, meretrix*, etc.), that contest arose from the clash between old and new forms of the subjectivity and subjection of women.

Despite my insistence on focusing on secular culture throughout this study, the appeal of "dominism" can probably best be appreciated by looking at the most radical religious movement of the era, that of an itinerant preacher—in fact of the first official itinerant preacher of the High Middle Ages, Robert of Arbrissel (ca. 1045–1116).[21] Robert had been a married local priest in Brittany until Reformers drove him from office in the late 1070s. After studying and working in Paris, Rennes, and Angers, he withdrew to the forest of Craon as a hermit in 1095. His eloquence in Angers before Urban II brought him apostolic status as "God's word-sower" (*seminiuerbius Dei*) a year later,[22] and he traveled about France over the two remaining decades of his life preaching against the luxury of the world.

Because the great number of women drawn to his ragged and disorderly band upset church officials, Robert founded Fontevrault in 1101, locating it just south of the Loire at the intersection of the counties of Poitou, Anjou, and Touraine. Although in origin a double monastery, Fontevrault soon became a convent of women served by a small number of men as an increasing number of noble and wealthy women entered, motivated to escape the social and religious limitations placed on them. Largely because its governance remained in the hands of women, it alone of all such High Medieval foundations avoided being reabsorbed into the male ecclesiastic and moral hierarchy during its transformation into a proper order.[23]

Within two decades Fontevrault counted two to three thousand members in sixteen chapters on the Continent and another ten in England, and it remained the most important religious institution for the female elite of France until the end of the eighteenth century. The enormous success with women of this and other popular religious movements signals clearly their great disatisfaction with traditional institutions and rules (of all sorts) at the turn of the twelfth century.[24]

Robert coupled his effort to change the status of women with an effort to change the feminine subject. We can see this second effort most clearly through an analysis of the *accubitus*, his practice of having men and women sleep alongside each other. We first hear of it around 1098, when his former teacher Marbod, recently elected Bishop of Rennes, wrote him a long epistle which begins with a disturbing rumor:

> You are said to prefer living together with women, a gender with which you once sinned, as if you were striving to expiate the stain of the old evil through the example of a new religious order around the same material. It is reported that you deem them worthy not only of a common table during the day, but also of a common bed at night, along with your flock of followers, so that you obstruct for both sexes the laws of sleep and wakefulness by lying in the midst of both.[25]

Although Marbod must have been pleased in general with this former student who had translated the Angevin curriculum into a social and religious movement, whether intentionally or not, he sharply disagrees here with Robert because of his own experience with the irresistible power of sexual pleasure and because of the new *persona* of bishop through which he now speaks.[26] That the *accubitus* was not simply a figment of Marbod's very active fantasy and that it continued even after the foundation of Fontevrault is shown by a second letter similar in content, though more hostile in tone, from Geoffrey, the grasping abbot of the Benedictine abbey of Vendôme situated nearby. Arguing that women are too evil to be treated gently and too delicate to be treated harshly, he tells Robert to consider them all equally as children.[27]

But in what sense can I use our word "woman" to translate the connotations of *femina* or *mulier*, the terms used indiscriminately by Marbod and Geoffrey in their letters, at a time when the feminine subject was under such cultural pressure? Significantly, Robert himself was more careful. In his only extant piece of first-person writing, a "discourse" (*sermo*) sent to Ermengard of Anjou after she had been forced to leave Fonte-vrault and return to her husband in 1109, he consoles her as a nun (calling her "beloved," "sister," "daughter"), but chastises her as wife (*mulier*).[28] He strikingly rejects both her rejection of the world and its rejection of her: she is bound by law, but not condemned by nature.[29] Robert conceives then of this "woman" not in terms of her essential sex (*femina*, a word he does not use) but in terms of her determinant persons (*mulier, soror*). She remains now split within the world between "wife" and "nun," the power of necessity (*lex*) and the language of will (*voluntas*). The differences be-tween his usage and that of his accusers suggest that we need to become much more cautious about "medieval attitudes toward women," even "the clerical view," if we are to perceive the diversity and change of medieval opinion rather than be content to underscore its constancy.[30]

This vision of a new split feminine subject helps interpret Robert's *accubitus*. In originally requiring men and women to sleep alongside one another, he sought to reform the determining moment of human nature by defeating the desire which, both writers note, Robert intentionally "ignited." It seems to me that he must have considered this form of martyr-dom to be modern and natural, using those words with all the lattitude and significance one finds in early twelfth-century texts. Marbod's letter, more-over, like Baudri of Bourgueil's *Vita*, makes it patent that Robert sought a community free of the distinctions introduced by class, wealth, and sex. Female, commoner, poor, sick—they were equally welcome. Thus I see no reason to assume with some historians that this martyrdom of desire and "salve of penance" applied only to men, especially given the contempo-rary example of the similar martyrdom of his companion Hervaeus and the English nun Eva.[31]

Once institutionalized, however, the ritual was soon reframed in a dif-ferent sexual and social context, one dominated by women and directed by ladies who—as Geoffrey's letter seems to reflect—were little interested in Robert's extreme asceticism. The aristocratic origins of the nuns at Fonte-vrault, especially those he selected to rule, could not finally be suppressed—a tribute to the conservative forces of class and family—despite the leveling strictures (such as the sumptuary regulations) set in place upon its founda-tion.[32] Furthermore, Robert actually preferred married noblewomen (*ma-tronae*) for governance (as his second biographer has him state in his final days), as well as for companionship. In this he still denied an essentialist position on women, since *matrona* also designated a person and not a sex.

Thus the *accubitus* within this institutional setting, as Jean-Marc Bienvenu seems to me to have deduced correctly, tested men alone. Existing notions of the martyrdom of desire and the service to ladies could be fused and re-formed within an institutional and programmatic context structured by the Benedictine Rule which preached in its prologue a gradual purification of the soul through humility and service "like gold in the furnace" (*ut aurum in fornacio*). (In fact, it is a likely source for the metallurgic metaphor behind the fundamental notion of "courtly love" with which vernacular lyric would soon become obsessed.) [33] The two different usages of the *accubitus* identify two divergent programs: a popular program to grant women the status of equality, and an elite program to grant ladies the status of superiority. The former's universalism and the latter's dominism helped define contradictory goals for the new feminine subject, whose tension can be seen throughout High Medieval secular representations of women.

Robert's reconstruction of the feminine subject combined a number of new images of feminine subjectivity which had developed independently across the last decades of the eleventh century. In the religious sphere, the most important was without doubt the radical Romanesque model of Mary Magdalene. The cult of this *sancta meretrix*, unlike that of the Virgin Mary, reveals much about the image of and hope for women *in* the world, even though it has only recently begun to attract scholarly attention. Victor Saxer has shown that its rapid spread must be dated to the last decades of the eleventh century and that it was particularly popular in Anjou and Brittany.[34] Significantly, "Magdalena" first appears as a proper name in the same time and space, supplying good evidence not only of the popularity of the cult but also of the use of the new subject by a family in its primal interpellation of the child. In 1093 a new church was dedicated to her in Angers, the most likely moment for Marbod's three hymns (PL 171.1647–49) to "this disreputable woman whom God made an *apostola*" which open, emblematically, the first part of his lyric collection, preceeding even those to God, Christ, and the Virgin Mary. One of his students, Geoffrey of Vendôme, wrote a *sermo* describing her role as the model and mediator for female penitents, a role she also played with particular currency for Robert of Arbrissel, who originally housed "widows and continents" at Fontevrault in a Priory dedicated to the prostitute-saint.[35] In the account of the "miracle" at Menelay, moreover, Robert provoked a scandal by bringing women into a church which had refused them, asking "who would dare say there would be any church into which it would be legitimate for a woman to enter, if [Mary Magdalene] was not prohibited because of her faults and sins?"[36] Like most conversion stories of "prostitutes," historical or literary, the sudden popularity of the Magdalene "example" indicates the perception of a strong need to alter religious thinking and practice with respect to sexuality and women.

A second important current of feminine subjectivity can be found in women writers whose work begins to appear during the Romanesque period. Increasingly well trained in Classical Latin letters and language, these "Sibyls" could be found throughout the schools attached to European convents by the late eleventh century.[37] Most of their work has not been preserved, the most striking case being that of Muriel, a nun at Wilton ca. 1090-ca. 1110: the complete oeuvre of this "famous versemaker" (*inclyta versificatrix*) has apparently been lost. Still, indirect evidence permits us to see the interaction between her literate person and her natural sex. Of the twenty lines Hildebert of Le Mans devoted to her poetry while he was an exile in England (1099–1100), for instance, only a single couplet (ed. Scott, 26.13–14) actually acknowledges her authorship by lauding her genius and eloquence and even permitting her (as *tu*) for the only time to be a grammatical subject. The remainder undercuts that status by expanding a simple topos (your inspired writing qualifies you as a *uates*) into a protracted portrait of her as a passive vessel of *diuinum opus* through whom the gods speak: *non te, sed per te numina credo loqui* (18).[38]

It would be nice to hear what Muriel herself thought, or at least said, about all this. The closest we can come may be through analogy with an anonymous complaint written by a nun-poet more or less during this period and in this region, which consists of 29 distichs grouped by a refrain into five stanzas of varying length and which I translate in the Appendix.[39] Borrowing from Ovid's exilic poems, the poet begins by lamenting the lack of love for learning in a "new world" with a "new law," relating how her *ars* and *ingenium* now anger the princes of the realm. In the third stanza she defends the study and practice of Classical letters against the charge of sacrilege with an ardent credo presumably dear to all Romanesque *literati*: "If God is grasped by the senses or grasped by reason, That one will grasp the more in whom there is already more reason. Great learned writing will not prohibit me from being good, learned writing does not prohibit, but allows me to know God" (29–32). She then counterattacks with irony: "Oh what new cunning (but known to me): under the guise Of correctness Envy seeks to have a place. It is not for religious women to compose verses, Nor ours to ask who Aristotle might be" (43–46). Finally, she addresses the unknown "good man" who tears apart her verses without knowing anything about composition, concluding that he would like her if he had her creative power (*ingenium*).

The raw contest of subjects here cannot be missed. To begin with, the speaker ignores interpellation as a woman (*mulier*), a "natural" subject in whose voice she never speaks. She does respond to interpellation as a nun, yet refuses the judgment on that person by making an impassioned and lengthy defense—the poem's entire middle stanza—of the sanctity of the study of pagan letters. But in the eleven distichs which precede her use of that voice, as in the eleven which follow, she speaks exclusively as a student and writer of Classical literature and history (*littera*). This clearly constitutes her primary identity in her own eyes, and it is as this "Humanist" subject that she insists on being addressed and judged. She emphasizes the point, moreover, by interpellating her accuser in turn as a natural subject, the creative male, in order to mock his impotence in the striking and sarcastic apostrophe (*uir bone*, 54) dominating the final stanza.

When religious and erotic forces weigh more heavily upon a lettered woman, the anguish caused by the conflict among new forms of feminine subjectivity becomes even greater. One of the most eloquent expressions of such anguish preceeding the letters of Heloise can be found in the response of a lady (*domina*) named Constance, a nun probably at Le Ronceray in Angers ca. 1090–1106, in a letter-poem to Baudri of Bourgueil which I translate in the Appendix.[40] For all its apparent sincerity, her confessional text (ed. Hilbert, carmen 201) represents a construct, as it constructs a representation, of conflicting subject positions. It affords an early and remarkable view of one noblewoman's struggle with the competing demands of religious ideology, literary discourse, and physical desire.

Constance first describes how she spent the day reading Baudri's letter and the night tossing in bed, sleepless from the heat raised by his request for her love. She turns away from that disturbing material to talk about his poem, praising him at length (201.19–52) as both *uates* and *poeta*. But the mention of his singular beauty brings her back to her original topic, and she begins to complain about his year-long absence and her fear of losing him. Then her professional voice enters, noting the difficulties raised by her dedication to chastity and to her "husband," God. Yet, she reasons, she is obliged to love her husband's friends and vassals, and thus she will love Baudri chastely and poetically (201.120). Two possible wrongs threaten her:

that he is lying and actually loves another, or that he is telling the truth and asking for unchaste love: "if you are deceiving me, you are bad; if you are telling the truth, evil" (201.127). Now giving in to the justified expression of her yearning, she concludes by exhorting him to take advantage of his freedom to travel: "you who have been expected, delay no longer," she warns; "I have called you often, now come, you who have been often called!" (201.177–78).

As this last couplet indicates, Constance derives the fundamental voice of her letter (1–18, 53–100, 133–78) from the female voices of desire in the *Heroides*.[41] Her *translatio studii* makes their authoritative emotions her own, and they suffuse the text: we hear her desire, awe, doubt, joy, and fear. This "Sapphic" content, protected by the poem's fictional immunity, allows her to work out a representation of an inner world, now hers, by making full use of the power of *persona* to voice a semi-public desiring self. She contends with this dangerous self-impersonation by tapping into three discrete discourses which dictate subjects of discipline: nun (wife of God), educated writer/reader, and noblewoman.[42] In this way, the referent she constructs for the name "Constance" can be viewed as a dialectic between the Classical *persona* on one side and the three Romanesque subjects on the other, with the speaking voice weaving its way among them.

In the courts, finally, equally new forms of female subjectivity had developed, although our access to them is even more limited than to those in the church and the schools. I know of no first-person text by a noblewoman speaking as a court lady until the second half of the twelfth century. Before then we must rely upon the indirect evidence provided by male ecclesiastic moralists, satirists, and "ventriloquists." In a quietly revolutionary article, Henri Platelle collected a number of texts from the eleventh century which decry a change in masculine style at court. But the threat posed by the altered behavior, clothing, and hairstyle which they all report derives not simply from a deviation from the social norm and structure associated with it, but also from a reversal of accepted signs of gender, as Platelle points out.[43] By the early twelfth century, satirical passages by Peter the Painter and Guibert of Nogent supply ample if distorted evidence about the centrality of desire; the former describes at length the lady's methods of seduction which the husband attempts to control with a guard (*custos*), the latter the fact that "on [the modern lady's] crowds of suitors rests her claim to nobility and courtly pride."[44] Lastly, one finds sympathetic poets who use impersonation to attempt to ventriloquize the court lady. Such is the portrait of "Helen" by Baudri of Bourgueil, for instance, with whose tragic logic he seems to have sought an apologia for Bertrada of Mont-fort.[45] But the most significant, complete, intriguing act of ventriloquism can be found in the Romanesque praise of ladies, especially that associated with Adela of Blois, to whom I now want to return.

The panegyrics written for Adela have long been known, yet their significance remains curiously unacknowledged. In addition, the explicit evidence found in a poem of Godfrey of Reims, that Adela began order-ing panegyric while still in her teens, also has been ignored, although it requires that her agency in the radical transformation of the image of the lady and of its vehicle be recognized and evaluated. Finally, analysis con-tinues to be largely absent, even traditional "close reading"; panegyric does not invite meditation. What interests me particularly here are the twinned subjects constructed on both sides of the text: the subject(s) of praise.[46]

In order to analyze those subjects, I need to raise certain theoretical considerations. As specialists will notice in the following analyses, I have restricted my use of the tools typically applied to Medieval Latin texts, namely philology and "topology" (*Toposforschung*), whose respective truths lie in the authorial text and the Classical tradition. Within this study, both those methods tend to eliminate the significance of texts like panegyric and satire by isolating their verbal creation and ignoring the conditions and agents of production and consumption. And it has been amply dem-onstrated that we must include those conditions and agents within our analyses if we wish to counteract the distortions of factors such as institu-tion, class, and gender which have buried themselves within Western high cultural values.[47]

By trying to balance sociopolitical and aesthetic analyses, I hope to "overread" for Adela's missing "signature," using and slightly altering Nancy K. Miller's terms.[48] Though necessarily speculative, this approach proves especially productive because panegyric operates in a relatively im-mediate and unbrokered market where the poet-craftsman shapes wares to sell to a specific patron by targeting the patron's known tastes, interests, and pleasures. Such dedicated pieces can be said already to project *passively* the patron's voice. Because of Adela's innovative and continual patronage, moreover, her panegyrics are better treated like commissioned pieces where the craftsman begins with a specific order and the patron reviews the work in progress (as Adela did with Baudri's poem). Such "bespoken" articles (to pun on a British phrase for made-to-order goods) *actively* project the patron's voice—although clearly pleasure, meaning, and value cannot be reduced to the patron's idea for, or of, the text. In fact, it seems to me that all bespoken work is perforce duplicit in the sense that it results from the interaction and interference of two intentions, that each "intender" has ulterior designs at least partially irrelevant and/or incomprehensible to the other, and that the product largely masks the process for ideological reasons.

If "overreading" serves to change the object of analysis by rendering the site and investments of production and consumption more visible, it also serves to change the subject of analytic discourse by contesting universal categories of perception and judgment guaranteed by the cult of individual genius. In this particular case, how can I hope to avoid the interference of my own class (or classlessness) and gender in "looking for Adela's signature" in the frame of panegyric production? To some extent, I cannot—there is simply too much I cannot experience or know. This is equally true of many if not all of the agents I study here, since their lived experience little resembles my own. Even if gender constitutes a separate case, my person is no more determined or exhausted by my gender than Adela's was by any, or even all of the subjects to which she was called; the gaps within and between subjects make possible my construction of a valid interpretation as they do her construction of a flexible and "personal" politics. Moreover, by not seeking some unique and natural identity for Adela (mother, beloved, daughter, courtly lady, individual, woman), I am less subjected to the corresponding position (son, lover, father, and so forth) which any exclusive identity would appear to offer me as observer and from which I would want to make sense.

With this theoretical support, I want to turn now to the task of analyzing the panegyric lyric (in the widest sense) addressed to Adela. The earliest extant praise written about and, obliquely, to her came from the pen of Godfrey, chancellor at Reims (ca. 1076–ca. 1095), who embedded it within a larger panegyric probably written in the early 1080s for one Ingelrann, then archdeacon at Soissons (ca. 1077–98).[49] In this letter-poem of 78 distichs, Godfrey begins by congratulating Ingelrann on his conversion from a frivolous to a serious life (1–26) and himself for having predicted it (27–42). In the poem's second section he lists the archdeacon's outstanding qualities: noble birth (43–56), learning (57–76), eloquence (77–94) and poetic talent (95–114). In this last category, Godfrey cites particularly "the poems which the king's daughter has had sent to her" (*poemata . . . quae directa sibi filia regis habet*, 117–18). This explicit testimony that Adela had

already solicited panegyric as a young woman of fifteen or so is precious,
and I shall return to its implications later. After digressing on William the
Conqueror's achievements and praising Adela's prenatal influence upon
her father's success (119–38), Godfrey closes the letter-poem with a critique
of Ingelrann's poem (139–56), concluding that her beauty required a better
writer. Eclipsed between author and father, Adela has in actuality only tan-
gential interest for Godfrey, though his poem supplies the only evidence
of her birth date, the first indication of her patronage, and a partial list of
the traits of the first impersonation of herself she is known to have sought:
virtue, generosity, and beauty (141–46).

   Unfortunately, no poem ascribed to the infamous Ingelrann has ever
been found. One anonymous late eleventh-century panegyric, written in
hexameter couplets tied by internal and end rhymes and found in two
closely related manuscripts representing the most significant extant anthology of the Loire School, however, could very well be one of those
he wrote to Adela. In any event it is interesting in its own right, and the
subjects of praise it projects deserve attention:

Superb Verses Composed in Meter

Oh famous progeny and special flower of the fatherland,
Be the general subject matter for my verses.
My Muse tells of you in her marvelous measures,
She sets you before all others by recounting so many praises.
If, oh Goddess, nobility or fame rich in deeds,   5
And if candor, judgment were to speak the truth,
They could escape the fated dangers of Death:
Adorned with such things, how fearless you could live!
Everyone knows how rich you are in ancestors,
I cannot count the whole family line of men.   10
If you had been alive, more suited that all others for deeds,
Greece would not have mourned, I know, for its captured spouse.
But although others would mourn your seizure by the Trojan,
Nevertheless the royal staff of empire would suit you:
You are said—and justly—to be worthy of a royal crown,   15
Your right hand has quickly bestowed most generous gifts.
Your reading of Ovid does not lie hidden, your worship,
Nor the perception of Cato [ed: Plato] which tests for truths.

You also know how to speak publicly in the vernacular:
You have learned to versify in an amazing arrangement.   20
But grant me your mercy, my veins empty of blood.
Since now I am failing, I cannot sing to the fullest,
My mind lies conquered; I undertook lofty doings,
My spirit has been returned stunned and senseless.[50]

Thematically structured by quatrains, the poem lauds her male ancestors, royal nature, and literary ability before its bloodless, beaten, stunned, and loving speaker "fails" to recount the rest of her praises, particularly her beauty. It has been dismissed with some disdain as the piece of an apprentice poet,[51] but that is more or less what Godfrey himself insinuates about Ingelrann's efforts, and I consider this poem likely to have been sent by Ingelrann to the princess Adela. Not only do all its praises fit her youthful state particularly well, but its wording finds echoes in Godfrey's poem: *deficiam—deficis*; *Phrige—Phrigio*; *diva—dea*. Furthermore, the comments about her suitability for manly deeds and her early generosity (9, 16) are repeated by Baudri (134.35–6 and 49–50), who also, curiously, hails her as "special flower" (*Et [carta] dictura tibi "flos specialis, aue"*, 134.1356). Even if this is not written to Adela, the image of an educated noblewoman writing poetry in the vernacular at this time is fascinating.

The location, tone, and length of Godfrey's criticism imply that he had written a poem for her as well. Another of his poems, "Parce, precor, virgo, tociens michi culta videri," fulfills that expectation, though no name is ever given to the young woman it lauds. Despite being described by John Williams as "immeasurably the most satisfactory of Godfrey's poems," it has seen bad summaries and even worse analyses. I include a full translation in the Appendix, for it deserves a closer look, especially since it directly influenced subsequent Latin panegyric to ladies.[52]

Divided into three sections, the 50 distichs (frequently Leonine) are directed toward a young woman with red hair and shining dark eyes. The first (1–32) contains the critique of ornament which has probably earned it the label *satyra*: hairdo, silken hairbands, artificial curls, gold earrings, glass necklace. The poet's tone changes as his gaze descends (19–22), and his nascent desire establishes a second level of meaning to his plea for a lack of covering. He ends with the request, "Let no external beauty adorn you any more than a horse, Although you are more beautiful with your beauty than a horse" (27–28). This piece of putative flattery only makes sense if Godfrey is speaking through the girl to her father beside her, for whom a beautiful woman and a powerful horse could function equally well as signs of power.

In the second segment (33–56) Godfrey expands the significance of the first segment's laudatory message. The girl's "natural beauty" exceeds not only the artifice of man, but also that of nature. Her eyes outshine the sun and stars, her neck gleams whiter than fresh snow, her chest and forehead seem like warm goat's milk, and the color of her face surpasses all the flowers: "The odorous glory of the blooming woods yields to you Nor does the well-watered garden have anything it might prefer to you" (47–8). These hyperboles, borrowed to some extent from the "Song of Songs," imply that the girl *is* Nature, a virginal Nature characterized not by procreation but by a pristine beauty unspoiled by insertion into time (53–4). A Christian reader would want another Garden and another Virgin, but Godfrey never makes the tropological *translatio*. Here the virtual naturalism we found in Marbod's Angevin program reaches its aesthetic consequence in the apology for the goodness of beauty and woman in their natural state.

If the second section placed the girl's beauty outside nature, the third and longest (57–100) places it outside history; if the second took its spoils from the Bible, the third takes them from the Classics. Jove would have relinquished his divinity, Priam would not have grieved for the loss of Troy, any god wandering through the woody grottos would think her the goddess Diana, and Paris would have chosen her over Venus: "If the apple were to be given to the more powerful beauty, It would have been given rather to your beauty" (95–6). Here Godfrey again retains the literal text by refusing to support moralizing readings which had gathered about the myths since Late Antiquity, and the entire section works as well by the presence of Diana and Ovid as by the absence of Mary and Christ.

Godfrey's critique of Ingelrann implies that he intended to mirror the girl's beauty in the poem's *sollempnis forma* (100), and to this end he has painted his portrait with the "colors" and "figures" of rhetoric, beginning with antithesis (*contentio*). Ironically, such a style relies upon the use of the very artifice that he rejects for the girl, an artifice they both need to compete at court for status and power. Godfrey's bad faith—using artifice to decry artifice—and hypocrisy—masking the poet's pride with a lover's humility (*pronus amo*, 33)—identify a male subject split in the production of female panegyric between the sociopolitical demands on a useful performance and the poetic demands on an appropriate text.[53]

Within a decade or so, Baudri of Bourgueil "dictated" a long and partially fictional poem about the marvelous tapestries in Adela's chamber, whose panegyric beginning I included at the start of this chapter (text 3). The poem has been little examined beyond the question of possible affiliation with the Bayeux Tapestry.[54] I sketched out its poetic, intellectual, and political interests in Chapter 2, suggesting that its anticipation of the "School of Chartres" probably reflects Adela's close relations after 1090 with Ivo, bishop of Chartres and supporter of the Reform, whose antipathy for Baudri surely derived from more than just the latter's attempt to buy the bishopric of Orléans which he reports in a scathing letter of 1096 (PL 162.84–85). After an introductory discussion of the royalty of Adela's parents (ed. Hilbert, 134.1–32), the poet apostrophizes and comforts his frightened poem by lauding the Countess's taste in poetry (37–38, 51–60), generosity (39–50), and marital fidelity (61–66). He then describes both his fear and her divine beauty (67–88), using Classical material with an ease and originality which signal the increasing maturity of Romanesque poetics:

Her unusual honor and unequaled beauty commend her,
As does the grace of her conversation.
But who would be able to soften such hard granite?
They gaze without cause; but it is pleasing to gaze.   70
They think of great rewards when they feed on empty hope,
And by gaping at her they irritate their eyes.
This is not surprising, becuase her beauty shines forth
So much that she ought to surpass all other young women.
I would have seen her except that I would have blushed like a
       country bumpkin;   75
In fact, while speaking I blushed to look upon her.
If I had not turned my wandering eyes aside,
She would then quickly have drained all my words from me.
In the same way very many abandon their proper duties
On the spot, once having gazed upon the Gorgon,   80
And many stiffened thus before Circe;
For they could not tolerate the goddess's majesty.
I scarcely saw her then, yet I remember having seen her,
I remember having seen her as I remember having seen dreams.
Thus I recall often having seen the new moon or,   85

When I barely see it, think I am seeing it.
I scarcely saw her; but as even I recall,
Her beauty is to be preferred to that of Diana.[55]

The evocative passage completes the description of the court culture
around Adela made by Godfrey by depicting the patronage of secular
poetry, the competition among poets, the praise of beauty, the courting of
married ladies, the "gaping" of suitors, and the stupefaction of the poet-
lover.[56]

Baudri "steps out" from the text by rendering its stylistic signs palpable. Here that takes the form of an arresting comparison: the sight of
Adela is to Baudri as that of Medusa was to most men, making them forget
their duties at once (79–80). Like the subsequent reference to the witch
Circe, this comparison is risky: how can he escape being the victim of the
power with which he toys? Allegory, of course, was invented to solve such
delicate problems of reading, and his defense appears to rely upon Adela's
ability to make use of that technique. For in his mythological poem Baudri
described the Gorgon as a very rich and crafty woman who doubled her
wealth while in power, outstripping her father and other kings (ed. Hilbert, 154.253–60). He goes on to gloss (154.275–90) the name "Medusa" as
"not being able to see" (*nequeat uidere*), one of three causes of Fear, which
only Perseus (as *sapientia*) can conquer with an oblique glance at his glassy
shield, where he can imagine *bona spes*.[57] Thus at the very moment that one
might expect finally to see Adela's beauty, one sees instead the speaker's
crafty and oblique references eliciting her presence as allegorical reader.
His learning enables him to elude the anger evoked by his craft, and in this
way to speak about the politics and poetics of the gaze.

Baudri's statement (in text 3, 134.55–56), that Adela had approved an
early fragment of the poem and urged him to continue, supports Godfrey's
mention of "the poems she has had sent to her." In fact, similarities among
the poems of (perhaps) Ingelrann, Godfrey, and Baudri suggest the existence of a kind of in-house "trait set" for her panegyric. Clearly, she wanted
to be represented as a king's daughter, to be praised for secular attributes
such as beauty, literary taste, intelligence, and generosity, and to be compared through Classical borrowings and reminiscences with a Roman goddess (*dea*), often Diana the virgin huntress.[58] All these may well have been
actual personal traits, but their isolation and inscription in representation
are finally ideological. The novelty and repetition of these traits seem to
point to Adela's appropriation and modification of the discourse of cour-

tesy and the loving subject at its center, elevating the symbolic power of both the "lady" and the sophisticated court around her.

Somewhere around the turn of the century, her impersonation changed dramatically from a courtly *domina* to Christian *matrona*. It is intriguing to speculate that Baudri's image of the faithful wife surrounded by spurned lovers was designed to evoke and reject Bertrada's paradigmatic figuration as *pellex*, especially since Anjou and Capetian France—the two sites of the Bertrada scandal—surrounded the Countess's domain and were its most dangerous adversaries. I see no other reason for his gratuitous mention of the possibility of marital infidelity (63–72), except that it had become useful to Adela to distance herself from the generic "Bad Lady" who ruined reputations and family lines by taking lovers at their word. Such a rejection would have attracted support from Ivo of Chartres, who had become the primary adversary of the efforts by Philip and Bertrada to legitimize their marriage and its offspring. In any case, Baudri's text shows us Adela as the lady of a court of poetry and desire for the last time. After the turn of the century, she will never again be represented as the object of the loving subject's gaze within a cult of elegance.

This fundamental change is presaged by a panegyric which Hildebert of Le Mans sent the Countess perhaps as early as 1096, the year Stephen left on the First Crusade and Hildebert was promoted. More sophisticated in form and content than his half-hearted epigram quoted earlier (text 4), this short paean expands upon the house theme of Adela's "divinity" in a novel manner:

Oh imperial progeny of a sublime ancestral line,
I ask that what I am sending, be it ever so little, please you.
I do not want your hand or head, worthy of scepter and crown,
To be turned toward my reward; favor me in your mind.
Just as it is enough for the common people to have earned the goodwill
        of those above
When the small sacrifice to the great gods falls,
So your grace (alone) fulfills my plea. I err more than Man
If I aspire to more than to have pleased you.[59]

The fact that Hildebert would even use feminine panegyric for a "favor" says a great deal about the status of the genre at Adela's court by that time. For even if this Christian humanist grasped the utility of the *persona* of ladies, he seems to have reviled their *sexus*, at least in his writings, despite having lived with a woman and fathered a son.[60] For these reasons, perhaps, the poem to Adela works more as an anti-panegyric, carefully placing her completely out of sight. Her power is suggested by its absence, that mercy which is itself only rendered "visible" by a dark image of hope. Refering to Roman religious practices that the poem's maker rejected ex officio, the speaker adopts the most abject of positions: that of the terrified and insignificant subject of distant and inconstant gods.

The last line assures everyone indirectly that the speaker does not want her "love," but Hildebert in fact did want more than her gratification. To begin with, we know he also sought money, goods, and favor from her, for in letters written about the same time he seeks a chasuble (PL 171.284) or safe conduct (171.288–89). Moreover, he wanted protection against the Anglo-Norman aggression in Maine by her brother William Rufus (1087–1100), which would lead in 1099 to a year of imprisonment and exile.[61] His panegyric subject, like that of Godfrey and Baudri, thus becomes more complex as the speaking self's humble performance on center stage is seen to disguise the ambitious desires of his authorial prompter in the wings.

That distinction says much about the venal elasticity of panegyric, and the slippery simile of lines 5–7 now become a trope of the actual agent of eloquence. The speaking subject is merely a pronominal fiction waiting for an antecedent like an empty mask waiting for an actor, suggesting that the final object of the sale was neither the content (secular praise) nor the style (Romanesque elegance) as much as the portrait of the insignificant subject. Because it hid its fictive status behind the veil of confession, it offered itself with particular ease to ideological appropriation.

As I think Hildebert must have intended, we see nothing of Adela in his poem—in fact we see her *as* nothing, a cipher or placeholder for family power—and I have difficulty believing she was pleased by the disappearance of both her *persona* and her *sexus* from the text. Some time later, however, Hildebert wrote a very different epistle to her about governance which I translate in the Appendix; it offers a clear view of the reformed subjects of praise which served both their interests. The opening is striking: "A more onerous concern for the county lies on you with the absence of your husband. Yet you administer it as a woman and by yourself in such a way that there is no need either for a man or for asking advice."[62] The wording implies that Adela had sought out this letter after the death of her husband with the question: "What authority do I have to rule?" In asking this she turned less to a spiritual adviser, as one might traditionally put it, than to an agent of verbal *auctoritas* who could tell her what she wanted to hear—and to be heard: "You have with you whatever is required for governance of the realm" (*Apud te est quidquid ad regni gubernacula postulatur*). Responding to new regional factors (the condemnation of Bertrada, the death of her husband, the majority of her son, the pressure for reform), Adela seems to have determined to have her *persona* altered by an apologetic epistle which would justify the authority of a "virtuous wife" in order to subjugate the male and religious establishments from whom she needed both peace and support.

Hildebert's voice differs from that of his earlier writings to her. Dropping humility, pride, and fear, he follows Late Carolingian precedents of adapting Stoic philosophy (especially that of Cicero and Seneca) to the demands for a useful and brief secular ethic by constructing an ungendered ideal ruler in whom Chastity removes the woman and Clemency the man. If she controls the natural subjection of desire and aggression, he argues, Adela can free herself from the constraints of gendered existence altogether. The means of this metamorphosis is *Ratio*, that human faculty which combines the judgment, discipline, and proportion essential to Hildebert's humanism, as Peter von Moos has shown convincingly.[63]

Hildebert betrays himself in a clever final gesture, when he depicts Clemency following Rationality "as a servant girl [does] the mistress of the house" (*quasi pedissequa matremfamilias*) in order to emphasize the deep homology among the governments of the realm, the household, and the soul. This slip into allegory is doubly revealing. First, it puts Adela in her place, the wife's place, and keeps her there by extending the simile for the rest of the section; withdrawing the independence and power he offered at the beginning of the letter, Hildebert restores normative gender relations by resubjecting her to dominant ideology. Moreover, his eloquence, too, follows Rationality, moderating, mediating, and finally betraying itself with its accommodating ways. This persuasive trope, the trope of persuasion, finally tropes by mistake its own pliancy and with it the suspicious utility of ornament within both sets of intentions which lend fascination to this well-crafted text.

The metamorphosis of Adela's textual person at the turn of the twelfth century can be seen in the anonymous poem written 1096–1102 and translated at the beginning of this chapter (text 7). Divided thematically into four units of three distichs apiece (assuming the last line to be missing), it combines an exordium, a statement of her outstanding qualities, a moral defense of her wealth and beauty, and a refutation of attacks on her sex. Three aspects of the poem help us understand the changes in its representation. First, although Adela's beauty is defended, it is pointedly neither described nor even included in the list of her "advantages" (*commoda*), and her patronage of poetry mentioned prominently by all previous panegyrists remains out of sight. Second, the style itself gradually changes gender, in a manner of speaking, moving from a florid style reminiscent of Godfrey and his praise of the body to a sententious style reminiscent of Hildebert and his praise of the soul. Finally, the speaking subject switches from an Ovidian voice to a Virgilian voice—if he starts by seeking favor as a crafter of words, he finishes by granting it as a seer of truths. These changes from earlier panegyric to her reveal a single desire, which I take to be Adela's, to reconstruct the representation of "the countess of Blois."

Adela's self-reformation received its strongest support in the last known panegyric "lyric" she received, an epistle from Hugh of Sainte-Marie, a monk at Fleury, sent in 1109 to dedicate to her what is now called his ecclesiastical history. Its actual content is better described by Hugh himself: "Here you have something you might read when you have free time: namely the acts of the ancient emperors and equally memorable acts of certain men beloved to God, from the incarnation of the Lord up to [the death of Charlemagne]."[64] A universal history and self-styled "anthology" (*haec . . . ab antiquis historiologis velut apis a diversis floribus mel colligens aggregavi*), Hugh's text enjoyed substantial success in the twelfth century, though it has yet to be examined with care.[65]

Although the author postpones a true panegyric (*preconium*) of Adela's virtues, the laudatory text and freestanding status of his dedicatory letter qualify it as "praise lyric" in the wider senses of both words. Whether or not she actually sought out the history, Adela's intentions resound loudly within it.[66] In fact, the ambitious project as a whole recalls the appropriation of Roman history and historiography which characterized the authors patronized by her father to legitimize his rule. Also, one sees for the first time her concern with the wider role of the secular aristocracy and its history, a concern she shared with many of her contemporaries. The astonishing success of the *miles Christi* in 1099 seemed to imply both that the martial class could be a true Order, and that its deeds belonged in some hitherto unseen manner to "ecclesiastical" history.

The most striking aspect of the epistle is its redemption of woman— at least, of the *domina*—within a universal framework. This redemption occurs in both the moral and the historical dimension. Hugh's repeated praise of the Countess over other "barons," including her own brothers, already sets up a moral dimension that his defense of dedicating a work of universal history to a woman makes explicit:

But also a woman sitting at the Lord's feet heard the words of His mouth not only better but also more devoutly than the Pharisees and Sadducees and even Christ's disciples. For the feminine sex does not lack understanding of profound matters but, as I shall state plainly in the following reading, now and then there is sometimes in women great mental industry and the most virtuous elegance of behavior.[67]

Taking the actions of the figure universally acknowledged at that time to be Mary Magdalene as his example, Hugh makes the astonishing and possibly unparalleled claim that *industria* and *elegantia* are potential properties of woman's reading which even the disciples did not possess.

In the second half of the epistle, sacred history itself is revised in order to eliminate any generic fault in the female sex. No woman is present in Hugh's 1109 version of the Fall, which is reduced to the following single sentence: "Inspired by God, Adam received from him on the sixth day of the week the power of his free will." Woman's unique role, the *genetrix* dear to the Marian cult, occupies a central position in his digest of sacred history from the Fall to the Redemption:

Whence [God] took flesh from a woman so that human nature itself might have with His incarnation something with which it could move back with His aid to the blessedness which it had lost. . . . Because [the Lord] wanted to be born of a woman he showed us the great benevolence of his graciousness and the immeasurable example of his humility.[68]

Clearly, Hugh believes that Adela wants to have the myth of Eve buried in order to replace it with the virtuous activity of the Lady in power as reader and ruler, the concluding image of the epistle.[69] Whether that represents his guess or her command remains unresolvable, finally, but the boldness of the design seems to me to speak more for Adela's prescribing patronage than Hugh's creative genius.

This cleansing of the female sex attests eloquently to the extraordinary degree to which the *domina* was ultimately elevated during the second period of the dominist revolution at Adela's court. Her decision toward the end of the eleventh century to have the representation of "the countess of Blois" reformed brought her gendered person inevitably into direct confrontation with the essential feminine subject of ecclesiastic ideology for the first time. Hugh's solution to include the lady within universal history contrasts usefully with Godfrey's to exclude her, and leaves us with a measure of the distance between the extremes set by the authoritative impersonations Adela paid for. Her legacy offered secular Romanesque French

ideology a loving subject which could respond to traditional class questions of dominance and permanence without betraying its construction of
gender.

The analysis of this panegyric has illuminated an important facet of the
story and history of Adela of Blois because it revealed shifts in the subject
of the lady and its eminently useful correlative, the loving subject. These
results suggest that if we change the object of analysis and the subject of
discourse, we can expand and deepen our understanding of the history and
theory of women during this crucial stage in the formation of the dominant
Western ideology.

Because of the clear evidence that Adela began near the beginning of
the 1080s to hire poets to publicize and magnify her secular traits, it seems
to me difficult to deny her an innovative and influential role in the use of
poetry at the secular court. Aristocratic women had long been patrons,
of course, but of religious artifacts rather than poetry; Adela initiated
a quantitatively and qualitatively different program with her support of
panegyric. She perceived clearly, probably through the patronage of history and lyric by her father and uncle, that she would do well to authorize
her own fame, exercising symbolic power to her own advantage through
a sort of reverse impersonation. Appropriating the revolutionary poetics
blossoming in Romanesque French schools, Adela and her money mediated between Medieval Latin poetry and the court at least two decades
before any other aristocratic woman—including her sister-in-law Mathilde
of England (who only began to reign in 1101), whose praise by William
of Malmesbury is often cited in this regard.[70] The extant poems are not
love poems, as Bezzola rightly observed, but to my mind her introduction
into French court culture of support by women of formal praise poems
based upon a Romanesque poetics took the crucial step toward the emergence into writing of the vernacular lyric poetry associated with the cult of
courtly love.

"Every discussion of the status of woman is complicated by the existence of the lady."[71] Emily James Putnam's classic assertion speaks well to
the extended implications of this material. For the young Countess of Blois
seems to have impersonated the new lady whose elegance and beauty had
established a highly eroticized set of values at many Romanesque French
courts, gradually making her over into a "lovely," literate, and increasingly
virtuous lady, a composite subject new to official culture. Other forms of
"dominism," as I have suggested calling it, arose about the same time, but

the one Adela created around her as a woman of power and status seems to me the most likely source for the idealized construct adopted by High Medieval French culture. Because her Lady promised to redeem Woman and because it reinforced the closure of the social formation, the radical subject of praise which Adela promoted was remarkably successful.

That success appears to have come at the expense of renouncing female voice and sexuality; Adela's Lady was safely "bespoken" and beloved, not speaking and loving like Constance of Le Ronceray or the anonymous nun-poet, both writing at about the same time. The traits of eloquence and desire we saw in the figure of Ælfgyva seem to have been displaced under the pressure of the dominant ideologies to her alter ego in the panel, the clerk, where they fuse with those not of a preacher but of a flatterer. When, guided by rhetoric and ideology, these impersonators learned increasingly well to hide artifice and greed behind nature and service, they succeeded in creating the complex and deceptive loving subject which proved so successful in twelfth-century court culture and beyond.

Finally, this study of Adela and the writers she supported has allowed us to perceive a variety of Romanesque critiques of the admixture of misogyny and essentialism which dominated ecclesiastic and secular representations of women. The multiple versions of this critique attest to the importance of the problem for Adela and her contemporaries, and to their self-conscious search for solutions. Godfrey constructed a "pre-essential" or supernatural woman; Adela impersonated first the courteous lady and then the virtuous wife; Robert argued for an "extra-essential" or agendered *homo*; Hildebert proposed a "trans-essential" or ungendered *ratio*; the anonymous poet composed an "anti-essential" and regendered vision; and Hugh of Sainte-Marie's "super-essentialism" inserted her into universal history. Reactionary and "sub-essential" texts, such as Hildebert's praise of the nun Adela stripped of both sex and person, or William of Poitiers's reduction of the lady to just her sexual drive and utility, only reinforce the sense of the extent to which the intense dominist speculation of Adela's generation had destabilized traditional secular feminine subjects. This speculation seems to me to mark the "woman's Renaissance" that Joan Kelly sought with such insight, even if its products should finally be seen as more complex and more ambiguous than she might have thought.[72]

Conclusion

In studying the loving subject in Romanesque France, I opted for a tight focus and an oblique perspective in order to bring out details in the shadows. Those details have disclosed the formation and gradual closure of a heterogeneous group within the schools and courts of central and northern France which intensely pursued secularity through the defense of the body and the means of its representation. The existence and interests of this group raise questions about current interpretations of the period, shedding light on the early history of the subject.

I have argued that by 1075 new secular subjects begin to appear in French cultural documents that indicate epochal changes in elite society. In the courts the figures of lady and lover and their cult of desire and elegance showed up alongside those of warrior and lord concerned with prowess and justice. In the schools the figures of the clerk and the poet-prophet and their cult of eloquence and genius accompanied those of ascetics and administrators concerned with chastity and orthodoxy. These figures were at first marginalized—and more often condemned or suppressed—in representation, but by the late eleventh century they had started moving rapidly toward a more central position. That movement seems to have been accelerated by a sort of "feedback loop" between changing mechanisms of subjection and subjectivity. As reformers began to condemn the sexual and material desires of the lower clergy, they unavoidably had to grant representational status to previously unspeakable subjects in order for the work of ideology to proceed. This new status, in turn, rendered the representation of attempts to resist or elude suppression both more possible and more profitable. Such a consequence helps explain why "personal" texts of all sorts suddenly become visible within the Latin culture of France during the last quarter of the eleventh century. The success of such texts, in turn, seems to have incited reformers during the 1090s to bring eloquence and composition themselves under control through a combination of attack and appropriation. Those efforts further drove clerks pursuing secular desires of all kinds outside the schools, where they could hope to sell their literacy, learning, and taste as elite tokens.

An analogous loop seems to have operated in the courts. The eleventh century witnessed the mounting success of new court figures supported by aristocratic investment in such areas as the pursuit of private pleasure, the desire for internal peace, and the need for alternative class markers. As the relative importance of these figures rose, ecclesiastic observers began to condemn ladies and lovers more frequently for behavior which appeared to undermine the role of the martial elite in the world order. This critique rendered in turn radical lyric practices more attractive to court society, whose members by that time in much of central and northern France were being routinely sent to school, as a means of deflecting and eluding the attacks on court culture. By the early twelfth century, finally, the capacity and significance of that lyric and its *persona* began to be appropriated by regional rulers in order to construct new subjects of power, a phenomenon which helps account for the sudden documentation of court lyric in Latin and Romance.

Complex products require complex production, and it seems to me that the new secular culture which emerged into view in France around the turn of the twelfth century cannot be explained or analyzed without an awareness of the movement between court and school, the interaction between Latin and vernacular culture, and the increasing pressure from conservative agents of martial and monastic ideologies. Yet in using the phrase "the new secular culture" I do not want to suggest that the product was either simple or singular. In fact, neither the two agents of experimentation nor the two agents of appropriation I have examined closely would have agreed on the culture's details, even though they agreed on its general interest and utility. Marbod was an academic of upper mercantile orgin; Baudri an esthete probably of noble origin. Where the former worked darkly with Classical letters and his own soul in a search for general utility, the latter played brightly with both for elite pleasure. In the courts, Adela moved toward religious conservatism, adopting its humility, service, and chastity for her *persona* by the turn of the century; William moved toward martial conservatism, adopting its insistence on pride, loyalty, and deeds. These early constructions of desire, eloquence, and power exercised great influence, yet others would continue for many centuries to appear with equal success.

The extent and influence of this manifold secular culture carries certain implications for the interpretation of secular practices, images, and documents in Romanesque France. It seems to me that our current views remain colored by the inherent bias in the extant documents and artifacts from this period, a bias which results from a strong selection for the moral, the institutional, and the masculine. Much has been preserved and therefore written about chivalry and feudalism, but little about sexuality and elegance; much about religion and reform, but little about composition and eloquence. The tacit equation of the present distribution of extant Romanesque documents with the former distribution of Romanesque interests renders interpretations often overly clerical and overly coherent.

The secular culture I have studied here diverges strongly from that of traditional views of Romanesque France, suggesting that certain cautions and revisions are necessary. Clearly those constructing new secular visions in the courts and schools made as much use of Roman culture as architects or writers working for ecclesiastic magnates. Yet one cannot characterize their work with the same terms used for Romanesque literature and art that seeks to celebrate divine power and portray human hubris. No one would deny such a *usage* of Roman culture, a usage which lay after all at the heart of the dominant eleventh-century ideological program associated with Cluny, but by the last quarter of the century other usages competed with it. Many differing, secular usages of things Roman in French cathedral schools and comital courts flourished in this period. Their unity lies in the turn to pagan Roman culture for "modernity" (as they often called it) and authority in exploring and redefining the secular; their plurality lies in what was looked at, what was seen, and how it was used.

Attempts to restore a certain balance in the interpretation of Romanesque culture have been made before. One of the most relevant to this study came from the great art critic and theorist Meyer Schapiro in an iconoclastic article published a half century ago. Examining a wide range of artifacts and documents, he concluded that "by the eleventh and twelfth centuries, there had emerged in western Europe within church art a new sphere of artistic creation without religious content and imbued with the values of spontaneity, individual fantasy, delight in color and movement, and the expression of feeling that anticipate modern art."[1] My analyses of aspects generally ignored in Romanesque studies lend credence to these conclusions, but they critique implicitly their Romantic vocabulary. Instead of concluding that Romanesque artists *existed* as creative and feeling individuals spontaneously and naturally expressing their genius, I conclude that there is good evidence that many artists (as well as writers and public figures) consciously *constructed* images of themselves as creative and desiring individuals from Roman sources with a good eye on social and economic advantage. They were aware of many of the psychological, discursive, and ideological constraints upon and implications of such constructions, and turned to the theory and practice of self-impersonation in order to negotiate the demands and desires they experienced.

This Romanesque *persona* was embodied voice—and hence must be carefully distinguished from its Modernist and New Critical analogues. Its semantic value lay somewhere between English "character" and "person," between the belief that a given role is created by language and distinct from the observer's self, on the one side, and the belief that it is expressed in language and part of that self on the other. The crucial position of *persona* in rhetoric, especially Horatian rhetoric, which figured so prominently in central French schools, helped placed a cultural premium upon the construction and manipulation of images of the self for the purposes of self-promotion and self-defense. A split subject of discourse seems almost to have been viewed as "normal" during the Romanesque period, especially in the secular culture, and constitutes one of its most significant traits.

The Romanesque *persona*, finally, could be made into a subject; this was the discovery, I think, that caused "lyric" to spread so rapidly. Powerful individuals realized that they could exploit the traits of self-impersonation for their own ends, and began consciously to manipulate their self-image within stylized first-person discourse and image, transforming individuality into ideology. Since they exercised great symbolic power within their domain, they could control the nature and extent of the "publication" of a new voice for themselves whose new eliteness and secularity derived from the cultural capital invested in lover and artist. This appropriation thus served to disguise the truth of social control with the fiction of personal freedom, the subject with the *persona*. Most Romanesque "individuals" we hear or see expressing themselves, in other words, use the voice of authority.

This conclusion links the Romanesque construction of the loving subject to the general history of the subject. That history, originally conceived on a grand scale and emphasizing systems, remains conceptually and temporally incomplete. Michel Foucault's groundbreaking work examined the beginnings of the modern subject in France during the eighteenth and nineteenth centuries, emphasizing the profound break with traditional Christian discourse of the subject. In the latter part of his career, Foucault discovered in Greek Antiquity an elaborate structure for the "care of the self" that preceded Christianity. Roman and Medieval texts represented for him but examples of Greek and Christian practices, respectively, and even the sixteenth century, which he acknowledged to be important, rarely attracted his careful attention.[2]

Much has been published since then on the Early Modern or Renaissance period, placing us in a better position to evaluate the shifts in the discourse of the subject. As David Aers has observed in his recent review, however, that research has been conducted with such a conviction of the privileged position of the Early Modern period in the history of the subject that it radically collapses and demonizes "the medieval"—unwittingly following the fifteenth-century humanists who coined the term. His counterclaim seems to me to be beyond dispute: "There is no reason to think that languages and experiences of inwardness, of interiority, of divided selves, of splits between outer realities and inner forms of being, were unknown before the seventeenth century."[3] Whatever exactly the appearance of the Early Modern subject represents, one cannot claim for it the invention of true or proper subjectivity.

My study of the Romanesque period, then, presents three broad considerations to historians of the subject. First, the evidence I have found joins that of other studies to confirm the twelfth century as a period of intense speculation about and reconstruction of the subject.[4] I do not claim, however, that here one finds at last the beginnings—much less the origins—of Western subjectivity. In fact, it seems more likely to me that significant moments can be found whenever and wherever changes occur in such areas as writing technology, production modes, social formation, and cultural consciousness that are strong enough to disturb the equilibrium between mechanisms of subjection and subjectivity. Fragmented by lines of geography, culture, politics, class, gender, and race, these multiple moments resist a single and coherent history.

Second, there seems no reason to assume the existence of some unique source for Western subjectivity. There can be little doubt, for instance, about the eminence of Augustine's *Confessions*, which many medievalists have claimed, for his agonizing search to stabilize knowledge by stabilizing the self repeatedly attracted serious attention. But it was not the only paradigm of subjectivity inherited from Antiquity; as we have seen here, Ovid attracted equal attention. His *Heroides* and *Metamorphoses* have provided an inexhaustible source for the last one thousand years of Western speculation about the destabilizing effects upon identity of sexuality, language, beauty, power, and change. In fact, the tradition of Western writing about subjectivity can be conceived abstractly but usefully as a set of complex reactions to the fundamental disagreements between the positions represented by Ovid and Augustine—between what Richard Lanham once characterized as the referential mystics and the rhetorical stylists.[5] From this perspective, again, a monologic history of the subject escapes us.

Finally, the documentary presence in Western culture (at least through the eighteenth century) of multiple and competing discourses of subjectivity with ancient authority sheds a somewhat more complex light on "the Humanist subject" which has attracted such critical fire since the analyses of Louis Althusser thirty years ago.[6] I have tried to argue in this study that "the subject of Humanism" is inherently no more stable, coherent, or unique than other subjects. It has been privileged in elite written culture, but since its beginnings in Roman theory it has always been a site of contention. In Romanesque France, some students of *humanitas* (like Hildebert of Le Mans) found a stable subject in the Roman past; others (like Baudri of Bourgueil) found an instable subject; still others (like Marbod of Rennes) seem to have found both. All agreed upon the centrality of eloquence, but they disagreed upon its relations with the erotic, material, and ideological forces operating on the speaker. The alleged unity and stability of the Humanist subject results, to my mind, rather from the cumulative labor of two millennia of Christian Humanism, that is, those Humanistic interpreters, interpretations, and institutions up through the present which insist one way or another on the harmony of Classical letters with revealed Truth.

Moreover, a curious sort of cultural amnesia seems to have rendered invisible the capacity of Humanistic writing to facilitate the articulation of new discourses of subjectivity and subjection at various cultural moments in the past. In the Romanesque period in France, I have found a whole cluster of figures exploiting the instable and discursive character of identity to elude "interpellation" by agents of the dominant ideologies. Yet another cluster of figures was reappropriating that same Humanistic technique in order to create new modes of subjection. Both consequences, it seems to me, always attend the Humanist subject, whether in fourteenth-century Italy, sixteenth-century England, eighteenth-century France, or elsewhere. Its ethical value derives from the use to which it is put by particular agents with particular intentions, and from the perspective of particular observers within particular institutions.

All that I have attempted to describe and analyze in this book took place a long time ago, and I often have had trouble explaining its "relevance" to students, colleagues, friends, and family. Yet I remain convinced about the value of understanding the complex actions and motivations of these people who were attempting the first thorough reworking of the natural and social self since the Christianization of Ancient culture. The very remoteness of their influential efforts creates a critical distance for the observer that helps to keep the object and subject of cultural history from collapsing. Yet we ourselves are in the picture we paint of them, both because we as natural and social agents are making sense of them, and because the sense they made of themselves has become part of the sense we make of ourselves. This reciprocity first drew me to this material, and I hope that I have persuaded others that it deserves and rewards more careful attention.

Appendix

*I. Complaint by an anonymous nun-poet, late eleventh
or early twelfth century.*

Laudis honor, probitatis amor, gentilis honestas,
    Cuncta simul quali, quo periere modo?
Liuor edax, ignaua quies, detractio turpis,
    Quid prosunt regni totius imperio?
Caesaribus dilecta uiris hoc tempore sordent   5
    Gratia Pieridum Pegaseusque liquor.
Romanae quondam non ultima gloria gentis,
    Vergilius, Naso, nomina uana iacent.
Pellimur orbe nouo, studium quia littera nostrum.
    Clio, fida comes, pellimur, egredere!   10

Principibus si quod placuit noua lectio nostris,
    Subque nouis regnat lex noua principibus.
Carmine leniri dudum fera corda solebant,
    At modo carminibus mollia corda tument.
Mitius exilium meruerunt carmina uatis   15
    Carminibusque fuit Caesaris ira minor.
Nostris principium dat littera nostra furoris,
    Nostris nulla placent carmina principibus.
Accusor, sed enim quo praecedente reatu?
    Ars mihi si quaeras crimen et ingenium,   20
Grande mihi crimen genuit mea littera grandis.
    Clio, . . .

O noua relligio uitae discretio sancta
    Iam si quod quid sit littera nosse scelus!
Illa uel ille bonus cui cernua semper imago,   25
    Qui, quoniam nil scit, se putat esse bonum.
Esse tamen sanctum cui de nihilo meditari
    Vel cui scire nihil contulit esse nihil?

    Ed. André Boutemy, "Recueil poétique du manuscrit Additional British Museum
24199," *Latomus* 2 (1938): 30–52 at 42–44.

The honor of praise, love of probity, noble virtue—
    How, in what way could they all perish at the same time?
Gnawing envy, idle inaction, base slander,
    What good are they to the rule of the whole kingdom?
The grace of the Muses and the fountain of Pegasus   5
    so beloved to the emperors are worthless to men
        nowadays.
Once not the least glory of the Roman people,
    Virgil, Ovid lie dead as empty names.
I am expelled from the new world because my effort is in
    learned writing.[1]
    Clio, faithful companion, leave: I am expelled!   10

Though new reading (once) pleased our princes,
    Under new princes a new law rules.
Formerly fierce hearts used to be softened by poetry,
    But now weak hearts are enraged by poems.
The poems of the poet [Ovid] earned a milder exile   15
    And Caesar's anger toward poetry was less.
My learned writing provides a source of rage to ours,
    No poems please our princes.
I am indicted, but in fact for what foregoing misdeed?
    If you want to know: my art is my crime, and my
        imagination.   20
My great learned writing gave birth to my great crime.
    Clio, . . .

Oh new religion, holy withdrawal from life,
    Now if only I knew what crime learned writing might be.
She or he (is) good whose face (is) always turned down,   25
    Who, since s/he knows nothing, thinks that s/he is good.
Yet (is) that existence holy to which meditating about nothing
    Or knowing nothing has brought being nothing?[2]

---

[1] The poet's use of *littera* here, like that of many of her contemporaries, seems to refer simultaneously to the literate mind and the learned document it produces.

[2] These difficult lines test the Latin and philosophy of the reader, and underscore the point about the value of learning.

Si capitur sensu deus et capitur ratione,
    Plus capiet cui plus iam rationis inest.   30
Esse bonum non me prohibebit littera multa,
    Dat mihi, non prohibet, littera nosse deum.
Credimus et ratione deum cognoscimus esse,
    Hoc quoque quod facimus non prohibere deum.
Quod facimus prohibet, uos quod facitis prohibemus.   35
    Clio, . . .

Carminibus recitare nouis bene uel male gesta:
    Iste fuit noster, si tamen error erat.
Detrectare bonis, si quae laudanda fuerunt,
    Quodque nequit uestra mens cupit arguere,   40
Si tamen ad laudem uos uel pudor impulit illud,
    Heu quam [. . .] esse bonum![3]
O noua calliditas—sed nobis cognita: quaerit
    Sub specie recti liuor habere locum.
Non est sanctarum mulierum frangere uersus,[4]   45
    Quaerere nec nostrum quis sit Aristotiles.
Ista uetus probitas, nil carmina tempore uestro,
    Nil genus aut species rethoricusue color.
Quid seruare modos iuuat, argumenta notare?
    Clio, . . .   50

Scire tamen magis est hoc quod reprehendere sanctum:
    Quid carpat nescit, carpit at illa tamen.
Quisquis es, hoc quod tam sapienter corrigis in me,
    Si uelles in te, uir bone, tunc saperes.
Carmina componas, lacertor carminis, ut te   55
    Posse quidem sed te fingere nolle putem.
Et tibi grata forem, si littera grata fuisset:
    Par solet ingenium conciliare duos!

---

[3] No break is indicated in the manuscript.

[4] By context, the phrase *frangere uersus* must mean "to write poetry," but *frangere* carries no such sense that I know of, and I suspect it is an error for *fingere* (as in 56).

If God is grasped by sense and grasped by reason,
    That one will grasp more in whom there is already more
        reason.   30
Great learned writing will not prohibit me from being good,
    learned writing does not prohibit, but allows me to know God.
I believe and know rationally that God exists
    And also that what I do God does not prohibit.
(If) he prohibits what I do, I will prohibit what you do.   35
    Clio, . . .

To recite in new verses good and bad deeds—
    That was my mistake, if such it was.
Your mind desired to condemn what it could not (do),
    To disparage the good things, if they were worthy of
        praise.   40
Yet even if shame compelled you to praise it,
    Alas how [. . .] being good!
Oh what new cunning—but known to me: under the guise
    of correctness Envy seeks to have a place.
It is not for religious women to compose verses   45
    Nor ours to ask who Aristotle might be.
This virtue (is) old: poems (are) nothing in your age,
    Nothing genus or species, or rhetorical ornamentation.
What good is it to keep proper measures, to record disputes?
    Clio, . . .   50

Yet knowing this holy thing[5] is better than faulting it;
    He does not know what he criticizes, but still criticizes it.
Whoever you are, what you so wisely correct in me
    You would know (to do) in you, good man, if you
        wanted to.
Compose verses, you slanderer of verse, so that I may think   55
    That you of course can create (poetry), but do not
        want to.
I would be acceptable even to you if my learned writing were
        acceptable:
    Equal genius usually reconciles two people!

---

[5] "This holy thing" refers, significantly, to *littera*.

*II. Baudri of Bourgueil to Lady Constance (of Le Ronceray?),
probably 1096–1106.*

Perlege, perlectam caute complectere cartam,
    Ne noceat fame lingua maligna meae.
Perlege sola meos uersus indagine cauta,
    Perlege, quicquid id est; scripsit amica manus.
Scripsit amica manus et idem dictauit amicus;   5
    Idem, qui scripsit, carmina composuit.
Quod sonat iste breuis, amor est et carmen amoris
    Inque breuis tactu nulla uenena latent.
Sanguine Gorgoneo non est lita pagina nostra
    Nec Medea meum subcomitatur opus.   10
Non timeas Ydram, noli dubitare Chymeram,
    Dum tanget nudum nuda manus folium.
Ipsa potes nostram secura reuoluere cartam
    Inque tuo gremio ponere tuta potes.
O utinam nosses, sicut mea uiscera norunt,   15
    Quanti sis mecum, quam michi te facio.
Pluris es et melior, maior michi denique uiuis
    Quam dea, quam uirgo quamue sit ullus amor;
Pluris es ipsa michi Paridi quam filia Ledae
    Quamque Venus Marti, quam dea Iuno Ioui.   20
Nec tanti Dane [ms, ed: Dafnes][2] necque tanti constitit Io,
    Pro quibus aurum et bos Iupiter ipse fuit.
Vates ad Stygias querulus cum tenderet undas,
    Non habuit pluris Orpheus Euridicen.
Hos autem populis commendat fabula Greca;   25
    Nam nebula quadam res adoperta uenit.
Sed me uerus amor nugis nebulisque remotis
    Esse tui nusquam desinit[3] inmemorem.
Inmemor esse mei citius, Constantia, possem,
    Quam tua forma tui non sinit inmemorem;   30

    Ed. Karlheinz Hilbert, *Baldricus Burgulianus Carmina* (Heidelberg, 1979), carmen 200: 266–71.   [2] Baudri knows the name as *Dane* both later in the poem (103) and in 154.235: *Danem corrupit aurum, non aureus imber.*   [3] I understand *desinit* not in its Classical sense ("stop) but as an intensified form of *sinit* ("allow"), the prefix *de-* serving to mark love's elevated status.

Read through this letter, and carefully clasp it once read,
    Lest malignant tongues harm my reputation.
Read through my verse by yourself with careful hunting,
    Read through it, whatever it is; a friend's hand wrote it.
A friend's hand wrote it, and the same friend fashioned it;   5
    The same man who wrote these verses, composed them.
What this letter speaks of is love and love poetry,
    And yet no venom lies hidden in the letter's touch.
My page is not smeared with the Gorgon's blood,[1]
    Nor does Medea secretly accompany my work.   10
Fear not the Hydra, waver not before the Chimaera
    As (your) bare hand touches the bare page.
You yourself can safely open this letter,
    And you can safely put it in your lap.
Oh, if only you knew, as my heart knows,   15
    How valuable you are to me, how much I make you mine.
To me you are more valuable and better, greater finally
        than a Goddess to mortals, than a girl, or than any love
            might be.
You are more valuable to me than Leda's daughter to Paris,
    Than Venus to Mars, than the goddess Juno to Jupiter.   20
Neither Danae [ms, ed: Daphne] nor Io were worth so much,
    For whom Jupiter was a shower of gold and a bull.
When Orpheus, the mournful bard, braved the Stygian waves,
    He did not regard Eurydice [to be] of greater value.
But Greek myth commends these men to people,   25
    For the deed comes to us covered in some sort of mist.
But once mists and trifles have been dispersed,
    true love does not allow me to forget you anywhere.
I can never forget you, Constance,
    Your beauty does not allow me to forget you;   30

---

[1] The following figures of unrestrained desire reappear with glosses in his other allegorical poems 134 and, especially, 154.

Inmemor esse mei citius, Constancia, possem,
    Quam compellar ego non memor esse tui;
Inmemor esse mei nunquam, Constancia, possis,
    Vt michi persoluas foedus amoris idem.
Sic nos o utinam natura deusque ligasset,   35
    Vt neuter uiuat inmemor alterius.
Crede michi credasque uolo credantque legentes:
    In te me nunquam foedus adegit amor.
In te conciuem uolo uiuere uirginitatem,
    In te confringi nolo pudiciciam.   40
Tu uirgo, uir ego; iuuenis sum, iunior es tu.
    Iuro per omne, quod est: nolo uir esse tibi.
Nolo uir esse tibi neque tu sis femina nobis;
    Os et cor nostram firmet amiciciam.
Pectora iungantur, sed corpora semoueantur;   45
    Sit pudor in facto, sit iocus in calamo.
Crede michi credasque uolo credantque legentes:
    In te me nunquam foedus adegit amor
Nec lasciuus amor nec amor petulantis amoris
    Pro te subuertit corque iecurque meum;   50
In te sed nostrum mouit tua littera sensum
    Et penitus iunxit me tua Musa tibi.
Denique tanta tuae uiuit facundia lingue,
    Vt possis credi sisque Sibilla michi.
Non rutilat Veneris tam clara binomia stella,   55
    Quam rutilant ambo lumina clara tibi.
Crinibus inspectis fuluum minus arbitror aurum;
    Colla nitent plus quam lilia nixue recens.
Dentes plus ebore, Pario plus marmore candent,
    Spirat et in labiis gratia uiua tuis.   60
Labra tument modicum; calor et color igneus illis,
    Que tamen ambo decens temperies foueat.
Iure rosis malas preponi dico tenellas,
    Quas rubor et candor uestit et omne decus.
Corporis ut breuiter complectar composituram: 65
    Est corpus, talem quod deceat faciem.
Ipsa Iouem summum posses deducere celo,

I could sooner forget myself, Constance,
    Than myself be compelled to forget you.
May you never be able so to forget me, Constance,
    That you dissolve the very bond of my love.
Oh, if only God and nature had bound us together   35
    So that neither should live forgetting the other.
Believe me (and I want both you and the readers to believe):
    A filthy love has never driven me to you.
I want virginity to live in you as a fellow citizen,
    I do not want chastity to be shattered in you;   40
You are a girl, I a man: I am young, you are younger.
    I swear by all that is: I do not want to be your husband.
I do not want to be your husband, nor you to be my wife:
    Let mouth and heart confirm our friendship.
Let our hearts[4] be joined, but our bodies remain apart;   45
    Let the shame be in the act, let the game be in the pen.
Believe me (and I want both you and the readers to believe):
    A filthy love has never driven me to you.
Neither lascivious love nor a love of wanton love
    Stirs up the depths of my heart[5] on account of you.   50
Your learned writing has moved my feeling for you,
    And your Muse has joined me to you deep within.
In short, so much eloquence lives in your tongue
    That you could be believed to be, a Sibyl, and are to me.
The binomial planet Venus[6] does not shine so bright   55
    As both your bright eyes shine.
One look at your hair, and I judge gold to be less yellow;
    Your neck gleams more than lilies or fresh snow.
Your teeth shine whiter than ivory, than Parian marble,
    And a lively grace breathes upon your lips.   60
Your lips swell somewhat; they have a firey warmth and color,
    But an appropriate modesty caresses them both.
It is right that I put your tender little cheeks before the roses,
    Cheeks dressed in red and white and every charm.
Let me express briefly the composition of (your) body: 65
    It is a body which suits such beauty.
You yourself could seduce high Jupiter from the heavens,

[4] The common poetic use of *pectora* ("chests") for "hearts" gains an ambiguous overtone in this context.
    [5] Literally: "stirs up my heart and liver."
    [6] "Hesperus" in the evening and "Lucifer" in the morning; see his carmen 134.705–12.

De Ioue si uerax fabula Greca foret.
In quascumque uelis se formas effigiasset,
    Si⁷ sua te seclis tempora prestiterint.   70
Sed quicquid facias quemcumque auertere possis,
    Non pro te partes distrahor in varias.
Nec caro titillat pro te neque uiscea nostra;
    Attamen absque dolo te uehementer amo.
Te uehementer amo, te totam totus amabo,   75
    Te solam nostris implico uisceribus.
Ergo patet liquido, quoniam genus istud amoris
    Non commune aliquid, sed speciale sapit.
Est spetialis amor, quem nec caro subcomitatur
    Nec desiderium sauciat illicitum.   80
Ipse tue semper sum uirginitatis amator,
    Ipse tue carnis diligo mundiciam.
Nolo uel ad modicum pro me tua mens uioletur;
    Irrita spes esset, irrita suspitio.
Propter id ergo tuam depinxi carmine formam,   85
    Vt morum formam extima forma notet.
Mores florigeros pretendat florida uirgo,
    Vt plus quam exterius floreat interius.
[I]nseritur metro gentilis pagina nostro,
    [Vt] te de falsis gentibus amoueam,   90
Vt tibi gentilis sit gens et pagina uilis,
    Quae colit impuros semimaresque deos,
Qui meretricales potius coluere tabernas,
    Rebus honestatis quam dederint operam.
Et tamen est uerum, quoniam tua forma uenusta   95
    Sydera transcendit, cum sit imago Dei.
Iupiter instat adhuc et tecum ludere temptat,
    [M]ars quoque, si Marti faueris atque Ioui.
Sunt multi iuuenes Iouis impia facta sequentes,
    Quos non inmerito dicimus esse Ioues.   100
Sunt multi Martes, scelerum uestigia prisca;
    Hi nimis infestant regna pudicicie.
Hi faciunt Veneres, Iunones, Danen et Io;

----

⁷Because of the context, I assume that Baudri has replaced either *etiam si* ("although") or *nisi* ("except that") with *si* for the sake of the meter.

If the Greek myth about Jupiter were true;
He would have fashioned himself in whatever shape you wish,
    If his age had [not] preceeded you by centuries.   70
But whatever you do, and whoever you can divert,
    I am not distracted in different directions because of you.
Neither my flesh nor my heart itches for you;
    But, nevertheless, I ardently love you without deceit.
I love you ardently, all of me will love all of you,   75
    You alone do I enfold within my heart.
Therefore, it is clearly visible that this kind of love
    Tastes of something not common, but special.
It is a special love, which neither the flesh accompanies
    Secretly nor illicit desire wounds.   80
I myself am always the lover of your virginity,
    I love the cleanness of your flesh.
I do not wish that your mind be violated even a little bit on
        account of me:
    Hope would be aroused, suspicion aroused.
For this reason I depicted your beauty in verse   85
    So that your outer beauty expresses the beauty of your
        character.
Let the girl as beautiful as a flower show her flowery ways,
    So that she flowers more inside than outside.
This pagan page is inserted in my poem
    In order that I might distance you from false people,   90
So that for you that people might be pagan and that page base
    Which worships the impure and half-male gods
Who frequented the whoring brothels, rather
    Than give this service to virtuous matters.
But nevertheless it is true that your charming beauty   95
    Transcends the stars, since it is the image of God.
Jupiter exists even today, and tries to play with you,
    And Mars, too, if you should favor Mars and Jupiter.
There are many youths following the impious deeds of Jupiter.
    And I say, not undeservedly, that they are Jupiters.   100
There are many Marses, and traces of his old crimes;
    These youths foul the realms of chastity beyond measure.
They create Venuses and Junos, Danae and Io;

Astreae uero uix latet una comes.
Vt sunt in ueterum libris exempla malorum,   105
    [S]ic bona, que facias, sunt in eis posita.
Laudatur propria pro uirginitate Diana;
    Portenti uictor Perseus exprimitur;
Alcidis uirtus per multos panditur actus;
    Omnia, si nosti, talia mistica sunt.   110
Ergo sepositis lenonibus et maculosis
    Alterius partis aggrediamur iter.
Virtutum gradiamur iter, gradiamur ad astra;
    Gentiles etiam sic properare monent.
Si mea uiuere uis, uiues mea, uiue Diana;   115
    Alcidem uolo uel Bellorofonta sequi.
Quodsi de libris nostris exempla requiris,
    Ipsa tot inuenies, quot uideas aspices.
In nostris non unus apex, non linea libris,
    Que nos non doceat alta sitire, uacat.   120
Sed uolui Grecas ideo pretendere nugas,
    Vt queuis mundi littera nos doceat,
Vt totus mundus uelut unica lingua loquatur
    Et nos erudiat omnis et omnis homo.
Captiuas ideo gentiles adueho nugas;   125
    Letor captiuis uictor ego spoliis.
Diues captiuos habeat Pregnaria seruos,
    Letetur Grais Cambio mancipiis;
Burgulii uictae nunc captiuantur Athenae,
    Barbara nunc seruit Grecia Burgulio.   130
Hostili preda ditetur lingua Latina;
    Grecus et Hebreus seruiat edomitus.
In nullis nobis desit doctrina legendi;
    Lectio sit nobis et liber omne, quod est.
Hanc igitur summam pertemptat epistola nostra,   135
    Vt, uirgo, uiuas uirgo Deo placita.
Sponsa mei domini sis tanti coniugis aula,
    Sis coniunx tanti coniugis et thalamus.

In truth, hardly one companion of Astrea[8] escapes them.
Just as there are examples of old evils in books,   105
 So too are good deeds placed in them which you might do.
Diana is praised for her proper virginity:
 Perseus is exalted as the victor of the monster.
The might of Alcidean Hercules is revealed through many acts.
 All such things, if you know them, are allegorical.   110
Therefore, let us put aside the perverse and foul men,
 And undertake our journey in another direction.
Let us tread the path of virtues, let us walk to the stars;
 Even pagans advise us to hasten thus.
If you wish to live as mine, you will live as mine; live (as) Diana!   115
 I wish to imitate Alcidean Hercules or Bellerophon.[9]
But if you require examples from my books,
 You will find as many as you see tips (of letters).
Not one tip, not one stroke spends time in my books
 that does not teach us to thirst for lofty things.   120
But I wanted to put forward the Greek trifles as proof
 That every literature of the world teaches us,
That the whole world speaks as with one tongue
 And that each and every man educates us.
I bring here the captive pagan trifles;   125
 I, the victor, rejoice in my captive spoils.
Let the rich Pregnaria have captive servants;
 Let the Cambio rejoice in Greek slaves.[10]
Captive Athens is now being captured at Bourgueil,
 Barbaric Greece now serves Bourgueil.   130
Let the Latin tongue be enriched by enemy booty;
 Let the vanquished Greek and Hebrew serve.
Let us not miss reading's lesson in any (of them);
 Let everything that is, be book and text for us.
Thus my letter attempts this lofty goal   135
 So that you, girl, may live as a virgin pleasing to God.
As the bride of my Lord, may you be the court of such a spouse,
 And as spouse be the bridal chamber of such a spouse.

---

 [8] Astrea is the goddess of Justice, the last immortal in Book I of Ovid's *Metamorphoses* to abandon earth.
 [9] Baudri recounts the allegorical myths of these two conquerors of desire in his carmen 154.445–518 and 989–1062.
 [10] The two streams, the *Cambio* and its tributary the *Pregnaria*, run through Bourgueil.

Subruat hunc dominus, qui templum subruit eius,
    Qui lapides uiuos ipse lapis perimit.   140
Nos autem nobis uigor uniat integritatis;
    Sint casti accessus castaque colloquia.
Quodsi nos aliquis dixisse iocosa remordet,
    Non sum durus homo; quicquid ago, iocus est.
Leta michi uitam fecit natura iocosam   145
    Et mores hylares uena benigna dedit.
Sed quicquid dicam, teneant mea facta pudorem;
    Cor mundum uigeat mensque pudica michi.
Tristes obscenos alit hec prouincia multos
    Et castos hylares educat hec eadem.   150
Nouimus et multos, qui Baccanalia uiuunt,
    Quos Curios simulat triste supercilium.
Nec despero, iocos quin etas auferat istos;
    Fructus maturos tempora sera dabunt.
Fronte seuerus tunc tantummodo seria scribam,   155
    Vt michi tunc pectus consonet et calamus.
Interea, mea uirgo, meis sis credula scriptis
    Et, sicut scripsi, sic mea uiue, uale.
Inquam uiue, uale; fac, quod uolo, uiue, quod opto.
    Quod uolo, non nescis; omne, quod opto, sapis.   160
Nulla mei cordis potuit te uena latere;
    Omne tibi scripsi, quod uolo, quod uolui.
Amodo maiori studio mea Musa uacabit;
    Inceptum Moysen iam repetunt socii.
Scilicet insultant, Genesim quia dimidiaui   165

Let the Lord cast him down who cast down his temple,
>He who, himself a stone, destroys living stones.   140
But let the strength of our integrity unite us to each other;
>Let there be chaste entrances and chaste conversations.
But if someone should blame us for having said playful things,
>I am not a solemn man: whatever I do is a game.
A happy nature has made life playful for me,   145
>And a congenial vein has given me a cheerful character.
But whatever I say, let my deeds retain modesty;
>Let my heart live in honor as pure, my mind as chaste.
This province rears many to be sad and lewd,
>And this same province raises others chaste and cheerful.   150
I also know many who live their lives like a Bacchic festival,
>Whose sad brow makes them resemble the Curii.[11]
I do not despair that age may take away these games;
>The later years will give ripe fruits.
With a serious face I will then write only serious things   155
>So that my heart and pen may then be in harmony.
Meanwhile, my girl, believe in what I have written
>And, as I wrote, so live and fare well as mine.
Live, I say, farewell: do what I want, live as I wish.
>You are not ignorant of what I want: everything I wish,
>you know.   160
No vein of my heart could lie hidden from you;
>I have written you everthing that I want, that I have wanted.
From now on my Muse will spend time with a greater task;
>Now colleagues demand anew the [exegesis of] Moses I began.
No doubt they jump up (in anger)[12] because I split Genesis in half, 165

[11] As also in carmen 1.35–50, Baudri gives the name of this Roman family famed for moderation and virute to hypocritical enemies of his verse; it may be a pun on *curia* ("[papal] court").

[12] Because of the context, I take this word in its literal sense rather than in the common, broader sense ("exult, rejoice").

Defessusque uia substiterim media.
Improperant nugas, quas scriptito sedulus ad te.
    Nullam preter te carmina nostra sciunt.
Si tamen ipsa michi quicquam rescribere temptas,
    Attendam, quicquid miseris, ut uideam.   170
Nec studii nostri post interualla silebo,
    Quin tibi rescribam saltem aliquando uale.
Dum tibi dico uale, uale hoc intellige salue;
    Vltima uox ad te non erit ista: uale.
Quamuis hoc uerbum soleant prestare sepultis,   175
    Nos tamen hoc uiuis et damus et dabimus.
Si uis, ostendas, si uis, hec scripta recondas;
    Nam pedagoga bone non timor est dominae.

And that, exhausted, I halted in the middle of the road.
They reproach the trifles I busily compose for you;
    My verses know none but you.
But if you should attempt to write back anything to me,
    Make sure that I see whatever you have sent.   170
I will not be silent after the interruption of my task
    And not write back sometime, at least to say "farewell."
But when I say "farewell," understand this "farewell" as "hello";
    My last spoken word to you will not be that "farewell."
Even though they usually offer this word to the dead,   175
    I give and will give this word to the living.
If you wish, display what I have written; hide it if you wish;
    For fear is not the teacher for a good lady.

III. Lady Constance (of Le Ronceray?) to Baudri of Bourgueil, probably 1096–1106.

Perlegi uestram studiosa indagine cartam
    Et tetigi nuda carmina uestra manu.
Explicui gaudens bis terque quaterque uolumen
    Nec poteram refici singula discutiens.
Ille liber michi gratus erat, gratissima dicta;   5
    Ergo consumpsi sepe legendo diem.
Nox studiis odiosa meis, inuisa legenti
    Me cessare meo compulit a studio.
Composui gremio posuique sub ubere leuo
    Scedam, quod cordi iunctius esse ferunt.   10
Si possem cordi mandare uolumina uestra,
    Cordi mandarem singula, non gremio.
Tandem fessa dedi nocturno membra sopori;
    Sed nescit noctem sollicitatus amor.
Quid non sperabam? quid non sperare licebat?   15
    Spem liber ediderat, ocia nox dederat.
In somnis insomnis eram, quia pagina uestra
    Scilicet in gremio uiscera torruerat.
O michi si dabitur tantum spectare prophetam,
    O michi se dabitur colloquii morula.   20
O quantus uates, quam preditus iste poeta,
    O quam diuino quelibet ore canit,
Quis sapor in dictis, o que sapientia uerbi,
    O quam discretus iste uir in calamo.
[Et] reor in factis est uir discretior iste;   25
    Omnia prudenter et facit et loquitur.
Hunc si Roma sibi quondam meruisset alumnum,
    Iste Cato rigidus, Tullius iste foret.
Hunc facerent uerba Ciceronem, facta Catonem;
    Multos iste ualet solus Aristotiles.   30

Ed. Hilbert, *Baldricus*, carmen 201: 271–76.

I have read through your letter with studious hunting,
  And I have touched your verses with my bare hand.
I have delighted in unrolling the volume two, three, four times,
  Nor could I be satisfied by picking apart single (verses).
That book was welcome to me, the words most welcome, 5
  So I spent the day reading them often.
The night, hostile to my studies, envious of my reading,
  Compelled me to cease from my study.
I put together the sheet in my lap and put it beneath my left breast
  Which, as they say, is more closely joined to the heart. 10
If I could send your volumes to my heart,
  I would send each one to my heart, not to my lap.
At last I gave my weary limbs over to the night's sleep;
  But troubled love does not recognize the night.
What did I not hope? What was I not permitted to hope? 15
  Your book produced hope; night had given free time.
In sleep I was sleepless, because your page
  In my lap had, of course, heated up my heart.
Oh, if only it might be granted for me to gaze on such a prophet,
  Oh, if only a moment might be granted for conversation! 20
Oh, how great a prophet, how gifted this poet,
  Oh, with what a divine mouth he sings whatever he pleases!
What elegance is in his sayings, oh what wisdom in his words,
  Oh how distinguished by his pen is this man!
But I think the man even more distinguished by his deeds: 25
  He both does and says everything wisely.
If long ago Rome had earned him (as) a foster-child for itself,
  He would be stern Cato, or Tully.
His words would make him Cicero, his deeds would make him Cato.
  He alone is worth many Aristotles. 30

Iste uidetur et est et dicitur alter Homerus;
    O quanta uersus commoditate canit.
Hystorias Grecas et earum mistica nouit
    Atque, quid hec aut hec fabula significet.
Vtque michi credas, metro mandauit idipsum;   35
    Adsensus fecit copia multiplices.
Euaginato David mucrone Goliae
    Eiusdem uictor perculit ense caput.
Taliter hic uates adiit penitralia Greca
    Gentilesque domos despoliauit eas.   40
Decipulas ensesque suos detorsit in hostes
    Aduectans nobis carmine gentis opes.
Inuexit nugas nobis gazasque Pelasgas
    Ex locuplete penu deripiens spolia.
Quid Mars, quid Iuno, quid cetera turba deorum   45
    Significent, nouit, nouit et exposuit.
Si de deuinis insurgat questio dictis,
    Nectareo nodos explicat eloquio.
Immo quid est, queso, quod sensum effugerit eius?
    Omnia sollerti circuit ingenio.   50
Si sermo fiat de forme compositura,
    Impar est tante nostra Camena rei.
Inter mortales tanquam flos unicus ille
    Formosis aliis corpore et ore preest;
Inter celicolas ut conspectissima stella   55
    Gratior aurora est soleque lucidior.
O qualis, quantus michi carmine significatur;
    Versibus hunc uideo, namque aliter nequeo.
Ve michi, cum nequeam, quem diligo, sepe uidere;
    Me miseram, nequeo cernere, quod cupio.   60
Afficior desiderio precibusque diurnis;
    In cassum fundo uota precesque Deo.
Annus abit, ex quo, quem quero, uidere nequiui;

He seems to be, and he is, and he is said to be another Homer:
    Oh with what appropriate measure he sings his verses!
He knows the Greek stories and their allegorical meanings,
    And also what each and every myth signifies.
Just so you believe me: he put it to verse;   35
    His (interpretive) ability makes multiple meanings.[1]
With blade unsheathed victorious David struck off
    Goliath's head with his own sword.
Similarly, this poet-prophet approached the inner chambers of
      the Greeks
    And plundered those pagan homes.   40
He turned their own traps and swords against the enemy,
    Conveying to us in verse that people's wealth.
He transported to us Pelasgian trifles and treasures,
    Tearing the spoils out of their rich pantry.
He knows what Mars, Juno, and the rest of that crowd   45
    Of gods means, he knows and has explained.
If a question arises concerning the utterances of the gods,
    He explains the difficulties[2] with nectar-sweet eloquence.
And what is there, I ask, which could elude his mind?
    He encompasses everything with his clever genius.   50
If talk should arise about the composition of his beauty,
    My Muse is unequal to such a thing.
Just like a flower he stands alone among mortals,
    He exceeds in body and face other handsome men.
Like the most conspicuous star among the heaven-dwellers,   55
    He is more pleasing than the dawn, and brighter than the sun.
Oh how much and how great is explained to me by his poetry,
    I see him in his verses, for I cannot (do) otherwise.
Alas that I cannot often see the one I love!
    Miserable me! I cannot behold what I desire.   60
I am weakened by desire and by day-long prayers;
    In vain I pour out vows and prayers to God.
A year has gone by in which I could not see the man I seek;

---

[1] I understand *adsensus* not in its Classical sense ("approvals") but as an intensive form of *sensus*.

[2] Literally: "he unties the knots."

Attamen ipsius carmina sepe lego.
O quales uersus, quam dulces, quam spetiosos   65
    Ad me misit heri perditus ille michi.
Hoc iacet in gremio dilecti scedula nostri;
    Ecce locata meis subiacet uberibus.
O utinam noster nunc hic dilectus adesset,
    Qui sensum proprii carminis exprimeret.   70
At circumstarent comites michi uel duo uel tres,
    Quamuis ipse sue sufficiat fidei;
Ne tamen ulla foret de suspitione querela,
    Saltem nobiscum sit mea fida soror.
Clara dies essset nec solos nos statuisset   75
    Hoc fortuna loco, sed magis in triuio.
Ecce uigil uigilo, quia me liber euigilauit
    Lectus multotiens, quem michi misit heri.
Sed quid ago? nichil est, quod tota nocte uoluto,
    Nil est, quod rogito pectore sollicito.   80
Ad me non ueniet nec eum sitibunda uidebo,
    Quem nimium tellus Pictaua sollicitat.
Forsitan idcirco, miseram me, carmina misit,
    Que me corrigerent, que michi uerba darent,
Vt se dissimulet, ut me sua littera fallat,   85
    Leniat ut nostrum callida carta metum.
Heu, quid non timeam? nunquam secura quiescam;
    Nec michi tutus amor, nec michi tuta fides.
Dum noua dat precepta michi, plus ipsa fatigor;
    Nunquam non possum suspiciosa fore.   90
Hunc timeo rapiat, dum nescio, quilibet error;
    Omnis uirgo meis inuidet auspiciis.
Nulla quidem uirgo me fortunatior esset,
    Si michi tutus amor tutaque pacta forent.
Firma fides nostrum quamuis michi firmet amicum,   95
    Credere non possum tuta sue fidei;
Nec fidei discredo sue nichil inde timendum,
    Perdere sed timeo, quod uehementer amo.

But (now) I read his verses often.
Oh, what verses, how sweet, how beautiful;   65
    He who is lost to me sent them to me yesterday.
My beloved's little sheet lies in this lap;
    Look, it lies placed beneath my breasts!
Oh, if only my beloved were now here
    Who would explain the meaning of his own poem.   70
But two or three of his companions would stand around me
    Even though he himself would suffice for my trust.
But lest there should be any complaint of suspicion,
    Let my faithful sister be with me, at least.
Bright would be that day, nor would fortune have placed us   75
    Alone in this place, but rather at the public square.
Look, wakeful I lie awake, because the book which he sent me
    Yesterday has been read many times and kept me awake.
But what am I doing? What I ponder the whole night is nothing,
    What I beg for with troubled heart is nothing.   80
He will not come to me, nor will I who thirst for him see him
    Whom the Poitevin land troubles greatly.[3]
Perhaps for that reason, miserable me!, he sent his verses
    To correct me and give me his words,
So that he might disguise himself, his letter deceive me,   85
    In order that his crafty letter might allay my fear.
Alas, what should I not fear? I will never rest secure;
    Nor will my love nor my trust ever be safe.
When he gives me new instructions, I am more tormented;
    I can never not be suspicious.   90
When I do not know (where he is), I fear some wandering
      might snatch him away:
    Every girl envies my hopes.
Indeed, no girl would be more fortunate than me
    If I had safe love and safe pacts.
Although firm fidelity affirms my friend for me,   95
    I cannot believe that I am secure in his fidelity.
And I do not doubt that there is anything to be feared about
      this in his fidelity,
    But I fear to lose what I violently love.

---

[3] This trouble in Poitou may be the adultery of count William VII to which Baudri elsewhere makes reference; see Chapter 4.

Pectore fluctiuago deduxi tempora noctis;
    Ergo satis licuit multa referre michi.   100
En Aurora suos producit lucida currus,
    Arbuta iam uolucrum garrulitate sonant.
Aggrediar ceram, quia nescit cera pudorem,
    Que referat domino congrua uerba meo.
Multa quidem scribam, que nolim dicere presens;   105
    Virgineos ausus sepe pudor reprimit.
O utinam placenat, que mens dictabit amantis;
    Carminis oda mei gratificetur ei.
Ipse iubes, dilecte meus, tu precipis, inquam,
    Vt castis operam legibus attribuam.   110
Attribuam; sic ipse iubes, sic ipsa preopto,
    Sic hucusque dies disposui proprios.
Casta fui, sum casta modo, uolo uiuere casta;
    O utinam possim uiuere sponsa Dei.
Non ob id ipsa tamen uestrum detestor amorem;   115
    Seruos sponsa Dei debet amare sui.
Tu sponsi seruus, tu frater tuque coheres,
    Tu quoque, tu sponsi dignus amore mei.
Sponsa sui sponsi uenerari debet amicos;
    Ergo te ueneror, te uigilanter amo.   120
Ius et lex nostrum semper tueatur amorem;
    Commendet nostros uita pudica iocos.
Ergo columbinam teneamus simplicitatem
    Nec michi pretendas quamlibet ulterius.
Quodsi preponis, quodsi pretenderis ullam,   125
    Scito, quod non est hic iocus in domino.
Si fallis, malus es, si uerum dicis, iniquus;
    Obsidet atque tenet crimen utrumque iocum.
Damnat falsiloquos Deus et praue facientes;
    Aut hoc aut illud uel simul ambo facis.   130
Sed Deus emendet, Deus in te corrigat ista;
    Hec me cura tui non sinit immemorem.
Virginis alterius sic nomen abominor, ut sim
    Virginis ad nomen frigidior glacie.
Sed, sicut tibi uis, credam credamque uolenti,   135
    Credam dictanti; tu quoque credi michi.

With fluctuating heart I have passed the hours of the night;
    Thus I was able enough to tell myself many things.   100
Look! now bright Aurora drives forth her chariot,
    And the arbutus trees resound with the chattering of birds.
I shall turn to the wax, because wax knows no shame
    And it can deliver words suitable to my Lord [or: lord].
Indeed, I will write many things which I do not want to say in
        person;   105
    Shame often curbs a girl's daring acts.
Oh, if only the things a lover's mind will compose might please!
    If only the lyric of my poem might please him!
You yourself, my beloved, you order and, I say, instruct
    me to apply my efforts to the laws of chastity.   110
And I will: just as you order, so do I choose.
    And thus have I arranged my own days until now.
I have been chaste, I am chaste now, I want to live chaste;
    Oh, if only I could live as a bride of God.
Yet not for this do I myself detest your love;   115
    The bride of God should love God's servants.
You are a servant of the bridegroom, you are brother and co-heir;
    You, too, you are worthy by my bridegroom's love.
The bride should respect the friends of her bridegroom.
    Therefore I respect you, I love you vigilantly.   120
May law and rule always watch over our love.
    May a chaste life commend our games.
Let us therefore have a simplicity pure as a dove,
    And do not prefer any (girl) more than me.
But if you favor, if your prefer any other (girl),   125
    Know that this game is not in the Lord.
If you deceive, you are bad, if you tell the truth, wicked;
    Either crime besieges and emprisons the game.
God condemns liars and those acting perversely;
    You do one or the other, or both at the same time.   130
But let God emend, let God correct these things in you;
    This worry does not allow me to forget you.
I hate the name of another girl so much, that
    I am colder than ice at the name of (any) girl.
But I will trust you, as you wish, and I will trust your wanting   135
    and trust your writing; you, too, trust in me.

Si te Roma uocat, si te Magontia temptat,
    Si meus es, retrahas mox ab utraque pedem.
Vade uiam tutam; petat alter barbara regna.
    Est grauis indomitas poena domare feras   140
Atque tibi digne uix respondere ualebunt,
    [C]um sint indocte, protinus edomitae.
Pullos indomitos alii multi domuerunt;
    Sic fortasse labor uester inanis erit.
Si michi discredens incassum forte laboras   145
    Subripiatque alter iugera uix domita,
Affectus nimio tandem tunc ipse pudore
    Ad ueteres sero regrediere uias.
Ridebunt alii; sed ego fidissima semper
    Planctibus et lacrimis participabo tuis.   150
Ergo dico tibi: me pretermittere noli;
    Nullam maioris inuenies fidei.
Si potes, et poteris, si tantum uelle uideris,
    Fac, ut te uideam, meque uidere ueni.
Ad te, si possem, pedes aut eques ultro uenirem;   155
    Non essent honeri pena pudorque michi.
Venero, si potero, uenissem, si potuissem;
    Sed disturbat iter seua nouerca meum.
At tu, qui dominus nullo custode teneris,
    Quem, quia multa potes, ipsa nouerca timet,   160
Maturato gradus et me uisurus adesto;
    Sumptus et comites sufficienter habes.
Cur ad nos uenias, occasio multa paratur:
    "Ad quem sermo michi, presul in urbe manet;
Clerus me mandat, abbates, ille uel ille;   165
    Me trahit ad comitem res facienda michi."
Demens! quem doceo? me debes ipse docere.

If Rome calls you, if Mayenne tempts you,[4]
    Quickly draw back your foot from each, if you are mine.
Go the safe way: let someone else seek barbarous kingdoms.
    It is a grievous torment to tame untameable beasts,   140
And those just completely tamed will hardly be able to answer you
    appropriately, since they are unlearned.
Many others have tamed the young and untamed;
    Thus perhaps your effort will be in vain.
If by chance you work (the land) in vain, not believing me,   145
    And another man should steal away the acres just tamed,
Then, eventually, broken by too much shame,
    You will return to your old paths too late.
Others will laugh; but I, always the most faithful,
    Will share your laments and tears.   150
Therefore I say to you: do not neglect me!
    You will find no (girl) of greater faith.
If you can and will be able, as you seem to want so much,
    Arrange that I can see you, and come to see me.
If I could, I would come over to you as a footsoldier or a
        knight;   155
    Punishment and shame would not be a burden to me.
I will come, if I am able; I would have come if I had been able;
    But my mean step-mother[5] disrupts my journey.
But you, who (as) a lord are not held by any guard,
    Who step-mother herself fears because you can do many
        things,   160
Hasten your steps and be here to see me;
    You have sufficient means and companions.
Many an occasion is contrived why you might come to me:
    "The bishop I must talk to is staying in the city;
The clergy summons me, the abbots, or so-and-so and
        what's-his-name;   165
    Some affair I must take care of calls me to the count."
Fool! who am I teaching? You yourself should teach me.

---

[4]The reference to Mayenne is unclear to me, although the passage (137–50) seems to indicate that the promotion for Baudri to bishop of Dol (elected 1107) was under consideration.

[5]Constance apparently uses this injurious term to describe her mother superior.

Si tibi causa deest, negligis, ut uenias.
Cura tibi de me non est, nisi ueneris ad me,
    Nec tua uel modicus uiscera tangit amor.   170
Hoc argumentum posui michi, si pigritaris;
    Hoc habeam certum federis inditium.
Visere me debes; nescis, quo langeo morbo,
    Quo desiderio scilicet affitior.
Grande tibi crimen, nisi paueris esurientem,   175
    Oranti si non ipse satisfatias.
Expectate, ueni nolique diu remorari;
    Sepe uocaui te; sepe uocate, ueni.

If you lack some cause, you are neglecting to come!
You do not care about me, unless you come to me,
    Nor does even the slightest love touch your heart.   170
I have set down this argument for myself (so that), if you
      delay,
    I would have this sure indication of (our) contract.
You should visit me; you do not know what illness ails me,
    That is to say, what desire afflicts me.
Your crime is great if you do not feed one hungering for you,   175
    If you yourself do not satisfy one pleading to you.
O long awaited one, come, and do not linger long;
    Often have I called you: you who are called often, come!

IV. Godfrey of Reims writing to a young girl, possibly Adela of Blois, in the early 1080s.

Parce, precor, virgo, tociens michi culta videri,
    Meque tuum forma perdere parce tua.
Parce supervacuo culto componere membra:
    Augeri studio tam bona forma nequit.
Ne tibi sit tanto caput et coma pexa labore,   5
    Nam caput hoc placuit, cum coma mixta fuit.
Ne stringant rutilos tibi serica vincla capillos,
    Cum vincant rutile serica vincla come.
Ne tibi multiplicem crines revocentur in orbem,
    Nam cum forte jacent, absque labore placent.   10
Aurea non video cur vertice flammea portes,
    Aurea nam nudo vertice tota nites.
Utraque fert auris aurum, fert utraque gemmas,
    Utraque nuda novis anteferenda rosis.
Ora facis vitreo tibi splendidiora nitore,   15
    Cum tamen [ms: tantum] ora vitro splendidiora geras.
Incendunt niveum lunata monilia collum,
    Nec collum simplex dedecuisse potest.
Contegis occulta candentes veste papillas,
    Candida cum nolit veste papilla tegi.   20
Ne toga fluxa volet, reprimit tibi fascia corpus,
    Cum corpus venerer, si toga fluxa volet!
Dic, teretes digitos cur annulus et lapis ambit,
    Cum teretes digiti dent precium lapidi.
Ornatu nullo potes exornatior esse,   25
    Et tamen [ms, ed: tantum] ornaris in mea dampna nimis.
Ne te plus equo species externa perornet,
    Cum sis plus equo pulcra decore tuo!
Ergo tam mire cessabis culta venire:
    Culta placere vales, que neque culta places.   30

Ed. Wilhelm Wattenbach, "Lateinische Gedichte aus Frankreich im elften Jahrhundert," in *Sitzungsberichte der Akademie der Wissenschaften zu Berlin* (Berlin, 1891): 97–114 at 107–9.

Please stop, girl, seeming totally artificial to me,
 And stop destroying me with your beauty, I who am yours.
Stop assembling the parts with vain artifice:
 Such fine beauty can not be increased with effort.
Do not work to have your head and hair be neat,   5
 For this head was pleasing when the hair was tousled.
Do not let silken bands tie the red strands of hair,
 Since the red strands of hair overwhelm the silken bands.
Do not let your locks be turned up in many circles,
 For as they lie haphazardly they please without effort.   10
I do not see why you wear flaming gold on your neck,
 For with your neck bare you gleam as if all gold.
Each ear bears gold, each bears jewels,
 And yet each (when) bare is preferable to young roses.
You make your face shinier with a glass-like gleam,   15
 Although you have a face shinier than glass.
Crescent-shaped necklaces ignite your snowy neck,
 And yet a plain neck could not have caused shame.
You cover your gleaming breasts with a dress that hides,
 Although the gleaming breast does not want to be
  covered.   20
A tie restrains the body lest the loose dress should fly open,
 Although I would adore the body if the loose dress
  should fly open!
Tell me why a ring and stone circle your smooth fingers,
 Although the smooth fingers give value to the stone.
You cannot become more adorned with any adornment,   25
 Yet you adorn too much, and it is ruining me.
Let no external beauty adorn you any more than a horse,
 Although you are more beautiful than a horse with your beauty.
Will you stop, therefore, coming so amazingly made up:
 You who do not please (me) when made up, can please
  (others) when made up.   30

Non ego sum, pro quo te componendo labores,
    Nec qui te talem non nisi cogar amem.
Pronus amo: non sum tenero qui pugnet amori,
    Nec qui te roseam velit [ed: nolit] amare deam.
Cum radiis certare Jovis tua lumina possent,   35
    Et possent radiis vincere signa Jovis.
Sole nichil toto melius splendescit in orbe,
    Sole tamen melius splendidiusque nites.
Sunt tibi colle quidem nive candidiora recenti,
    Et modo labente candidiora nive;   40
Nec nive, quam lapsam Phebi tepefecerit ardor,
    Set nive, que nullo marcida sole jacet.
Conveniunt tepido tua frons et pectora lacti,
    Set lacti, sature quod posuere capre,
Lacti, quod per agros celesti rore refecta   45
    Graminibusque novis pasta creavit ovis.
Cedit odora tibi vernantis gloria silve,
    Nec tibi quod riguus preferat ortus habet.
Nulla colorati speties tibi proxima prati,
    Nec cum floruerit par tibi campus erit.   50
Alba ligustra tue nequeunt accedere laudi,
    Fixaque cespitibus lilia laude premis.
Nulla tuos possunt equare rosaria vultus,
    Cum nec adhuc spinis sit rosa vulsa suis.
Gratia quam viole maturo flore merentur,   55
    Si [ms, ed: sit] quod contulerit se tibi, vilis erit.
Non Helene mater nec par tibi filia Lede,
    Quamvis hec Paridem moverit, illa Jovem.
Compulit illa Jovem cigni latuisse sub alis,
    Compulit illa Phriges seva sub arma duces.   60
Leda per albentes humeros fluitante capillo,
    Dum legit Argive florea serta dee,
Erranti super astra Jovi de nube suprema
    Cognita, fluvialem de Jove fecit avem,

I am not one for whom you should work so to put yourself
    together,
    Nor who unless forced would not love you as you are.
Humble, I love: I am not one who would resist a tender love,
    Nor who would want to love you (as) a rosy goddess.
Your eyes can compete with the rays of Jove,   35
    And can conquer with their rays the constellations of Jove.
Nothing shines better than the sun in the whole world,
    Yet you shine better and more splendidly than the sun.
Your neck is indeed whiter than recent snow,
    And whiter than the snow now falling—   40
Not snow which the heat of Phoebus had heated to ruin
    But snow which lies wasted by no sun.
Your forehead and chest are just like warm milk,
    But milk which sated goats have given,
Milk which the sheep in the fields produced when refreshed   45
    By divine dew and fed with new grass.
The odorous glory of the springtime wood yields to you
    Nor does the well-watered garden have anything
        preferable to you.
No face of the colored meadow will come close to you,
    Nor the field when it has flowered.   50
The white ligustra cannot approach your praise
    And you defeat in praise the lilies planted in the grass.
No rosebushes can equal your face
    Since up to now no rose has been plucked without its thorns.
The grace which violets earn in mature bloom,   55
    If it were compared to you, will be vile.
Neither Helen's mother nor Leda's daughter is equal to you,
    Even though the former inspired Paris, the latter Jove.
The one forced Jove to hide beneath the wings of a swan,
    The other forced the Trojan princes (to hide) beneath
        fierce arms.   60
While Leda was gathering flowered garlands of the Greek goddess
    With flowing hair on white shoulders,
And when, wandering above the stars, Jove recognized her from the
    highest cloud, she made a river bird out of Jove.

Tuque, puellari dum ludis in agmine princeps,   65
    Inter virgineos lucida stella choros.
Si magno conspecta Jovi de nube fuisses,
    Deposuisse deum non puduisset eum.
Ast Helene facies et opima potentia forme
    Dardanio Paridi per mare preda fuit.   70
Grecia conjurat repetendam mille carinis,
    Jurat, et hanc ratibus Grecia mille petit.
Te tam conspicuam Phrigius se predo videret,
    Et te vel velo vel rapuisset equo,
Grecia juraret populis te mille petendam,   75
    Et merito populis mille petita fores.
Annis tracta decem sunt Troica bella, set uno,
    Si pro te fierent, mense peracta forent.
Virgine Ledea me judice dignior esses,
    Pro qua Trojanas flamma cremaret opes.   80
Tu poteras Priamo validissima causa fuisse,
    Nulla sit ut cura, regna perisse sua.
Si succinta togam ritu pharetrata Diane
    Venatrix toto crine soluta fores,
Si Driadum comitata choro, si nudata [ms, ed: nuda] lacertos,   85
    Arcu fulmineos insequereris apros,
Te quicunque deus silvosa per antra vagantem
    Conspiceret, veram crederet esse deam.
De pretio forme cum tres certamen inissent,
    Electusque Paris arbiter esset eis,   90
Prefecit Venerem Paridis censura deabus,
    Deque tribus victe succubuere due.
Cum tribus a Paride quarta probanda venires,
    De tribus a Paride quarta probata fores;

You also, when you play the leader in the girls' line dance,   65
    A shining star among the girl dancers,
If you were spotted by great Jove from a cloud,
    He would not be ashamed to lay down his deity.
But the loveliness of Helen and the full power of her beauty
    was booty for Dardanian Paris (to be taken) by sea.   70
Greece swore that she would be taken back with a thousand ships,
    Greece swore, and sought her with a thousand barks.
If the Phrygian robber were to see you so conspicuous
    And had seized you by ship or by horse,
Greece would swear that you were to be sought by a thousand
      people   75
    And you would be sought in fairness by one thousand people.
The Trojan war went on for ten years, but in one
    Month, if it happened for you, it would be completed.
In my judgment you would be worthier than Leda's girl,
    For whom the flames burned up Trojan wealth.   80
You could have been Priam's most powerful excuse
    So that it would be no concern that his kingdom perished.
If you had tied on the toga and quiver in Diana's manner,
    if you had let down your hair and were a huntress,
If with a dancing band of Driads you had bared your arms   85
    And pursued with a bow the fulminating boars,
Any god wandering through the woody grottos
    Who spotted you would think you were a true goddess.
When three had set up a contest for the prize in beauty
    And elected Paris to be their judge,   90
Paris's judgment preferred Venus to the other goddesses:
    Of the three two succumbed, vanquished.
If you came as a fourth to be judged by Paris with the (other) three,
    You would be judged by Paris as the fourth of the three;[6]

[6] I understand this to mean that her beauty would entitle her to enter such a contest among goddesses.

Pomaque si forme potiori danda fuerunt,   95
    Hec potius forme danda fuere tue.
Corda gerit dura, quem tam divina figura
    Vel tam purpuree non tetigere gene.
Robore vel scopulo genitum convincere possem,
    Quem tam sollempnis forma movere nequit.   100

And if the apple were to be given to the more powerful
     beauty,   95
   This would have been given rather to your beauty.
He who is not moved by such a divine face
   or such shining dark eyes has a hard heart:
I could be convinced that he was born of oak or stone
   Who cannot be moved by such grand beauty.   100

V. Hildebert of Le Mans writing to Adela of Blois about 1101–2

Absentia mariti laboriosior tibi cura consulatus incubuit. Eam tamen et femina sic administras et una, ut nec viro nec precariis consiliis necesse est adiuvari. Apud te est quidquid ad regni gubernacula postulatur. Sane tantus bonorum conventus in femina gratiae est, non naturae. Gratia dei praedicandos tibi titulos cumulavit, quibus et sexui esses ad gloriam et potestatem temperares. Defers enim feminam [ed: feminae], dum colis in pulchritudine castitatem; comitissam reprimis, dum servas in potestate clementiam. Illa tibi virum conciliat, haec populum. Inde nomen acquiris, hinc favorem. Utrumque bonum per se quidem satis insigne est atque conspicuum, nec linguae supplicat alienae. Caeterum clementiae plurimum laudis accedit, quia pluribus prodest. Quippe formosa pudica sibi providet; mitis autem principatus regnum servat incolume.

Huius profecto virtutis locus est apud potentes, qui iure parentum, vel vi, vel electionis beneficio caeteris principantur. Apud populum vero non ita, cui nulla est potestas puniendi. Ipse autem ex alto crudelitatem detestatur, adorat clementiam, quorum alterum feris, alterum hominibus natura docuit assignandum. Ea sanxit oportere homines mansuescere clementia, timeri feras crudelitate. Igitur crudelem esse cum feris est habere commercium et hominem diffiteri. Praeterea suum est hominis ratio qua caetera supergreditur animantia, deo cedit; atqui rationi nullum est penitus cum crudelitate consortium. Illa cum deo et cum sapientibus divinam pepigit mansionem; haec ad infima et sanguine gaudentia demigravit. Quae igitur societas homini ad crudelitatem, cuius lares ratio tam superne despicit, tam longe relinquit, tam constanter abiurat, tam penitus ignorat. Aliud habet illa contubernium, atque aliis cohabitatoribus constipatur, inter quos clementia non ultimum possidet locum, qua sicut humanitati nihil est affinius, ita nihil gloriosius in principe. Ea rationem, quasi pedissequa matremfamilias, comitetur oportet, ciuis arbitrio severas potestates emolliat, mitiores animos advocet, reis parcat. Omnibus enim virtutibus ratio praesidet, omnibus fines ordinat, omnibus suorum tempora denuntiat officiorum.

Ed. Peter von Moos, *Hildebert von Lavardin, 1056–1133. Humanitas an der Schwelle des höfischen Zeitalters* (Stuttgart, 1965), 341–42 (=PL 171.144–45).

Because of your husband's absence a more toilsome concern about the county has fallen upon you. Yet you administer it as a woman and as a single person in such a way that you do not need to be helped by either a husband [or: man] or by dubious advice. You have with you whatever is required for the governance of the realm. But such an assemblage of good qualities in a woman comes from grace, not from nature. The grace of God piled praiseworthy honors upon you, with which you would both be a model for your gender and would moderate power. For you indict the Woman when you pursue chastity in beauty; you curb the Countess when you retain mercy in power. The former reconciles your husband to you, the latter the people. Thus you acquire reputation, and from that, approval. Both these good qualities are, of course, quite visible and illustrious by themselves, and do not require someone else's tongue. Besides, the most praise befalls clemency, because it benefits the most people. To be sure, a chaste beauty looks after herself, but a merciful leader keeps the realm safe.

There is a place for the pursuit of this virtue with the powerful who rule others by right of parents, by force, or by the benefit of election. But it is not so with the populace, which has no power to punish. From long ago, however, it detests cruelty and adores clemency; the one Nature has taught as belonging to wild animals, the other to men. She ordained it to be proper for men to be softened by clemency, wild animals to be feared for cruelty. Thus to be cruel is to have commerce with wild animals and to disavow man. Besides, the essential trait of man is reason, in which he surpasses other animals, yields to God; and reason has absolutely no commerce with cruelty. The former contracts for the divine mansion with God and the wise; the latter leads down to the depths and to those taking pleasure in blood, a society for cruelty to man whose household gods reason so loftily despises, so long relinquishes, so constantly abjures, so thoroughly knows. The former has a different living-arrangement and is pressed by other cohabitants, among whom clemency does not have the last place; just as nothing is more closely related to man that this, so nothing is more glorious in a prince. It is proper that it follow reason like a servant-girl does the woman of the house, by whose judgment it softens severe powers, recalls a milder spirit, spares the condemned. For reason presides over all virtues, sets the limits for all, announces to all the times of their duties.

De clementia quoque compendiosa principibus capitula Senecae vigilavit, in quibus ideo brevitatem dilexit non obscuram, ut magnis occupatos legere non taederet. Ea igitur pro te et ad te suscepta suscipe atque recordare, quae dudum didicisti ex te et pro te. Pauca ea sunt: "Clementiae est aliquid ultrici detrahere sententiae. Quisquis nihil reatus impunitum relinquit, delinquit. Culpa est totam persequi culpam. Immisericordem profitetur, cui quidquid licet libet." Item: "Gloriosa virtus est in principe citra punire quam liceat. Virtus est ad vindictam necessitate trahi, non voluntate venire. Magnum quid et divinum sapit offensus clemens." Item: "Bonus princeps neminem sine poena punit, neminem sine dolore proscribit. Bonus princeps ita crimen insequitur, ut quem punit hominem reminiscatur." Item: "Bonus princeps sibi dominatur, populo servit. Nullius sanguinem contemnit: inimici, sed eius qui amicus fieri potest; nocentis, sed hominis. Cuiuscunque sit, quia non potuit dare crimen, putat auferre. Ideo quoties funditur, confunditur." Sufficiunt haec animo docili amanti disciplinam. Ex quibus diligentiores facile percipient quantum vel crudelitas obsit, vel prosit clementia potestati. Vale.

An abridged chapter by Seneca[1] also about clemency has kept watch over princes, in which he loved a brevity which was not obscure so that reading it would not bore those occupied by great matters. Therefore adapt and remember these (words) adapted for you and to you, which until now you learned from and for yourself. They are few: "Clemency is to remove something from a vengeful feeling. Whoever leaves none of the guilt unpunished, fails. It is a wrong to prosecute the whole wrong. Let him profess no clemency who likes whatever is permitted." Likewise: "It is a praiseworthy virtue in the leader to punish less than is permitted. It is a virtue to be drawn by necessity to revenge, not to come by will. Someone with clemency for an offense knows what (is) great and divine." Likewise: "A good leader punishes no one without pain, condemns no one without sorrow. A good leader pursues a crime so that he remembers the man he punishes." Likewise: "A good leader (who) governs himself, leads the people. He condemn's no one's blood: (it is the blood) of an enemy, but one who could become a friend; (it is that) of a wrongdoer, but a man. Whoever's (blood) it is, because he could not give (a sentence which is) a crime, he thinks to remove (it). Thus he confounds as often as he conquers." These (words) suffice a mind that is teachable and loves study. From them the more diligent easily will perceive how much either cruelty blocks power or clemency aids it. Farewell.

[1] For the Senecan reminiscences, see von Moos, 58–59.

Notes

Abbreviations Used in Notes

AFW Alfred Tobler and Erhard Lommatzsch, *Altfranzösisches Wörterbuch* (Wiesbaden, 1925–)

DuCange Charles DuCange et al., *Glossarium Mediae et Infimae Latinitatis* (Niort, 1883–87)

LwSh Carlton Lewis and Charles Short, *A Latin Dictionary* (Oxford, 1879)

Nier J. F. Niermeyer, *Mediae Latinitatis Lexicon Minus* (Leiden, 1976)

MLW *Mittellateinisches Wörterbuch*, ed. Otto Prinz et al (Munich, 1967–)

NovGlos *Novum Glossarium Mediae Latinitatis* (Hafnia, 1957–)

OxLat *Oxford Latin Dictionary* (Oxford, 1968)

PL *Patrologia Latina*, ed. J.-P. Migne (Paris, 1844–82)

TLL *Thesaurus Linguae Latinae* (Leipzig, 1900–)

Introduction

1. Useful overviews in English of the ferment within the political and religious Romanesque establishments can now be found in Georges Duby, *The Knight, the Lady and the Priest: The Making of Modern Marriage in Medieval France*, tr. Barbara Bray (New York, 1983); Jean Dunabin, *France in the Making, 843–1180* (Oxford, 1985); and Henrietta Leyser, *Hermits and the New Monasticism: A Study of Religious Communities in Western Europe, 1000–1150* (New York, 1984).

2. Writing about 1115, Guibert de Nogent reports that King Edward of England often had sent a certain chaplain on business to France "because he understood French elegance" (quia Francicam elegantiam norat, III.2); *Autobiographie*, ed. and tr. Edmond-René Labande (Paris, 1981), 270–71. I use the term "France" in this study more or less as Guibert does here to designate the region of Carolingian Neustria bounded roughly by the Meuse, the Loire and the Atlantic.

3. Although I join others in not being persuaded that our notion of "individual person" was a medieval discovery, as Colin Morris proclaimed, it certainly took on a new importance in twelfth-century thought and letters; see his *The Discovery of the Individual, 1050–1200* (London, 1972). Major disagreements with Morris (from the perspective of religious history) are voiced by Caroline Walker Bynum, "Did the Twelfth Century Discover the Individual?" in her *Jesus as Mother: Studies in the Spirituality of the High Middle Ages* (Berkeley, 1982), 82–109; and John F. Benton, "Consciousness of Self and Perceptions of Individuality," in *Renaissance*

and Renewal in the Twelfth Century, ed. Robert L. Benson and Giles Constable (Cambridge, Mass., 1982), 263–95.

4. In the opening chapter of *Romanesque Art* (New York, 1977), 1–27, Meyer Schapiro examines the relationships among material pleasure, Roman tradition, and the image of the self, traits which seem to me indispensible to any definition of Romanesque. The ideological aspects are considered by Linda Seidel in her careful study, *Songs of Glory: The Romanesque Façades of Aquitaine* (Chicago, 1981). The close link between the concepts of Romance languages and Romanesque art is shown by Wayne Dynes, "Art, Language and Romanesque," *Gesta* 28 (1989): 3–10.

5. See Stephen G. Nichols, Jr., "Romanesque Imitation or Imitating the Romans?" in *Mimesis: From Mirror to Method, Augustine to Descartes*, ed. John D. Lyons and Stephen G. Nichols, Jr. (Hanover, N.H., and London, 1982), 36–59: "Representation in Romanesque texts, then, when properly understood, leads not to a discovery of the absence of an enunciating subject or of an alienated subject. We find, rather, a rigorously intellectual *cogito* ascending from history and differentiation toward a metaphysical epiphany" (59). My only argument with Nichols's conclusion, based on the careful and ingenious analyses which appeared subsequently in *Romanesque Signs: Early Medieval Narrative and Iconography* (New Haven, Conn., 1983), lies with his claim that it is unique and universal.

6. A succinct overview of the semantic range of *amor* in France during this period can be obtained from John C. Moore, "Love in Twelfth-Century France: A Failure in Synthesis," *Traditio* 24 (1968): 429–43; and Glyn S. Burgess, *Contribution à l'étude du vocabulaire pré-courtois* (Geneva, 1970), 141–58. Still widely ignored, unfortunately, is the insight of George Fenwick Jones in *The Ethos of the Song of Roland* (Baltimore, 1963), 115: ". . . medieval men protected themselves with all sorts of personal and political alliances in addition to their natural ties of kinship. Although these alliances were conventionally negotiated in terms of the words *amer*, *amis*, *amor*, and *amistiet*, they were often a matter of practicality rather than affection."

7. The fine article by Martin Stevens, "The Performing Self in Twelfth-Century Culture," *Viator* 9 (1978): 193–212, loses some of its interpretive value by excluding desire from creativity.

8. I am using the word "discourse" more or less in the sense given it by Michel Foucault, but without the degree of singularity, concordance, and hegemony that he grants it. See Hubert L. Dreyfus and Paul Rabinow, *Michel Foucault: Beyond Structuralism and Hermeneutics*, 2d ed. (Chicago, 1983), 44–78.

9. The perception of individuality is probably universal, as Marcel Mauss claimed in a classic study, "A Category of the Human Mind: The Notion of Person," in *The Category of the Person*, ed. M. Carrithers, S. Collins, and S. Lukes (New York, 1979 [1938]), 1–25. Yet in Western discourse the "peculiar idea" of the unique and discrete self has found nothing but support from the dominant cultures; see Clifford Geertz, *Local Knowledge* (New York, 1983), 59.

10. Adolf Trendelenburg's catalogue makes the contradictions clear: "A Contribution to the History of the Word Person," tr. Carl Haessler, *The Monist* 20 (1910): 336–63. The OxLat lists the following meanings: mask, dramatic character, social role, personality, actual individual being, litigant, personification, and grammatical person. Although the etymology from *personare*, "to sound through," may

indeed be false, the word was understood thus in Roman Antiquity; Robert Elliott provides a succinct discussion in *The Literary Persona* (Chicago, 1982), 19–20.

11. Elliott, *Literary*, 21. Mauss stressed the theatrical origins and deceptive essence of the Western person in much of his work; see, for instance, the pieces in *Sociology and Psychology: Essays*, tr. Ben Brewster (London, 1979). His assumptions have been interestingly elaborated as well as criticized in *Semiotics, Self and Society*, ed. Benjamin Lee and Greg Urban (Berlin and New York, 1989).

12. Intellegendum etiam est duabus quasi nos a natura indutos esse personis: quarum una communis est ex eo quod omnes participes sumus rationis . . . altera autem, quae proprie singulis est tributa (I.30). Neal Wood, *Cicero's Social and Political Thought* (Berkeley, 1988), 84–85, has a useful discussion. See Elliott, *Literary*, 25–27, for an overview of Cicero's enormous influence.

13. Si plosoris eges aulaea manentis et usque sessuri donec cantor "uos plaudite" dicat, aetatis cuiusque notandi sunt tibi mores mobilibusque decor naturis dandus et annis. Tr. Smith Palmer Bovie, *The Satires and Epistles of Horace* (Chicago, 1959), 277.

14. C. O. Brink, *Horace on Poetry: The "Ars Poetica"* (Cambridge, 1971), 468–523. In the poem, lines 119–78 treat character as a poetic concern, 309–22 as an ethical concern. Horace himself speaks throughout as critic, friend, poet, satirist, historian, and so forth.

15. *Institutiones*, 9.2.29. He elsewhere speaks of Socrates, "with whose character Plato seems to indicate what he is thinking" (cuius persona uidetur Plato significare quid sentiat, 2.15.26).

16. The Velleius citation comes from LewSh, 1355: nihil ex persona poetae disserunt. Neither Virgil nor Ovid, the two exemplary literary *auctores* for the Latin Middle Ages, makes much use of the word *persona*, but their conceptions of "person" and rhetoric lie in an opposition which was long held to be paradigmatic. See the rich essay by Richard Lanham, "The Fundamental Strategies: Plato and Ovid," in *The Motives of Eloquence* (New Haven, Conn., 1976), 36–64.

17. Robert Kaster's fine study is helpful: *Guardians of Language: The Grammarian and Society in Late Antiquity* (Berkeley, 1988).

18. The christianized concept's potential for figuring absolute power in the temporal domain attracted conservative Romanesque writers such as the anonymous Norman theorist of kingship studied by Ernst Kantarowicz, *The King's Two Bodies: A Study in Medieval Political Theology* (Princeton, N.J., 1957), 42–61; or the mythologists of Charlemagne probed by Nichols in *Romanesque*.

19. For Augustine's concept of person (but not his use of the word *persona*) see Gareth B. Matthews, "The Inner Man," and A. C. Lloyd, "On Augustine's Concept of a Person," in *Augustine: A Collection of Critical Essays* (New York, 1972), 176–90, 191–205; also Eugene Vance, "Augustine's Confession and the Grammar of Selfhood," *Genre* 6 (1973): 1–28. Augustine was influenced by Jerome's Christian interpretation of Cicero's *persona (communis)*; see Adele Fiske, "Hieronymus Ciceronianus," in *Transactions and Proceedings of the American Philological Association* 96 (1965): 119–38.

20. Hans Rheinfelder, *Das Wort "Persona": Geschichte seiner Bedeutung mit besonderer Berücksichtigung des französischen und italienischen Mittelalters*, Beiheft zur

Zeitschrift für Romanische Philologie, vol. 77 (Halle, 1928). Two very different analyses in English of the relation between language and public person (but not the rhetorical *persona*) can be found in C. Stephen Jaeger, *The Origins of Courtliness: Civilizing Trends and the Formation of Courtly Ideals* (Philadelphia, 1985); and Laura Kendrick, *The Game of Love: Troubadour Wordplay* (Berkeley, 1988).

21. Leo Spitzer, "Note on the Poetic and Empirical 'I' in Medieval Authors," *Traditio* 4 (1946): 414–22; see also Evelyn B. Vitz, "The *I* of the *Roman de la Rose*," *Genre* 6 (1973): 49–75, and Charles Dahlberg, "First Person and Personification in the *Roman de la Rose*: Amant and Dangier," *Mediaevalia* 3 (1977): 37–58. Stevens, "Performing," makes a strong case for the limitations of Spitzer's view. High Medieval lyric has provoked important studies. See, for instance, D. R. Sutherland, "L'élément théatral dans la canso chez les troubadours," *Revue de Langue et Littérature d'Oc* 12–13 (1962–63): 95–101; W. T. H. Jackson, "Persona and Audience in Two Medieval Love-Lyrics," *Mosaic* 8 (1975): 147–59; Paul Zumthor, "Le *je* du poète," in his *Langue, Texte, Enigme* (Paris, 1975), 163–216; William D. Paden, Jr., "Utrum copularentur: Of *Cors*," *Esprit Créateur* 19 (1979): 70–83; and Jill Mann, "Satiric Subject and Satiric Object in Goliardic Literature," *Mittellateinisches Jahrbuch* 15 (1980): 63–86. A. J. Minnis's excellent study of scholastic theory, *Medieval Theory of Authorship: Scholastic Literary Attitudes in the Later Middle Ages*, 2d ed. (Philadephia, 1988), makes only passing reference to *persona*.

22. Karlheinz Hilbert, *Baldricus Burgulianus Carmina* (Heidelberg, 1979), 85.35–46: Quod uero tanquam de certis scriptito rebus Et quod personis impono uocabula multis Et modo gaudentem, modo me describo dolentem Aut puerile loquens uel amo uel quidlibet odi, Crede michi: non uera loquor magis omnia fingo: Nullus amor foedus michi quidlibet associauit. Sed modus iste michi dictandi plus inoleuit Sicque figuraui, quod multis competat in me, Nec plus inde michi nisi semen materiei Et michi quod genus hoc iocundius esse putaui. Quocirca sodes mea sit sententia uerbi, Et sua, non mea sit intentio materiei. The central verse (*Nullus amor foedus michi quidlibet associauit*) could also be translated "no vile desire attached anything at all to me." In both cases, I treat *associare* as a transitive verb.

23. The point is elaborated well by Elliott, *Literary*, 32.

24. Heinrich Sedlmayer collects a number of later medieval comments upon this problem in *Prolegomena Critica ad Heroides Ovidianas* (Vendôme, 1878). Compare also Minnis, *Medieval*, 20–21 and passim.

25. See G. E. M. Anscombe, "The First Person," in *Mind and Language*, ed. Samuel Guttenplan (New York, 1975), 45–65; and the discussion by Carol A. Rovane, "The Epistemology of First-person Reference," *Journal of Philosophy* 84 (1987): 147–67 at 149–51.

26. Murray Krieger, "The Semiotic Desire for the Natural Sign: Poetic Uses and Political Abuses," in *The States of Theory: History, Art and Critical Discourse*, ed. David Carroll (New York, 1990), 221–53.

27. Erving Goffman, *The Presentation of the Self in Everyday Life* (Garden City, N.Y., 1957). I profited from the review and critique by Philip Manning, *Erving Goffman and Modern Sociology* (Stanford, Calif., 1992). In his *Literacy and the Survival of Humanism* (New Haven, Conn., 1983), Richard Lanham constructs an intriguing

defense of Humanism by arguing that if the self is finally dramatic, then verbal play becomes essential instead of superfluous (129).

28. Walter Ullmann's *The Individual and Society in the Middle Ages* (Baltimore, 1966), provides a convenient and learned survey.

29. Catherine Belsey's tight and lucid argument remains for me one of the best short introductions to the fundamental questions, with bibliographic indications which remain useful; see *Critical Practice* (London, 1980), especially "Addressing the Subject," 56–84. Paul Smith analyzes the major theories in depth in *Discerning the Subject* (Minneapolis, 1988).

30. Louis Althusser, "Ideology and Ideological State Apparatuses (Notes Toward an Investigation)," in *Lenin and Philosophy and Other Essays*, tr. Ben Brewster (London, 1971), 123–73: 169, 161. Foucault notes that "both meanings suggest a form of power which subjugates and which makes subject to"; see "Afterword: The Subject and Power," in Dreyfus and Rabinow, *Foucault*, 208–26: 212.

31. I take this useful concept of "official culture" from Dominick LaCapra, *Soundings in Critical Theory* (Ithaca, N.Y., 1989), 136.

32. Althusser had already made a more extended and more subtle analysis of ideology, "Marxism and Humanism," in *For Marx*, tr. Ben Brewster (New York, 1969), 219–41, esp. 231–36.

33. See Smith, *Subject*, 3–23. I have found valuable the analyses and critiques by Diane Macdonell, *Theories of Discourse* (Oxford, 1986), 24–42; Gregory Elliott, *Althusser: The Detour of Theory* (London, 1987), 224–35; and Susan James, "Althusserian Materialism in England," in *Studies in Anglo-French Cultural Relations: Imagining France*, ed. Ceri Crossley and Ian Small (London, 1988), 187–209.

34. Macdonell, *Theories*, 40–41. Elliott, *Althusser*, notes (231) that this idealist nature of the subject derives not only from the great influence of Jacques Lacan, as is well known, but also from Spinoza, whom Althusser considered the precursor of a properly Marxist conception of ideology.

35. Macdonell, *Theories*, 39; James, "Materialism," 195.

36. Goffman details a similar range of response in *Presentation*, 19–21.

37. For Brecht and Althusser, see Stephen Heath, "Lessons from Brecht," *Screen* 15, 2 (1974): 103–28. Foucault argues the centrality of confession in *Discipline and Punish*, tr. Alan Sheridan (New York, 1979), though the topic is recurrent in his writings.

38. Anthony Giddens, *Central Problems in Social Theory: Action, Structure and Contradiction in Social Analysis* (Berkeley, 1979), 52. See now also Terry Eagleton, *Ideology* (London, 1991), esp. 136–46.

39. Smith, *Discerning*, xxix, his emphasis.

40. I make exception for a qualified usage such as "the subject of discourse" or "the subject of satire," where I specify the identity imposed by the power granted to a particular medium or mode.

41. I do not mean this analogy lightly, for it seems to me that any system of such common, public subjects can be analyzed for variants in traits, forms, functions, and significances to reveal its social, spatial, and temporal nature. As such a language, the artificial and arbitrary "systems of differences" which it transmits are stabilized by the conventional and material "systems of distinctions" lived by

its users. See Pierre Bourdieu, *Outline of a Theory of Practice* (Cambridge and New York, 1977), with its careful discussion of *habitus*: the detailed system of values carefully engrained in the individual through education and culture and lived out in particular life styles.

42. Emile Benveniste, "Subjectivity in Language," in *Problems in General Linguistics*, tr. Mary Elizabeth Meek (Miami, 1971), 223–30. Contrast Anthony Giddens, "Action, Subjectivity, and Meaning," in *The Aims of Representation: Subject/Text/History*, ed. Murray Krieger (Stanford, Calif., 1987), 159–74: "Terms like 'I' and 'me' may not have as their meaning the object (the body) to which they relate, but they nevertheless gain their significance from the context of activities in which human agents are implicated" (164). In my own view, "I" can only designate the particular self-impersonation through which an empirical agent speaks—consciously or unconsciously—at any given moment.

43. A good overview of the theoretical discussions on the "projection" of subject positions by cultural media can be had from the selection of work from the journal *Screen* published as *Culture, Ideology and Social Process*, ed. Tony Bennett et al (London, 1981). For a succinct discussion of "subject position," see Belsey, *Critical*, 67. The general tone was set by books like Roland Barthes, *Mythologies*, tr. A. Lavers (London, 1972); John Berger, *Ways of Seeing* (London, 1972); and Clifford Geertz, *The Interpretation of Cultures* (London, 1973).

44. Lacan's two volumes of essays, *Ecrits* (Paris, 1966–71), supply a first entry into his theory of the subject, especially "Le stade du miroir comme formateur de la fonction du Je" and "Du suject enfin en question," vol. 1, 89–109. I rely for detailed knowledge on Kaja Silverman, *The Subject of Semiotics* (Oxford, 1983), esp. 126–93. For the specificity and multiplicity of subjects, see also Smith, *Discerning*, 74–75.

45. For this important notion, see Brian Stock, *Listening for the Text: On the Uses of the Past* (Baltimore, 1990); and the discussion by Jan Ziolkowski, "Cultural Diglossia and the nature of Medieval Latin Literature," in *The Ballad and Oral Literature*, ed. Joseph Harris (Cambridge, Mass., 1991), 193–213.

Chapter 1

1. Although he is speaking about the eighteenth-century *régime du savoir*, Michel Foucault's comment about the nature of subjection seems to me appropriate here: "This form of power applies itself to immediate everyday life[, an act] which categorizes the individual, marks him by his own individuality, attaches him to his own identity, imposes a law of truth upon him which he must recognize and which others have to recognize in him. It is a form of power which makes individuals subjects"; see "Afterword: The Subject and Power," in *Michel Foucault: Beyond Structuralism and Hermeneutics*, ed. Hubert Dreyfus and Paul Rabinow, 2d ed. (Chicago, 1983), 208–26: 212.

2. General orientation to the Tapestry, now hung in the Centre Guillaume le Conquérant in Bayeux, can be had through the fine reproduction of David M. Wilson, *The Bayeux Tapestry* (New York, 1985), where the Ælfgyva panel is Plate 17b;

the review of scholarship by David Bernstein in the first part of his *The Mystery of the Bayeux Tapestry* (Chicago, 1986); the bibliography of Shirley Ann Brown, *The Bayeux Tapestry* (London, 1988); the careful analyses in *The Bayeux Tapestry: A Comprehensive Survey*, ed. Frank Stenton (London, 1957); and the careful scene-by-scene analysis by Lucien Musset, *La tapisserie de Bayeux* (Paris, 1989). Despite the lack of a "critical edition," the restorers generally seem to have gotten the design right by following the original thread holes, even if their colors do not always match well (Wilson, *Bayeux*, 10). The curator and I compared this panel with careful early eighteenth-century drawings (Montfaucon) and found no changes.

3. Wilson, *Bayeux*, 217. The geography seems to be indicated by the tower complex just to the right of the *clericus*, which, following a convention used elsewhere in the Tapestry, balances another standing to the left of the preceding scene set in William's court.

4. The crude, cruciform plants are replaced in the middle of the Tapestry by a more realistic plant with elaborate tendrils. See Nicolas Hallé, *Inventaire de la flore et de la faune de la Tapisserie de Bayeux* (Paris, 1987); more generally, Francis Wormwald, "Style and Design," in *Bayeux*, ed. Stenton, 25–36; Wilson, *Bayeux*, 208–10; and Bernstein, *Mystery*, 82–88.

5. A smaller female figure flees with child from a burning house (Pl. 50b), another mourns the death of King Edward (Pl. 30b). The latter is no doubt Queen Edith, Harold's sister, a powerful woman whose strategies as daughter and wife have been analyzed by Kenneth E. Cutler, "Edith, Queen of England, 1045–1066," *Mediaeval Studies* 35 (1973): 222–31. Small nude females also appear twice in the border (Pl. 14a and 53a). Frank Stenton exposes women's place in the Tapestry and in its modern interpretation when he notes that "they would have provided good decorative elements in the various indoor scenes, or scenes involving crowds. This almost misogynistic scarcity is paralleled by the designer's strong partiality for horses," in *Bayeux*, ed. Stenton, 166. The vigor and beauty of horses and ships ("horses of the sea") supply a striking index to the tight relationship between art and ideology in the period.

6. The efforts to identify the content of this panel are well reviewed by J. Bard McNulty, "The Lady Ælfgyva in the Bayeux Tapestry," *Speculum* 55 (1980): 659–68; M. W. Campbell, "Ælfgyva: The Mysterious Lady of the Bayeux Tapestry," *Annales de Normandie* 34 (1984): 124–45; and Eric Freeman, "The Identity of Ælfgyva in the Bayeux Tapestry," *Annales de Normandie* 41 (1991): 117–34. The evidence for erotic content includes the caption itself with its missing verb, the face-fondling gesture, and the naked man aping the cleric in the border; McNulty, 665, note. McNulty denies actual sex (ibid.), and Campbell apparently agrees (144, repeated 145).

7. McNulty's insight ("Lady," 663) that the scene is "iconographic" and refers to a topic of discussion rather than an event is important, though I find his identification, like the others which have been proposed, cannot account for the image.

8. The standard view is well represented by Edgar De Bruyne's *Etudes d'esthétique médiévale* (Bruges, 1946), which begins with the Christian Neoplatonist Boethius, from whose interest in numbers and their ratios one derives "the"

medieval aesthetic. An insight into the ideology of this hermeneutic can be found in the fascinating study by Stephen G. Nichols, Jr., *Romanesque Signs: Early Medieval Narrative and Iconography* (New Haven, Conn., 1983); and by Linda Seidel, *Songs of Glory: The Romanesque Façades of Aquitaine* (Chicago, 1981), whose introduction offers a critical overview of the term "Romanesque," its implications, and its origins.

9. The close relationship between embroidery and femininity has been explored by Rozsika Parker, *The Subversive Stitch: Embroidery and the Making of the Feminine* (London, 1982). For the medieval period, see A. G. I. Christie, *English Medieval Embroidery* (Oxford, 1938); and Simone Bertrand, *La tapisserie de Bayeux et la manière de vivre au onzième siècle* (La-Pierre-qui-Vire, 1966). The topic of women in the Middle Ages, once so ignored, now enjoys a substantial literature. For general orientation, see Michela Pereira, ed., *Né Eva né Maria: Condizione femminile e immagine della donna nel Medioevo* (Bologna, 1981); A. M. Lucas, *Women in the Middle Ages: Religion, Family, Letters* (Brighton, 1983); Penny Shine Gold, *The Lady and the Virgin: Image, Attitude and Experience in Twelfth-Century France* (Chicago, 1985); Susan Mosher Stuard, ed., *Women in Medieval History and Historiography* (Philadelphia, 1987); M. Erler and M. Kowaleski, eds., *Women and Power in the Middle Ages* (Athens, Ga., 1988); and Georges Duby and Philippe Ariès, eds., *L'histoire des femmes en Occident, II: le moyen âge* (Paris, 1991).

10. This last designation seems to me surprisingly apt, despite the obvious anachronism, since it alone stresses the sense of motion which characterizes this epic representation. See the fine elaboration of the implications of this term by Michel Parisse, *La tapisserie de Bayeux* (Vitry, 1983), 54–56.

11. Une tente tres longue et estroicte de telle a broderie de ymages et escripteaulx faisans representation du conquest d'Angleterre, laquelle est tendue environ la nef de l'eglise le jour et par les octaves des reliques." Brown, *Bayeux*, 161. The apparently fictitious role given to the relics at Bayeux in the Tapestry has led to the proposal that it was crafted in 1077 for the dedication of its cathedral; but see the counter-evidence assembled by Bernstein, *Mystery*, 104–7. A folk tradition (first attested 1730) associated the Tapestry with William's wife, Mathilde, but no foundation exists for that belief either (Bernstein, 28–30).

12. See N. Brooks and H. E. Walker, "The Authority and Interpretation of the Bayeux Tapestry," in *Proceedings of the Battle Conference of Anglo-Norman Studies, 1978*, ed. R. A. Brown (Ipswich, 1979), 1–34; and the first half of Bernstein, *Mystery*.

13. See his long portrait in *The Ecclesiastical History*, ed. and tr. Marjorie Chibnall (Oxford, 1969–80), VIII.1, ed. 4.114–19; and David R. Bates, "The Character and Career of Odo, Bishop of Bayeux (1049/50–1097)," *Speculum* 50 (1975): 1–20. The Tapestry may have been designed as a gift to appease William in 1082: Otto Werkmeister, "The Political Ideology of the Bayeux Tapestry," *Studi Medievali* ser. 3, 17 (1976): 535–95; and Shirley Ann Brown, "The Bayeux Tapestry: Why Eustace, Odo and William?" *Anglo-Norman Studies* 12, Proceedings of the 1989 Battle Conference, ed. Marjorie Chibnall (Woodbridge, 1990), 7–28.

14. See Orderic Vitalis, *Ecclesiastical*, ed. and tr. Chibnall, 4.116 and note.

15. Dominick LaCapra, *Soundings in Critical Theory* (Ithaca, N.Y., 1989), 136.

16. In the court scene at Rouen, Harold is shown pointing at a bearded man on his left (and not, *pace* McNulty, 663, to the Ælfgyva panel), who stands apart from William's retainers and who points back at him. Apparently this scene shows Harold arguing for the release of his nephew Hakon, who, as Norman historians themselves confirm, returned to England with Harold. On the events of 1052–54, see Campbell, "Ælfgyva"; and his "A Pre-Conquest Norman Occupation of England?" *Speculum* 46 (1971): 21–31.

17. Haroldum vero sufficientissime cum honore in urbem sui principatus caput Rotomagum introduxit, ubi multiplex hospitalitatis officiositas viae laborem perpessos juncundissime recrearet. William of Poitiers, *Gesta Normannorum ducum*, ed. and tr. R. Foreville (Paris, 1952), 102. The unique manuscript and its unique seventeenth-century copy have both disappeared. On the sources of William's history, see Foreville's Introduction; and R. H. C. Davis, "William of Poitiers and his *History of William the Conqueror*," in *The Writing of History in the Middle Ages*, ed. R. H. C. Davis and J. M. Wallace-Hadrill (Oxford, 1981), 71–100.

18. A good idea of the importance of hospitality in the idealized portrait of the "good lord" can be had from Matilda Tomaryn Bruckner, *Narrative Invention in Twelfth-century French Romance: the Convention of Hospitality* (Lexington, Ky., 1980).

19. In addition to the material already cited above, see Kay Staniland's beautiful *Medieval Craftsmen: Embroiderers* (Toronto, 1991).

20. George Wingfield Digby, "Technique and Production," in *Bayeux*, ed. Stenton, 37–55: 40.

21. A theoretically grounded analysis of legibility has been made by Richard Brilliant, "The Bayeux Tapestry: A Stripped Narrative for their Eyes and Ears," *Word and Image* 7 (1991): 98–126.

22. Digby, "Technique," 42.

23. Tunc cujusdam matronae frequenti ac religioso rogatu compellatus est ut ei stolam sacerdotalem artificiosa operatione praepingeret, quam postea ad divinos cultos aurifactoria imitatione figuravit. *Memorials of Saint Dunstan*, ed. William Stubbs (London, 1874), 80. Digby quotes the anonymous version of about 1000 but does not consider it to have had any particular relevance to the Bayeux Tapestry. The fact that Osbern alters the wording but not the substance of the description (ibid.) suggests that it was still accurate.

24. See Wendy Steiner's excellent discussion, *The Colors of Rhetoric* (Chicago, 1982), 33–50.

25. E. H. Gombrich argues instead for a plodding purposiveness here: "[The designer] was obviously trained in the intricate interlace work of eleventh-century ornament and adjusted these forms as far as he thought necessary to signify trees"; *Art and Illusion: A Study in the Psychology of Pictorial Representation* (Princeton, N.J., 1960), 77.

26. Persuasive evidence for the hanging's having been at least designed at Saint Augustine's in Canterbury has been assembled by Brooks and Walker, "Authority"; Wilson (212) prefers Winchester, where there was a tradition of royal patronage of embroidery.

27. Brooks and Walker, "Authority," 11.

28. Christie (*English*, 31–32) lists nine different eleventh-century references to the wondrous emboidery of Anglo-Saxon women.

29. Cortinam gestis viri sui intextam atque depositam, depictam in memoriam probitatis eius. See Mildred Budny, "The Byrhtnoth Tapestry or Embroidery," in *The Battle of Maldon*, ed. Donald Scragg (Oxford, 1991), 263–78. This is the only secular tapestry mentioned in eleventh-century English sources; the documentation and preservation of tapestry, like that of so much medieval art, depended heavily upon its utility to ecclesiastic institutions.

30. William Brandt, *The Shape of Medieval History: Studies in Modes of Perception* (New Haven, Conn., 1966), 85–88. For a discussion of legal attitudes toward rape, see Kathryn Gravdal, *Ravishing Maidens: Writing Rape in Medieval French Literature and Law* (Philadelphia, 1991).

31. Mieke Bal, *Narratology: Introduction to the Theory of Narrative* (Toronto, 1985), 104–5.

32. Digby, "Technique," 41.

33. McNulty, "Lady," 664. For frame-breaking as a medieval convention for motion, see Meyer Schapiro, "On Some Problems in the Semiotics of Visual Art: Field and Vehicle in Image-Signs," *Semiotica* 1 (1969): 223–42 at 227. The clerk's gestures belong to the general category of index, of which two types can be seen in the Tapestry: referential and syntagmatic. Referential index, established by the representation of known persons, places, objects, and actions, attempts to "point" to the official Norman version of the Conquest. Syntagmatic index, marked by the ubiquitous first finger, attempts to dictate the eye's motion through the images' complex signifying space. Musset (*Tapisserie*, 255) proposes that the clerk's gesture is an appeal for memory which can be found elsewhere in eleventh-century images and documents, though he cites no sources.

34. Nudes and dragons show up once earlier in the border (Pl. 14), underneath the panel showing Harold being led to William.

35. See Seidel, *Songs*, 56–66; and Adolf Katzenellenbogen, *Allegories of the Virtues and the Vices in Medieval Art from Early Christian Times to the Thirteenth Century*, tr. Alan Crick, Studies of the Warburg Institute 10 (London, 1939; rpr. New York, 1964). A figure carrying what has been taken to be a rope in Pl. 45b has been identified as a "citation" from a Prudentius manuscript; see Wormwald, "Style," 32. The caption (. . . *ut cibum raperentur*) and context (the other figures are bringing the animals slaughtered, cooked, and eaten in the next four scenes) suggest to me the object might be more likely something like sausage.

36. See David Douglas, *William the Conqueror: the Norman Impact upon England* (London, 1964), esp. 265–88; and Margaret Gibson, *Lanfranc of Bec* (Oxford, 1978), 116–61.

37. Pierre Bec, *La lyrique française au moyen âge*, vol. 1 (Paris, 1977), 107–19, comments that the speaking subject of such Old French lyric is always "une jeune fille simple, qui aime avec force et naturel" (108). See also his "Trobairitz et chansons de femme: contribution à la connaissance du lyrisme féminin au moyen âge," *Cahiers de Civilisation Médiévale* 22 (1979): 235–62. The implications of ethno-

graphic evidence have been drawn by Eva Gasparini, "A proposito delle 'chansons de toile,'" in *Studi in onore di Italo Siciliano* (Florence, 1966), 457–66.

38. Wilson remarks: "Because of the thickness of the wool and the manner of stitching, the surface is a mass of light and shade, which gives a lively feeling to the embroidery and sometimes makes it difficult to be precise in a description of the colour of a particular feature" (*Bayeux*, 11). I have taken the general premises for my argument from Schapiro's two essays, "Problems" and "Aesthetic"; also Svetlana Alpers, *Rembrandt's Enterprise* (Chicago, 1988), 14–33; and Julia Kristeva, "Giotto's Joy," in *Calligram: Essays in New Art History from France*, ed. Norman Bryson (Cambridge, 1988), 27–52, despite the very different material, aesthetic, and ideological programs in question.

39. See Pierre Bourdieu's extended discussion, *Language and Symbolic Power* (Cambridge, Mass., 1991).

40. Roman Jakobson, "Linguistics and Poetics," in *Selected Writings*, vol. 3 (The Hague, 1981), 18–51; see Linda Waugh, "The Poetic Function and the Nature of Language," *Poetics Today* 2 (1980): 57–82.

41. Ernst Robert Curtius, "Sodomy," in *European Literature and the Latin Middle Ages*, tr. Willard Trask (New York, 1953), 113–17; Gombrich, *Art*, 93–115; and Leonard Barkan's meditation, *Transuming Passion: Ganymede and the Erotics of Humanism* (Stanford, Calif., 1991).

42. See Steiner's discussion in *Colors*. She treats the modern era, but the connections between the art of portraiture and the art of language dates from Horace and the *Ars poetica*.

43. Nancy K. Miller, "Arachnologies," in *Subject to Change: Reading Feminist Writing* (New York, 1988), 77–101, makes a superb argument for unraveling "the sometimes brutal traces of the culture of gender, the inscriptions of its political structures" to be found in the representations of writing itself (84). The modern connections between detail and gender, that Naomi Schor investigates in *Reading in Detail* (New York, 1987), have good ancient and medieval roots.

44. Brilliant denies this entire premise: "the Tapestry is not a book to be held close to the eye of a reader and to be seen, or read, in small, isolated bits" ("Bayeux," 117); yet he must treat the Ælfgyva panel as an inexplicable aside.

45. I intend "stare" to be a technical term: the focus of visual attention upon the signifier to the relative exclusion of the signified. It has the effect of rendering the spectator conscious of the bodily presence of both the producer and the consumer of the image, and could profitably be added to Norman Bryson's "Gaze" and "Glance," *Vision and Painting: The Logic of the Gaze* (New Haven, Conn., 1983), 87–131.

46. Steiner, *Colors*, 40.

47. Otto Werkmeister, for instance, found a formal source in Trajan's Column at Rome in "The Political Ideology of the Bayeux Tapestry," *Studi Medievali* ser. 3, 17 (1976): 535–95. That suggestion has been refuted by Brooks and Walker (5–6). Their own proposal (17), that the banquet scene before the battle of Hastings (Plate 48a) imitates an illustration of the Last Supper in a manuscript from St. Augustine's, ignores its own implications. Cluniac interest in the parallelism be-

tween the martyrdom of Christ and the combat of the just warrior lay at the base of the notion of the *miles Christi*, and helps account for the papal banner which William of Poitiers says was carried in battle, and which may appear in Pl. 68b; see Douglas, *William*, 192–98.

48. Important contributions on this topic have been made by Georges Duby in *Mâle moyen âge: De l'amour et autres essais* (Paris, 1988). More generally, see Susan Suleiman, *The Female Body in Western Culture* (Cambridge, Mass., 1986); and Alison Jaggar and Susan Bordo, *Gender/Body/Knowledge* (New Brunswick, N.J., 1989). R. Howard Bloch's "Medieval Misogyny: Woman as Riot," *Representations* 20 (1987): 1–15, stresses the perception of the threat of the female body which underlies this panel.

49. Gravdal, *Ravishing*, 3.

50. Voluit in omne seculum et progeniei suae optime consultum fuisse prudens victor, pius parens. Idcirco germanam Hereberti ex partibus Teutonum suae munificentiae maximis impensis adductam, nato suo conjugare decrevit, ut per eam ipse et progeniti ex ipso, jure quod nulla controversia convelli posset vel infirmari, Hereberti haereditatem possiderent sororius et nepotes. Et quoniam pueri aetas nondum fuit matura conjugio, in locis tutis illam prope nubilem magno cum honore custodiri fecit, nobilium atque sapientium virorum atque matronarum curae commissam. Haec generosa virgo, nomine Margarita, insigni specie decentior fuit omni margarita. Sed ipsam non longe ante diem quo mortali sponso jungeretur, hominibus abstulit Virginis filius, virginum sponsus, caelicus imperator: cujus igne salutifero pia puella flagrabat, pro cujus desiderio orationibus, abstinentiae, misericordiae, humilitati, denique plurimae bonitati studebat, vehementer exoptans, praeter ipsius connubium, aliud perpetuo ignorare. *Gesta Guillelmi Ducis*, cap. 39; ed. Foreville, 92–95.

51. Orderic Vitalis tells things very differently a half-century later (*Ecclesiastical*, ed. and tr. Chibnall, 2.116): "The young count his son took the advice of his mother Bertha and commended himself and his patrimony to the powerful duke of Normandy, giving his sister Margaret in marriage to the duke's son Robert. With her he gave her inheritance, which was the county of Maine if he died without children." Elsewhere (2.304) Orderic notes that she "died whilst still a maiden in the guardianship (*tutela*) of the duke."

52. Gravdal, *Ravishing*, demonstrates the ubiquity of such a subject. Friedrich Panzer supports its pan-European distribution in "Der älteste Troubadour und der älteste Minnesinger," *Dichtung und Volkstum* 40 (1939): 133–45. Boasts about sexual conquest appear prominently in court discourse in the *Pèlerinage de Charlemagne à Constantinople*, dated about 1120, and implicitly in the various condemnations of court behavior which I examine later.

53. See, for instance, Joan Ferrante, "The Education of Women in the Middle Ages in Theory, Fact and Fantasy," in *Beyond Their Sex: Learned Women of the European Past*, ed. Patricia Labalme (New York, 1980), 9–42; Peter Dronke, *Women Writers of the Middle Ages: A Critical Study of Texts from Perpetua (†203) to Marguerite* (Cambridge, 1984).

54. Leo Spitzer, "The Mozarabic Lyric and Theodor Frings' Theories," *Comparative Literature* 4 (1952): 1–22; John Plummer, ed., *Vox Feminae: Studies in Medi-*

eval Woman's Song (Kalamazoo, Mich., 1981); Nancy Ann Jones, *The Medieval Female Lyric: The Poetics of Gender and Genre*, Ph.D. dissertation, Brown University, 1987; Doris Earnshaw, *The Female Voice in Medieval Romance Lyric* (New York, 1988); and Georges Duby, "La matrone et la mal mariée," in *Mâle*, 50–73.

55. For the ties with St. Augustine's, see *Carmina Cantabrigiensia*, ed. Karl Strecker (Berlin, 1926), vii–x; on the French origin of the love songs, xvii–xviii, and see Werner Ross, "Die Liebesgedichte im Cambridger Liederbuch (CC): Das Problem des 'Frauenliedes' im Mittelalter," *Der altsprachliche Unterricht* 20 (1977): 40–62. An excellent introduction in English to the anthology can now be had from *The Cambridge Songs (Carmina Cantabrigiensia)*, ed. and tr. Jan M. Ziolkowski (New York, 1994).

56. Leuis exsurgit zephirus Et sol procedit tepidus, Iam terra sinus aperit, Dulcore suo difluit. Ver purpuratum exiit, Ornatus suos induit, Aspergit terra[m] floribus, Ligna siluarum frondibus. Struunt lustra quadrupedes, Et dulces nidos uolucres Inter ligna florentia Sua decantant gaudia. Quod oculis dum uideo, Et auribus dum audio, Heu pro tantis gaudiis Tantis inflor suspiriis. Cum mihi sola sedeo Et hec reuoluens palleo, Si forte capud subleuo, Nec audio nec uideo. Tu, saltim ueris gratia, Exaudi et considera Fronde[s], flores et gramina; Nam mea languet anima. Ed. Ziolkowski, *Cambridge*, 116–17, with translation slightly altered. Why spring would be "crimson" is unclear, but the editor adduces a parallel (289) suggesting that the adjective serves to connote royalty or divinity, although I hesitate to see specific reference to Christ. The punctuation and translation of *tu saltim ueris gratia* remains conjectural, since everything about this crucial line is ambiguous (ibid.). A useful parallel might be drawn from a poem by Marbod of Rennes that I examine in the third chapter, DESCRIPTIO VERNAE PULCHRITUDINIS (PL 171.1717), where *ueris gratia* forces the speaker to abandon his bad mood.

57. On the Clerk's dress, see Wilson, *Bayeux*, 220. The secular appearance of curial clerks was apparently infectious, to judge from the following decision by the Council of Troyes in 1107 whose ideological investment is signalled by the awkward latinization of the vernacular terms: "Presbiteris et diaconibus longos capillos, rostratos sotulares, fixas uestes, laqueos in blial[d]ibus [ed: blialdis] uel camisiis habere uel aleis seruire prohibemus"; see Uta-Renate Blumenthal, *The Early Councils of Pope Paschal II, 1100–1110* (Toronto, 1978), 94.

58. Such "confusion" is endemic to Ovid's *Metamorphoses*; see Leo Curran, "Rape and Rape Victims in the *Metamorphoses*," *Arethusa* 2 (1978): 213–41; and Patricia Kleindienst Joplin, "The Voice of the Shuttle is Ours," *Stanford Literature Review* 1 (1984): 25–53.

59. DuCange (s.v.) cites William of Jumieges, 7.10: Cognomento clericus, quia copiose literatus erat. See also Orderic Vitalis (*Ecclesiastical*, ed. Chibnall, II.28): Radulfus enim quintus frater clericus cognominatus est quia peritia literarum aliarumque artium apprime imbutus est; and Rupert of Deutz: clericum, quo nomine designare mos est cuiuscumque ordinis uel habitus valenter litteratum (Nier s.v.).

60. See Peter Damian, "Contra Clericos Aulicos ut ad Dignatates Provehantur" (PL 145, 463–72), written about 1072 against the German Emperor's appointing a bishop from outside the clergy proper. C. Stephen Jaeger, *The Origins*

of Courtliness (Philadelphia, 1985), 54–67, discusses the context of such criticism. For the conflict itself, see Uta-Renate Blumenthal's overview, *The Investiture Controversy: Church and Monarchy from the Ninth to the Twelfth Century* (Philadelphia, 1988).

61. Habebam plane contra me amicos, qui, etsi bona mihi suadebant, crebro tamen et laudes et ex literis claritudines ingerebant, et per haec culminum opumque assecutiones. Tr. John Benton, *Self and Society in Medieval France* (New York, 1970), 79; I have modified it for greater literalism. Ed. Guibert de Nogent, *Autobiographie*, ed. and tr. Edmond-René Labande (Paris, 1981), 112.

62. Fundamental here is Herbert Grundmann, "Litteratus—illitteratus," *Archiv für Kulturgeschichte* 40 (1958): 1–65. See also the discussion by Peter Classen, "Die Hohen Schulen und die Gesellschaft im 12. Jahrhundert," *Archiv für Kulturgeschichte* 48 (1966): 155–80, where this statement by Abelard is cited. This group or class, he concludes (171), was created by education rather than birth. See also the important study of Rolf Köhn, " 'Militia curialis'. Die Kritik am geistlichen Hofdienst bei Peter von Blois und in der lateinischen Literatur des 9.-12. Jahrhunderts," in *Soziale Ordnungen im Selbstverständnis des Mittelalters*, ed. Albert Zimmermann (Berlin, 1979), 227–57. Jaeger's *Origins* provides the best overview of the primary and secondary literature surrounding this curial clerk.

63. For the international figure of the clerk-lover-poet, see the comparative studies of Edwin Zeydel, "Vagantes, Goliardi, Joculatores: Three Vagabond Types," in *Helen Adolf Festschrift*, ed. Sheema Buehne et al. (New York, 1968), 42–46; Stephen Wailes, "*Vagantes* and the Fabliaux," in *The Humor of the Fabliaux*, ed. Thomas Cooke and Benjamin Honeycutt (Columbia, Mo., 1974), 43–58, whose notes point to earlier work; and George Rigg, "Golias and Other Pseudonyms," *Studi medievali* ser. 3, 18 (1977): 65–109. A good survey of the Romanesque French clerk's analogous role in the emerging epic has been made by Hans-Erich Keller, "Changes in Old French Epic Poetry and Changes in the Taste of its Audience," in *The Epic in Medieval Society*, ed. Harald Scholler (Tübingen, 1977), 150–77.

64. Aeole, rex fortis, ventosae cura cohortis, De vento nequam si rem mihi feceris aequam, Thus et aroma dabo, vitulum tibi sacrificabo. Unde querar dicam: jam complexabar amicam, Ecce furens ventus, quem non amet ulla juventus; Dum sumus in latebris, ferit ictibus ostia crebris; Credidimus flantem fore quemlibet insidiantem, Qui complexantes deprendere vellet amantes. Res erat in tactu, modicum distabat ab actu. Surgimus haud lente, mutantur cuncta repente, Oscula rumpuntur, quae nuda fuere teguntur. Hunc igitur ventum claudas per secula centum; Carcere claudatur ne, si foris egrediatur, Quaslibet in partes similes exerceat artes. Ed. Maurice Delbouille, "Un mystérieux ami de Marbode: le 'redoutable poète' Gautier," *Moyen Age* 57 (1951): 205–40 at 222, with altered punctuation. I have followed his edition of the only eleventh-century manuscript; for a composite edition of the three extant versions, see Walther Bulst, *Carmina Leodiensia* (Heidelberg, 1975), 9.

65. The term Goliardic is normally associated with a later period, but see G. Walsh, "Golias and Goliardic Poetry," *Medium Aevum* 52 (1983): 1–9.

66. Branislow Malinowski indicates with "charter" the definition a group gives itself about the value, goal, and significance of its institutions; see *A Scientific*

Theory of Culture (New York, 1960), 140, 162. I extend the term here to designate any document of official culture which explicitly represents the value structure underlying the institution which produced it.

67. This topic dominates Duby's pieces in *The Chivalrous Society*, tr. Cynthia Postan (Berkeley, 1977); and, to a lesser extent, in the later collection *Mâle*.

68. The messenger before William in Pl. 13a, Harold before Edward in Pl. 28a, and—with the variation of the head rotated—Isengrimus before Noble in the margin of Pl. 5b.

69. R. Howard Bloch, *Etymologies and Genealogies: A Literary Anthropology of the French Middle Ages* (Chicago, 1983), 35.

70. Compare Peter Dronke, "The Rise of the Medieval Fabliau: Latin and Vernacular Evidence," *Romanische Forschungen* 85 (1973): 275–97.

71. Contrast Natalie Zemon Davis, "Women on Top," in *Society and Culture in Early Modern France* (London, 1975), 124–52 at 131: "The image of the disorderly woman did not always function to keep women in their place. On the contrary, it was a multivalent image that could operate, first, to widen behavioral options for women within and even outside marriage, and second, to sanction riot and political disobedience for both men and women in a society that allowed the lower orders few formal means of protest. Play with an unruly woman is partly a chance for temporary release from the traditional and stable hierarchy, but it is also part of the conflict over efforts to change the basic distribution of power within society."

Chapter 2

1. The first complete edition by Phyllis Abrahams, *Les Oeuvres poétiques de Baudri de Bourgueil (1046–1130)* (Paris, 1926) made this intriguing oeuvre available for the first time. A detailed list of textual corrections has been compiled by Karlheinz Hilbert, *Studien zu den Carmina des Baudri von Bourgueil* (Ph.D. dissertation, University of Heidelberg, 1967), 1–56. That author's excellent edition, *Baldricus Burgulianus Carmina* (Heidelberg, 1979), unfortunately lacks commentary, so I refer always to both editions, Hilbert's in Arabic numerals and Abrahams's in Roman numerals. Citations are taken unaltered from Hilbert unless otherwise noted, with the exception that I have replaced his raised period with a semi-colon. All translations are my own in lieu of any contrary indication.

2. Basic treatment of the non-religious poetry of Baudri can be found in Max Manitius, *Geschichte der lateinischen Literaur des Mittelalters*, vol. 3 (Munich, 1931), 885–96, where earlier literature is cited; Hennig Brinkmann, *Entstehungsgeschichte des Minnesangs* (Halle, 1925): 13–61; Otto Schumann, "Baudri von Bourgueil als Dichter," in *Studien zur lateinischen Dichtung des Mittelalters: Ehrengabe für Karl Strecker* (Dresden, 1931), 158–70, rpr. in *Mittellateinische Dichtung*, ed. Karl Langosch (Darmstadt, 1969), 330–42; F. J. E. Raby, *A History of Secular Latin Poetry in the Middle Ages*, 2d ed., vol. 1 (Oxford, 1957), 337–48; and in Reto Bezzola, *Les origines et la formation de la littérature courtoise en Occident (500–1200)*, vol. 2, part 2 (Paris, 1960), 371–82. For Baudri's life and works, see Henri Pasquier, *Un poète latin*

du XIème siècle: Baudri, Abbé de Bourgueil, Archevêque de Dol, 1046–1130 (Paris, 1878);
a fine succinct overview has been made by Jean-Yves Tilliette, "Culture classique et
humanisme monastique: les poèmes de Baudri de Bourgueil," in *La littérature angevine médiévale: Actes du Colloque du samedi 22 mars 1980* (Angers, 1981), 77–88. I have
not seen his thesis, *Rhétorique et poétique chez les poètes latins médiévaux: recherches sur
Baudri de Bourgueil*, thèse de 3ème cycle, Université de Paris IV, 1981.

3. Ludwig Traube, *Vorlesungen und Abhandlungen*, vol. 2: *Einführung in die
lateinische Philologie des Mittelalters*, ed. Paul Lehmann (Munich, 1911), 113.

4. These characteristic traits are singled out at the beginning of an analysis
of youth culture by John Clarke et al., "Sub Cultures, Cultures and Class," in *Culture, Ideology and Social Process: A Reader*, ed. Tony Bennett et al. (London, 1981),
53–79.

5. The contemporary manuscript (Reginensis Latinus 1351) came to the
Vatican Library in the late seventeenth century, along with those of other French
Romanesque poets. It is made up of four discrete sections collected at different
times, but probably all written down during the poet's lifetime. The first and longest section (poems 1–153) seems to have been written about 1096, given the known
dates (see Abrahams) for nearly all the epitaphs it contains. For a detailed analysis
of the manuscript, see Hilbert, *Studien*, 7–25. Despite the presence of textual errors,
it is most likely an authorized copy; Jean-Yves Tilliette, "Note sur le manuscrit des
poèmes de Baudri de Bourgueil," *Scriptorium* 37 (1983): 241–45. Abrahams lists the
remainder of his works, *(Oeuvres*, xxiii–iv), though the data need much revision;
and add now Jean-Yves Tilliette, "Une lettre inédite sur le mépris du monde et la
componction du coeur adressée par Baudri de Bourgueil à Pierre de Jumièges,"
Revue des Etudes Augustiniennes 28 (1982): 257–79.

6. 201/CCXXXIX was written by the noblewoman and nun, Constance, and
204/CCXLII by a certain Odo. Baudri and his contemporaries frequently use *littera (littera multa, littera grandis*, and so forth) in an abstract, Ciceronian sense to
indicate simultaneously a liberal education based on the *auctores* and the learning
and eloquence associated with such an education.

7. The Vatican manuscript transmits almost one hundred epitaphic laments,
averaging about ten lines in length (see Hilbert, *Studien*, 77–181). Written as poetic
inscriptions for inclusion in the death-rolls (*rotuli*) circulated among religious
establishments, they form the major subgroup of the *titulus*, or inscription poem,
a genre widely cultivated in the eleventh century and in many ways characteristic of its approach to language and ornament. See Günter Bernt, *Das lateinische
Epigramm im Übergang von der Spätantike zum frühen Mittelalter* (Munich, 1968);
Léopold Delisle, "Les monuments paléographiques concernant l'usage de prier
pour les morts," *Bibliothèque de l'Ecole des Chartes* 3 (1846): 361–411; and his *Rouleaux
des morts du XIème au XVème siècle* (Paris, 1866).

8. Baudri never actually links the words *amor* and *iocus* grammatically. The
strong sexual connotation of the phrase *iocus amoris* would have destroyed the
delicate ambiguity upon which the poetry thrives, and further angered Baudri's
ever-present critics.

9. AD EVM QUI TABULAS EI PROMISERAT Rumores de te frater

michi rettulit unus, Quos ego complector colloquiumque precor. Rettulit ipse, mei quoniam non immemor esses, Meque salutando mox tua uerba dedit; Rettulit ipse michi, quia me uehementer amares Meque semel uisum pectore congereres; Rettulit ipse michi, quia, si tibi fidus adesset Portitor, ipse michi dirigeres tabulas. Suscepi gaudens, quicquid michi rettulit ex te, Iamque rependo tibi fedus amicitie. Ecce salutantem me uerbo te resaluto, Si tamen alludas uersibus ipse meis. Verbaque carminibus, uerbis quoque carmina iunxi, Vt saltem placeam quolibet ipse modo. Et precor, ut detur locus alter colloquiorum, Vt si[c] te nostris contigues occulis. Ergo per hunc nostrum michi dirige, queso, tabellas, Dirige, que deceant, ut michi plus placeant. Si uero queras, proprie cui dirigo carmen, Clausula signat in hoc, quod gerit: Odo, uale. 105/CLXVII.

10. 252/XXXI.1–4; 191/CCXXIX, passim; 88/CL.4; etc. The word has a complex history within both the Classical and the Christian traditions. See Franz Quadlbauer, *Die antike Theorie der Genera dicendi im lateinischen Mittelalter* (Vienna, 1962), s.v.; and Christine Mohrmann, "Saint Augustine and the 'Eloquentia,'" in her *Etudes sur le latin des Chrétiens*, vol. 1 (Rome, 1961), 351–70.

11. Jean Leclercq, "L'amitié dans les lettres au moyen âge," *Revue du Moyen Age Latin* 1 (1945): 391–410 at 409.

12. Schumann, "Dichter," 342: "Bedeutend kann man Baudri nicht nennen." In the seventeenth century, the Benedictines refused even to consider a body of poems inappropriate to the monastic spirit, see *Histoire littéraire de la France*, vol. 11 (Paris, 1869), 97–9.

13. Michel Banniard, "Théorie et pratique de la langue et du style chez Alcuin: rusticité feinte et rusticité masquée," *Francia* 13 (1985): 579–601.

14. Rhetorical terms are employed here in the form and with the definitions used by Marbod in his *De Ornamentis Verborum* (PL 171.1687–92), which Baudri must have known and which I analyze in the next chapter. Other sources were available: Manegold of Lautenbach, whose student Gerald of Loudun was enticed by Baudri to Bourgueil (76/CXXXVIII), wrote an extant but unpublished commentary on the *De Inventione* and probably one on the *Ad Herennium* as well. Both texts were completed before 1084 in France, according to Mary Dickey, "Some Commentaries on the *De Inventione* and *Ad Herennium* of the Eleventh and Early Twelfth Centuries," *Medieval and Renaissance Studies* 6 (1968): 1–41 at 9–12.

15. Giles Constable, *The Letters of Peter the Venerable*, vol. 2 (Cambridge, Mass., 1967), 25. The Introduction constitutes an excellent overview of the letter in this period, and I have made liberal use of it. Reappraisals of the *ars dictaminis* have been made by William Patt, "The Early 'Ars Dictaminis' as Response to a Changing Society," *Viator* 9 (1978): 133–55; and Franz Josef Worstborck, "Die Anfänge der mittelalterlichen Ars dictandi," *Frühmittelalterliche Studien* 23 (1989): 1–42.

16. Jean Leclercq, "The Monastic Crisis of the Eleventh and Twelfth Centuries," in *Cluniac Monasticism in the Central Middle Ages*, ed. Noreen Hunt (Hamden, Conn., 1971), 217–37: 222. Contrast John Van Engen, "'The Crisis of Cenobitism' Reconsidered: Benedictine Monasticism in the Years 1050–1150," *Speculum* 61 (1986): 269–304. Herman Haberg, *Taxae pro communibus servitiis* (Rome, 1949), 293, reveals that in the fourteenth century Bourgueil was being taxed the same

amount as Ripoll, Savigny, and Préaux. Rabelais still cites it as a wealthy abbey in the sixteenth century (*Gargantua*, ch. 52); and see Alfred Baudrillart, ed., *Dictionnaire d'Histoire et de Géographie Ecclésiastique* (Paris, 1912–), 10.233.

17. The monastic ideal of *otium* has been well described by Jean Leclercq, *Otia monastica: études sur le vocabulaire de la contemplation au moyen âge* (Rome, 1963), esp. 37–40 and 59.

18. 1/XXXVI.56: Dices 'nolebat uiuere tempus iners; 99/CLXI.153–54: Sed malo libris incumbere carminibusque Quam par iumentis ducere tempus iners. In both quotations, the word *iners* carries the etymlogical connotation "without *ars*, lacking discipline." See also Siegfreid Wenzel, *The Sin of Sloth: Acedia in Medieval Thought and Literature* (Chapel Hill, N.C., 1960).

19. The relationship between literacy and the Benedictine tradition is discussed in broad terms by Jean Leclercq in his classic study, *The Love of Learning and the Desire for God*, 2d ed. (New York, 1974).

20. A particularly useful view can be had from Wolfram von den Steinen, "Humanismus um 1100," in his *Menschen im Mittelalter* (Bern and Munich, 1967), 196–214. Although limited to Hildebert of Le Mans, the article carries implications for the entire Loire School.

21. Leclercq, *Love*, 226; also his articles "L'amitié," cited above, and "Le genre épistolaire au moyen âge," *Revue du Moyen Age Latin* 2 (1946), 63–70. So many letters were being written that some reformers condemned the practice; see Constable, *Letters*, 2.2.

22. In his list of synonyms for "letter" (vol. 2, 3 and note), Constable does not include *tabulae*, yet see Wilhelm Wattenbach, *Das Schriftwesen im Mittelalter*, 3rd ed. (Leipzig, 1896), 53, where the greater secrecy is rendered explicit in a passage written in 1075: Anno Coloniensis cuidam familiares litteras, a se ipso in tabulis propter maiorem secreti cautelam conscriptas, dedit episcopo Halberstadensi preferendas.

23. Ernstpeter Ruhe, *De Amasio ad Amasiam* (Munich, 1975), esp. 7–21. See also Jean Leclercq, "Lettres de S. Bernard: histoire ou littérature?" *Studi Medievali* ser. 3, 12 (1971): 1–74. Interesting theoretical observations are provided by Heinrich Dörrie, *Der heroische Brief* (Berlin, 1968), 7–30.

24. Leclercq, *Love*, 226. This position excludes the political, social, and economic utility of friendship, even among monks.

25. At the end of poem 144/CCVI, for instance, one finds a prose addendum written in the manuscript in smaller letters: Quicunque hos uersus legeritis, imperfectum meum uideant oculi uestri et uos imperfecti mei supplementum estote (144/CCVI, after 36: whoever you are who will have read these lines, may your eyes see my imperfection, and may you be the supplement of my imperfection). See Constable, *Letters*, 23–29, for interesting details about the procedures for sending letters in this period.

26. Ad alios uerba, ad te intencionem dirigo; Ewald Könsgen, *Epistolae Duorum Amantium* (Leiden, 1974), 11.

27. See Jean Leclercq, *Monks and Love in Twelfth-Century France: Psychohistorical Essays* (Oxford, 1979), 66–69, where he agrees with Paule Demats, *Fabula: trois études de mythographie antique et médiévale* (Geneva, 1973), 116. Brian McGuire comments that "Marbod and Baudri remain outside . . . harbingers of a new secu-

lar expression of friendship that came in the later Middle Ages;" *Friendship and Community* (Kalamazoo, Mich., 1988), 248.

28. See the discussion by Adelle Fiske, "Alcuin and mystical friendship," *Studi Medievali* ser. 3, 2 (1961): 551–75; rpr. in her *Friends and Friendship in the Monastic Tradition* (Cuernavaca, 1970), 8/1–8/25.

29. Leclercq, "L'amitié;" and, with a perspective less restricted to monastic spirituality, McGuire, *Friendship*.

30. Leclercq, "L'amitié," 404. Godfrey of Reims is not an "ordinary" friend, but "special" (99/CLXI.213–14), as are the friends and poets Teucer, Galo, Hildebert, and Marbod. Also "special" can be *honestas* (95/CLVII.4), *amor* (200/CCXXXVIII.77), *amator* (206/CCXLIV.13), *pignus* (148/CCX.9), *corque iecurque* (142/CCIV.46), and even *aue* (142/CCIV.2) and *ualeto* (90/CLII.33).

31. 13/XLVIII.7–8: Alter ego uel ego, si sint duo spiritus unus Sique duo fiant corpora corpus idem; compare 74/CXXXVI.21: alter ego, sed magis idem.

32. *De Amicitia*, xxi: est enim is [uerus amicus] qui est tamquam alter idem. In his edition for the Guillaume Budé series, L. Laurand has a lengthy comment about the proverbial nature of this concept: *L'amitié* (Paris, 1928), 43, note.

33. Philosophus quidam quaesitus quid sit amicus, Pauca prius meditans, sic ait: 'alter ego'; T. Wright, *The Anglo-Latin Satirical Poets and Epigrammatists of the Twelfth Century*, vol. 2 (London, 1872), 219.

34. Ed. Antonio Viscardi, "Una epistola di Rodolfo Tortario," *Studi romanzi* 19 (1928): 7–45; rpr. in *Saggi neolatini* (Rome, 1945), 249–87; the friends' tale has been translated (very roughly) by MacEdward Leach, *Amis and Amiloun* (London, 1937), 101–5.

35. *De Amicitia*, xxvii: ex [uirtute] exardescit siue amor siue amicitia, utrumque enim ductum est ab amando; amare autem nihil est aliud nisi eum ipsum deligere, quem ames, nulla indigentia, nulla utilitate quaesita. The range of Latin *amor* is best appreciated through the entries in the TLL, s.v., and Peter Dronke, *Medieval Latin and the Rise of European Love-Lyric*, vol. 1, 2d ed. (Oxford, 1968), 195–200.

36. Baudri did not begin to write to women until long after he started writing to men (137/CXCIX.35–40). His eleven letter-poems to women range from religious (138/CC) to literary (153/CCXV).

37. John Boswell, *Christianity, Social Tolerance and Homosexuality: Gay People in Western Europe from the Beginning of the Christian Era to the Fourteenth Century* (Chicago, 1980), supplies a valuable general history. Peter Damian's text (PL 145.169–90) has been translated by Pierre Payer as *The Book of Gomorrah: An Eleventh-Century Treatise Against Clerical Homosexual Practices* (Waterloo, Ont., 1982).

38. Thomas Stehling, *Medieval Latin Poems of Male Love and Friendship* (New York, 1984), makes a succinct overview in his Introduction. See also Boswell, *Christianity*, 243–66; R. W. Southern, *Saint Anselm and His Biographer* (Cambridge, 1963), 67–76; Peter von Moos, *Humanismus an der Schwelle des höfischen Zeitalters* (Stuttgart, 1965), 236–39; Thomas Stehling, "To Love a Medieval Boy," *Journal of Homosexuality* 8 (1983): 151–70; Helmut Birkhan, "Qu'est-ce qui est préférable de l'hétérosexualité ou de l'homosexualité? Le témoignage d'un poème latin," in

Amour, mariage et transgressions au moyen âge, ed. Danielle Buschinger and André Crépin (Göppingen, 1984), 25–45; and Ernst Robert Curtius, *European Literature and the Latin Middle Ages*, tr. Willard Trask (New York, 1953), 113–17.

39. I give the full list in "Iocus," 187–88, notes. The overlapping terms *puer* and *iuuenis* have great chronological range in medieval texts, extending to include men in their thirties.

40. 193/CCXXXI.49–50: Viuo michi, si uiuo tibi; mea summa uoluptas Est, ut agam, quicuid me tibi gratificet.

41. Naturam nostram plenam deus egit amoris; Nos natura docet, quod deus hanc docuit. Si culpatur amor, actor culpatur amoris; Actor amoris enim criminis actor erit. Quod sumus, est crimen, si crimen sit, quod amamus; Qui dedit esse, deus prestat amare michi. Nec deus ipse odium fecit, qui fecit amorem; Namque, quod est odium, nascitur ex uicio. Tu recitator eras nec eras inuentor amoris; Nulla magisterio flamma reperta tuo est. 97/CLIX.51–60. The context suggests that *actor* here is a variant of *auctor*, as frequently attested elsewhere; see MLW s.v.; and M. D. Chenu, "Auctor, Actor, Autor," *Bulletin DuCange* 3 (1927): 81–86. The fusion of the two words neatly expresses the problem of a natural and virtuous self.

42. Noted also by Boswell, *Christianity*, 247; and Sabine Schuelper, "Ovid aus der Sicht des Balderich von Bourgueil, dargestellt anhand des Briefwechsels Florus-Ovid," *Mittellateinisches Jahrbuch* 14 (1979): 93–118 at 117, who found no Ovidian source for this passage.

43. 102/CLXIV.5–6: Iam stilus et tabule, iam nuncius omnis abesto; Nos simus nobis ista, quod esse solent.

44. A general discussion of the use of wax tablets in the medieval period can be found in Wattenbach, *Schriftwesen*, 51–89; the specific terminology has been studied by R. H. Rouse and M. A. Rouse, "The Vocabulary of Wax Tablets," *Harvard Library Bulletin* n. ser., 1 (1990): 12–19, from which I quote (18).

45. Baudri describes with great detail the original fabrication of a broken iron stylus in a mock lament with muted Neoplatonic overtones (92/CLIV).

46. 101/CLXIII.11–13: Matutinus ego tabulas grafiumque pararam Inuitaturus nostras ex more Camenas. Ergo solus eram solusque uacare solebam . . . .

47. Wattenbach (*Schriftwesen*) mentions only a few instances in which the tablets were sent as *epistola*. Baudri's poems often leave unclear whether *tabulae* refers literally to the object or by metonymy to the text it carries. Abrahams's assertion (*Oeuvres*, xxvi) that Baudri dictated to his scribe is without basis.

48. H. Wagenvoort, *"Ludus poeticus": Studies in Roman Literature, Culture and Religion* (Leiden, 1956), 37. See the TLL, s.v. Contrast *vester ludus mecum* in 12/XLVII.44 with *uobiscum iocos . . . meos* in 109/CLXXI.16.

49. See the glossary in Abrahams under *alludo* for most of these compounds. She does not list *preludo* (126/CLXXXVIII.107) or *eludo* (101/CLXIII.16). In its context (*eludere uoces*), the latter appears to mean "to pun."

50. Abrahams (*Oeuvres*, 391, note) identifies the *dux Rotgerius* of 192/CCXXX as Roger II of Sicily (born 1097). Her dating of this poem (1107–30) is erroneous, since Baudri calls himself *Burgulianus* (4). If Roger II is indeed the recipient and not his father (d. 1101), then he was at most ten years old when Baudri left Bourgueil, and this is another letter-poem to a *puer*.

51. See "Early Medieval Grammar" by R. Howard Bloch, *Etymologies and Genealogies: A Literary Anthropology of the French Middle Ages* (Chicago, 1983), 30–63. The contrast between the view of grammar explicated there and Baudri's attitude here is striking.

52. See, for instance, 99/CLXI.195–99, where he talks about the technique, and 122/CLXXXIV, where he practices it; both seem under Marbod's influence.

53. The cultural importance of the concept of "play" or "game" has been a topic of detailed research since the publication of Johan Huizinga's *Homo Ludens: A Study of the Play-Element in Culture* (Boston, 1950). See Roger Caillois, *Man, Play and Games* (New York, 1979); Jacques Ehrmann, *Game, Play and Literature* (Boston, 1968); Brian Sutton-Smith, *The Folkgames of Children* (Austin, Tex., 1972); Paul Zumthor, *Langue, texte, énigme* (Paris, 1975); Glending Olson, *Literature as Recreation in the Later Middle Ages* (Ithaca, N.Y., 1982); and Laura Kendrick, *The Game of Love: Troubadour Wordplay* (Berkeley, 1988).

54. Huizinga, *Homo*, 8–13.

55. Franco Munari, *Ovid im Mittelalter* (Zurich, 1960), 3. Among the many treatments of "the medieval Ovid," I have found the following most helpful: Max Manitius, "Beiträge zur Geschichte des Ovidius und anderer römischer Schriftsteller im Mittelalter," *Philologus, Supplementband* 7 (1899): 723–68; Salvatore Battaglia, "La tradizione di Ovidio nel Medioevo," *Filologia Romanza* 6 (1959): 185–224; E. K. Rand, *Ovid and His Influence* (New York, 1963); Simone Viarre, *La survie d'Ovide dans la littérature scientifique des XIIème et XIIIème siècles* (Poitiers, 1966); Winfried Offermanns, *Die Wirkung Ovids auf die literarische Sprache der lateinischen Liebesdichtung des XI. und XII. Jahrhunderts* (Wuppertal, 1970); Demats, "L'Ovide médiévale: du philosophe au mythographe," in *Fabula*, 107–77; John Fyler, *Chaucer and Ovid* (New Haven, 1979); Roy Rosenstein, *"Iocus amoenus:" Love, Play and Poetry in Troubadour Lyric*, Ph.D. dissertation, Columbia University, 1980; Kurt Smolak, "Der verbannte Dichter (Identifizierungen mit Ovid in Mittelalter und Neuzeit)," *Wiener Studien* n. F., 14 (1980), 158–91; L. D. Reynolds, ed., *Texts and Transmissions: A Survey of the Latin Classics*, (Oxford, 1983), 257–84; Allison Goddard Elliot, "Ovid and the Critics," *Helios* 2 (1985): 9–20; Ralph Hexter, *Ovid and Medieval Schooling* (Munich, 1986); and the special issue dedicated to "Ovid in Medieval Culture," ed. Marilynn Desmond, *Mediaevalia: A Journal of Medieval Studies* 13 (1989 for 1987).

56. Demats, *Fabula*, 5–60; Brian Stock, *Myth and Science in the Twelfth Century* (Princeton, N.J., 1972); Winthrop Wetherbee, *Platonism and Poetry in the Twelfth Century* (Princeton, N.J., 1972); Peter Dronke, *Fabula: Explorations into the Uses of Myth in Medieval Platonism* (Leiden, 1974); and Jon Whitman, *Allegory: The Dynamics of an Ancient and Medieval Technique* (Cambridge, Mass., 1987). On the medieval popularity of Martianus Capella, see William Harris Stahl, *Martianus Capella and the Seven Liberal Arts*, vol. 1 (New York, 1971), 55–71.

57. Léopold Delisle, "Les Ecoles d'Orléans au XIIème et au XIIIème siècles," *Annuaire: Bulletin de la Société de l'Histoire de France* 7 (1869): 139–54; F. Ghisalberti, *Arnolfo d'Orleans—un cultore di Ovidio nel secolo XII* (Milan, 1932); Edwin A. Quain, "The Medieval Accessus ad Auctores," *Traditio* 3 (1945): 215–64; R. H. Rouse, "Florilegia and Latin Classical Authors in Twelfth- and Thirteenth-Century

Orléans," *Viator* 10 (1979): 131–60; B. Roy and H. Shooner, "Querelles de maîtres au 12ème siècle," *Sandalion* 8–9 (1985–86): 315–41; and Hexter, *Ovid*, passim. The *sompnium* by Godfrey of Reims about Odo of Orléans around 1080 is probably the best primary source for the intellectual and literary interests of the school during the Romanesque period; see André Boutemy, "Trois oeuvres inédites de Godefroid de Reims," *Revue du Moyen Age* 3 (1947): 335–66 at 344–51.

   58. The pseudo-Ovidiana were studied by Paul Lehmann in *Die Parodie im Mittelalter* (Munich, 1922) and *Pseudoantike Literatur des Mittelalters* (Leipzig, 1927); see also Friedrich Lenz, "Einführende Bemerkungen zu den mittelalterlichen Pseudo-Ovidiana," *Das Altertum* 5 (1959): 171–82; rpr. *Ovid*, ed. Michael von Albrecht and Ernst Zinn (Darmstadt, 1968), 546–66.

   59. Curtius, *European*, 367.

   60. Vt sunt in ueterum libris exempla malorum, [S]ic bona, que facias, sunt in eis posita. Laudatur propria pro uirginitate Diana; Portenti uictor Perseus exprimitur; Alcidis uirtus per multos panditur actus; Omnia, si nosti, talia mistica sunt. . . . In nostris non unus apex, non linea libris, Que nos non doceat alta sitire, uacat. Sed uolui Grecas ideo pretendere nugas, Vt totus mundus uelut unica lingua loquatur Et nos erudiat omnis et omnis homo . . . Hostili preda ditetur lingua Latina; Grecus et Hebreus seruiat edomitus. In nullis nobis desit doctrina legendi; Lectio sit nobis et liber omne, quod est. 200/CCXXXVIII.105–10 and 119–34.

   61. For its correct constitution see Hilbert, *Studien*, 7–25; summarized in *Baldricus*, 308–10.

   62. Demats, *Fabula*, 56. A detailed examination and interpretaton of Baudri's reworking would be useful. For Fulgentius, see Emil Jungmann, "Quaestiones Fulgentianae," in *Acta Societatis philologiae lipsiensis* 1 (1872): 61–71; Hans Liebeschutz, *Fulgentius Metaforalis: ein Beitrag zur Geschichte der antiken Mythologie im Mittelalter* (Leipzig, 1926), 1–43; M. L. W. Laistner, "Fulgentius in the Carolingian Age," in his *The Intellectual Heritage of the Early Middle Ages* (Ithaca, N.Y., 1957), 202–15; Pierre Langlois, "Les oeuvres de Fulgence le mythographe et le problème des deux Fulgence," *Jahrbuch für Antike und Christentum* 7 (1964): 94–105; and the two articles by Robert Edwards, "Fulgentius and the Collapse of Meaning," *Helios* 3 (1976): 17–35, and "The Heritage of Fulgentius," in *The Classics in the Middle Ages*, ed. Bernard Aldo (Binghamton, N.Y., 1990), 141–51. Primary material in 154/CCXVI.239–40, 651–54, and 833–34.

   63. Baudri speaks of *ingenium* as the human faculty responsible for creation ("genius" or "inventiveness") that is most concentrated in the craftsman (*artifex*), but shows little awareness of its epistemological function. See Murray Bundy, *The Theory of Imagination in Classical and Mediaeval Thought* (Urbana, 1927); Theodore Silverstein, "The Fabulous Cosmogony of Bernardus Silvestris," *Modern Philology* 46 (1948–49): 92–116; Wetherbee, *Platonism*; Stock, *Myth*; Jane Chance Nitzsche, *The Genius Figure in Antiquity and the Middle Ages* (New York, 1975); and Denise N. Baker, "The Priesthood of Genius: A Study of the Medieval Tradition," *Speculum* 51 (1976): 277–91.

   64. DE TEMPESTATE Tempestas oritur; obducunt ethera nubes; Aer densatus intonuit modicum. Ad sua formice pernices castra recurrunt Obliquis celum tramitibus radiat. Nec tamen hac satis est pro tempestate timendum; Clara dies

aderit post modicam pluuiam. Quid michi significet tempestas signaque, noui: Iuppiter et Iuno nunc ineunt thalamos. Hanc tempestatem si gens pauefacta refellit,Hanc ego complector, hec michi sit propria; Hec michi tempestas haut est grauis, haut odiosa, Hec michi portendit difficiles aditus. Ergo secunda ueni, tempestas accelerata; Iam tempestiuos non renuam monitus. Te ueniente quidem discam secreta deorum Et, michi quid sit opus, te redeunte legam. Nam post secessus nubis reditusque choruscos Te quoque tranquilla spero quiete frui. 198/CCXXXVI. The context has led me to translate *te redeunte* (16) and *reditus* (17) with a literal "turn back, withdraw" instead of the usual "return."

65. Bond, "Composing."

66. For historical and interpretative implications of the *Heroides*, see Howard Jacobson, *Ovid's "Heroides"* (Princeton, N.J., 1974); Florence Verducci, *Ovid's Toyshop of the Heart: 'Epistulae Heroidum'* (Princeton, N.J. 1985); and Dörrie, *Brief.* Ovid is thought to have added the six paired letters (16–21) one or two decades later. See Walther Kraus, "Die Briefpaare in Ovids Heroiden," in *Ovid*, ed. Albrecht and Zinn, 269–94.

67. Jacobson, *"Heroides"*, 277–300. Helen's philosophizing about the interrelation of desire, fate, and human nature (8/XLIII.95–116) resembles the position Baudri argues in other letter-poems.

68. Baudri urges someone he has never met: "let me be Paris, judge of beauty, (your) other self" (forme iudex sim Paris alter ego, 10/XLV.18).

69. The extended apologia which constitutes the second book of Ovid's *Tristia* was clearly an important source for Baudri here, as for many later poets (Smolak, "Verbannte").

70. I cannot find that he called himself an *exul* until after he left for Brittany in 1107, though he was already a kind of *exul Nasonis* and *exul potestatis* (97/ CLIX.84) at this time, having just been denied the bishopric of Orléans (the center of Ovidian studies) in a particularly unpleasant manner by his own "Caesar," Philip I of France. If the poems are to be dated after 1107, then much of Baudri's direct experience is reflected here, since exile, bad weather, and misery are common topics in his description of coming to Brittany in his *Itinerarium*. A similar conclusion has been reached by Christine Ratkowitsch, "Baudri von Bourgueil—ein Dichter der inneren Emigration," *Mittellateinisches Jahrbuch* 22 (1987): 142–65.

71. Both letters have been well analyzed; see Offermanns, *Wirkung*, 106–111; and Dronke, *Women*, 84–90 and notes. For a fine review, see Jean-Yves Tilliette, "Hermès amoureux, ou les métamorphoses de la Chimère: réflexions sur les *carmina* 200 et 201 de Baudri de Bourgueil," in *Mélanges de l'Ecole Française de Rome: Moyen Age* 104 (1992): 121–61. I remain persuaded of her letter's authenticity by its very different tone, by the three other poems by Baudri to a Constance (including a similarly worded epitaph), and by the presence at this time of a Constance at the convent of Le Ronceray in Angers (Sancta Maria Caritatis) noted for the noble origins and literate instruction of its students. See Paul Marchegay, ed., *Chroniques des églises d'Anjou*, vol. 3 (Paris, 1869), 282 and passim. Baudri's funereal lament for Constance is included in a small group of epitaphs (209–14/LXXXII–LXXXVI) whose date of composition, where it can be determined, is 1106 (Abrahams, *Oeuvres*, notes).

72. Baudri certainly knew of polyphony (*concentus, harmonia, symphonia*),

although its practice was still in infancy. In the long poem for Adela of Blois, he comments that "the symphony of my voice is like applause to her" (huic uelut applaudit nostre simphonia uocis, 154.993 = CCXVI.806). The words "fundamental" and "overtone," *uox principalis* and *uox organalis*, were already being used in the Romanesque period (Nier).

73. O utinam legatus ego meus iste fuissem Vel quam palparet cartula uestra manus, Et michi, qui nunc est, tunc idem sensus inesset, Sed neque me nosses, donec ego cuperem. Tunc explorarem uultumque animumque legentis, Si tamen et possem me cohibere diu. Cetera propiciis diis fortuneque daremus; Nam Deus ad ueniam promptior est homine. 108/CLXX.

74. Offermanns, *Wirkung*, 18.

75. Citations in the TLL and Nier, s.v., are helpful. Romanesque evidence comes from F. J. E. Raby, "*Amor* and *Amicitia*: A Medieval Poem," *Speculum* 40 (1965): 599–610 at 605; *Rodulfi Tortarii Carmina*, ed. M. B. Ogle and D. M. Sullivan (Rome, 1933), II.18–20 and IX.52; and the Regensburg love-verses edited by Dronke, *Medieval*, vol. 2, 422–47: IX.1, XXV.8, etc.

76. 252/XXXI.9–10: O utinam te iungat idem michi fedus amoris Vt michi te iungit (ms: iungat) sollicitatus amor. The denial is made in 85/CXLVII.40: Nullus amor foedus michi quidlibet associauit.

77. 1/XXXVI.11–68; 85/CXLVII.1–50; 86/CXLVIII.29–35; 91/CLIII.13–16; 97/CLIX.45–60; 98/CLX.57–70; 99/CLXI.137–212; 109/CLXXI.11–12; 142/CCIV.3–4; 193/CCXXXI.97–108; 196/CCXXXIV.1–14.

78. Abrahams compiled a "liste classée des destinataires" in her edition (lvii–lx), but unfortunately it is neither accurate nor complete. I have counted two letter-poems to abbots, five to priors, twelve to archbishops, one to a bishop, one to an archdeacon, three or four to nobles, and two to an architect; details in "Iocus."

79. Seven to monks, eight to clerics, fifteen to teachers, nine to young women; details in "Iocus." Two members of this large group are further described as noble, of the rest nothing explicit about their status is said.

80. Hexter, *Ovid*, passim; for the school education of young nobles in central France, see Jaeger, *Origins*, 225 and note.

81. That poetic reputations at this time were primarily regional is pointed out with interesting examples by André Wilmart, "Le florilège de Saint-Gatien: contribution à l'étude des poèmes d'Hildebert et de Marbode," *Revue Bénédictine* 48 (1950): 3–40 at 6 and note. The "region" defined by Baudri's literary correspondents is roughly the northwest quadrant of France.

82. Brian Stock, *The Implications of Literacy* (Princeton, N.J., 1983), 90–92.

83. 130/CXCII.1–3: Format tibi littera mores; Moribus es, qualis clericus esse solet: Scilicet urbanus, alacer, iocundus, amicus. Compare Offermanns, *Wirkung*, 5, note 5.

84. See especially Georges Duby's articles "The Nobility in Medieval France" and "The Origins of Knighthood," both in *The Chivalrous Society*, tr. Cynthia Postan (Berkeley and Los Angeles, 1977), 94–111, 158–70.

85. 192/CCXXX.45–46: Tales multimodis ludos intersere curis; Ex hoc publica res te sentiet uberiorem. Lurking here is one of the *distichia* of Cato: Interpone tuis interdum gaudia curis, Ut possis animo quemuis sufferre laborem. The distich

was repeatedly cited in defense of literary gaming; see Olson, *Literature*, 93 and elsewhere. The latter's discussion of monastic *recreatio* (109–14) reveals how unusual Baudri's theories are for this time and context.

86. The Ovidian tendencies of some of the more famous poets of this period are well known. John R. Williams comments that Godfrey of Reims seems to have been even more deeply indebted to Ovid than he was to Virgil; "Godfrey of Rheims, A Humanist of the Eleventh Century," *Speculum* 22 (1947): 29–45 at 39. Godfrey wrote a letter-poem to Hugh (Rainard), bishop of Langres (1065–85), who had "a penchant for light and spicy verse," and to Ingelrann, archdeacon of Soissons (1077–98) who indulged in *nenia, risus iners, iocus et sine pondere uerba* (Williams, 37 and 33). Baudri praises Hildebert of Le Mans (87/CXLIX.15): *Doctiloquus Naso non nunc urbanior esset*; and calls a certain Stephen, author of a poem "De Talpa," a *Naso nouus* (90/CLII.22). See also Delbouille, "Mystérieux," and Offermanns, *Wirkung*, who assembles much useful data on this question.

Chapter 3

1. For basic work on Marbod's life and writings, see Léon Ernault, *Marbode, évêque de Rennes, sa vie et ses oeuvres* (Rennes, 1890); Max Manitius, *Geschichte der lateinischen Literatur des Mittelalters*, vol. 3 (Munich, 1931), 719–30; F. J. E. Raby, *A History of Secular Latin Poetry in the Middle Ages*, 2d ed. (Oxford, 1957), 329–37. The *carmina varia* (PL 171.1647–86 and 171.1717–36) include a host of anonymous texts ("Doctrinae Commendatio" through "Elogium Milonis," 171.1684–85) added by J.-J. Bourassé to the censured 1708 edition of Antoine Beaugendre, who himself had added many anonymous texts ("Epitaphium Caroli" through "Proverbia Catonis," 171.1726–36). For the suppressed texts, see Walther Bulst "Liebesbriefgedichte Marbods," in *Liber Floridus: mittellateinische Studien Paul Lehmann . . . gewidmet*, ed. Bernhard Bischoff (St. Ottilien, 1950), 287–301, rpr. in his *Lateinisches Mittelalter: Gesammelte Beiträge* (Heidelberg, 1984), 182–96. The result of the suppressions and additions is far from satisfactory. The *carmina* were already divided into two sections (on an unknown basis) in the *editio princeps* of 1524 ed. by Yves Mayeuc, bishop of Rennes (1507–41), a copy of which resides at the Bibliothèque Nationale in Paris. A second copy exists, according to Felicitas Corrigan, commenting in Helen Waddell's *More Latin Lyrics* (New York, 1976), 238: "The Bodleian has recently acquired a precious little volume of Marbod's poems printed in double columns in black letter in 1524. Its opening poem decorated with a handsome floriated initial is that in honour of St. Mary Magdalen." Three texts missing in PL were published by Jakob Werner, *Beiträge zur Kunde der lateinischen Literatur des Mittelalters* (Aarau, 1905), 5–7. Any detailed study of Marbod's poetry must use Bulst's "Studien zu Marbods Carmina varia und Liber decem capitulorum," in *Nachrichten von der Gesellschaft der Wissenschaften zu Göttingen*, phil.-hist. Klasse n. F. II, vol. 10 (Göttingen, 1939), 173–241; his *Carmina Leodiensia* (Heidelberg, 1975); and Hans Walther, *Initia carminum ac versuum medii aevi posterioris latinorum: Alphabetisches Verzeichnis der Versanfänge mittellateinischer Dichtungen*, 2d ed. (Göttingen, 1969). Good English translations

in Thomas Stehling, *Medieval Latin Poems of Male Love and Friendship* (New York, 1984), 30–39.

2. Parents Robert and Hildeburg, brothers Hugh, Salomon, and Paganel are attested; Marbod comments about a nephew Robert that he was *nec dives homo nec egenus* (PL 171.1721). His father is qualified as *pelliciarius* or *paramentarius* in the documents, indicating that he dealt in luxury clothing. See Ernault, *Marbode*, 10; Olivier Guillot, *Le comte d'Anjou et son entourage au XIème siècle* (Paris, 1972), vol. 1: 150, 161, 195; vol. 2: notes to document C402bis; and Jacques Dalarun, "La Madeleine dans l'Ouest de la France au tournant des XIème–XIIème siècles," in *Mélanges de l'Ecole Française de Rome: Moyen Age* 104, "La Madeleine (VIIIème–XIIème siècle)" (1992): 71–119 at 74–79. On Angevin culture, see Jacques Boussard, "La vie en Anjou aux XIème et XIIème siècles," *Le Moyen Age* 56 (1950): 29–68; and Jean Vézin's fine study, "La vie en Anjou aux XIème et XIIème siècles," in his *Les scriptoria d'Angers au XIème siècle* (Paris, 1974), 1–25, which repeatedly comments on Fulbert's influence.

3. Ad pueri propero lacrimas, quem verbere saeuo Iratus cogit dictata referre magister, Dediscenda docens que confinxere poetae Stupra nefanda Iovis seu Martis adultera facta, Lasciuos recitans iuvenes turpesque puellas, Mutua quos iunxit sed detestanda voluptas. Imbuit ad culpam similem rude fabula pectus Praeventusque puer vitii ferventis odore Iam cupit exemplo committere foeda deorum. *Marbodi Liber Decem Capitulorum*, ed. Rosario Leotta (Rome, 1984), 79–80. Dalarun ("Madeleine," 77) points out that the date of 1102 traditionally assigned to this poem, which would put Marbod's birth in 1035, clashes with the dedication to Hildebert, with whom Marbod had very serious conflicts at that time. He suggests that both the birth year and the poem should be dated a few years later, which seems reasonable.

4. Bulst, "Liebesbriefgedichte," reproduces the complete series. One of the texts ("Puella Ad Amicum Munera Promittentem") also appears among those of a small collection in a contemporary manuscript put together by a friend of Marbod's, and has led Bulst (*Carmina*, 26) to conclude that Marbod did not compose the poem.

5. Marbod sent an obsequious letter-poem to Odo of Bayeux (PL 171.1724) not long after 1066, and Bulst has found direct and indirect evidence which places Marbod among Odo's protégés in Normandy not long after the Conquest; see "Studien," 180–84, for the account of a certain *Britannicus quidam clericus Marbodo* who uttered the following Leonine hexameter when handed a silver drinking vessel at a dinner with Odo and the King: "Nec pice nec clavis eget hec argentea navis" (this silver vessel needs neither pitch nor nails). He also shows (185–88) that Marbod maintained close ties with Bayeux through an old friend, Samson, bishop of Bayeux 1082–96. A marvelous satirical portrait (subsequently removed) of Samson's gluttony exists in a holograph by William of Malmesbury of his *Gesta pontificum*; see Hugh Farmer, "William of Malmesbury's Life and Works," *Journal of Ecclesiastical History* 13 (1962): 39–54 at 45–46.

6. For the dates of the office, see Guillot, *Comte*, vol. 1, 257 note, 261 note.

7. Guillot, *Comte*, vol. 1, 122.

8. For the program of Christian Humanism associated with this figure, see

Peter von Moos, *Hildebert von Lavardin, 1056–1133; Humanitas an der Schwelle des höfischen Zeitalters* (Stuttgart, 1965); and Wolfram von den Steinen, "Humanismus um 1100," in *Menschen im Mittelalter* (Bern, 1967), 196–214. The general situation can be appreciated in C. Stephen Jaeger's "Cathedral Schools and Humanist Learning," *Deutsche Vierteljahrsschrift* 61 (1987): 569–616. For the ignored but enormous role of Cicero's writings in this period, see Jaeger's *The Origins of Courtliness: Civilizing Trends and the Formation of Courtly Ideals 939–1210* (Philadelphia, 1985); and the astonishing list of texts and anthologies in Birger Munk Olsen, *L'étude des auteurs classiques latins aux XIème et XIIème siècles*, vol. 1 (Paris, 1982), 99–350. Ernault, *Marbode*, 24–30, describes Marbod's general Ciceronian interests, and detailed studies have been made by Patrizia Scotti, "Marbodo di Rennes e la fortuna del *Laelius*," *Acme: Annali della Facoltà di Lettere e Filosofia* 33 (1980): 313–29; and Rosario Leotta, "Il 'De Ornamentis verborum' di Marbodo di Rennes," *Studi medievali* ser. 3, 29 (1988): 103–27.

9. One might reasonably date the poem from Marbod's tenure at Angers, given the "youthful" topic and grammatical licence (20), where I assume that *oscula fusa super* represents an adjustment of *oscula superfusa* for the sake of the Leonine rhyme. Rhetoricians called this metaplasm ("change in a word for the sake of metrical ornament"); see James J. Murphy, *Rhetoric in the Middle Ages* (Berkeley, 1974), 33–34.

10. DE MOLESTA RECREATIONE Ad sonitum cithare solitus sum me recreare, Pellere sollicite quotiens volo tedia vite. Est citharista meus non ipse puer Cithereus, Sed puer ipse deo paulominus a Cithereo Cuius dulce melos transcendit acumine celos. Concinit hic odam misero de milite quodam, Cuius amica gemit quod eum sibi casus ademit. Vulnera sunt mentis mihi singula verba gementis, Tacta sonora chelis replet atria tota querelis, Ad cithare questum fit cor mihi flebile mestum. Membra iacentis humo iam pallida iam sine fumo Virgo leuare parat, quem lancea lata forarat. Corpus ad exertis cadit amplexura lacertis, In medio nisu sine mente fit et sine visu; Vixque refecta mora crudis secat vnguibus ora. Inmoritur terre, loquitur que nolo referre. Est recitare metus grauis irritamina fletus: Os oculos vultum gelida iam morte sepultum, Singula commemorat, non sunt ea qualia norat, Oscula fusa super dat ei non qualia nuper. Collige, quid dicat, dum vulnera sanguine siccat! Collige, quid memoret, dum vultibus eius inheret! Hec puer effigiat, quasi res non cantio fiat; Dum citharizatur, plus quam satis imitatur Virginis amplexus fidium vocisque reflexus. Transit in affectus varios mihi mobile pectus Meque pati credo, quicquid sonat a citharedo. Sic michi pro ludo succedit sollicitudo. Que dum me ledit, res in contraria cedit, Grata fit ingratus recreatio nam cruciatus. Ed. Bulst, "Liebesbriefgedichte," 296. For *sine fumo*, see TLL, 6.1542: *fumus flatus est in naribus nostris*. MedLat *colligere* commonly means "gather, conclude, understand, perceive"; see MLW, s.v. I understand the word in 21–22 to mean "gather a conclusion from [this example]," as in the *Liber decem capitulorum*, 2.5–6; ed. Leotta, 74.

11. See "Interaction between Text and Reader," in *The Reader in the Text*, ed. Susan Suleiman and Inge Crosman (Princeton, N.J., 1980), 106–19: "The blank in the fictional text appears to be a paradigmatic structure; its function consists in initiating structured operations in the reader, the execution of which transmits the

reciprocal interaction of textual positions into consciousness" (119). This interpretation neglects mechanisms of play and pleasure for those of meaning, a neglect he rectifies somewhat in his *Prospecting: From Reader Response to Literary Anthropology* (Baltimore, 1989), 249–61.

12. In translating the word *miles* with "knight," I do not wish to imply the existence of some single, coherent, empirical, and stable concept. Marbod seems to use it here in the generic sense of "professional man of arms." In the fragmentary dynastic history written ca. 1098 by Fulk Rechin, Count of Anjou (1068–1109), *miles* designates the professional title, while *eques* names the mounted fighter; Paul Marchegay, ed., *Chroniques des églises d'Anjou*, vol. 1 (Paris, 1856), 375–83.

13. Gerd Althoff, "Nunc fiant Christi milites, qui dudum extiterunt raptores: Zur Entstehung von Rittertum und Ritterethos," *Saeculum* 32 (1981): 317–33, argues that one cannot separate the early use of the word *miles* from Cluniac ideology. Important along these lines are also Franco Cardini, *Alle radici della cavalleria medievale* (Florence, 1981); Jean Flori, *L'Essor de la chevalerie, XIème–XIIème siècles* (Geneva, 1986); and Alessandro Barbero, *L'Aristocrazia nella società francese del medioevo: Analisi delle fonti letterarie (secoli X–XIII)* (Bologna, 1987). Marbod criticized *bella domestica* about 1098 in a poem praising Bohemond of Antioch and the holy war (PL 171.1672).

14. Literally, of course, *amica* means "(girl) friend"; Latin and Romance languages mark the gender of "friend," facilitating a useful sexual euphemism. But its connotations vary greatly by context: monks found in them a figure of the world's evil, knights just the opposite. An interesting fusion of common sense and the commonplace (NUGAE POETICAE) condemns her specifically: "the countryside is fertile, corruption is pus, and a girl-friend is a pig in the mud" (fertile rus, corruptio pus, et amica luto sus, PL 171.1685). This anonymous poem was added to Marbod's oeuvre by Bourassé, though I see no particular reason to think it his.

15. The Girl-Friend's performance was ritualized by gestural and verbal formulas of the "mourning woman" found throughout heroic and Christian literature. In *The Book of Memory: A Study of Memory in Medieval Culture* (Cambridge, 1990), Mary J. Carruthers examines the formation of the self as a "subject-who-remembers" (182–84).

16. Speaking as a Christian in his popular *Vita Sanctae Thaisidis*, Marbod blamed feminine desire for the destruction of the nobility; on this text, see Antonella Degl'Innocenti, *L'opera agiografica di Marbodo di Rennes* (Spoleto, 1990); and Dalarun, "Madeleine."

17. Marbod defined the figure in the *De Ornamentis Verborum* as "the repetition of one or more words for the sake of amplification or pity" (conduplicatio est, cum ratione amplificationis aut miserationis, unius aut plurimum verborum iteratio fit, PL 171.1691). This definition comes from *Rhetorica ad Herennium* 4.28, where the discussion of the figure concludes with a tantalizing metaphor: "The reiteration of the same word makes a deep impression upon the hearer and inflicts a major wound upon the opposition—as if a weapon should repeatedly pierce the same part of the body" (Vehementer auditorem commovet eiusdem redintegratio verbi et vulnus maius efficit in contrario causae, quasi aliquod telum saepius perveniat in eandem corporis partem); text and translation from the Loeb edition by Harry Caplan (Cambridge, Mass., 1954).

18. In the *Liber decem capitulorum* 2.9–23 and 52–74, Marbod separates *puer* from *iuvenis* with the simultaneous arrival of sexuality and rationality at puberty.

19. In Marbod's DISSUASIO MUNDANAE CUPIDITATIS (PL 171.1667), the first temptation mentioned arises from the beauty of young women and the looks of young men.

20. For Marbod's belief in this Isidorian principle, see PL 1671: Nomen commendat res nomine significata. Ergo debemus naturam quaerere rerum, Ex quo possimus de nomine cernere verum. More generally: Ernst Robert Curtius, "Etymology as a Category of Thought," in *European Literature and the Latin Middle Ages*, tr. Willard Trask (Princeton, N.J., 1953), 495–500; and the first chapter of R. Howard Bloch, *Etymologies and Genealogies: A Literary Anthropology of the French Middle Ages* (Chicago, 1983).

21. In POENITUDO LASCIVI AMORIS (PL 171.1655–56), the speaker renounces the desire of both sexes, concluding: Ergo maneto foris, puer aliger, auctor amoris; Nullus in aede mea tibi sit locus, o Cytherea! Displicet amplexus utriusque quidem mihi sexus . . . .

22. Like Baudri, Marbod held the fusion of "friend" and "critic" to be an important ideal; see the intriguing prologue to his *Vita Sancti Gualterii* (PL 171.1565), likely written sometime reasonably soon after the saint's death in 1071.

23. Emile Benveniste, "Subjectivity in Language," in *Problems in General Linguistics*, tr. Mary Elizabeth Meek (Coral Gables, Fla., 1971), 223–30.

24. John Boswell views this last theme biographically, and laments that such poems by Marbod, whom he unfortunately calls "master of the extremely influential school of Chartres," lack critical attention; *Christianity, Social Tolerance, and Homosexuality: Gay People in Western Europe from the Beginning of the Christian Era to the Fourteenth Century* (Chicago, 1980), 248 and note. His comments and translations do not do much to remedy the problem.

25. Neither the source nor the date of the rubrics is known. Given the presence of similar rubrics in the authorized copy of Baudri of Bourgueil's poetry, I see no reason not to think that these originated with Marbod.

26. For some recent suggestive explorations of the linkage between writing, texts, and ideas of the self, see Franz Bäuml, "Varieties and Consequences of Medieval Literacy and Illiteracy," *Speculum* 55 (1980): 237–65; Walter Ong, *Orality and Literacy* (London, 1982), chapter 4; Daniella Regnier-Bohler, "Imagining the Self," in *A History of Private Life*, vol. 2, *Revelations of the Medieval World*, ed. Georges Duby and Philippe Ariès, tr. Arthur Goldhammer (Cambridge, Mass., 1988), 311–94; and the fascinating first chapter of M. S. Regan, *Love Words: The Self and the Text in Medieval and Renaissance Poetry* (Ithaca, N.Y., 1982).

27. Contrast Michel Foucaut's frequently cited "What is an Author?" in *Language, Counter-Memory, Practice*, tr. D. Bouchard and S. Simon, ed. D. Bouchard (Ithaca, N.Y., 1977), 113–38. On medieval reading, see the suggestive observations by Paul Saenger, "Silent Reading: Its Impact on Late Medieval Script and Society," *Viator* 13 (1982): 367–414.

28. Denuntiamus vobis obitum domini Marbodi venerabilis episcopi, semper cum laude memorandi, lingua facundi, religione praecipui, morum honestate praeclari, litterarurm eruditione doctissimi; cujus sermo sale semper conditus erat, et ex ore illius omni dulcior melle fluebat oratio. Et quamvis eodem tempore variis

studiis tota Gallia resonaret, ipse tamen oratorum rex, Gallicanae arcem eloquentiae obtinebat. Léopold Delisle, *Rouleaux des morts du XIème au XVème siècle* (Paris, 1866), 347–48, with other funeral poems from Marbod's death roll.

29. The evidence for dating his texts about nature and language to the Angers period remains somewhat scanty. Of those written after 1096, however, only the *Liber decem capitulorum* examines nature at all, and there only as the order of things to which mortals are subject (see Bulst, *Studien*, 221).

30. See *Renaissance and Renewal in the Twelfth Century*, ed. Robert L. Benson and Giles Constable (Cambridge, Mass., 1982); and Charles Haskins, *The Renaissance of the Twelfth Century* (Cambridge, Mass., 1927), who pays careful attention to the history of science.

31. See the Introduction by John Riddle, *Marbod of Rennes, De Lapidibus* (Wiesbaden, 1977); Robert Halleux, "Damigéron, Evax et Marbode. L'héritage alexandrin dans les lapidaires médiévaux," *Studi medievali* ser. 3, 15 (1977): 327–47; Serenella Baggio, "Censure lapidarie," *Medioevo romanzo* 11 (1986): 207–28; and H. F. Haefele, "Zum Lapidarius des Marbods von Rennes," in *Scire Litteras: Forschungen zum mittelalterlichen Geistesleben*, ed. M. Bernhard and S. Krämer (Munich, 1988), 211–19. Manitius (724) and Riddle (6) are probably right to date the treatise toward the end of the Angevin period; see also Baggio's comments, 210–11 and note.

32. *Liber Lapidum*, 5–10: . . . componere duxi Aptim gestanti forma breviora libellum, Qui mihi praecipue paucisque pateret amicis; Nam majestatem minuit qui mystica vulgat Nec secreta manent, quorum fit conscia turba (PL 171.1738–39).

33. At Chrysoprassum lapidum domus India mittit. Hic porri succum referens, mistusque colore, Aureolis guttis quasi purpura tincta renidet. Quas habeat vires potui cognoscere nondum; Sed tamen esse reor, nec fas est omnia nosse. PL 171.1749. See Riddle, *Marbod*, 53, for comments.

34. Chrisoprasus est purpureus interguttatus guttis aureis: eos significat qui semper in tribulatione et labore passionum vitam suam agunt, semper manendo in charitate. Ed. Riddle, *Marbod*, 128, where he ascribes it to Marbod. The text provides a figurative meaning ("Mystica seu moralis applicatio") of the twelve stones on the walls of the heavenly Jerusalem, following Revelations xxi.

35. Riddle, *Marbod*, ix and 6.

36. See Bruce Flood, Jr., "The Medieval Herbal Tradition of Macer Floridus," *Pharmacy in History* 18 (1976): 62–66.

37. Dici flos florum nobis rosa iure videtur Quod specie cunctos praecedat odoreque flores. Non tamen haec specie tantum nec odore iuvare Nos valet, at variis nos adiuvat illa medelis. Eius sicca gradu vis est et frigida primo: Compescit sacrum, si trita apponitur, ignem, Sic quoque, si stomachus calet aut praecordia, sedat . . . . *Macer Floridus, De Viribus Herbarum*, ed. Ludwig Choulant (Leipzig, 1832), 60.

38. See *Theobaldi "Physiologus"*, ed. T. Eden (Leiden, 1972); Nikolaus Henkel, *Studien zum Physiologus im Mittelalter* (Tübingen, 1976); and H. Diekstra, "The Physiologus, the Bestiaries and Medieval Animal Lore," *Neophilologus* 69 (1985): 142–55.

39. Quicumque igitur physiognomoniam assequitur, primo memoriae man-

dare debet significationes signorum, secundo dignitates eorum cognitas habere, tertio quaecunque signa reppererit, conicere atque ea inter se conferre, ut ita verbi causa constituat. . . . Latera tenuia et angusta et depressa timiditatis arguunt, et quae referta sunt carnibus et dura, indociles homines ostendunt. quae autem rotunda sunt tanquam tumentia, loquacem, inanem declarant; nam refertur ad ranas. Ed. Richard Foerster, *Scriptores Physiognomonici Graeci et Latini*, vol. 2 (Leipzig, 1893), 17–18, 86. See Maurice Delbouille, "Un mystérieux ami de Marbode: le 'redoutable poète' Gautier," *Moyen Age* 57 (1951): 205–40; and the Introduction of Bulst, *Carmina*.

40. DESCRIPTIO VERNAE PULCHRITUDINIS Moribus esse feris prohibet me gratia veris Et formam mentis mihi mutuor ex elementis: Ipsi naturae congratulor, ut puto, jure. Distingu[u]nt flores diversi mille colores; Gramineum vellus superinduxit sibi tellus. Fronde virere nemus et fructificare videmus. Aurioli, merulae, graculi, pici [ed: pisci], philomenae Certant laude pari varios cantus modulari. Nidus nonnullis stat in arbore non sine pullis Et latet in dumis nova progenies sine plumis. Egrediente rosa viridaria sunt speciosa. Adjungas istis campum qui canet aristis; Adjungas vites, uvas quoque, postmodo nuces. Adnumerare queas nurum matrumque choreas Et ludos juvenum [ed: jevenum], festumque diemque serenum. Qui tot pulchra videt, nisi flectitur et nisi ridet, Intractabilis est et in ejus pectore lis est. Qui speciem terrae non vult cum laude referre, Invidet auctori cujus subservit honori Bruma rigens, aestas, autumnus, veris honestas. PL 171.1717, with punctuation somewhat simplified. The phrase "matrum nurumque" may be a reminiscence of Ovid's "matrum nurumque caterva" (*Metamorphoses*, 12.216), which occurs in the same metrical position. A reading of *uirginum matrumque* has been made from one manuscript by R. N. B. Goddard, "Eugenius of Toledo and Marbod of Rennes in Marcabru's 'Pois la fuoilla revirola,'" *Medium Aevum* 57 (1988): 27–37 at 32; his translation (36 note 28) is faulty, and the evidence for influence seems dubious.

41. For the *descriptio*, see Curtius, *European*, s.v.; Annette Georgi, *Das lateinische und deutsche Preisgedicht* (Berlin, 1969), who pays particular attention to Romanesque France; and Therese Latzke, "Der Fürstinnenpreis," *Mittellateinisches Jahrbuch* 14 (1979): 22–65. Good background in George Economou, *The Goddess Natura in Medieval Literature* (Cambridge, Mass., 1972).

42. These Marian echoes are even more distinct in the fourth chapter ("De Matrona") of the *Liber decem capitulorum*.

43. Marbod uses the word *auctor* in a variety of ways. Cupid is called *auctor amoris* (171.1656) or "agent of desire"; Bohemond is called the *auctor et exemplum violentis* (171.1672) or "paragon of ferocity"; and God, here, is called the *auctor naturae*, and in the *Liber decem capitulorum* the *bonus auctor* (10.86). The passage preceding the last (10.63–73) reworks the argument of this poem.

44. I refer here more to the general rhetorical strategies found behind genres such as dialogues rather than specific philosophical doctrines of any kind.

45. See M. D. Chenu, "The Symbolist Mentality," in *Nature, Man and Society in the Twelfth Century: Essays on New Theological Perspectives in the Latin West*, ed. and tr. Jerome Taylor and Lester K. Little (Chicago, 1968), 99–145: 104.

46. Text in PL 171.1685–92; certain "very probable" corrections are made by Rosario Leotta, "Il 'De Ornamentis,'" 105 note. See Edmond Faral, *Les arts poétiques*

du XIIème et du XIIIème siècle (Paris, 1924), 48–51; Murphy, *Rhetoric*, with frequent references to the importance of Marbod's digest; and the collection Murphy edited on *Medieval Eloquence: Studies in the Theory and Practice of Medieval Rhetoric* (Berkeley, 1978).

47. Si potes his [scematibus verborum] veluti gemmis et floribus uti, Fiet opus clarum velut ortus deliciarum, Quo diversorum fragrantia spirat odorum Nec deerit fructus florum de germine ductus, Mens auditoris persuasa nitore coloris (PL 171.1687–88). Leotta, "'Ornamentis,'" 107, lists the reminiscences of the *Rhetorica*.

48. Six of the original figures have been eliminated (*interrogatio, continuatio, conpar, interpretatio, permissio, expeditio*), and a new one added (*commistum*). Leotta gives a detailed discussion of their interrelationships.

49. Marbod laments its monotony in his retraction of 1102 in the *Liber decem capitulorum*, 1.29–33; ed. Leotta, 65.

50. Criminis est formam componere, spernere famam, Scortum sectari, *miracunnum vocitari. Hic qui magnanimum se vult fortemque videri, Corde pavet leporis cum territet ore leonis: Sicut dama fugit, quasi bos ad vulnera mugit. PL 171.1690. The last verse is missing in the *editio princeps* but can be found in some of the best manuscripts, according to a note in PL. The word *miracunnum/miraconnum* is a hapax transmitted by sixteen manuscripts and supported by six others, according to Leotta (112 note), who conjectures an unattested *mirum cunnum*. Marbod's humorous *commistum* seems to twist an understood *miraculum* into *miracunnum*; I have tried to imitate that by twisting "marvelous" into "marvelass." Leotta shows that the content of the gloss comes from the *Rhetorica ad Herennium*, 4.28: Perditissima ratio est amorem petere, pudorem fugere, diligere formam, neglegere famam.

51. See Geoffrey of Vinsauf's *Poetria nova*, 1134ff, ed. Faral, *Arts*, 232.

52. Prava sequi, perversa loqui, tormenta minari. *Notices et extraits des manuscrits* vol. 31 (Paris, 1884), 102. The manuscript (Bibliothèque de Saint-Omer 115) is filled with works of Loire poets, including a fascinating elaboration of Marbod's injunctions here in an anonymous text of 100 lines (f. 97r, ed. 132–35).

53. Interea tanquam speculum formamque poetae, Rerum naturam, qui scribere vultis, habete, Cuius ad exemplar, veluti qui pingere discit, Aptet opus proprium quisquis bene fingere gliscit. Ars a natura ratione ciente profecta, Principii formam proprii retinere laborat. Ergo qui laudem sibi vult scribendo parare, Sexus, aetates, affectus, condiciones Sicut sunt in re, studeat distincta referre. Ed. Leotta, "'Ornamentis,'" 122. Compare Horace, *Ars poetica*, 317–22. The words "in the meantime" refer to the interval during which the students try these figures in their poetry before committing the full rhetorical art to memory.

54. Compare Horace, *Ars Poetica*, 125–27, 408–11; *Rhetorica ad Herennium*, 3.16–22; and Leotta, "'Ornamentis,'" 124. More generally, Edouard Galletier, "L'Imitation et les souvenirs d'Horace chez Marbode, évêque de Rennes," in *Mélanges bretons et celtiques offerts à M. J. Loth* (Rennes, 1927), 79–91. For the little appreciated importance of Horace's writings in the Romanesque period, see Angelo Monteverdi, "Orazio nel Medio Evo," *Studi Medievali* n. s., 9 (1936): 162–80; Kindermann, *Satyra*, passim; and the list of manuscripts in Munk Olsen, *L'étude*, 421–522.

55. Robert Kaster, *Guardians of Language: The Grammarian and Society in Late Antiquity* (Berkeley, 1988), is particularly good on these questions.

56. Insipiens opifex reprehendendusque videtur, Cuius opus vanum veluti vas fictile transit. Sic faber ignavus per opus culpatur ineptum Artificemque suum reprehendit fabrica nutans. *Liber decem capitulorum*, 2.136–39; ed. Leotta, 89. The remainder of the second chapter continues and expands this argument. The passage is cited without comment by Curtius, *European*, 544–45.

57. Tres res convenit habere narrationem: ut brevis, ut dilucida, ut veri similis sit. *Rhetorica ad Herennium*, 1.9. Compare Marbod, PL 171.1565: quatenus quae dicenda sunt breviter et dilucide, nec inornate omnino, valeam explicare.

58. In his prose religious texts, Marbod defended simplicity as appropriate for Christian texts. Furthermore, as a teacher, he frequently stressed that "a short text drives away boredom and a simple style permits easy understanding" (PL 171.1505). But as a rhetorician, he lauded a Virgilian *mediocritas*: "I will strive therefore for the sake of the power [of this material] to conserve this middle style in composing, so that the diction seem neither abject nor too elaborate" (PL 171.1565). In his lyric poetry, Marbod usually prefers a simpler style.

59. Singula distingens facili brevitate notavi, Quae quo plana forent, magis haec placitura putavi, PL 171.1692; Haec aditu facili rudibus doctisque patescunt, PL 171.1653; Nam cum Gesta Sanctorum ob hoc litteris mandentur, ut omnium legentium vel audientium ad imitandum accendatur intentio, curandum est summopere scriptori ut, in quantum fieri potest, nullius excedat capacitatem, quod ad omnium spectat utilitatem, PL 171.1505. To Hildebert he writes: Nobis directo satis est procedere calle (PL 171.1653).

60. See Michel Banniard, "Théorie et pratique de la langue et du style chez Alcuin: rusticité feinte et rusticité masquée," *Francia* 13 (1985): 579–601 at 582.

61. Kindermann, *Satyra*, 1–30 and passim. Raby gives an overview of Romanesque satire in *History* 2: 45–54. For the Classical term and concept, see Robert Elliott's *The Power of Satire: Magic, Ritual, Art* (Princeton, N.J., 1960), esp. the second chapter.

62. IN PUERUM TURPI AMATORI DEDITUM Sordidus et fedus nimis est, et fetet ut hedus, Cuius amas tactus, turpis sibi culcitra factus. Quem quociens audes digitis emundere, gaudes, Et quasi munus habes, cum te maculat sua labes. Cum quo dum flumen petis, ut lavet unda bitumen, Non undis mundas te, sed tu polluis undas. Non inpune feres, quod sordibus eius adheres Nec metuas dorsum, quia tendo minas aliorsum. Sis licet inberbis, utar pro verbere verbis; Verbera cessabunt, sed plus te verba gravabunt: Fies infamia nostris per secula grammis, Dum nox atque dies durabunt, fabula fies. Werner, *Beiträge*, 6. For *bitumen*, see the entries in TLL, s.v.; and MLW, s.v.: bitumen significat retinacula mundi.

63. Jill Mann, "Satiric Subject and Satiric Object in Goliardic Literature," *Mittellateinisches Jahrbuch* 15 (1980): 63–86.

64. AD EANDEM RESIPISCENTEM Ploro cum ploras, labor est michi quando laboras, Nec tua teste deo vulnera ferre queo, Dissimulemque licet, vultus meus hoc tibi dicet, Parent in facie nubila tristicie. Penitet vt scribis, nec talia rursus inibis, Quod me tam subito leseris immerito. Ora rigas lacrimis, suspiria ducis ab imis, Pro danda venia voce rogando pia. Ad supplex verbum michi cor nequit

esse superbum, Zelus et ira iacet cum fera lingua tacet. Do veniam fasse, satis est tibi pena rogasse, Tantum me nolis fallere [Bulst: fallera] queso dolis. Ars simulat verum mutatque vocabula rerum, Quemque vocat carum, nouit amare parum. Presertim multas simulat res docta facultas, Dum mouet ingenium quodlibet ad studium. Quod rogo ne facias neque rethor in hoc michi fias: Ostendas [ed. pr.: Ostendes; Bulst: Ostendens] alias quid simulare scias! Me non ex libris, sed totis dilige fibris: Qua te mente colo, me cole, digna polo. Bulst, "Liebesbriefgedichte," 293.

65. AD AMICAM GEMENTEM, in Bulst, "Liebesbriefgedichte," 294.

66. DE VASE SAPHIRINO Porticus est Rome, quo dum spatiando fero me; Res querendo novas, inveni de saphiro vas. Institor ignotus vendebat cum saphiro thus; Thus socius noster tres emit denarios ter, Vas tribus et semi solidis ego prodigus emi. Hoc inconcussum dum tollere sollicitus sum, Pro cofino mundo de viminibus pretium do. Ponitur introrsum sanum vas, inde memor sum, Extrahitur fissum: tristis miser inde nimis sum. Inter convivas magni foret hoc pretii vas Si foret allatum sicut positum fuerat tum; Lator at hoc pressit, cui prospera nulla dies sit. Ed. Bulst, *Studien*, 204–5. A useful contrast is provided by the subtle study of Charles Witke, "Rome as 'Region of Difference' in the Poetry of Hildebert of Lavardin," in *Classics in the Middle Ages*, ed. Aldo S. Bernardo and Saul Levin (Binghamton, N.Y., 1990), 403–11.

67. Bulst, ibid.; Walther, *Initia*, lists fifteen manuscripts for this poem (his no. 14284).

68. With the last interpretation I am thinking of Marbod's frequent image in his Christian texts (PL 171.1348, 1519, etc.) of the verbal text as a "vase of clay" *vas fictilis* (from II Corinthians, iv, 7: Habemus autem thesaurum istum [sc. illuminationem scientiae claritatis Dei] in vasis fictilibus: ut sublimitas sit virtutis Dei, et non ex nobis).

69. DISSUASIO INTEMPESTIUI AMORIS SUB ASSUMPTA PERSONA Mens mea tristatur, virtus mea debilitatur, Corpus tabescit, flet vena, medulla liquescit,Pellis mutatur, facies mea flendo rigatur, Nec satis effundo lachrimas, quibus intus abundo; Cum via nulla datur qua quo volo perueniatur, Prorsus despero rem, quam contingere quero, Nec desisto tamen nec habet mea cura leuamen. Claudus agens leporem frustra consumo laborem, Improba testudo ceruum sequor et mihi ludo, Sed neque sic cesso, nec dat furor ocia fesso. O si quid nossem, per quod desistere possem. Quam felix fierem, si quod volo nolle valerem, Nolle sed ex toto, nequaquam duplice voto. Langueo quippe volens medicinam flagito nolens, Rursum quero volens medicinam, langueo nolens. Sic quod nolo volo rursum quoque quod volo nolo. In me diuisus de me michi concito risus, Risus exosos, risus tristes, lachrimosos. Nunquid in hoc tabo putrescens semper amabo? Aut quis erit finis tantis, bone Christe, ruinis? Num semper prisco cupiam me tradere visco Et semel egressus rursum laqueis dare gressus? Dilexi multas paruas puer et vir adultas, Dilexi multos paruos puer et vir adultos. Quotquot dilexi, facili conamine flexi. Etas consimilis, decor et risus puerilis, Aspectus letus, vox dulcis, sermo facetus Quas affectabat facile sibi conciliabat Et paribus lignis ardebat mutuus ignis. Nunc dispar etas cogit viciis dare metas, Iam dat ad amplexus neuter mihi brachia sexus, Nec bene, si cupiam, quod eram tunc denuo fiam. Quis iam pene senis

iuuenum parebit habenis? An sectabor anus incanaque timpora canus? Lasciuum pectus non debet habere senectus Et contemptibilis solet esse libido senilis. Ergo mori restat, si me mala cura molestat, Vt voto solo sim mechus, viuere nolo. Ed. Bulst, "Liebesbriefgedichte," 297–98.

70. Inde senectutem mala consuetudo molestat, Et cum iam coitus sibi sit subtracta facultas, Utpote cui gelidus cohibet penitralia sanguis, Insatiata tamen prurit sub corde voluptas Et petit affectu quod non procedit in actum. . . . Heu miser! illa dies mihi quae tormenta parabit, Qui laevum per iter semper devexa secutus Illecebris carnis superata mente vacavi, Cuius in omne nefas intentio prompta cucurrit, Cuius opus virtus a crimine nulla redemit! *Liber decem capitulorum* 2.81–85 and 173–77, ed. Leotta, 82–83 and 92–93.

71. Although the influence of his rhetorical theory cannot be doubted, specific examples of the influence of Marbod's lyric are few. This may be because of the disruption of secular poetic production in central France by Urban II's crucial visit in 1095–96, because its circulation was limited to close friends, or because conservative pressures to reform content and style along the lines of Hildebert's successful oeuvre marginalized it. Baudri, of course, knew Marbod's work very well, and later poets such as Hilary of Orléans and particularly Serlo of Wilton also seem to have been well acquainted with it. A clear example of influence has been found by Therese Latzke in the Ripoll collection, see "Die Carmina erotica der Ripollsammlung," *Mittellateinisches Jahrbuch* 10 (1975): 138–201, where poem 18, "Nimium ne crede mulieri," cites his "Quisquis eris" (PL 171.1684).

Chapter 4

1. See above all Georges Duby, *The Knight, the Lady, and the Priest: The Making of Modern Marriage in Medieval France*, tr. Barbara Bray (New York, 1983). He had already provided a short and useful discussion of the affair in *Medieval Marriage* (Baltimore, 1978), 25–45; in a passage quoted there (121, note 47), Orderic Vitalis says that the king *in malitia perduravit* ("persisted in this evil"). Crusade ideology around 1100 is well treated by Jonathan Riley-Smith, *The First Crusade and the Idea of Crusading* (Philadelphia, 1986); the role of the tournament, a more ignored topic, has been carefully examined by Maurice Keen, *Chivalry* (New Haven, Conn., 1984).

2. Urban's papacy has been studied in detail by Alfons Becker, *Papst Urban II. (1088–1099)* (Stuttgart, 1964). The pope's policy in France is discussed 187–226; the French trip ("the high point of his French politics, the world-historic highpoint of his papacy") 213–16. See also René Crozet, "Le Voyage d'Urbain II et ses négociations avec le clergé de France (1095–1096)," *Revue Historique* 179 (1937): 271–310; and Jean-Marc Bienvenu, "Les caractères originaux de la réforme grégorienne dans le diocèse d'Angers," *Bulletin Philologique et Historique* (1968): 545–60.

3. See Brian Stock's valuable comments in the opening chapters of *The Implications of Literacy* (Princeton, N.J., 1983). Aristocratic literacy at this time extended in central France well beyond the levels of much of Europe. Marbod notes

that Angevin nobles routinely sent their children to school; see C. Stephen Jaeger, *The Origins of Courtliness: Civilizing Trends and the Formation of Courtly Ideals 939–1210* (Philadelphia, 1985), 225 and note. Lay literacy was also important even below the aristocracy; see, for instance, Alfred Leroux, "Quelques manuscrits du château de Las Tours en Limousin," *Bulletin de la Société Archéologique et Historique du Limousin* 56 (1907): 299–302.

4. The historical summary that follows represents a digest of the lengthy introductory essay on William's life which I included in my *The Poetry of William VII, Count of Poitiers, IX Duke of Aquitaine* (New York, 1982), xv–xlix, where full sources are indicated. Until George Beech completes his biography, the primary source remains Alfred Richard, *Histoire des comtes de Poitou* (Paris, 1910). Beech has reviewed medieval evaluations in his useful survey, "Contemporary Views of William the Troubadour, IXth Duke of Aquitaine," in *Medieval Lives and the Historian*, ed. Neithard Bulst and Jean-Philippe Genet (Kalamazoo, Mich., 1986), 73–89. See also the important overview by Jane Martindale, "'Cavalaria et Orgueil': Duke William IX of Aquitaine and the Historian," in *The Ideals and Practice of Medieval Knighthood: II*, ed. Christopher Harper-Bill and Ruth Harvey (Woodbridge, 1988), 87–116, who stresses the traditional nature of the Count's political and social policies.

5. The affair with Maubergeonne has been carefully examined by François Villard, "Guillaume IX d'Aquitaine et le concile de Reims de 1119," *Cahiers de Civilisation Médiévale* 16 (1973): 295–302.

6. Song 1.1–3: Companho, farai un vers tot covinen Ez aura.i mais de foudatz no.i a de sen Ez er totz mesclatz d'amor e de joi e de joven. Song 2.13–15: Qu'eu anc non vi nulla domn'ab tan gran fei Qui no vol prendre son plait on sap mercei, S'om la loigna de proessa, que ab malvastatz non plaidei. Song 3.4–6: Pero dirai vos de con, cals es sa leis, Com sel hom que mal n'a fait e peitz n'a pres: Si com autra res en merma, qui.n pana, e cons en creis. Song 4.25–30: Amigu'ai ieu, non sai qui s'es C'anc no la vi, si m'aiut fes; Ni.m fes que.m plassa ni que.m pes, Ni no m'en cau; C'anc non ac Norman ni Frances Dins mon ostau. Song 5.1–6: Farai un vers, pos mi sonelh E.m vauc e m'estauc al solelh. Donnas i a de mal conselh, E sai dir cals: Cellas c'amor de cavalier Tornon a mals. Song 6.22–28: Ben aia celui que.m noiri Que tan bon mester m'escari Que anc a negun non failli: Qu'ieu sai joguar sobre coisi A totz tocatz; Mas ne sai de nuill mon vezi, Qual que.m vejatz. Song 7.31–36: Obediensa deu portar A maintas gens, qui vol amar; E cove li que sapcha far Faitz avinens, E que.s gart en cort de parlar Vilanamens. Song 9.7–12: Ieu, so sabetz, no.m dey gabar, Ni de grans laus no.m say formir; Mas si anc nulhs joys poc florir, Aquest deu sobre totz granar E part los autres esmerar, Si cum sol brus jorns esclarzir. Song 10.13–18: La nostr'amor va enaissi Com la branca de l'albespi, Qu'esta sobre l'arbre tremblan La nuoit, a la ploia ez al gel, Tro l'endeman, que.l sols s'espan Per la fueilla vert el ramel. Song 11.33–36: Tot ai guerpit cant amar sueill: Cavalaria et orgoill; E pos Dieu platz, tot o acueill, E prec li que.m reteng'am si. Ed. and tr. Bond, Poetry; I have not included the disputed Song 8. Philological details can be found in Nicolò Pasero, *Guglielmo IX d'Aquitania* (Modena, 1973); and Frede Jensen, *Provençal Philology and the Poetry of Guillaume of Poitiers* (Odense, 1983).

7. Three examples should suffice: the sexuality and aggression of Song 1 versus the service and poetics of Song 7; the plain style of the heroic Song 11 versus the *ornatus difficilis* of the encomiastic Song 9; and the deep use of feudal concepts in Song 10 versus the equally deep use of Ovidian concepts in Song 6. I have examined these questions in detail in "Origins," a contribution to the *Handbook of the Troubadours*, ed. F. R. P. Akehurst (Stanford, 1995). That chapter revises and expands my views in *Poetry*, lv–lxxi. See also the important contributions from Hans-Erich Keller, "Le climat pré-troubadouresque en Aquitaine: Erich Köhler zum Gedenken," in *Mittelalterliche Studien*, ed. Hennig Krauss and Dietmar Rieger (Heidelberg, 1984), 120–32; and Laura Kendrick, *The Game of Love* (Berkeley, 1988).

8. The earliest theory of contradiction is probably the famous article of Pio Rajna, "Guglielmo, Conte di Poitiers, trovatore bifronte," in *Mélanges de linguistique et de littérature offerts à M. Alfred Jeanroy* (Paris, 1928), 349–60. For an early and clear exposition of the theory of progression, see Karl Vossler, "Die Kunst des ältesten Troubadours," in *Miscellanea di studi in onore di Attilio Hortis* (Trieste, 1910), 419–40. Ezra Pound may have articulated the first theory of multiple voices in his *Spirit of Romance* (New York, 1910; rpr. 1968), 39; its latest versions can be found in Kendrick, *Game*, passim; and Hans Ulrich Gumbrecht, "The Transgression(s) of the First Troubadour," *Stanford French Review* 14 (1990): 117–41. Maria Dumitrescu, finally, attempted to reassign Songs 7–10, "Eble II de Ventadorn et Guillaume IX d'Aquitaine," *Cahiers de Civilisation Médiévale* 11 (1968): 379–412. Lynne Lawner, "'Norman ni Frances,'" *Cultura Neolatina* 30 (1970): 223–32, interprets Song 4 as an attack on poets of the Loire School. For William's documented contact with Marbod and Baudri, see Beech, "Contemporary," 86, note 32.

9. The following discussion looks at developments outside the schools and is not limited to appearances of the abstract noun *curialitas* in MedLat, which have been documented by Jaeger (*Origins*, 152–73). He finds its earliest known occurrence in a German document of 1080, about two decades after the adjective "in the sense of courtly sophistication" first appeared coupled with *facetus* in a central French tract against Berengar of Tours. The rare vernacular derivative *cortezia* appears first in the poems of the moralist troubadour Marcabru (fl. 1130–50).

10. Is in aetate positus florulenta, cum gratissimae esset elegantiae, praesertim cum sicuti nobilitate genus ejus, ita et mirabili specierum conspicuitate polleret, aliorum quoque municipiorum, divitiarum etiam omnium claritate pateret. . . . Dum in aliquo, die quodam nescio quid acturus operis, esset vico, ecce quispiam ei astitit sub tiria lacerna, tibialibus sericis pedulum abscisione damnatis, muliebriter diductis a fronte crinibus et summas attingentibus ulnas, amasium potius exhibens quam exulem. . . . Hunc ipsum audivimus tantas, dum seculo viveret, cultiorum vestium habuisse curas, ut nullis ditioribus impar esset, adeo autem indignabundae habitudinis, ut facile cuipiam, vel verbo, aggressibilis nequaquam videri posset. . . . Cui inolitum quiddam curialissimum fuit ut, si quos reperiret, quos praeminere literis sciret, in libellulo, quem ad id operis secum ipse crebro gestaret, quemque pro suo captu dictitare prosa seu versibus cogeret, ut dum quorumque, qui super eo praedicabantur studio, dicta colligeret, ex dictis etiam singulorum sensa libraret. Quae siquidem quamvis per se non caperet, ex eorum tamen, quibus haec legenda pandebat, indubie sententia mox teneret, in quo potissimum

quis, aut in sensu aut carmine, accuratiora dixisset. Tr. (modified at times for greater literalism) John Benton, *Self and Society in Medieval France* (New York, 1970), 54–55. Ed. Guibert de Nogent, *Autobiographie*, ed. and tr. Edmond-René Labande (Paris, 1981), 52–59.

11. See the Introduction of Benton, *Self*, with bibliography; and the subtle reading of Seth Lerer, "Writing and Sexuality in Guibert of Nogent," *Stanford French Review* 14 (1990): 243–66. The *exemplum* about Evrard occurs in a section (I.8–11) where a series of such acts prepared the young Guibert, as their accounts prepare the reader, for conversion.

12. The appearance of this doubly didactic device (operating on the protagonist as on the reader) here within a context of individual conversion and class reform attests to an early interest in the development of mythopoetic means for the religious reform of the secular court.

13. See the discussion by Jacques Paul, "Le démoniaque et l'imaginaire dans le *De vita sua* de Guibert de Nogent," *Sénéfiance* 6, "Le diable au moyen âge" (1979): 371–99. Because his interest lies in monastic mentality, he does not analyze this anecdote.

14. The primary power of Evrard's tale for Guibert as well as for the reader derives from its role as reliable testimony, as he repeats in telling the story. The double conversion mattered greatly to the author, writing when popular religious movements—like those of Robert of Arbrissel and his disciples—threatened the black monk Guibert and his order. As Benton points out (8), Guibert's fame for objectivity rests upon his sharp critique of the authenticity of relics in *De Pignoribus Sanctorum* (PL 156.607–80).

15. Unless the French can be considered somehow naturally elegant, an assertion a foreigner is inclined to doubt, their model must have developed from certain antecedents. The Carolingian combination of poetry and politics might be a good place to start; see Peter Godman, *Poets and Emperors: Frankish Politics and Carolingian Poetry* (Oxford, 1987). But it lacked the cults of ladies and desire, as did the Ciceronian *elegantia morum* that functioned (Jaeger, *Origins*, 128–52) as the ideal for upper clergy in later court service; both may be necessary to explain the origins of the new French courtesy, but neither is sufficient.

16. For the French and English sources, see Henri Platelle, "Le Problème du scandale: les nouvelles modes masculines aux XIème et XIIème siècles," *Revue Belge de Philologie et d'Histoire* 53 (1975): 1071–96. Perhaps because of the date of the document, Platelle does not include Guibert's testimony. The German material has been carefully examined by Jaeger, *Origins*.

17. Tunc effeminati passim in orbe dominabantur indisciplinate debachabantur sodomiticisque spurciciis foedi catamitae flammis urendi turpiter abutebantur. . . . Patres antiqui . . . modestis uestiebantur indumentis, optimeque coaptatis ad sui mensuram corporis; et erant habiles ad equitandum et currendum, et ad omne opus quod ratio suggereret agendum. Ast in diebus istis ueterum ritus pene totus nouis adinuentionibus commutatus est. Femineam mollitiem petulans iuuentus amplectitur, feminisque uiri curiales in omni lasciuia summopere adulantur. *Ecclesiastical*, 8.10; ed. and tr. Chibnall, 4.188–91.

18. On the eleventh-century use of *curialis*, see Jaeger, *Origins*, 152–61.

19. Interea cum versificandi studio ultra omnem modum meum animum immersissem . . . ad hoc ipsum, duce mea levitate, jam veneram ut ovidiana et bucolicorum dicta praesumerem, et lepores amatorios in specierum distributionibus epistolisque nexilibus affectarem . . . talibus virulentae hujus licentiae lenociniis laetabatur, hoc solum trutinans, si poetae cuipiam comportari poterat quod curialiter dicebatur. Ed. Labande, 134–35; tr. Benton, *Self,* 79, 87, modified for greater literalism. My rendering of *in distributionibus specierum* (literally, "in the distributions of types") links it to the rhetorical technique of *distributio* (*divisio, dispositio*), dividing out a topic into several parts; see TLL, s.v.; *Rhetorica ad Herrenium,* 4.35.47: distributio est, cum in plures res aut personas negotia quaedam certa dispertiuntur. This suggests that Guibert might be describing the use of fictive voices to represent different aspects of a topic.

20. One can now gain a good understanding of the complex genealogy of these subjects by contrasting the treatments of Jaeger, *Origins,* passim; and Kendrik, *Game,* 53–73.

21. See Georges Duby, *The Three Orders: Feudal Society Imagined,* tr. Arthur Goldhammer (Chicago, 1980); and Jean Dunabin, *France in the Making* (Oxford, 1985), esp. 162–222.

22. The term "quasi-literate" was proposed by Franz Bäuml, "Varieties and Consequences of Medieval Literacy and Illiteracy," *Speculum* 55 (1980): 237–65 at 246, to describe "*illiterati* who must and do have access to literacy." On the general argument of the *Ruodlieb* see Werner Braun, *Studien zum Ruodlieb* (Berlin, 1962); Peter Dronke, *Poetic Individuality in the Middle Ages* (Oxford, 1970), 33–65; John Hirsch, "The Argument of the *Ruodlieb*," *Classical Folia* 27 (1973): 74–83; and Dennis Kratz, "Ruodlieb: Christian Epic Hero," *Classical Folia* 27 (1973): 252–66.

23. See the work of Rita Lejeune, *Recherches sur le thème: les chansons de geste et l'histoire* (Liège, 1948); and, with Jacques Stiennon, *La Légende de Roland dans l'art du moyen âge* (Brussels, 1963).

24. The existence of stories about Gauvain by 1100 has been demonstrated by Pierre Gallais, "Bleheri, la cour de Poitiers et la diffusion des récits arthuriens sur le continent," in *Actes du VIIème congrès national de la société française de littérature comparée* (Paris, 1967), 47–79. A later source says that "the count of Poitiers" loved to hear stories about Gauvain from a famous Welsh storyteller; see Jessie Weston, "Wauchier de Denain and Bleheris," *Romania* 34 (1905): 100–05.

25. [Historia] Quae . . . Creditur a grauibus fabula ficta uiris; Vera tamen falsis quaedam permixta uidentur Quae protestantur quanta facessat amor (119–22). His version of the tale occupies lines 117–320 of the letter-poem *Ad Bernardum,* edited by Angelo Monteverdi, "Una epistola di Rodolfo Tortario," *Studi romanzi* 19 (1928): 7–45; rpr. in *Saggi neolatini* (Rome, 1945), 249–87. The manuscript (Rome, Bib. Vat., Reg. 1357) contains only his works, dates from the early twelfth century, and probably comes from Fleury (Monteverdi, *Saggi,* 273), and thus is very likely an authorized copy if not an autograph. The collected works have been published by M. B. Ogle and D. M. Sullivan, *Rodulfi Tortarii Carmina* (Rome, 1933); and the letter-poems have been studied by Francis Bar, *Les Epîtres de Raoul le Tourtier (1065?–1114?)* (Paris, 1937).

26. Similarly Gumbrecht, "Transgression(s)," 128.

27. Erat tunc Willelmus comes Pictavorum fatuus et lubricus; qui, postquam de Jerosolima . . . rediit, ita omne vitiorum volutabrum premebat quasi crederet omnia fortuitu agi, non providentia regi. Nugas porro suas, falsa quadam venustate condiens, ad facetias revocabat, audientium rictus cachinno distendens. Denique apud castellum quoddam, Niort, habitacula quaedam quasi monasteriola construens, abbatiam pellicum ibi se positurum delirabat; nuncupatim illam et illam, quaecunque famosioris prostibuli esset, abbatissam vel priorem, ceterasve officiales institutorum cantitans. Legitima quoque uxore depulsa, vicecomitis cujusdam conjugem surripuit, quam adeo ardebat ut clypeo suo simulacrum mulierculae insereret, perinde dictitans se illam velle ferre in praelio sicut illa portabat eum in triclinio. William of Malmesbury, *Gestis*, ed. Stubbs, 670–71. I have translated *prostibulum* as "whore" (as in Leviticus 21.7) rather than "whorehouse," as earlier scholars have done, and interpreted *quaecumque famosioris prostibuli* as a genitive of quality; it seems much more relevant to the satire that the women rather than their establishment be well known. For MedLat *reuocare ad*, see Nier, 919. On William of Malmesbury, see Hugh Farmer, "William of Malmesbury's Life and Works," *Journal of Ecclesiastical History* 13 (1962): 39–54. The point that these are songs was made long ago by Pio Rajna, "La badia di Niort," *Romania* 6 (1876): 249–53.

28. See Richard, *Histoire*, 453–54. The early date for the Count's relationship with Maubergeonne depends upon the *Itinerarium* of Baudri of Bourgueil who, writing about IIII as bishop of Dol to the monks at Fécamp, explained his departure from Bourgueil with a transparent metaphor: "I emigrated voluntarily to Brittany, and chiefly because illicit shrubs (*adulterina fruteta*) were growing up in my rose garden—and many of them, as usual—from which I fled, since I could neither pluck them out nor hide them: because I preferred to transmigrate than to persist in pulling out the thorn bushes. I was afraid that I might fail under the burden of the task, and already the restless Poitevin storm had begun to blow foully"; PL 166.1173, where I correct *cum evellerem vel dissimularem vel non possem* to *cum vel evellere vel dissimulare non possem*.

29. An excellent account of ecclesiastic efforts to explain away the failure of the Crusade of 1101 has been made by Riley-Smith, *First*, 120–52.

30. The importance of contemporary Latin satire for the cultural elevation of vernacular lyric has not been well explored, despite the fact that William of Poitiers and others had a specific term (*casteis/castejars*, "chastisement") for the genre.

31. Reto Bezzola, *Les origines et la formation de la littérature courtoise en Occident (500–1200)*, vol. 2, part 2 (Paris, 1960), 293. See also Villard, "Guillaume"; and my *Poetry*, xxxvii–xl. Since the Count and Robert interacted intensely and repeatedly from 1100 onward, since William of Malmesbury's unusual term (*monasteriola*) for William's fictional foundation matches that of Robert's biographer Baudri of Bourgueil, and since the Count himself actually promoted a monastic foundation by one of Robert's companions, Bezzola's proposal seems likely. Both William's bishop, Peter, and William's wife, Mathilde, were strong supporters of Robert and Fontevrault.

32. Bezzola, *Origines* vol. 2.2, 293, points to the late legend of Robert of

Arbrissel's conversion of whores in Rouen, a connection I find as unconvincing as it is unproductive.

33. En Alvergnhe, part Lemozi, M'en anei totz sols a tapi; Trobei la moiller d'en Guari E d'en Bernart; Saluderon mi sinplamentz Per Sant Launart. . . . So dix n'Agnes a n'Ermessen: "Mutz es, qe ben es conoissen; Sor, del bainh nos apareillm E del sojorn." Ueit jorn ez ancar m'en estei Az aqel torn. Tant las fotei com auziretz: Cen e qatrevint e ueit vetz! Qe a pauc no.i rompet mos conretz E mos arnes, E no.us pues dir lo malaveig Tan gran m'en pres. 5.13–18, 73–84; ed. Bond, *Poetry*, 20–23.

34. While in Songs 2 and 3 William describes the women as *con* ("vagina, cunt"), a product of nature with its own "law," Songs 1 and 5 identify them as specific and historic individuals. On the former technique, similar to that of Horace and Marcabru (fl. 1130–45), see Stephen G. Nichols, Jr., "'Canso—conso': Structures of Parodic Humor in Three Songs of Guilhem IX," *L'Esprit Créateur* 16 (1976): 16–29.

35. Dos cavals ai a ma seilla ben e gen; Bon son ez ardit per armas e valen, Mas no.ls puesc tener amdos que l'uns l'autre no consen. Si.ls pogues adomesgar a mon talen, Ja no volgr'aillors mudar mon garnimen, Que meils for'encavalguatz de negun home viven. Song 1.7–12; ed. Bond, *Poetry*, 2.

36. Leo Pollmann, *Die Liebe in der hochmittelalterlichen Literatur Frankreichs* (Frankfurt, 1966), 77–99.

37. The topic of chivalry is often treated from a perspective which is both too ahistorical and too clerical. Keen, *Chivalry*, works hard to correct both distortions, and is particularly good on the importance of the tournament and its audience of ladies in the early development of chivalry. He connects the adoption of individualized devices for shields with the rise of the tournament and the new importance of identifying particular knights (126). Martindale, "'Cavalaria,'" analyzes as a historian William's concept of knighthood and power.

38. See Georges Duby's "Youth in Aristocratic Society: Northwestern France in the Twelfth Century," in *The Chivalrous Society*, tr. Cynthia Postan (Berkeley, 1977), 112–22; and Jean Flori, "Qu'est-ce qu'un *bacheler*?" *Romania* 96 (1975): 289–314.

39. I included a particularly mournful charter issued in 1119, a likely date for the lament, in my *Poetry*, 134–35.

40. See the work of Gerd Althoff, "'Nunc fiant Christi milites, qui dudum extiterunt raptores.' Zur Entstehung von Rittertum und Ritterethos," *Saeculum* 32 (1981): 317–33; Jean Flori, *L'Essor de la chevalerie, XIème–XIIème siècles* (Geneva, 1986); and Alessandro Barbero's thoughtful *L'Aristocrazia nella società francese del medeioevo* (Bologna, 1987). They all reformulate the problems of nobility and knighthood in a complex understanding of ideological and discursive factors. Barbero's analysis of William's chivalric poetry is important: "L'idealizzazione della vita cavalleresca non è, beninteso, un fenomeno puramente letterario; essa è radicata nella vita della società di corte, nel tono dei rapporti che uniscono il principe ai suoi uomini" (67).

41. The only other secular noble from this period known to have composed

vernacular songs was Eble II, Viscount of Ventadorn (1106–45), "who loved songs of joy until his old age. Ebolus . . . was very charming in singing songs, for which reason he attained for himself the greatest favor with [count] William, son of Guy," as Geoffroy of Vigeois puts it in the 1180s. See *Recueil des historiens des Gaules et de la France*, vol. 12 (Paris, 1877), 424, 445.

42. [Guillelmus Pictauensium dux] audax fuit et probus nimiumque iocundus, facetos etiam histriones facetiis superans multiplicibus. . . . Pictauensis uero dux peractis in Ierusalem orationibus, cum quibusdam aliis consortibus suis est ad sua reuersus, et miserias captiuitatis suae, ut erat iocundus et lepidus, postmodum prosperitate fultus coram regibus et magnatis atque Christianis cetibus multotiens retulit rithmicis uersibus cum facetis modulationibus. *Ecclesiastical*, 10.21; ed. and tr. Chibnall, 5.324–25 and 342–43. I have altered the translation of the last occurrence of *facetus* (Chibnall: "skillful") to underscore the word's repetition in the passage. Compare P. Rousset, "La description du monde chevaleresque chez Orderic Vital," *Le Moyen Age* 3–4 (1969): 427–44.

43. On William of Malmesbury and Hildebert, see Rodney Thompson, *William of Malmesbury* (Woodbridge, 1987), 71–72; on Orderic and Baudri, Chibnall, *Ecclesiastical*, 5.13–15.

44. Albert Poncelet, "Boémond et Saint Léonard," *Annalecta Bollandiana* 31 (1912): 24–44; Rita Lejeune, "L'extraordinaire insolence du troubadour Guillaume IX d'Aquitaine," in *Mélanges de langue et de littérature offerts à Pierre Le Gentil*, ed. Jean Dufournet and Daniel Poirion (Paris, 1973), 485–503: 499. I add to the evidence for the identification in my *Poetry*, l–li, where I also argue that this is the earliest extant song. It can be neither proven nor disproven that William attended the wedding at Chartres, if the testimony from that year listed by Richard, *Histoire*, is complete.

45. On this song, see Yves Lefèvre, "Réflexions sur une chanson de Guillaume IX," in *Actes du IXème Congrès d'Etudes Régionales de la Fédération Historique du Sud-Ouest* (Bordeaux, 1956), 1–7; Lejeune, "L'extraordinaire"; Alan Press, "Quelques observations sur la chanson V de Guillaume IX: 'Farai un vers pos mi sonelh,'" in *Etudes de civilisation médiévale: mélanges offerts à Edmond-René Labande* (Poitiers, 1974), 603–9; Allison Elliot, "The Manipulative Poet: Guilhem IX and the 'Fabliau of the Red Cat,'" *Romance Philology* 38 (1984–85): 293–99; Michel Stanesco, "L'étrange aventure d'un faux muet: blessures symboliques et performances sexuelles dans un poème de Guillaume IX d'Aquitaine," *Cahiers de Civilisation Médiévale* 32 (1989): 115–24.

46. Ab la dolchor del temps novel Foillo li bosc, e li aucel Chanton, chascus en lor lati, Segon lo vers del novel chan; Adonc esta ben c'om s'aisi D'acho dont hom a plus talan. De lai don plus m'es bon e bel Non vei mesager ni sagel, Per que mos cors non dorm ni ri Ni no m'aus traire adenan, Tro que eu sacha ben de la fi S'el'es aissi com eu deman. Song 10.1–12; ed. Bond, *Poetry*, 36–37.

47. Pos vezem de novel florir Pratz, e vergiers reverdezir, Rius e fontainas esclarzir, Auras e vens, Ben deu cascus lo joi jauzir Don es jauzens. Song 7.1–6. Del vers vos dic que mais ne vau, Qui be l'enten, e n'a plus lau; Que.ls motz son faitz tug per egau Comunalmens, E.l sonetz, ieu meteus m'en lau, Bos e valens. Song 7.37–42. Ed. Bond, *Poetry*, 28–29.

48. W. T. H. Jackson, "Persona and Audience in Two Medieval Love-Lyrics," *Mosaic* 8 (1975): 147–59. Leslie Cahoon's fine analysis, "The Anxieties of Influence: Ovid's Reception by the Early Troubadours," *Mediaevalia: A Journal of Medieval Studies* 13 (1989 for 1987): 119–55, seems to me to supersede earlier discussions by virtue of its subtle understanding of ancient as well as medieval authors.

49. See the discussion of this key term by Hubert L. Dreyfus and Paul Rabinow, *Michel Foucault: Beyond Structuralism and Hermeneutics*, 2d ed. (Chicago, 1983), 44–78.

50. Martin Stevens, "The Performing Self in Twelfth-Century Culture," *Viator* 9 (1978): 193–212.

51. Cited by Beech, "Contemporary," 87, note 45, with comments upon the source and its reliability, 82–83.

52. Kendrick, *Game*, esp. 53 and 157; and Jaeger, *Origins*, 161–68. Neither cites the important contribution of Antonio Viscardi, "'Stropha' e 'gab,'" in *Ricerche e interpretazioni mediolatine e romanze* (Milan, 1970), 179–89.

53. Unde increpitus et excommunicatus a Girardo Engolismorum episcopo, jussusque illicitam venerem abjicere, "Antea," inquit, "crispabis pectine refugum a fronte capillum quam ego vicecomitissae indicam repudium"; cavillatus in virum, cujus pertenuis caesaries pectinem non desideraret. Ed. Stubbs, *Gestis*, 671.

54. Sigmund Freud, *Jokes and Their Relation to the Unconscious*, tr. James Strachey (New York, 1960), 132.

55. TORTA CAPUT id est habens capillos refugos et tortos, scilicet crispos, quod contigit ex nimio calore et siccitate capillorum. Arnulf of Orléans, *Glosule Super Lucanum*, ed. Berthe Marti (Rome, 1958), 503. In William of Malmesbury's *Vita sancti Dunstani*, when the Devil is defeated, he howls "oh what has he done, this bald man?!" (o quid fecit calvus iste). The author adds that "[he was] taunting, or rather attacking a man who had ruinous locks with hair flying back from his forehead" (Jocatus vel potius grassatus in hominem cui, refugis a fronte capillis, damnosa caesaries erat); ed. William Stubbs, *Memorials of Saint Dunstan* (London, 1874), 262–63, who dates the book containing it to 1120–29 (xxxv). Here, as in Lucan, the word appears to refer to the presence, rather than the absence, of hair; and here, as there, that hair signifies potential harm (interestingly, *damnosa* replaces *formosa* in an earlier version). I found the parallel through the indices of Thomson, *William*. Joan Gluckauf Haahr has demonstrated that the monk-historian used Lucan to characterize William Rufus; "William of Malmesbury's Roman Models: Suetonius and Lucan," in *Classics*, ed. Aldo, 165–173 at 171.

56. Cicero, *De Oratore*, 2.61: "Men are most delighted with a joke when the laugh is raised by the thought and the language in conjunction." Freud, *Jokes*, 132: "a good joke makes, as it were, a *total* impression of enjoyment on us, without our being able to decide at once what share of the pleasure arises from its joking form and what share from its apt thought-content." Freud appears to owe a large and unacknowledged debt to Cicero's analysis, especially in the discussion of technique.

57. Platelle, "Problème," collects the repeated denunciations of long and curly hair in the Romanesque court.

58. Pero no m'auzetz tan gabier Qu'ieu no fos raüsatz l'autrier, Que jogav'a un joc grossier Que.m fo trop bos al cap premier Tro fo taulatz; Quan gardei, no

m'ac plus mestier, Si.m fo camjatz. Mas ela.m dis un reprovier: "Don, vostres datz son menudier Ez ieu revit vos a doblier!" Fis m'ieu: "Qui.m dava Monpeslier Non er laisatz!" E levei un pauc son taulier Ab ams mos bratz. E quen l'aic levat lo tau-lier, Espeis los datz; E.ill dui foron cairat, vallier, E.l tertz plombatz. E fi.ls ben ferir al taulier E fon jogatz. 6.43–62; ed. Bond, *Poetry*, 26.

59. Further support from the chronicler Geoffroy of Vigeois, who reports four anecdotes about the Count which feature wax, nutshells, a packhorse, and pepper; see my *Poetry*, Appendix. For the locution *ne vaut un peinge*, see AFW, s.v. Marcabru satirizes courtiers as *los acropitz penchenat*, "the well-combed squat-ters," who lie with their ladies to remove *la dolor del penchinill*, "the pain of the little comb"; *Poésies complètes*, ed. J.-M.-L. Dejeanne (Toulouse, 1909), 39.59 and 38.27.

60. Raoul Glaber, "Vita domini Wilhelmi abbatis," in *Geschichte der deutschen Kaiserzeit*, ed. W. von Giesebrecht (Leipzig, 1929), 2.317–18: nugacissima pene uni-versorum et inanissima [ed.: insanissima] [j]actitatio . . . lasciva ad omnes pene sermones ore tetricrepo juramenta.

61. See his rich essay, "The History of the Anecdote: Fiction and Fiction," in *The New Historicism*, ed. H. Aram Veeser (New York, 1989), 49–76, esp. 57. I have used the word "anecdote," but that Enlightenment term ("things not made pub-lic") risks anachronism. William of Poitiers knew it as a *comte* which, like English "tale," literally meant "an accounting." Its ubiquitous presence as an oral narrative of "deeds" deserves better attention.

62. Some idea of the prevalence of such japing in the medieval court can be had from Hugo Theodor, *Die komischen Elemente der altfranzösischen chansons de geste* (Halle, 1913), 97–105; Philippe Ménard, *Le rire et le sourire dans le roman courtois en France au moyen âge* (Geneva, 1969), 20–28; and Mario Mancini, "Forme e funzioni del comico," in his *Società feudale e ideologia nel 'Charroi de Nîmes'* (Florence, 1972), 133–63, who links the humor to the "bachelors" (young, landless fighting men) in French Romanesque society.

63. Cicero notes: "it certainly becomes the orator to excite laughter; either because mirth itself attracts favor to him by whom it is raised; or because all admire wit, which is often comprised in a single word, especially in him who replies and sometimes in him who attacks; or because it overthrows the adversary, or hampers him, or makes light of him, or discourages or refutes him; or because it proves the orator himself to be a man of taste, or learning or polish; but chiefly because it mitigates and relaxes gravity and severity and often, by a joke or a laugh, breaks the force of offensive remarks which can not easily be overthrown by arguments." *De Oratore*, 2.58; tr. J. S. Watson, *Cicero on Oratory and Orators* (Carbondale, Ill., 1970), 150–51. Michael Mulkay's analyses in *On Humor* (Cambridge and New York, 1988) delineate the social functions of humor with remarkable clarity and insight. Also useful is the intriguing study by Robert Adams, *Bad Mouth: Fugitive Papers on the Dark Side* (Berkeley, 1977).

64. Lo coms de Peitieus si fo uns dels majors cortes del mon e dels majors trichadors de dompnas e bons cavalliers d'armas e larcs de dompnejar e saup ben trobar e cantar. *Biographies des troubadours*, ed. Jean Boutière and A.-H. Schutz (Toulouse, 1950), 7. The unique *larcs de domnejar* might be an error for the formulaic *larcs de donar*. At the same time, one finds in OFr examples of nobles who are "gen-

erous with the body;" see AFW 5.175. Charmaine Lee analyzes well the historical, critical, and ideological roles of this text in "La 'vida' di Guglielmo IX," *Medioevo romanzo* 12 (1987): 79–87.

65. Paul Smith, *Discerning the Subject* (Minneapolis, 1988), xxxv.

66. Pound, *Spirit of Romance*, 39.

Chapter 5

The empirical base of this chapter owes much to Professor Kimberly LoPrete at the University of Oklahoma, who shared unpublished portions of her *A Female Ruler in Feudal Society: Adela of Blois (ca. 1067–ca. 1137)* (Ph.D. dissertation, University of Chicago, 1992), and generally helped me to keep one foot on the ground with her comments, criticisms, and suggestions.

1. David Herlihy, "Land, Family and Women in Continental Europe," *Traditio* 18 (1962): 89–120; Jo Ann McNamara and Suzanne Wemple, "The Power of Women Through the Family in Medieval Europe, 500–1100," in *Women and Power in the Middle Ages*, ed. Mary Erler and Maryanne Kowaleski (Athens, Ga., 1988), 83–101.

2. On the county in general, see the second volume of Henri d'Arbois de Jubainville, *Histoire des ducs et des comtes de Champagne* (Paris, 1859–61), esp. 168–284; Adela herself is treated in some detail by Alexandre Dupré, *Les comtesses de Chartres et de Blois* (Chartres, 1870). More recent work has altered earlier conclusions; see Michel Bur, *La formation du comté de Champagne, v. 950–v. 1150* (Nancy, 1978); Sharon Farmer, "Persuasive Voices: Clerical Images of Medieval Wives," *Speculum* 61 (1986), 517–43; and the contributions of Kimberly LoPrete, "The Anglo-Norman Card of Adela of Blois," *Albion* 22 (1990): 569–89; and "Adela of Blois and Ivo of Chartres: Piety, Politics, and the Peace in the Diocese of Chartres," *Anglo-Norman Studies* 14 (1992): 131–52.

3. On the relations between Adela and Ivo, see Rolf Sprandel, *Ivo von Chartres und seine Stellung in der Kirchengeschichte* (Stuttgart, 1962), esp. 101–15, 183–98; and the counter-opinion of LoPrete, "Adela," whose persuasive argument I follow here.

4. Ego Adela Blesensium comitissa et Willelmi gloriosi regis Anglorum filia Stephanique palatini comitis quondam uxor karissima; Emile Mabille, ed., *Cartulaire de Marmoutier pour le Dunois*, (Châteaudun, 1874), 78–82.

5. Stephanus Blesensis palatinus comes cum Guillelmo rege uolens firmare amiciciam, requisiuit ab eo in coniugium Adelam eius filiam. Quae consultu prudentum a patre illi concessa est; et cum magno satis tripudio illi sociata est. Ille apud Bretolium eam desponsauit; et apud Carnotum honorabiles nuptias fecit (V.11). *The Ecclesiastical History*, ed. and tr. Marjorie Chibnall (Oxford, 1969–80), vol. 3, 116. I have altered the translation of *cum magno satis tripudio*, which Chibnall renders "with due ceremonial," since *satis* is used elliptically by Orderic and other MedLat writers for "very." The dates of Orderic's writing have been determined by Chibnall, 1.45–48. For an analysis of the strategy involved in this alliance, see LoPrete, "Anglo-Norman."

6. Regius in excellentia vestra sanguis ex utraque linea descendens, nobilitatem generis in oculis hominum manifeste commendat. Sed hanc apud religiosas mentes morum probitas et larga ad erogandum manus, quantum didici, vehementer exsuperat. Unde miror qua ratione consobrinam vestram Adalaidem sicut vos ipsam amare dicatis, cujus adulterinos cum Willelmo complexus vel defendere vel protelare tanto studio laboratis, nec saluti vestrae vel illorum satis commode providetis, neque quantum periculum vel quanta infamia mihi super hoc immineat aliquatenus praecavetis; *Yves de Chartres: Correspondence*, vol. 1, ed. Jean Leclercq (Paris, 1949), 14–16. The dating depends upon its position at the beginning of the collection of Ivo's letters. LoPrete discusses the affair in "Adela," 135–36.

7. Vna tamen res est, qua presit filia patri: Versibus applaudit scitque uacare libris. Hec etiam nouit sua merces esse poetis; A probitate sua nemo redit uacuus. Rursus inest illi ditandi [ms, ed: dictandi] copia torrens Et preferre sapit carmina carminibus. Ergo ne timeas; nimis est affabilis ipsa; Ipsa dabit tempus et dabit ipsa locum, Vtque reor, non te comitissa remittet inanem; Sis licet ipsa rudis, more suo faciet. Nec tibi prestabit tantillum, quod meruisiti; Prestabit, quod sit lausque decusque suum. Pene sua est orbi iam munificentia nota, Extremos homines iam sua dona uocant. Ipsa michi nota est, nec ego sum cognitus illi; Occuluit sibi me rustica simplicitas. Nec nunc auderem premittere carmen ad illam; Sed uoluit mandans carmen habere meum. Quidlibet audiuit nuper de carmine nostro, Innuit applaudens, quatenus adiciam. Adicio, non quod par esse sue probitati Possit, sed uigeat ex probitate sua. Materies grandis mea carmina nobilitauit, Non mea nobilitant carmina materiam. Hanc morum probitas, hanc castum pectus honestat, Nobilis hanc soboles ornat amorque uiri. Sunt tamen et multi quos commendare puellis Et decus et probitas et sua forma queat, Hanc qui temptassent; sed quid temptasse iuuaret? Seruat pacta sui non uiolanda thori. *Baldricus Burgulianus Carmina*, ed. Karlheinz Hilbert (Heidelberg, 1979), 134.37–66. I have emended *dictandi copia* to *ditandi copia*, "a flowing source of generosity," since the entire passage (39–50) concerns the poet's faith in Adela's *liberalitas*, and since *rursus* indicates a contradiction.

8. Desipit et peccat, qui te mortalibus equat; Est in laude parum, sed eris mihi prima dearum. *Hildebertus Carmina Minora*, ed. A. Brian Scott (Leipzig, 1969), 4.

9. Attritae frontis est egestas; nihil pudet, dummodo juvet. Egestas et ad crimen urget et intercedit ad veniam. Ignosces igitur si quid, ea urgente, supra meritum postulabo. Doces me sperare majora meritis, quae meritis majora largiri non desistis. Si quaeris quid aut qua fiducia postulem: planeta indigeo, eam mihi promisisti. Sicut arbitror, non deseres promissum quae etiam non promissa festinas erogare. Vale. PL 171.284.

10. Stephanus comes Adelae comitissae, dulcissimae amicae, uxori suae, quicquid mens sua melius aut benignius excogitare potest. Notum sit dilectioni tuae, Romaniam me cum omni honore omnique corporea sospitate iter beatum tenere. Vitae meae ac peregrinationis seriem a Constantinopoli litteratorie tibi mandare curaui; sed ne legato illi aliquod infortunium contigerit, tibi has rescribo litteras. Ad urbem Constantinopolim cum ingenti gaudio, Dei gratia, perueni. Imperator vero digne et honeste, et quasi filium suum me diligentissime suscepit, et amplissimis ac pretiosissimis donis dotauit; et in toto Dei exercitu non est dux neque

comes neque aliqua potens persona, cui magis credat vel faueat quam mihi. Vere mi dilecta, ejus imperialis dignitas me persaepe monuit et monet, ut unum ex filiis nostris ei commendemus: ipse uero tantum tamque praeclarum honorem se ei attributurum promisit, quod nostro minime inuidebit. In ueritate tibi dico, hodie talis uiuens homo non est sub caelo. Ipse enim omnes principes nostros largissime ditat, milites cunctos donis releuat, pauperes omnes dapibus recreat. . . . Pater, mi dilecta, tuus multa et magna dedit, sed ad hunc paene nihil fuit. Haec parua de eo tibi scribere dilexi, ut paululum quis esset cognosceres. . . .

Pauca certe sunt, carissima, quae tibi de multis scribo, et quia tibi exprimere non ualeo quae sunt in animo meo; carissima, mando ut bene agas, et [res] terrae tuae egregie disponas, et natos tuos et homines tuos honeste, ut decet te, tractes, quia quam citius potero me certe uidebis. Vale. *Epistulae et chartae: Die Kreuzzugsbriefe aus den Jahren 1088–1100*, ed. Heinrich Hagenmeyer (Innsbruck, 1901; rpr. Hildesheim, 1973), 138–39 and 152; I have altered the punctuation in the last sentence of the translation.

11. Stephanus quoque Blesensis palatinus comes pene ab omnibus derogabatur, et indesinenter uerecundabatur, eo quod de obsidione Antiochena turpiter aufugerit, et gloriosos sodales suos in martirio Christi agonizantes deseruerit. A multis personis multoties corripiebatur, et militiam Christi tam terrore quam confusione repetere cogebatur. Ad hoc etiam Adela uxor eius frequenter eum commonebat, et inter amicabilis coniugii blandimenta dicebat, 'Absit a te domine mi ut tantorum diu digneris hominum opprobria perpeti. Famosam strenuitatem iuuentutis tuae recole, et arma laudabilis militiae ad multorum salutem milium arripe, ut inde Christicolis ingens in toto orbe oriatur exultatio, ethnicisque formido suaeque scelerosae legis publica deiectio.' Haec et multa his similia mulier sagax et animosa uiro suo protulit. . . (X.20). *Ecclesiastical*, ed. and tr. Chibnall, 5.324. I have abandoned her rendering ("between conjugal caresses") of *inter amicabilis coniugii blandimenta* in order to see the means of Adela's persuasion. Interpretations of this passage in James Brundage, "An Errant Crusader: Stephen of Blois," *Traditio* 16 (1960): 380–95; and Farmer, "Persuasive."

12. Cum totus Blesis comitissam praedicet orbis, Inclinemus in hanc sub breuitate manum. Sed uariis intrans uernantem floribus ortum, Nescio quem de tot floribus ante legam. Tot bona concurrunt dum singula mente reuoluo, Vt dubius reddar quid prius excipiam! Femina nulla potest reperiri tempore nostro Cui data commoda sint tantaque totque simul: Si genus inquiris, soror est et filia regis; Si uitae meritum, relligiosa satis; Si maiestatem, ducis est et mater et uxor; Si rerum summam, res sibi multa domi. Res amplas fortuna dedit, natura decorem, Sed neque res fastus nec decor opprobrium. Quanto ditior est, tanto minus illa superbit; Et quanto plus est pulchra, pudica magis; Nec mores peruertit honor nec forma pudorem. Rara tamen res est forma pudorque simul. Femina res leuis est; haec, cum sit femina, non est Femina, femineae nil leuitatis habens! Est mulier sexu, sed agendo uiriliter uir, Qua duce stat regni gloria et usque uiget: In fragili sexu uigor est animusque uirilis [. . .]. In André Boutemy, "Deux pièces inédites du manuscrit 749 de Douai," *Latomus* 2 (1938): 123–30 at 126–27. One final verse is missing, since the poem is constructed of distichs but ends with a hexameter, as Boutemy notes. On the manuscript itself, where the poem appears on 105v–106r, see his "Notice sur le manuscrit 749 . . . de Douai," *Latomus* 3 (1939): 183–206, 264–98. He dates the

poem 1096–99 or post 1102, but, since the text describes her as *ducis est et mater et uxor*, it seems to me that it must have been written before Stephen's death in May 1102.

13. Anno ab incarnatione Domini MCVI in fine Februarii quando cometa longissimum crinem emittens in occiduis partibus apparuit, Buamundus famosus dux post captam Antiochiam in Gallias uenit, et Constantiam Philippi regis Francorum filiam uxorem duxit, et nuptias honorabiles apud Carnotum largiter administrante sufficientem apparatum Adela comitissa celebrauit (V.19). . . . Anno ab incarnatione Domini MCIII [for MCVII] Paschalis papa in Gallias uenit, et a Gallis honorifice susceptus diuinam seruitutem fideliter exercuit. Tunc uenerabilis Iuo Carnotenae urbis episcopus inter precipuos Franciae doctores eruditione litterarum tam diuinarum quam secularium floruit, a quo inuitatus papa solennitatem Paschae apud Carnotum celebrauit. Adela quoque comitissa largas ad ministerium papae impensas contulit; et benedictionem sibi domuique suae in aeternum a sede apostolica promeruit. Laudabilis era post peregrinationem mariti consulatum illius honorifice gubernauit, tenerosque pueros ad tutamen aecclesiae sanctae sollerter educauit (XI.5). *Ecclesiastical*, ed. and tr. Chibnall, 3.182 and 6.42.

14. Interdictus est, ut audiuimus, praecepto vestro filiis nostris canonicis Beatae Mariae exitus viarum, panis et aqua et omnia huic vitae necessaria quae sunt sub potestate vestra. Quod quid aliud est facere quam homines innocentes et arma non tenentes sine audientia et sine judicio morti destinare? Ita enim necat fames et sitis sicut gladius. Quod truces Turci, Christiani nominis persecutores possent truculentius edictum in Dei servos promulgare quam necessaria eis vitae subtrahere? Unde monendo consulo et consulendo moneo nobilitatem vestram, quatenus inconsideratum sententiae vestrae rigorem usque ad audientiam in melius commutetis, et non convictos, non judicatos tam severa sententia morti [non] addicatis. Ep. CLXXIX, in PL 162.180–81, understanding the capitalization of "Exitus Viarum" as a mistake.

15. Dignum censeo, serenissima domina, munus presentis operis mansuetudini vestrae supplici affectu dedicare, cum sitis nostri aevi multis preponenda proceribus, tum generositate preclara, tum probitate precipua, tum quoniam estis litteris erudita, quod est gentilitium sive civilitas magna. . . . Quibus si fueritis intenta, non deprimet inertia acumen ingenii vestri splendidum et honestum. Porro de virtutum vestrarum preconio, quas originis vestrae sublimitas et naturae felicitas nobis infuderunt, modo loqui erubesco, ne videar uti levitate parasitica. Loquor autem alias ubi fuerit oportunum. In *Monumenta Germaniae Historica: Scriptores*, ed. Georg Waitz (Hanover, 1851), 9.349–50. The prologue and epilogue are reprinted with excerpts from the chronicle in PL 163.821–30. Hugh's gloss (*sive civilitas magna*) indicates that *gentilitium* probably translates the vernacular *gentilesce*. The only other use of this word I have found comes from a late eleventh-century English monastic history, where the following interesting observation is made for the year 1043: "All the nobles began to speak the French language in their courts as a (sign of) great elegance" (Gallicum idioma [ceperunt] omnes magnates in suis curiis tanquam gentilicium magnum loqui); *Dictionary of Medeival Latin from British Sources*, fasc. 4 (Oxford, 1989), 1066.

16. Quoties quae circa te aguntur audio, laetatur et exsultat spiritus meus; audio enim te deduci in semitam mandatorum Dei, et ad terram viventium inoffenso currere vestigio. Audio etiam de locuplete pauperem spiritu, de splendidis-

sima et constipata cuneis obsequentium comitissa, humilem monacham, atque ad instar abjectioris ancillulae, caeteris filiabus Christi, quae tecum Domino serviunt, et providere quod necessarium est et officiosissime famulari. Sane haec mutatio, mutatio dexterae Excelsi. PL 171.145–46. Concerning the date of Adela's retirement to Marcigny, usually given as 1122 or later, see Chibnall's note in *Ecclesiastical*, 6.44.

17. Reto Bezzola, *Les origines et la formation de la littérature courtoise en Occident (500–1200)*, vol. 2.2 (Paris, 1957), 374. He argues there that she lacked the genius, imagination, and boldness of William VII of Poitou, and elsewhere flatly rejects influences from Medieval Latin panegyric (381).

18. I distinguish these two in the terms of Peter the Painter, a contemporary Flemish poet who complains about the shifting pattern of patronage: "For if a bishop's *ioculator* should sing to him, Then a *uersificator* should read him good verses, Which of them will he listen to and love the more? The one liked by the uncultured mob!" *Petri Pictoris Carmina*, ed. L. van Acker (Turnhout, 1972), 3.33–36. LoPrete has pointed out to me that one *Goffredus joculator* can be found in Adela's entourage in 1101, and that a document from 1132 confirms an earlier donation of two other *joculatores*, Radulfus and Ernulfus, to the abbey of Sainte Foy at Conques. See Mabille, *Cartulaire*, 60–62; and Gustave Desjardins, *Cartulaire de l'abbaye de Conques en Rouergue* (Paris, 1879), 353–54.

19. An appropriate example of the kind of panegyric that directly preceded the changes initiated by Adela can be found in the epitaph composed for her mother, Emma, in 1083 by Fulk of Beauvais. See H. Omont, "Epitaphes métriques composées par Fulcoie de Beauvais," in *Mélanges Julien Havet* (Paris, 1895), 223–24; and Eleanor Searle, "Emma the Conqueror," in *Studies in Medieval History Presented to R. Allen Brown*, ed. Christopher Harper-Bill et al. (Woodbridge, 1989), 281–88.

20. An excellent review can be found in Marjorie Chibnall, "Women in Orderic Vitalis," *Haskins Society Journal* 2 (1990): 105–21.

21. A good survey in English is Henrietta Leyser, *Hermits and the New Monasticism: A Study of Religious Communities in Western Europe, 1000–1150* (New York, 1984). See also L. Raison and R. Niderst, "Le mouvement érémitique dans l'ouest de la France à la fin du XI siècle et au début du XII siècle," *Annales de Bretagne* 55 (1948): 2–46; Herbert Grundmann, "Neue Beiträge zur Geschichte der religiösen Bewegungen im Mittelalter," *Archiv für Kulturgeschichte* 37 (1955): 129–82; Ernst Werner, *Pauperes Christi: Studien zu sozial-religiösen Bewegungen im Zeitalter des Reformpapsttums* (Leipzig, 1956); Jean Becquet, "L'érémitisme clérical et laïc dans l'ouest de la France," and Etienne Delaruelle, "Les ermites et la spiritualité populaire," both in *L'eremitismo in Occidente nei secoli XI e XII: Atti della seconda Settimana Internazionale di studio* (Milan, 1965), 182–211, 212–41; Jean Leclercq, "The Monastic Crisis of the Eleventh and Twelfth Centuries," in *Cluniac Monasticism in the Central Middle Ages*, ed. Noreen Hunt (Hamden, Conn., 1971), 217–37; Dominique Iogna-Prat, "La femme dans la perspective pénitentielle des ermites du Bas-Maine (fin XIème début XIIème)," *Revue de l'Histoire de la Spiritualité* 53 (1977): 47–64; Jacqueline Smith, "Robert of Arbrissel: *procurator mulierum*," *Studies in Church History*, Subsidia 1 (1978): 175–84; Jacques Dalarun, "Robert d'Arbrissel et les femmes," *Annales* 39 (1984): 1140–60; and his subtle revision and analysis, *Robert d'Abrissel, fondateur de Fontevraud* (Paris, 1986).

22. For Urban's deep interest in regular canons and apostolic life, see (in

addition to Becker, *Papst*) Horst Fuhrmann, "Un papa tra religiosità personale e politica ecclesiastica: Urbano II (1088–1099) ed il rapimento di un monaco benedettino," *Studi medievali* ser. 3, 27 (1986): 1–21. The term *seminiuerbius Dei* is taken from Acts 17.18.

23. Penny Shine Gold, *The Lady and the Virgin: Image, Attitude and Experience in Twelfth-Century France* (Chicago, 1985), 93–113.

24. The list of other itinerant preachers and former companions is given by Raison and Niderst, "Mouvement," 7–17.

25. Mulierum cohabitationem, in quo genere quondam peccasti, diceris plus amare, ut quasi antiquae iniquitatis contagium novae religionis exemplo circa eamdem materiam studeas expiare. Has ergo non solum communi mensa per diem, sed et communi accubitu per noctem dignaris, ut referunt, accubante simul et discipulorum grege, ut inter utrosque medius iacens utrique sexui vigiliarum et somni leges praefigas. Text edited by Johannes von Walter, *Die ersten Wanderprediger Frankreichs*, vol. 1: *Robert von Arbrissel* (Leipzig, 1903), 182.

26. Robert's beliefs in the power of a practical rhetoric, the promise of virtual naturalism, and the need for universal religious instruction seem to parallel closely those of Marbod, although the influence of the Angevin curriculum has never been considered.

27. For this interesting text, see PL 157.182–83; and Jean de Pétigny, "Robert d'Arbrissel et Geoffroi de Vendôme," *Bibliothèque de l'Ecole des Chartes* 5 (1854): 1–30. The terms being used here (*jucundus, alacer, humanitas*) indicate that Geoffrey, like Marbod and even Baudri, conceives of Robert as one of those new clerks whose success derived first from their eloquence.

28. Text, translation, and discussion by Jean de Pétigny, "Lettre inédite de Robert d'Arbrissel à la comtesse Ermengarde," *Bibliothèque de l'Ecole des Chartes* 5 (1854): 209–35. Not long after this letter, Marbod wrote Ermengard a sort of reactionary panegyric (PL 171.1659), that can be viewed as the end result of the reform pressure. Analyses of all related documents can be found in Therese Latzke, "Robert von Arbrissel, Ermengard und Eva," *Mittellateinisches Jahrbuch* 19 (1984): 116–54.

29. Smith, "Robert," 183.

30. See Marie-Thérèse d'Alverny, "Comment les théologiens et les philosophes voient la femme," *Cahiers de Civilisation Médiévale* 20 (1970): 105–21; and Jacques Dalarun, "Regards de clercs," in *L'histoire des femmes en Occident*, vol. 2, ed. Christiane Klapisch-Zuber (Paris, 1991), 31–54. The latter places useful restrictions on his conclusions, yet still collapses the three writers he examines and, in the case of Marbod, does not distinguish between his voices as schoolmaster and bishop.

31. Iogna-Prat ("Femme") and Bienvenu (*Etonnant*, 65–67) argue that only Robert's pathological sexual desire was in question, and that noble ladies must have objected to his perverted male desire.

32. See von Walter, *Ersten*, 156–59, on the social origins of the nuns, and 190 for the restrictions on dress in Robert's *Rule*; further details in Gold, *Lady*, 99–101.

33. Yet see Cicero, *Epistulae ad familiares*, 9.16: Nam etsi non facile diiudicatur amor verus et fictus, nisi aliquod incidit eiusmodi tempus ut, quasi aurum igni, sic benevolentia fidelis periculo aliquo perspici possit. For evidence of an

existing notion of service to ladies in the eleventh-century court, see the parodic passage (XIV.55–56) in the "proto-romance" *Ruodlieb* (1050–1075) where a young woman jokes about the man she is marrying, saying that "I want him night and day to serve me zealously; the better he does this the dearer he will be to me" ([S]erviat obnixe, volo, quo mihi nocte dieque, Quod quanto melius facit, est tanto mihi karus). Ed. and tr. Dennis Kratz, *Waltharius and Ruodlieb* (New York, 1984), 178–79. Peter Dronke, *Poetic Individuality in the Middle Ages* (Oxford, 1970), 33–65, analyzes the text as romance.

34. Victor Saxer, *Le culte de Marie Madeleine en Occident des origines à la fin du moyen âge* (Paris, 1959); Guy Lobrichon, "La Madeleine des Bourguignons aux XIème et XIIème siècles," in *Marie Madeleine dans la mystique, les arts et les lettres*, ed. Eve Duperray (Paris, 1989), 71–88; and Jacques Dalarun, "La Madeleine dans l'Ouest de la France au tournant des XIème–XIIème siècles," *Mélanges de l'Ecole Française de Rome: Moyen Age* 104, "La Madeleine (VIIIème–XIIème siècle)" (1992): 71–119.

35. For Geoffrey, see Dalarun, "Regards," 46–47, who notes in passing that "En 1084 et 1093 les premières femmes portant le nom de Madeleine sont repérées près de Tours et du Mans." Robert's interests have been described by Iogna-Prat, "Femme," 64; Delaruelle, "Ermites," 235–38; and Dalarun, "Robert," 1151–54.

36. Paris, Bibliothèque Nationale, f. fr. 2468, f. 111r: qui est celuy qui oseroyct dire qu'il auroit aulcune eglise en laquelle ne seroict licite femme entrer Sy per ses faultes et coulpes ne luy estoict prohibe? Ed. Jacques Dalarun, *L'impossible sainteté: La vie retrouvée de Robert d'Arbrissel (v. 1045–1116), fondateur de Fontevraud* (Paris, 1985), 297–98. There also exists a miracle about Robert's entering a brothel in Rouen to convert its prostitutes; see ibid., 349.

37. See Peter Dronke, *Women Writers of the Middle Ages: A Critical Study of Texts from Perpetua (†203) to Marguerite* (Cambridge, 1984), 84–97. Both Baudri and Hildebert call Muriel a "Sibyl," and the former also addresses other female correspondents with the same term. It would be interesting to see where and when the name "Sibyl" begins to appear in Romanesque France.

38. Hildebert inserts a hemistich from Ovid's *Ars amatoria* (3.549) at the end of the fifth verse, as Scott notes (17). The citation seems to hint at his private position on sex and authorship through its ironic reminder of Ovid's original usage (*est deus in nobis [uatibus] et sunt commercia caeli*), arguing that young women ought to love poets. Baudri of Bourgueil finds a similar disjunction between her great learned writing (*littera multa*) and her sex, although he typically restricts the frame: "when you recite . . . your words sound like a man, your voice was that of a woman" (ed. Hilbert, 137.9–10).

39. "Laudis honor, probitatis amor, gentilis honestas," in André Boutemy, "Recueil poétique du manuscrit Additional British Museum 24199," *Latomus* 2 (1938): 30–52 at 42–44. As he notes (34), form and content indicate that the collection is French and dates from the late eleventh or early twelfth century.

40. Helpful background is provided by Penelope Johnson's fine study, *Equal in Monastic Profession: Religious Women in Medieval France* (Chicago, 1991). I reviewed the arguments for the historicity of Constance and her letter-poem in Chapter 2, note 71.

41. Dronke, *Women*, 84–97, analyzes the debt to Ovid. Constance eliminates Ovid's irony, which so often works against the female voice. In this, she rescues the Sapphic narrator from her Ovidian master, and should be considered within the framework set by Joan DeJean, "Fictions of Sappho," *Critical Inquiry* 13 (1987): 787–805.

42. The privileged status of these subjects is stressed in the epitaph Baudri wrote for her (as I presume), where he devotes one couplet to each; ed. Hilbert, carmen 213.1–6.

43. Henri Platelle, "Le problème du scandale: les nouvelles modes masculines aux XIème et XIIème siècles," *Revue Belge de Philologie et d'Histoire* 53 (1975): 1071–96 at 1075.

44. Peter the Painter, *Carmina*, ed. van Acker, carmina 14 and 16, esp. 14.255–291; Guibert of Nogent, *Self and Society in Medieval France*, tr. John Benton (New York, 1970), 65–66; *Autobiographie*, ed. and tr. Edmond-René Labande (Paris, 1981), 78–82 at 80.

45. I have made an extended analysis of this letter-poem in "Composing Yourself: Ovid's *Heroides*, Baudri of Bourgueil and the Problem of Persona," *Mediaevalia* 13, "Ovid in Medieval Culture," ed. Marilynn R. Desmond (1989 for 1987): 83–117. A different example of the contemporary use of the *Heroides* in the Loire Valley (one of the manuscripts belonged to a library at Blois) has been published by Jürgen Stohlmann, " 'Deidamia Achilli': Eine Ovid-Imitation aus dem 11. Jahrhundert," in *Literatur und Sprache im europäischen Mittelalter: Festschrift für Karl Langosch zum 70. Geburtstag*, ed. Alf Oennerfors et al. (Darmstadt, 1973), 195–231.

46. Hennig Brinkmann examined female panegyric closely in "Anfänge lateinischer Liebesdichtung im Mittelalter," *Neophilologus* 9 (1924): 49–60, 203–21; *Geschichte der lateinischen Liebesdichtung im Mittelalter* (Halle, 1925); and *Entstehungsgeschichte des Minnesangs* (Halle, 1926). See also Bezzola's study of Adela's court culture in *Origines*, vol. 2.2, 366–91; the catalogue by Therese Latzke, "Fürstinnenpreis," *Mittellateinisches Jahrbuch* 14 (1979): 22–65; and Elisabeth van Houts, "Latin Poetry and the Anglo-Norman Court 1066–1135: The *Carmen de Hastingae Proelio*," *Journal of Medieval History* 15 (1989): 39–62.

47. Janet Wolff's lucid *Aesthetics and the Sociology of Art*, 2d ed. (Ann Arbor, Mich., 1993) provides a succinct examination of these debates from what seems to me to be a reasonable position founded on the "belief that the experience and evaluation of art are socially and ideologically situated and constructed, and at the same time irreducible to the social or the ideological" (84; similar position with respect to psychoanalysis, 102).

48. I take these terms from her suggestive essay "Arachnologies," in *Subject to Change* (New York, 1988), 77–101, which has influenced my approach in this chapter. Speaking in particular of the novel, she defines overreading as "a focus on the moments in the narrative which by their representation of writing itself might be said to figure the production of the female artist" and adds that it also means to wonder about the conditions for the production of literature (83).

49. Godfrey of Reims has been little studied: Wilhelm Wattenbach, "Lateinische Gedichte aus Frankreich im elften Jahrhundert," in *Sitzungsberichte der Akademie der Wissenschaften zu Berlin* (Berlin, 1891), 97–114; John R. Williams, "Godfrey

of Reims, a Humanist of the Eleventh Century," *Speculum* 22 (1947): 29–45; André Boutemy, "Trois oeuvres de Godefroid de Reims," *Revue du Moyen Age* 3 (1947): 335–66; and his "Autour de Godefroid de Reims," *Latomus* 6 (1947): 231–55. Van Houts, "Anglo-Norman," argues (48–49) persuasively that Godfrey also composed the anonymous poem to William the Conqueror, "Plus tibi fama dedit quam posset musa Maronis," which she reedits (56–57).

50. OPTIMI VERSUS METRICE DICTATI Inclita progenies, patrie flos et specialis, Sis michi materies in carminibus generalis. Te mea Musa refert, mirabiliter modulando, Te cunctis prefert preconia tot numerando. Si, dea, nobilitas aut dives gloria rerum, Et si simplicitas, prudentia dicere[nt] verum, Possent fatata vitare pericula mortis: Talibus ornata, quam posses vivere fortis! Omnibus est notum quantum sis dives avorum, Non valeo totum genus enumerare virorum. Pre cunctis apta rebus, si nata fuisses, Coniuge pro capta scio Grecia non doluisset, Sed quamvis alii te raptam Phrige dolerent, Te tamen imperii regalia sceptra decerent. Diceris et merito regali digna corona, Cuius dextra cito tribuit largissima dona. Lectio Nasonis non te latet, o veneranda, Sed neque Catonis [ed: Platonis] sententia vera probanda. Tu quoque barbarico nosti sermone profari: Ordine mirifico didicisti versificari. Sed michi da veniam,vacuantur sanguine vene. Cum iam deficiam, non possum psallere plene, Victa iacet mea mens; ingentes movimus actus, Redditus est amens animus meus et stupefactus. Wilhelm Wattenbach, "Beschreibung einer Handschrift mittelalterlicher Gedichte," *Neues Archiv* 17 (1892): 349–84 at 362. "Plato" is such an unlikely and inappropriate name in this context that I have emended to "Cato"; not only was Cato the Elder proverbial for his acuity, but the sententious *Disticha* of his fourth-century namesake Valerius Cato was used, like many of Ovid's texts, in elementary schooling. For Ingelrann's reputation, see the material cited by Boutemy, "Autour," 240–46.

51. Latzke, "Fürstinnenpreis," 63–64.

52. Williams, "Godfrey," 36. Ed. Wilhelm Wattenbach, "Lateinische Gedichte aus Frankreich im elften Jahrhundert," in *Sitzungsberichte der Akademie der Wissenschaften zu Berlin* (Berlin, 1891): 97–114 at 107–09. Latzke ("Fürstinnenpreis," 56) shows that Marbod's poem to Mathilde of England ("Ad reginam Anglorum," PL 171.1660) contains a similar catalogue of artificial beauty.

53. Viewed historically, Godfrey may well have adapted a model he developed for his former protector Manasses I, archbishop of Reims, the great prelate, politician, and patron who was forced from office by the Reformers in 1080; see John R. Williams, "Manasses I of Rheims and Gregory VII," *American Historical Review* 54 (1949): 804–24.

54. See Jean-Yves Tilliette, "La Chambre de la comtesse Adelle: Savoir scientifique et technique littéraire dans le c. CXCVI de Baudri de Bourgueil," *Romania* 102 (1987): 145–71; and with Patrick Gautier Dalché, "Un nouveau document sur la tradition du poème de Baudri de Bourgueil à la comtesse Adèle," *Bibliothèque de l'Ecole des Chartes* 144 (1986): 241–57.

55. Hanc decor insolitus et inequiperanda uenustas Commendatque simul gratia colloquii. Sed quis tam duram silicem molliri ualeret: Inspiciunt sine re; sed iuuat inspicere. Premia magna putant, dum spe pascuntur inani, Irritantque suos hanc inhiando oculos. Nec mirum, quoniam species sua tanta refulget, Debeat ut

cunctis prefore uirginibus. Hanc ego uidissem, nisi rusticus erubuissem; Ipsam quippe loquens inspicere erubui; Tunc nisi palantes obliquarentur ocelli, Mox exhausisset omnia uerba michi. Gorgone conspecta quamplures destituuntur Taliter a propriis protinus officiis Et coram Circe sic multi diriguere; Non etenim poterant numina [ed: lumina] ferre dee. Vix ideo uidi; uidisse tamen reminiscor, Vt reminiscor ego somnia uisa michi. Sic me sepe nouam lunam uidisse recordor Vel, cum uix uideo, meue uidere puto. Vix ipsam uidi; sed sicut et ipse recordor, Diane species anteferenda sua est. Ed. Hilbert, *Baldricus*, 134.67–88. I have restored the manuscript's reading in 82 because Horace speaks of the *Dianae numina* in Epodes 17.3.

56. In her edition, Abrahams dates the poem 1099–1102. But by virtue of its location in the unique authorized copy, the poem must be dated between the time of the birth of Adela's first son, William (implied by *soboles*, 62), ca. 1087 and the time Baudri had his early poetry copied in book form ca. 1096, as determined by the epitaphs it includes. Also, lines 64–65 and 73–74 imply that Adela is a "young woman" (*puella*, *virgo*), as does the comment about her generosity being "barely known to the world" (49–50). If the passage about her marital fidelity refers to Stephen's departure on the First Crusade, as scholars have assumed, then the poem was probably written in 1096.

57. Since Baudri's reworking of Fulgentius's *Mithologiae* lacks both beginning and end in its extant form, nothing is known about its immediate political context. Intellectually, it is closely linked to carmina 154 and 200.

58. Baudri's use of "Diana" for Adela, like Godfrey's "Marcellus" for Ingelrann, recalls the use of pseudonyms by the Carolingian court described by Peter Godman, *Poetry of the Carolingian Renaissance* (Norman, Okla., 1985), 6–8.

59. Augusti soboles, serie sublima avorum, Missa tibi placeant quantulacunque precor. Nolo manus sceptris, vel cervix apta corone Ad mea flectantur munera: mente fave. Ut satis est populo superum meruisse favorem, Cum cadit ad magnos hostia parva deos, Sic implet votum tua gratia. plus homine erro, Si plus affectem quam placuisse tibi. *Carmina*, ed. Scott, carmen 15.

60. Besides the thorough study of von Moos, see Wolfram von den Steinen, "Humanismus um 1100," in his *Menschen im Mittelalter* (Bern, 1967), 196–214; and Dalarun, "Regards." Hildebert's poem, "De Tribus Malis" (ed. Scott, carmen 50), cited by Baudri (ed. Hilbert, 87.19–21), is dated by its editor 1091–96.

61. See Alphonse Dieudonné, *Hildebert de Lavardin, évêque du Mans, archévêque de Tours (1056–1133)* (Paris, 1898), 44–47. Hildebert's fear suggests a possible date of 1098, as William Rufus's forces threatened Le Mans.

62. Absentia mariti laboriosior tibi cura consulatus incubuit. Eam tamen et femina sic administras et una, ut nec viro nec precariis consiliis necesse sit adiuvari; Peter von Moos, *Hildebert von Lavardin, 1056–1133: Humanitas an der Schwelle des höfischen Zeitalters* (Stuttgart, 1965), 341, discussion 58–59. Beaugendre dated the letter about 1101 (PL 171.144). Similar opening in another letter by Hildebert to Adela, PL 171.288.

63. See von Moos, *Hildebert*, passim; and on the late Carolingian use of those philosophers, Jaeger, *Origins*, passim. Adela adopts the voice of Reason in an unusual charter of 1104 where she describes herself as "having been instructed by

Stephen's governance by reason and being thoroughly terrified at the same time by the great number of my people who are missing" (Stephani magisterio rationis edocta simulque meorum mole perterrita delictorum); see M. Gemähling, *Monographie de l'abbaye de Saint-Satur de Sancerre* (Paris, 1867), 137–38.

64. Ecce habetis quod otiabunda legatis: actus videlicet antiquorum imperatorum et quorundam Deo amabilium virorum pariter memorabiles actus ab incarnatione dominica usque ad tempora prefinita. PL 163.822. In the translation, I have replaced the prologue's *ad tempora prefinita* with the epilogue's *usque ad obitum imperatoris Caroli Magni* (PL 163.828) for the sake of clarity. Two different dedicatory letters (1109 and 1110) exist, one to Adela and another to Ivo of Chartres; see André Wilmart, "L'histoire ecclésiastique composée par Hugues de Fleury et ses destinataires," *Revue Bénédictine* 50 (1938): 293–305. The longer letter to Ivo is much more cautious. Wilmart comments (301) upon the implications of substituting *diregere* for *dedicare* in the revision of 1110 for Ivo.

65. Waitz found fifteen manuscripts without looking very hard (PL 163.807); Nico Lettinck, "Pour une édition critique de l'histoire de Hugues de Fleury," *Revue Bénédictine* 91 (1981), 386–97, knows of 33. Manitius (*Geschichte*, Index) records Hugh's influence on Hugh of Saint-Victor, Orderic Vitalis, Gerald of Cambridge, and Ralph of Dicet. For Hugh's historical vision, see Lettinck, "Comment les historiens de la première moitié du XIIème siècle jugeaient-ils leur temps?" *Journal des Savants* (1984): 51–77.

66. It is worth noting that such ideas do not appear in the two other works Hugh wrote for her family: a *Tractatus de regia potestate* in 1100–1106 for her brother, Henry I of England; and the *Liber modernorum regum francorum*, originally promised to Adela but dedicated sometime after 1114 to Empress Mathilde, Henry's daughter and Adela's niece, the wife of Henry V of Germany.

67. Sed et mulier secus pedes Domini sedens audiebat verba oris ejus, tanto Phariseis et Saduceis non solummodo sed et ipsis Christi ministris melior, quanto devotior. Sexus enim femineus non privatur rerum profundarum intelligentia, verum, ut in sequenti lectione lucide declarabimus, solet aliquando feminis inesse magna mentis industria et morum probatissimorum elegantia. PL 163.823.

68. Unde sumpsit de femina carnem, ut haberet in ejus incarnatione ipsa humana natura, unde posset ad illam quam perdiderat beatitudinem ejus beneficio remeare . . . Quod autem de femina nasci voluit, magnum nobis benignitatis suae beneficium ostendit et immensum humilitatis exemplum. PL 163.823–24.

69. Ergo et vos Ecclesiae Domini filia haec eadem sacramenta intenta mente percipite, et letabunda legite, legendo credite.

Vive, vale, gaude, multa dignissima laude,
Progenies regum, cleri populique columpna,
Quam probitas morum, quam nobilitas atavorum
Exornant eque; cedant tibi prospera quaeque!

(Therefore with intent mind, oh daughter of the Church of the Lord, you too should learn these holy things and read the happy news and, in reading, believe. Live long, be well, rejoice, oh royal progeny most worthy of praise, pillar of the clergy and the people, whom upright behavior and nobility equally celebrate: may all good fortune come your way!). PL 163.824.

70. "Once her liberality had been planted throughout the world, schoolmen famous for both songs and verses came here in bands, and if the lady's ears were pleased by the novelty of someone's poem, he considered himself happy"; *Gesta Regum Anglorum*, ed. William Stubbs, vol. 2 (London, 1889), 494. Interestingly, Bezzola grants to Mathilde (*Origines*, vol. 2.2, 422–26) the literary court he denies to Adela.

71. Emily James Putnam, *The Lady* (New York, 1910), x.

72. Joan Kelly, "Did Women Have a Renaissance?" in her *Women, History and Theory* (Chicago, 1984), 19–50.

Conclusion

1. Meyer Schapiro, "On the Aesthetic Attitude in Romanesque Art," in his *Romanesque Art* (New York, 1977): 1–27 at 1.

2. Foucault provides a useful overview of his mature thinking about the history of the subject shortly before his death in the interview "Afterword (1983)," in Hubert L. Dreyfus and Paul Rabinow, *Michel Foucault: Beyond Structuralism and Hermeneutics*, 2nd ed. (Chicago, 1983), 229–52.

3. David Aers, "A Whisper in the Ear of Early Modernists," in *Culture and History 1350–1600*, ed. David Aers (Detroit, 1992), 177–202 at 186.

4. See, for instance, the very different studies by R. Howard Bloch, *Etymologies and Genealogies: A Literary Anthropology of the French Middle Ages* (Chicago, 1983); Evelyn Birge Vitz, *Medieval Narrative and Modern Narratology* (New York, 1989); and Sarah Kay, *Subjectivity in Troubadour Poetry* (Cambridge, 1990).

5. Richard Lanham, *Motives of Eloquence* (New Haven, Conn., 1976), 36. Lanham's "referential mystic" is Plato, not Augustine, in fact the latter plays no role in the author's conception of the Renaissance.

6. See "Marxism and Humanism," in *For Marx*, tr. Ben Brewster (New York, 1969), 219–41.

Select Bibliography

The following list is restricted to works of broad scope in order to provide an initial orientation for the general reader to topics addressed in this study. Specialists will find detailed documentation in the notes, and all editions and studies cited there can be found through the Index.

Aers, David. "A Whisper in the Ear of Early Modernists." In *Culture and History, 1350–1600*, ed. David Aers, 177–202. Detroit, 1992.

Althoff, Gerd. "'Nunc fiant Christi milites, qui dudum extiterunt raptores.' Zur Entstehung von Rittertum und Ritterethos." *Saeculum* 32 (1981): 317–33.

Althusser, Louis. "Ideology and Ideological State Apparatuses (Notes Toward an Investigation)." In *Lenin and Philosophy and Other Essays*. Trans. Ben Brewster, 123–73. London, 1971.

d'Alverny, Marie-Thérèse. "Comment les thélogiens et les philosophes voient la femme." *Cahiers de Civilisation Médiévale* 20 (1970): 105–29.

Barbero, Alessandro. *L'Aristocrazia nella società francese del medioevo*. Bologna, 1987.

Bates, David R. "The Character and Career of Odo, Bishop of Bayeux, 1049/50–1097." *Speculum* 50 (1975): 1–20.

Battaglia, Salvatore. "La tradizione di Ovidio nel Medioevo." *Filologia Romanza* 6 (1959): 185–224.

Bäuml, Franz. "Varieties and Consequences of Medieval Literacy and Illiteracy." *Speculum* 55 (1980): 237–65.

Becker, Alfons. *Papst Urban II. (1088–1099)*. Stuttgart, 1964.

Beech, George. "Contemporary Views of William the Troubadour, IXth Duke of Aquitaine." In *Medieval Lives and the Historian*, ed. Neithard Bulst and Jean-Philippe Genet, 73–89. Kalamazoo, Mich., 1986.

Belsey, Catherine. *Critical Practice*. London, 1980.

Bennett, Tony et al., eds. *Culture, Ideology and Social Process*. London, 1981.

Benson, Robert L. and Giles Constable, eds. *Renaissance and Renewal in the Twelfth Century*. Cambridge, Mass., 1982.

Bernstein, David. *The Mystery of the Bayeux Tapestry*. Chicago, 1986.

Bezzola, Reto. *Les origines et la formation de la littérature courtoise en Occident (500–1200)*. Paris, 1944–63.

Bienvenu, Jean-Marc. "Les caractères originaux de la réforme grégorienne dans le diocèse d'Angers." *Bulletin Philologique et Historique* (1968): 545–60.

Bloch, R. Howard. *Etymologies and Genealogies: A Literary Anthropology of the French Middle Ages*. Chicago, 1983.

Blumenthal, Uta-Renate. *The Investiture Controversy: Church and Monarchy from the Ninth to the Twelfth Century*. Philadelphia, 1988.

Bond, Gerald A. *The Poetry of William VII, Count of Poitiers, IX Duke of Aquitaine*. New York, 1982.

————. "*Iocus amoris*: The Poetry of Baudri of Bourgueil and the Formation of the Ovidian Subculture." *Traditio* 42 (1986): 143–93.

Boswell, John. *Christianity, Social Tolerance and Homosexuality: Gay People in Western Europe from the Beginning of the Christian Era to the Fourteenth Century*. Chicago, 1980.

Bourdieu, Pierre. *Outline of a Theory of Practice*. Cambridge and New York, 1977.

Boussard, Jacques. "La Vie en Anjou aux XIème et XIIème siècles." *Le Moyen Age* 56 (1950): 29–68.

Brinkmann, Hennig. *Geschichte der lateinischen Liebesdichtung im Mittelalter*. Halle, 1925.

Brown, Shirley Ann. *The Bayeux Tapestry*. London, 1988.

Bulst, Walther. *Studien zu Marbods Carmina varia und Liber decem capitulorum*. Nachrichten von der Gesellschaft der Wissenschaften zu Göttingen, phil.-hist. Klasse IV, n. F. ii, Nr. 10. Göttingen, 1939.

Bur, Michel. *La formation du comté de Champagne, v. 950–v. 1150*. Nancy, 1978.

Bynum, Caroline Walker. *Jesus as Mother: Studies in the Spirituality of the High Middle Ages*. Berkeley, 1982.

Cahoon, Leslie. "The Anxieties of Influence: Ovid's Reception by the Early Troubadours." *Mediaevalia: A Journal of Medieval Studies* 13, "Ovid in Medieval Culture," ed. Marilynn R. Desmond (1989 for 1987): 119–55.

Cardini, Franco. *Alle radici della cavalleria medievale*. Florence, 1986.

Chibnall, Marjorie. "Women in Orderic Vitalis." *Haskins Society Journal* 2 (1990): 105–21.

Classen, Peter. "Die Hohen Schulen und die Gesellschaft im 12. Jahrhundert." *Archiv für Kulturgeschichte* 48 (1966): 155–80.

Crozet, René. "Le Voyage d'Urbain II et ses négociations avec le clergé de France, 1095–1096." *Revue historique* 179 (1937): 271–310.

Dalarun, Jacques. *Robert d'Arbrissel, fondateur de Fontevraud*. Paris, 1986.

————. "Regards de clercs." In *L'Histoire des femmes en Occident*, vol. 2: *Le Moyen Age*, ed. Christiane Klapisch-Zuber, 31–54. Paris, 1991.

————. "La Madeleine dans l'Ouest de la France au tournant des XIème–XIIème siècles." In *Mélanges de l'Ecole Française de Rome: Moyen Age*, "La Madeleine (VIIIème–XIIème siècle)," 104 (1992): 71–119.

Delisle, Léopold. *Rouleaux des morts du XIème au XVème siècle*. Paris, 1866.

Demats, Paule. *Fabula: trois études de mythographie antique et médiévale*. Geneva, 1973.

Dörrie, Heinrich. *Der heroische Brief*. Berlin, 1968.

Douglas, David. *William the Conqueror: The Norman Impact upon England*. London, 1964.

Dronke, Peter. *Poetic Individuality in the Middle Ages*. Oxford, 1970.

————. *Women Writers of the Middle Ages: A Critical Study of Texts from Perpetua (†203) to Marguerite*. Cambridge, 1984.

Duby, Georges. *The Knight, the Lady, and the Priest: The Making of Modern Marriage in Medieval France*. Trans. Barbara Bray. New York, 1983.

————. *Mâle moyen âge: de l'amour et autres essais.* Paris, 1988.

————, and Philippe Ariès, eds. *L'histoire des femmes en Occident.* Paris, 1991.

Dunbabin, Jean. *France in the Making, 843–1180.* Oxford, 1985.

Dynes, Wayne. "Art, Language and Romanesque." *Gesta* 28 (1989): 3–10.

Economou, George. *The Goddess Natura in Medieval Literature.* Cambridge, Mass., 1972.

Elliott, Robert. *The Literary Persona.* Chicago, 1982.

Ernault, Léon. *Marbode, évêque de Rennes, sa vie et ses oeuvres.* Rennes, 1890.

Farmer, Hugh. "William of Malmesbury's Life and Works." *Journal of Ecclesiastical History* 13 (1962): 39–54.

Fiske, Adele. *Friends and Friendship in the Monastic Tradition.* Cuernavaca, 1970.

Flori, Jean. *L'Essor de la chevalerie, XIème–XIIème siècles.* Geneva, 1986.

Foucault, Michel. "Afterword: The Subject and Power." In *Michel Foucault: Beyond Structuralism and Hermeneutics*, ed. Hubert L. Dreyfus and Paul Rabinow. 2d ed., 229–52. Chicago, 1983.

Georgi, Annette. *Das lateinische und deutsche Preisgedicht.* Berlin, 1969.

Giddens, Anthony. "Action, Subjectivity, and Meaning." In *The Aims of Representation. Subject/Text/History*, ed. Murray Krieger, 159–74. Stanford, Calif., 1987.

Gold, Penny Shine. *The Lady and the Virgin: Image, Attitude and Experience in Twelfth-Century France.* Chicago, 1985.

Gravdal, Kathryn. *Ravishing Maidens: Writing Rape in Medieval French Literature and Law.* Philadelphia, 1991.

Grundmann, Herbert. "Litteratus—illitteratus." *Archiv für Kulturgeschichte* 40 (1958): 1–65.

Guillot, Olivier. *Le comte d'Anjou et son entourage au XIème siècle.* Paris, 1972.

Herlihy, David. "Land, Family and Women in Continental Europe." *Traditio* 18 (1962): 89–120.

Hexter, Ralph. *Ovid and Medieval Schooling.* Munich, 1986.

Jackson, W. T. H. "Persona and Audience in Two Medieval Love-Lyrics." *Mosaic* 8 (1975): 147–59.

Jaeger, C. Stephen. *The Origins of Courtliness: Civilizing Trends and the Formation of Courtly Ideals, 939–1210.* Philadelphia, 1985.

————. "Cathedral Schools and Humanist Learning." *Deutsche Vierteljahrsschrift* 61 (1987): 569–616.

Johnson, Penelope. *Equal in Monastic Profession: Religious Women in Medieval France.* Chicago, 1991.

Keen, Maurice. *Chivalry.* New Haven, Conn., 1984.

Keller, Hans-Erich. "Le climat pré-troubadouresque en Aquitaine: Erich Köhler zum Gedenken." In *Mittelalterliche Studien*, ed. Hennig Krauss and Dietmar Rieger, 120–32. Heidelberg, 1984.

Kelly, Joan. *Women, History and Theory.* Chicago, 1984.

Kendrick, Laura. *The Game of Love: Troubadour Wordplay.* Berkeley, 1988.

Kindermann, Udo. *Satyra: Die Theorie der Satire im Mittellateinischen; Vorstudie zu einer Gattungsgeschichte.* Nürnberg, 1978.

Köhn, Rolf. "'Militia curialis.' Die Kritik am geistlichen Hofdienst bei Peter von Blois und in der lateinischen Literatur des 9.-12. Jahrhunderts." In *Soziale Ord-*

nungen im Selbstverständnis des Mittelalters, ed. Albert Zimmermann, 227–57. Berlin, 1979–80.

Könsgen, Ewald. *Epistolae Duorum Amantium.* Leiden, 1974.

Latzke, Therese. "Der Fürstinnenpreis." *Mittellateinisches Jahrbuch* 14 (1979): 22–65.

Leclercq, Jean. "L'Amitié dans les lettres au moyen âge." *Revue du Moyen Age Latin* 1 (1945): 391–410.

———. "The Monastic Crisis of the Eleventh and Twelfth Centuries." In *Cluniac Monasticism in the Central Middle Ages*, ed. Noreen Hunt, 217–37. Hamden, Conn., 1971.

———. *The Love of Learning and the Desire for God.* 2d ed. New York, 1974.

Lenz, Friedrich. "Einführende Bemerkungen zu den mittelalterlichen Pseudo-Ovidiana." *Das Altertum* 5 (1959): 171–82. Repr. in *Ovid*, ed. Michael von Albrecht and Ernst Zinn, 546–66. Darmstadt, 1968.

Leotta, Rosario. "Il 'De Ornamentis Verborum' di Marbodo di Rennes." *Studi medievali* ser. 3, 29 (1988): 103–27.

Lerer, Seth. "Writing and Sexuality in Guibert of Nogent." *Stanford French Review* 14 (1990): 243–66.

Lettinck, Nico. "Comment les historiens de la première moitié du XIIème siècle jugeaient-ils leur temps?" *Journal des Savants* (1984): 51–77.

Leyser, Henrietta. *Hermits and the New Monasticism: A Study of Religious Communities in Western Europe, 1000–1150.* New York, 1984.

LoPrete, Kimberly. "Adela of Blois and Ivo of Chartres: Piety, Politics, and the Peace in the Diocese of Chartres." *Anglo-Norman Studies* 14 (1992): 131–52.

———. *A Female Ruler in Feudal Society: Adela of Blois ca. 1067–ca. 1137.* Ph.D. dissertation, University of Chicago, 1992.

Manitius, Max. *Geschichte der lateinischen Literatur des Mittelalters.* Munich, 1911–31.

———. "Beiträge zur Geschichte des Ovidius und anderer römischer Schriftsteller im Mittelalter." *Philologus, Supplementband* 7 (1899): 723–68.

Mann, Jill. "Satiric Subject and Satiric Object in Goliardic Literature." *Mittellateinisches Jahrbuch* 15 (1980): 63–86.

Martindale, Jane. "'Cavalaria et Orgueil': Duke William IX of Aquitaine and the Historian." In *The Ideals and Practice of Knighthood: II*, ed. Christopher Harper-Bill and Ruth Harvey, 87–116. Woodbridge, 1988.

Mauss, Marcel. "A Category of the Human Mind: the Notion of Person." In *The Category of the Person*, ed. M. Carrithers, S. Collins, and S. Lukes, 1–25. New York, 1979 [1938].

McGuire, Brian Patrick. *Friendship and Community.* Kalamazoo, Mich., 1988.

McNamara, Jo Ann, and Suzanne Wemple. "The Power of Women through the Family in Medieval Europe, 500–1100." In *Women and Power in the Middle Ages*, ed. Mary Erler and Maryanne Kowaleski, 83–101. Athens, Ga., 1988.

Monteverdi, Angelo. "Orazio nel Medio Evo." *Studi Medievali* n. s., 9 (1936): 162–80.

Moore, John C. "Love in Twelfth-Century France: A Failure in Synthesis." *Traditio* 24 (1968): 429–43.

Morris, Colin. *The Discovery of the Individual, 1050–1200.* London, 1972.

Munk Olsen, Birger. *L'étude des auteurs classiques latins aux XIème et XIIème siècles.* Paris, 1982–89.

Murphy, James J. *Rhetoric in the Middle Ages.* Berkeley, 1974.

Musset, Lucien. *La Tapisserie de Bayeux.* Paris, 1989.

Nichols, Stephen G., Jr. "Romanesque Imitation or Imitating the Romans?" In *Mimesis: From Mirror to Method, Augustine to Descartes,* ed. John D. Lyons and Stephen G. Nichols, Jr., 36–59. Hanover, N.H., and London, 1982.

———. *Romanesque Signs: Early Medieval Narrative and Iconography.* New Haven, Conn., 1983.

Offermanns, Winfried. *Die Wirkung Ovids auf die literarische Sprache der lateinischen Liebesdichtung des XI. und XII. Jahrhunderts.* Wuppertal, 1970.

Parker, Rozsika. *The Subversive Stitch: Embroidery and the Making of the Feminine.* London, 1982.

Pasquier, Henri. *Un poète latin du XIème siècle: Baudri, Abbé de Bourgueil, Archevêque de Dol, 1046–1130.* Paris, 1878.

Patt, William. "The Early 'Ars Dictaminis' as Response to a Changing Society." *Viator* 9 (1978): 133–55.

Platelle, Henri. "Le problème du scandale: les nouvelles modes masculines aux XIème et XIIème siècles." *Revue Belge de Philologie et d'Histoire* 53 (1975): 1071–96.

Plummer, John, ed. *Vox Feminae: Studies in Medieval Woman's Song.* Kalamazoo, Mich., 1981.

Raby, F. J. E. *A History of Secular Latin Poetry in the Middle Ages,* 2d ed. Oxford, 1957.

Rand, E. K. *Ovid and His Influence.* New York, 1963.

Regnier-Bohler, Daniella. "Imagining the Self." In *A History of Private Life,* vol. 2: *Revelations of the Medieval World,* ed. Georges Duby and Philippe Ariès, 311–94. Trans. Arthur Goldhammer. Cambridge, Mass., 1988.

Rheinfelder, Hans. *Das Wort 'Persona': Geschichte seiner Bedeutung mit besonderer Berücksichtigung des französischen und italienischen Mittelalters.* Beiheft zur Zeitschrift für Romanische Philologie, vol. 77. Halle, 1928.

Richard, Alfred. *Histoire des comtes de Poitou.* Paris, 1910.

Rigg, George. "Golias and Other Pseudonyms." *Studi medievali* ser. 3, 18 (1977): 65–109.

Riley-Smith, Jonathan. *The First Crusade and the Idea of Crusading.* Philadelphia, 1986.

Ruhe, Ernstpeter. *De Amasio ad Amasiam: Zur Gattungsgeschichte des mittellateinischen Liebesbriefes.* Munich, 1975.

Saxer, Victor. *Le culte de Marie Madeleine en Occident des origines à la fin du moyen âge.* Paris, 1959.

Schapiro, Meyer. *Romanesque Art.* New York, 1977.

Schumann, Otto. "Baudri von Bourgueil als Dichter." In *Studien zur lateinischen Dichtung des Mittelalters. Ehrengabe für Karl Strecker,* 158–70. Dresden, 1931. Repr. *Mittellateinische Dichtung,* ed. Karl Langosch, 330–42. Darmstadt, 1969.

Seidel, Linda. *Songs of Glory: The Romanesque Façades of Aquitaine.* Chicago, 1981.

Silverman, Kaja. *The Subject of Semiotics*. Oxford, 1983.

Smith, Paul. *Discerning the Subject*. Minneapolis, 1988.

Staniland, Kay. *Medieval Craftsmen: Embroiderers*. Toronto, 1991.

Stehling, Thomas. "To Love a Medieval Boy." *Journal of Homosexuality* 8 (1983): 151–70.

Stenton, Frank, ed. *The Bayeux Tapestry: A Comprehensive Survey*. London, 1957.

Stevens, Martin. "The Performing Self in Twelfth-Century Culture." *Viator* 9 (1978): 193–212.

Stock, Brian. *The Implications of Literacy*. Princeton, N.J., 1983.

Stuard, Susan Mosher, ed. *Women in Medieval History and Historiography*. Philadelphia, 1987.

Thompson, Rodney. *William of Malmesbury*. Woodbridge, 1987.

Tilliette, Jean-Yves. "Culture classique et humanisme monastique: les poèmes de Baudri de Bourgueil." In *La littérature angevine médiévale. Actes du Colloque du samedi 22 mars 1980*, 77–88. Angers, 1981.

———. "Hermès amoureux, ou les métamorphoses de la Chimère. Réflexions sur les *carmina* 200 et 201 de Baudri de Bourgueil." *Mélanges de l'Ecole Française de Rome: Moyen Age* 104 (1992): 121–61.

Traube, Ludwig. *Vorlesungen und Abhandlungen, II: Einführung in die lateinische Philologie des Mittelalters*, ed. Paul Lehmann. Munich, 1911.

Van Houts, Elisabeth. "Latin Poetry and the Anglo-Norman Court 1066–1135: the *Carmen de Hastingae Proelio*." *Journal of Medieval History* 15 (1989): 39–62.

Van Engen, John. " 'The Crisis of Cenobitism' Reconsidered: Benedictine Monasticism in the Years 1050–1150." *Speculum* 61 (1986): 269–304.

Vézin, Jean. *Les scriptoria d'Angers au XIème siècle*. Paris, 1974.

Viarre, Simone. *La survie d'Ovide dans la littérature scientifique des XIIème et XIIIème siècles*. Poitiers, 1966.

Von den Steinen, Wolfram. *Menschen im Mittelalter*. Bern/Munich, 1967.

Von Moos, Peter. *Hildebert von Lavardin, 1056–1133. Humanitas an der Schwelle des höfischen Zeitalters*. Stuttgart, 1965.

Werner, Ernst. *Pauperes Christi: Studien zu sozial-religiösen Bewegungen im Zeitalter des Reformpapsttums*. Leipzig, 1956.

Williams, John R. "Godfrey of Reims, a Humanist of the Eleventh Century." *Speculum* 22 (1947): 29–45.

Wilmart, André. "Le Florilège de Saint-Gatien: contribution à l'étude des poèmes d'Hildebert et de Marbode." *Revue Bénédictine* 48 (1950): 3–40.

Wilson, David, ed. *The Bayeux Tapestry*. London, 1985.

Witke, Charles. "Rome as 'Region of Difference' in the Poetry of Hildebert of Lavardin." In *Classics in the Middle Ages*, ed. Aldo S. Bernardo and Saul Levin, 403–11. Binghamton, N.Y., 1990.

Ziolkowski, Jan. "Cultural Diglossia and the Nature of Medieval Latin Literature." In *The Ballad and Oral Literature*, ed. Joseph Harris, 193–213. Cambridge, Mass., 1991.

Zumthor, Paul. *Langue, texte, énigme*. Paris, 1975.

Index

Abelard, 37
Abrahams, P., 221–22n, 226n, 229n, 230n,
    260n
accubitus, 138–40
Adams, R., 250n
Adela of Blois, 2, 16, 43, 58, 66, 68, 101, 109,
    119, 122, 128–37, 144–57, 159, 202, 251n,
    255n, 260–61nn
aditus, 57, 60, 73, 87
Ælfgyva, 18–19, 21, 23, 26–28, 31–36, 42, 74,
    157
Aers, D., 162, 262n
agency, 13, 16, 25, 30, 52, 77, 106, 128, 144–45
Agnes of Poitou, 108, 111
Alcuin, 48, 88
allegory, 27–8, 43, 85, 91, 107–8, 122, 148, 150,
    153
Alpers, S., 217n
alter ego, 36, 49–50
Althoff, G., 234n, 247n
Althusser, L., 11–14, 163, 211n, 262n
amica, 74, 116, 234n
Amis and Amile, 112
amor, 48, 50; *verus*, 50, 63, 112. *See also* desire,
    friendship
amplexus, 75
Andreas Capellanus, 49
Angers, 2, 8, 42, 79, 84, 130
Anscombe, G., 210n
Anselm of Bec, 47, 49
Aristotle, 6, 53, 80, 81
ars dictaminis, 45, 93
ars, 7, 22, 42, 83, 86, 141
Augustine, 8, 14, 49, 57, 86, 89, 96, 162–63,
    262n
author, 52, 77–78, 83, 86, 91, 93–95, 152, 237n

Baggio, S., 236n
Baker, D., 228n
Bal, M., 27, 216n
Banniard, M., 223n, 239n

Bar, F., 245n
Barbero, A., 234n, 247n
Barkan, L., 217n
Barthes, R., 212n
Bates, D., 214n
Battaglia, S., 227n
Battle of Maldon, 25, 39
Baudri of Bourgueil, 3, 8, 16, 42–69, 71, 99,
    100, 118, 122, 128, 131, 136, 142, 144, 147,
    149–50, 159, 163, 231n; correspondents,
    66–69
Bäuml, F., 235n, 245n
Bayeux Tapestry, 5, 18–41, 42, 58, 67, 73, 109,
    111, 149; artists of, 22–25
Bec, P., 216n
Becker, A., 241n, 256n
Becquet, J., 255n
Beech, G., 242n, 243n, 249n
Belsey, C., 211n, 212n
Benedictine order, 46–48, 70, 106, 109, 113,
    146
Bennett, T., 212n
Benson, R., 236n
Benton, J., 207n, 220n, 244n, 245n, 258n
Benvenuto, E., 13, 212n, 235n
Berengar of Tours, 71
Berger, J., 212n
Bernstein, D., 213n, 214n
Bernt, G., 222n
Bertrada of Montfort, 99, 114, 115, 119, 129,
    144
Bertrand, S., 214n
Bezzola, R., 114, 136, 156, 221n, 246n, 255n,
    258n, 262n
Bienvenu, J.-M., 241n, 256n
biography, 59, 63, 94, 97
Birkhan, H., 225n
Bloch, R., 40, 218n, 221n, 227n, 235n, 262n
Blumenthal, U., 219–20nn
Boethius, 7
Bohemond of Antioch, 119, 234n

Bordo, S., 218n
Boswell, J., 225n, 226n, 235n
Bourdieu, P., 212n, 217n
Bourgueil, 46
Boussard, J., 232n
Boutemy, A., 228n, 253n, 257n, 259n
Boutière, J., 250n
Bovie, S., 209n
Brandt, W., 26, 216n
Braun, W., 245n
Brecht, Berthold, 12
Brilliant, R., 215n, 217n
Brink, C., 7, 209n
Brinkmann, H., 221n, 258n
Brooks, N., 214n, 215n
Brown, S., 213–14nn
Bruckner, M., 215n
Brundage, J., 253n
Bryson, N., 31, 217n
Budny, M., 216n
Bulst, W., 94, 220n, 231n, 232n, 233n, 236n, 240n, 241n
Bundy, M., 228n
Bur, M., 251n
Burgess, G., 208n
Bynum, C., 207n
Byrhtnoth of Essex, 25, 39

Cahoon, L., 249n
Caillois, R., 227n
Campbell, M., 213n, 215n
Cambridge Songs, 35, 38
Canterbury, 23, 25, 35
Caplan, H., 234n
Cardini, F., 234n
Carmina Leodiensia, 38
Carolingian, 43, 48, 53, 56, 68, 69
Carruthers, M., 234n
censorship, 15, 38, 70, 99–100
chansons de toile, 29
character, 6–8, 61–62, 73, 112
Charlemagne, 111
charter, 221n
Chartres, 149
Chenu, M.-D., 84, 226n, 237n
Chibnall, M., 214n, 248n, 251n, 253n, 255n
Choulant, L., 236n
Christie, A., 214n, 216n
Cicero, 6, 7, 49, 50, 63, 85–88, 124, 126, 153, 222–23nn, 233n, 249n, 250n, 256n

Clarke, J., 222n
Classen, P., 220n
clerk, 13, 19, 29, 36–39, 67, 99, 122, 220n, 256n
close reading, 31, 144
clothing, 18–19, 29–31, 37, 107–9, 139, 143, 219n
Cluny, 113, 117, 160, 217n, 234
color, interpretation of, 29–30; rhetorical, 45, 55, 74, 76, 83, 84–88, 120, 124, 148
Constable, G., 223n, 224n, 236n
Constance (of Le Ronceray?), 63, 64, 142–43, 157, 229n, 258n
Constance of Arles, 108
Constance of France, 119
Council of Tours, 71, 106–13
court, 3, 38, 119, 122, 127
courtesy, 22, 40, 243n, 254n. See also elegance
craft, 29–30, 121, 127
crusade, 21, 100, 106, 112, 119, 123, 154, 234n
Crozet, R., 241n
culture, official, 21, 34, 39
Curran, L., 219n
Curtius, E., 57, 87, 217n, 226n, 228n, 235n, 237n, 239n
Cutler, K., 213n

d'Alverny, M.-T., 256n
d'Arbois de Jubainville, H., 251n
Dahlberg, C., 210n
Dalarun, J., 232n, 255n, 256n, 257n, 260n
Dalché, P., 259n
Dante, 120
Davis, N., 221n
Davis, R., 215n
DeBruyne, E., 213n
Degl'Innocenti, A., 234n
deixis, 30–31, 39, 216n
DeJean, J., 258n
Delaruelle, E., 255n, 257n
Delbouille, M., 220n, 231n, 237n
Delisle, L., 222n, 227n, 236n
Demats, P., 224n, 227n, 228n
desire, 3–5, 28, 34–36, 39–40, 44–45, 48–49, 62, 74–76, 100, 116–17, 136, 140, 143, 208n; and nature, 36, 52–53, 82–83. See also amor
Desjardins, G., 255n
Desmond, M., 227n
detail, 30, 217
De Viribus Herbarum, 80
dialectic, 47, 83

Diana, 148, 150
Dickey, M., 223n
Diekstra, H., 236n
Dieudonné, A., 260n
Digby, G., 22, 27, 215–16nn
discourse, 208n
dominism, 136–37, 155–56
Doomsday Book, 28
Dörrie, H., 224n, 229n
Douglas, D., 216n, 218n
Dreyfus, H., 208n, 249n
Dronke, P., 218n, 221n, 225n, 227n, 229n,
    230n, 245n, 257n, 258n
Duby, G., 33, 68, 207, 214n, 218n, 219n, 221n,
    230n, 241n, 245n, 247n
Dumitrescu, M., 243n
Dunabin, J., 207n, 245n
Dupré, A., 251n
Dynes, W., 208n

Eadmer, 25
Eagleton, T., 211n
Earnshaw, D., 219n
Economou, G., 237n
Eden, T., 236n
Edwards, R., 228n
Ehrmann, J., 227n
elegance, 2, 108, 207, 244n. *See also* courtesy
Elliot, A., 227n, 248n
Elliott, R., 6, 209n, 210n, 239n
Elliott, G., 211n
eloquence, 4–5, 20, 36, 39–40, 78, 86–88,
    100, 123, 153, 158
embroidery, 19–20, 22–25, 30–31
envy, 64
epistola, 47
epitaph, 43–44, 55
Erler, M., 214n
Ermengarde of Anjou, 101, 139
Ernault, L., 231–32nn
Evrard of Bretueil, 106–110, 112, 114, 118,
    244n
exile, 229n

fabula, 56–61, 239n, 245n
Faral, E., 84, 237–38nn
Farmer, S., 251n
Farmer, H., 232n, 246n
Ferrante, J., 218n
Fineman, J., 126, 250n

Fiske, A., 209n, 225n
Flood, B., 236n
Flori, J., 234n, 247n
Florus, 52, 53, 62
foedus, 45, 65
Foerster, R., 237n
Fontevrault, 137–38
Foreville, R., 215n, 218n
Foucault, M., 12, 28, 77, 121, 161–62, 211n,
    212n, 235n, 262n
France, 207n
Freeman, E., 213n
Freud, S., 14, 48, 124, 125, 249n
friendship, 48–53, 112. *See also amor*
Fuhrmann, H., 256n
Fulbert of Chartres, 70, 71, 87
Fulgentius, 58
Fyler, J., 227n

Gallais, P., 245n
Galletier, E., 238n
game, 38, 44, 54–56, 68–69, 75, 109, 222n. *See
    also* play
Ganymede, 51, 109
Gasparini, E., 217n
Gauvain, 112, 113, 117–18
Geertz, C., 208n, 212n
Gemähling, M., 261n
gender, 28, 137, 157
genetrix, 83
Geoffrey of Vendôme, 47, 138, 140
Geoffrey of Vigeois, 248n, 250n
Geoffrey of Vinsauf, 85, 238n
Geoffrey of Winchester, 90
Georgi, A., 237n
Gerald of Loudun, 47, 223n
Ghisalberti, F., 227n
Gibson, M., 216n
Giddens, A., 13, 211n, 212n
Girard of Angoulême, 123
Glaber, Raoul, 108, 126
Goddard, R., 237n
Godfrey of Reims, 47, 48, 53, 130, 144–48,
    157, 225n, 228n, 231n
Godman, P., 244n, 260n
Goffman, E., 10, 210–11nn
Gold, P., 214n, 256n
Goliard, 38
Gombrich, E., 215n
Gravdal, K., 33, 216n, 218n

Grundmann, H., 220n, 255n
Guibert of Nogent, 37, 106–110, 113, 114, 143, 207n, 244n, 258n
Guillot, O., 232n
Gumbrecht, H., 113, 243n, 245n

Haahr, J., 249n
Haberg, H., 223n
Haefele, H., 236
Hagenmeyer, H., 253n
Hallé, N., 213n
Halleux, R., 236n
Harold, earl of Wessex, 21, 25, 27
Haskins, C., 236n
Heath, S., 211n
Helen, 61, 144, 146
Henkel, N., 236n
Henry III, 108, 111
Herlihy, D., 251n
Hervaeus and Eva, 139
Hexter, R., 66, 227–28n, 230n
high story, 26
Hilbert, K., 113, 210n, 221n, 222n, 228n, 252n, 260n
Hildebert of Le Mans, 20, 48, 71, 72, 81, 87, 88, 100, 118, 132, 135, 141, 151, 157, 163, 225n, 231n
Hirsch, J., 245n
homosexuality, 3, 50–51. See also pedophilia
Horace, 6–7, 45, 86–90, 128, 161
hospitality, 22, 40, 215n
Hugh of Sainte-Marie, 135, 154–55, 157
Hugh of Langres, 231n
Huizinga, J., 56, 227n
humanism, 3, 120, 211n; Christian, 7–8, 71–72, 232n
Hume, D., 78
hypocrisy, 93, 98, 148. See also sincerity

ideology, 11–12, 15, 28, 106, 110, 126–27
imagination, 39, 56, 62, 89. See also ingenium
individual, 11, 13–15, 39, 68, 105, 122, 207–8nn
Ingelrann of Soissons, 145–47, 231n
ingenium, 7, 58, 62, 97, 142, 228n. See also imagination
intention, 8, 23, 26, 28, 78, 145
interpellation, 11–12, 29, 34, 41, 68, 112, 142
interrogation, 12
iocus, 58
Iogna-Prat, D., 255n, 256n, 257n

Iser, W., 73, 233n
Isidore of Seville, 55
Ivo of Chartres, 47, 130, 131, 135, 149, 151

Jackson, W., 121, 210n, 249n
Jacobson, H., 229n
Jaeger, S., 37, 111, 123, 210n, 219–20n, 230n, 233n, 242n, 243n, 244–5nn, 249n, 260n
Jagger, A., 218n
Jakobson, R., 30, 217n
James, S., 12, 211n
Jean de Meun, 8
Jensen, F., 242n
John, bishop of Orléans, 2–3, 100
John, Poitevin architect, 67
John Scotus, 83
Johnson, P., 257n
Jones, G., 208n
Jones, N., 219n
Joplin, P., 219n
Jungmann, E., 228n

Kantarowicz, E., 209n
Kaster, R., 209n, 239n
Katzenellenbogen, A., 216n
Kay, S., 262n
Keen, M., 247n
Keller, H.-E., 220n, 243n
Kelly, J., 157, 262n
Kendrick, L., 123, 210n, 227n, 243n, 245n, 249n
Kindermann, U., 90, 238–39nn
knight, 13, 73–74, 116–17, 234n
Köhn, R., 220n
Könsgen, E., 224n
Kowaleski, M., 214n
Kratz, D., 245n, 257n
Kraus, W., 229n
Krieger, M., 210n
Kristeva, J., 217n

Lacan, J., 14, 212n
LaCapra, D., 211n, 214n
lady, 13, 25–26, 137, 156
Laistner, M., 228n
Lanfranc, 40
Langlois, P., 228n
Lanham, R., 163, 209n, 210n, 262n
Latzke, T., 237n, 241n, 256n, 258–59nn
Laurand, L., 225n

Lawner, L., 243n
Leach, M., 225n
lecher, 28, 96
Leclercq, J., 45–47, 223–24nn, 225n, 255n
Lee, C., 250n
Lefèvre, Y., 248n
legibility, 22, 265n
Lehmann, P., 228n
leisure, 46–47, 71
Lejeune, R., 245n, 248n
Lenz, F., 228n
Leotta, R., 84, 232–33nn, 237–38n, 239n, 241n
Le Ronceray, 229n
Lerer, S., 244n
Leroux, A., 242n
letter, 47–8. See also *epistola*
letter-poem, 44, 46, 66, 71
Lettinck, N., 261n
Leyser, H., 207n, 255n
Liebeschutz, H., 228n
literacy, 2, 37, 100, 224n, 241–2nn
littera, 43, 67, 69, 141–42, 167n, 222n
Lloyd, A., 209n
Lobrichon, G., 257n
Loire School, 42, 46, 224n, 238n, 243n
Loire Valley, 4, 48, 80
LoPrete, K., 130, 251n, 255n
Lucan, 124
Lucas, A., 214n
lyric, 5, 45, 98, 100, 105, 128, 136, 154

Mabille, E., 251n, 255n
Macdonell, D., 12, 211n
Macrobius, 63
Malinowski, B., 220n
Mancini, M., 250n
Manegold of Lautenbach, 47, 223n
Manitius, M., 221n, 227n, 231n, 236n, 261n
Mann, J., 210n, 239n
Manning, P., 210n
Marbod of Rennes, 2, 8, 20, 31, 37, 38, 48, 49,
    52, 55, 71–98, 99–100, 117, 122, 128, 138, 140,
    148, 159, 163, 223n, 225n; *De Ornamentis
    Verborum*, 88; *Liber Decem Capitulorum*,
    49–50, 71–72, 87, 89, 97, 236n; *Liber
    Lapidum*, 79–80; influence, 241n, 256n
Marcabru, 120, 125, 250n
Marchegay, P., 229n, 234n
marriage, 99, 102
Martianus Capella, 58

Martindale, J., 242n, 247n
Marx, K., 11, 14
Mary Magdalene, 140–41, 155
matrona, 141. See also lady
Mathilde of England, 156
Matthews, G., 209n
Mauss, M., 208n, 209n
Maubergeonne of Châtellerault, 101, 114,
    116, 123
McGuire, B., 224n, 225n
McNamara, J., 251n
McNulty, J., 213n, 215–16nn
memory, 25, 39, 74, 234n
Ménard, P., 250n
Miller, N., 144, 217n, 258n
Minnis, A., 210n
Mohrmann, C., 223n
Monteverdi, A., 238n, 245n
Moore, J., 208n
Morris, C., 207n
Mulkay, M., 250n
Munari, F., 227n
Munk Olsen, B., 233n, 238n
Muriel of Wilton, 141, 257n
Murphy, J., 233n, 238n
Musset, L., 213n, 216n

names, 13, 34, 77, 111–12, 116, 137, 140
nature, 35, 42, 52–3, 59–60, 79–84, 91, 120,
    139, 148
naturalism, 80, 84
Neoplatonism, 7, 53, 56, 58, 81, 213n
Nichols, S., 208n, 214n, 247n
Niderst, R., 255n, 256n
Nitzsche, J., 228n
nugae, 38, 45, 63, 71, 92, 114, 123

Odo of Meung, 80
Odo of Bayeux, 20, 27, 31, 71, 78, 232n
Offermanns, W., 65, 227n, 229n, 230n, 231n
Ogle, M., 230n, 245n
Olivier, 112
Olson, G., 227n, 231n
omen, 27, 55, 76, 122
Omont, H., 255n
Ong, W., 235n
Orderic Vitalis, 20, 108, 109, 113, 118–120, 123,
    129, 131, 133, 134–36, 214n, 218n, 219n
Orléans, 2, 3, 57, 149
ornament, 27, 40, 120, 147, 153. See also color

overreading, 144–45, 258n
Ovid, 14, 30, 43, 53, 56–66, 71, 110, 120–21, 141, 146, 154, 162–63, 257n; *De Ponto*, 62; *Heroides*, 61–62, 143; *Metamorphoses*, 30, 56, 60, 237n; *Tristia*, 62, 96

Paden, W., 210n
panegyric, 20, 83, 144–45, 151–52
Panzer, F., 218n
Paris, 61–2, 148
Parisse, M., 214n
Parker, R., 214n
Pasero, N., 242n
Pasquier, H., 221n
patronage, 20, 131–32, 144, 156
Patt, W., 233n
Paul, J., 244n
Payer, P., 225n
pedophilia, 51–53, 61, 76
Pèlerinage de Charlemagne à Constantinople, 218n
Pereira, M., 214n
performance, 22, 41, 72–73, 75, 119
persona, 5–10, 60–64, 72, 77, 86–87, 89–98, 109, 117–18, 125, 138, 151–53, 159, 161, 209–10nn; and subject, 52, 105–6, 121, 143, 152. *See also* self-impersonation
Peter the Painter, 90, 143, 255n, 258n
Peter Damian, 50, 219n, 225n
Peter of Poitiers, 101, 102, 118, 123
Pétigny, J., 256n
Physiognomonia, 81
Physiologus, 81
pity, 63, 73–75, 97
Philip of France, 99, 100, 114, 115, 119
Philippa-Mathilde of Toulouse, 101
Platelle, H., 143, 244n, 249n, 258n
Plato, 6–7, 49, 146
play, 23, 73, 92, 122
Plummer, J., 218n
poetry, defense, 47, 65–66; and employment, 37, 92; and politics, 43, 122, 136, 150
Pollmann, L., 116, 247n
Poncelet, A., 248n
Pound, E., 128, 243n, 251n
power, 5, 28, 30, 61–62, 80, 116, 130, 152; symbolic, 30, 156
pregnant moment, 32
Press, A., 248n

production, 31, 54, 144
Putnam, E., 136, 262n

Quadlbauer, F., 223n
Quain, E., 227n
Quintillian, 85, 123

Rabinow, P., 208n, 249n
Raby, H., 221n, 230–31nn, 239n
Raison, L., 255–56nn
Rajna, P., 243n, 246n
Ralph of Dicet, 122, 123
Rand, E., 227n
Raoul Glaber, 250n
Ratkowitsch, C., 229n
reading, 47, 64, 77, 108, 137, 235n
recreatio, 65, 68, 72, 76
Reformers, 28, 68, 99, 102, 114, 117, 137
Regan, M., 235n
Regnier-Bohler, D., 235n
Renaissance, 28, 162–63; 12th-c., 3
resistance, 42
Rheinfelder, H., 8, 209n
rhetoric, 5, 21, 31, 38, 45, 55, 62, 84–89, 114, 154, 245n. *See also* color
Rhetorica ad Herennium, 84, 85, 223n, 238n
Richard, A., 242n, 246n, 248n
Riddle, J., 236n
Rigg, G., 220n
Riley-Smith, J., 241n, 246n
Robert of Arbrissel, 71, 100, 114, 137–41, 157
Rodolf Tortarius, 48, 50
Roger of Sicily, 55, 67, 68
Roman de la Rose, 8
Romanesque, 2, 4, 8–10, 16, 101, 122, 149, 160–61, 207–8nn
Rosenstein, R., 227n
Ross, W., 219n
Rouen, 18, 21
Rouse, M., 226n
Rouse, R., 226n, 227n
Rousset, P., 248n
Rovane, C., 210n
Roy, B., 228n
Ruhe, E., 47, 224n
Ruodlieb, 111, 257n
rusticitas, 45, 67, 87–88, 111

Saenger, P., 235n
Saint-Aubin, 70, 72

Samson of Bayeux, 232n
Sappho, 143, 258n
satire, 27–28, 90–91, 114, 119, 147, 246n
Saxer, V., 140, 257n
Schapiro, M., 160, 208n, 216n, 217n, 262n
schools, 2–3; lower, 66; cathedral, 37, 47, 70, 100
Schor, N., 217n
Schuelper, S., 226n
Schumann, O., 45, 221n, 223n
Schutz, A.-H., 250n
Scott, A., 252n, 260n
Scotti, P., 233n
Searle, E., 255n
secularity, 3, 20, 43, 67, 69, 75, 88, 113, 100, 122, 159
Sedlmayer, H., 210n
Seidel, L., 208n, 214n, 216n
self-impersonation, 6–8, 15, 38, 55, 68, 70, 89, 94, 106, 119. See also *persona*
Seneca, 153
Serlo of Bayeux, 20, 90
sexuality, 100, 102, 114, 141, 157
Shooner, H., 228n
Sibyl, 141, 257n
Silverman, K., 212n
Silverstein, T., 228n
sincerity, 9, 93. *See also* hypocrisy
Smith, J., 255–56nn
Smith, P., 13, 127, 211n, 212n, 251n
Smolak, K., 227n, 229n
Socrates, 7
Southern, R., 225n
Spitzer, L., 8, 210n, 218n
Sprandel, R., 251n
Stahl, W., 227n
Stanesco, M., 248n
Staniland, K., 215n
stare, 31, 75–76, 217n
Stehling, T., 225n, 232n
Steiner, W., 32, 215n, 217n
Stenton, F., 213n
Stephen of Blois, 129, 133
Stevens, M., 122, 208n, 249n
Stiennon, J., 245n
Stock, B., 67, 212n, 227–28nn, 230n, 241n
Stohlmann, J., 258n
Strecker, K., 219n
Stuard, S., 214n
Stubbs, W., 215n

subculture, 43
subject, 10–16, 40, 78, 88, 124, 143–44, 152, 158, 211–12nn; of academic discourse, 32, 65, 91, 145; of aggression, 111–12; Early Modern, 162; gendered, 29; history of, 111–12, 161–63; Humanist, 98, 127, 142, 147, 163; individual, 12, 14; loving 18, 41, 68, 100, 156; position, 14, 111, 127–28, 212; satiric, 91; split, 32, 76, 89, 119–21, 139, 148, 161
subjection, 12, 19, 33, 40, 51, 69, 153, 212n
subjectivity, 4, 12, 14, 40–42, 69, 142–43
subversion, 31, 40, 42
Suleiman, S., 218n
Sullivan, D., 230n, 245n
Sutherland, D., 210n
Sutton-Smith, B., 227n

textual community, 67
texture, 19, 29–30
Theodor, H., 250n
theory, medieval, 5, 70
Thompson, R., 248–49nn
Tilliette, J.-Y., 222n, 229n, 259n
tournament, 100
trait, 117–18
transgression, 27
translation, cultural, 18, 85, 124, 126
Traube, L., 43, 222n
Trendelenburg, A., 208n

Ullmann, W., 211n
Urban II, 3, 99, 100

Van Engen, J., 223n
Van Acker, L., 255n
Van Houts, E., 258–59nn
Vance, E., 209n
vates, 64, 88, 142
Velleius Paterculus, 7
Vézin, J., 232n
Viarre, S., 227n
Villard, F., 242n, 246n
Virgil, 53, 62
vis/virtus, 80, 84
Viscardi, A., 123, 225n, 249n
Vitz, E., 210n, 262n
voice, 4, 7, 16, 93, 97, 105, 117, 130, 142–43. *See also* self-impersonation, *persona*
von Moos, P., 153, 225n, 233n, 260n

von den Steinen, W., 224n, 233n, 260n
von Walter, J., 256n
Vossler, K., 243n

Waddell, H., 231n
Wagenvoort, H., 226n
Wailes, S., 220n
Waitz, G., 254n, 261n
Walker, H., 214n, 215n
Walsh, G., 220n
Walter, 81, 84, 88, 92
Walther, H., 231n, 240n
Watson, J., 250n
Wattenbach, W., 224n, 226n, 258–59nn
Waugh, L., 217n
wax tablets, 54
Wemple, S., 251n
Wenzel, S., 224n
Werkmeister, O., 214n, 217n
Werner, E., 255n
Werner, E., 255n
Werner, J., 231n, 239n
Weston, J., 245n
Wetherbee, W., 227n, 228n
Whitman, J., 227n
whore, 28, 114–16, 129, 140–41, 151

William the Conquerer, 18, 20–22, 58
William of Conches, 58
William, count of Poitiers, 2, 16, 21, 40,
    99–128, 136, 157, 215n
William of Malmesbury, 113, 118, 123, 124,
    126, 156
William Rufus of England, 20, 108, 124, 152
William of Poitiers, historian, 21, 33
Williams, J., 147, 231n, 258n, 259n
Wilmart, A., 230n, 261n
Wilson, D., 21, 212–13nn, 215n, 217n, 219n
wit, 38, 92, 101–2, 106, 113, 118, 122–27
Witke, C., 240n
Wolff, J., 258n
women, 3, 19, 25–29, 67, 83, 93, 116, 129,
    137–42, 154–55, 213. See also lady
Wood, N., 209n
Wormwald, F., 213n, 216n
Worstborck, F., 223n
Wright, T., 225n
writing, 48, 54, 77

Zeydel, E., 220n
Ziolkowski, J., 212n, 219n
Zumthor, P., 210n, 227n

University of Pennsylvania Press
MIDDLE AGES SERIES
Ruth Mazo Karras and Edward Peters, General Editors

F. R. P. Akehurst, trans. *The* Coutumes de Beauvaisis *of Philippe de Beaumanoir.*
1992

Peter L. Allen. *The Art of Love: Amatory Fiction from Ovid to the* Romance of the
Rose. 1992

David Anderson. *Before the Knight's Tale: Imitation of Classical Epic in Boccaccio's
Teseida.* 1988

Benjamin Arnold. *Count and Bishop in Medieval Germany: A Study of Regional Power,
1100–1350.* 1991

Mark C. Bartusis. *The Late Byzantine Army: Arms and Society, 1204–1453.* 1992

Thomas N. Bisson, ed. *Cultures of Power: Lordship, Status, and Process in Twelfth-
Century Europe.* 1995

Uta-Renate Blumenthal. *The Investiture Controversy: Church and Monarchy from the
Ninth to the Twelfth Century.* 1988

Gerald A. Bond. *The Loving Subject: Desire, Eloquence, and Power in Romanesque
France.* 1995

Daniel Bornstein, trans. *Dino Compagni's* Chronicle *of Florence.* 1986

Maureen Boulton. *The Song in the Story: Lyric Insertions in French Narrative Fiction,
1200–1400.* 1993

Betsy Bowden. *Chaucer Aloud: The Varieties of Textual Interpretation.* 1987

Charles R. Bowlus. *Franks, Moravians, and Magyars: The Struggle for the Middle
Danube, 788–907.* 1995

James William Brodman. *Ransoming Captives in Crusader Spain: The Order of Merced
on the Christian-Islamic Frontier.* 1986

Kevin Brownlee and Sylvia Huot, eds. *Rethinking the* Romance of the Rose*: Text,
Image, Reception.* 1992

Matilda Tomaryn Bruckner. *Shaping Romance: Interpretation, Truth, and Closure in
Twelfth-Century French Fictions.* 1993

Otto Brunner (Howard Kaminsky and James Van Horn Melton, eds. and trans.).
Land and Lordship: Structures of Governance in Medieval Austria. 1992

Robert I. Burns, S.J., ed. *Emperor of Culture: Alfonso X the Learned of Castile and
His Thirteenth-Century Renaissance.* 1990

David Burr. *Olivi and Franciscan Poverty: The Origins of the* Usus Pauper *Controversy.*
1989

David Burr. *Olivi's Peaceable Kingdom: A Reading of the Apocalypse Commentary.* 1993

Thomas Cable. *The English Alliterative Tradition.* 1991

Anthony K. Cassell and Victoria Kirkham, eds. and trans. *Diana's Hunt/Caccia di Diana: Boccaccio's First Fiction*. 1991

John C. Cavadini. *The Last Christology of the West: Adoptionism in Spain and Gaul, 785–820*. 1993

Brigitte Cazelles. *The Lady as Saint: A Collection of French Hagiographic Romances of the Thirteenth Century*. 1991

Karen Cherewatuk and Ulrike Wiethaus, eds. *Dear Sister: Medieval Women and the Epistolary Genre*. 1993

Anne L. Clark. *Elisabeth of Schönau: A Twelfth-Century Visionary*. 1992

Willene B. Clark and Meradith T. McMunn, eds. *Beasts and Birds of the Middle Ages: The Bestiary and Its Legacy*. 1989

Richard C. Dales. *The Scientific Achievement of the Middle Ages*. 1973

Charles T. Davis. *Dante's Italy and Other Essays*. 1984

William J. Dohar. *The Black Death and Pastoral Leadership: The Diocese of Hereford in the Fourteenth Century*. 1994

Katherine Fischer Drew, trans. *The Burgundian Code*. 1972

Katherine Fischer Drew, trans. *The Laws of the Salian Franks*. 1991

Katherine Fischer Drew, trans. *The Lombard Laws*. 1973

Nancy Edwards. *The Archaeology of Early Medieval Ireland*. 1990

Richard K. Emmerson and Ronald B. Herzman. *The Apocalyptic Imagination in Medieval Literature*. 1992

Theodore Evergates. *Feudal Society in Medieval France: Documents from the County of Champagne*. 1993

Felipe Fernández-Armesto. *Before Columbus: Exploration and Colonization from the Mediterranean to the Atlantic, 1229–1492*. 1987

Jerold C. Frakes. *Brides and Doom: Gender, Property, and Power in Medieval German Women's Epic*. 1994

R. D. Fulk. *A History of Old English Meter*. 1992

Patrick J. Geary. *Aristocracy in Provence: The Rhône Basin at the Dawn of the Carolingian Age*. 1985

Peter Heath. *Allegory and Philosophy in Avicenna (Ibn Sînâ), with a Translation of the Book of the Prophet Muḥammad's Ascent to Heaven*. 1992

J. N. Hillgarth, ed. *Christianity and Paganism, 350–750: The Conversion of Western Europe*. 1986

Richard C. Hoffmann. *Land, Liberties, and Lordship in a Late Medieval Countryside: Agrarian Structures and Change in the Duchy of Wrocław*. 1990

Robert Hollander. *Boccaccio's Last Fiction: Il Corbaccio*. 1988

John Y. B. Hood. *Aquinas and the Jews*. 1995

Edward B. Irving, Jr. *Rereading* Beowulf. 1989

Richard A. Jackson, ed. Ordines Coronationis Franciae: *Texts and Ordines for the Coronation of Frankish and French Kings and Queens in the Middle Ages*, Vol. I. 1995

C. Stephen Jaeger. *The Envy of Angels: Cathedral Schools and Social Ideals in Medieval Europe, 950–1200*. 1994

C. Stephen Jaeger. *The Origins of Courtliness: Civilizing Trends and the Formation of Courtly Ideals, 939–1210*. 1985

Donald J. Kagay, trans. *The Ustages of Barcelona: The Fundamental Law of Catalonia.* 1994

Richard Kay. *Dante's Christian Astrology.* 1994

Ellen E. Kittell. *From Ad Hoc to Routine: A Case Study in Medieval Bureaucracy.* 1991

Alan C. Kors and Edward Peters, eds. *Witchcraft in Europe, 1100–1700: A Documentary History.* 1972

Barbara M. Kreutz. *Before the Normans: Southern Italy in the Ninth and Tenth Centuries.* 1992

Michael P. Kuczynski. *Prophetic Song: The Psalms as Moral Discourse in Late Medieval England.* 1995

E. Ann Matter. *The Voice of My Beloved: The Song of Songs in Western Medieval Christianity.* 1990

Shannon McSheffrey. *Gender and Heresy: Women and Men in Lollard Communities, 1420–1530.*

A. J. Minnis. *Medieval Theory of Authorship.* 1988

Lawrence Nees. *A Tainted Mantle: Hercules and the Classical Tradition at the Carolingian Court.* 1991

Lynn H. Nelson, trans. *The Chronicle of San Juan de la Peña: A Fourteenth-Century Official History of the Crown of Aragon.* 1991

Barbara Newman. *From Virile Woman to WomanChrist: Studies in Medieval Religion and Literature.* 1995

Joseph F. O'Callaghan. *The Learned King: The Reign of Alfonso X of Castile.* 1993

Odo of Tournai (Irven M. Resnick, trans.). *Two Theological Treatises:* On Original Sin *and* A Disputation with the Jew, Leo, Concerning the Advent of Christ, the Son of God. 1994

David M. Olster. *Roman Defeat, Christian Response, and the Literary Construction of the Jew.* 1994

William D. Paden, ed. *The Voice of the Trobairitz: Perspectives on the Women Troubadours.* 1989

Edward Peters. *The Magician, the Witch, and the Law.* 1982

Edward Peters, ed. *Christian Society and the Crusades, 1198–1229: Sources in Translation, including* The Capture of Damietta *by Oliver of Paderborn.* 1971

Edward Peters, ed. *The First Crusade: The* Chronicle of Fulcher of Chartres *and Other Source Materials.* 1971

Edward Peters, ed. *Heresy and Authority in Medieval Europe.* 1980

James M. Powell. *Albertanus of Brescia: The Pursuit of Happiness in the Early Thirteenth Century.* 1992

James M. Powell. *Anatomy of a Crusade, 1213–1221.* 1986

Susan A. Rabe. *Faith, Art, and Politics at Saint-Riquier: The Symbolic Vision of Angilbert.* 1995

Jean Renart (Patricia Terry and Nancy Vine Durling, trans.). *The Romance of the Rose or Guillaume de Dole.* 1993

Michael Resler, trans. Erec *by Hartmann von Aue.* 1987

Pierre Riché (Michael Idomir Allen, trans.). *The Carolingians: A Family Who Forged Europe.* 1993

Pierre Riché (Jo Ann McNamara, trans.). *Daily Life in the World of Charlemagne.* 1978

Jonathan Riley-Smith. *The First Crusade and the Idea of Crusading.* 1986

Joel T. Rosenthal. *Patriarchy and Families of Privilege in Fifteenth-Century England.* 1991

Teofilo F. Ruiz. *Crisis and Continuity: Land and Town in Late Medieval Castile.* 1994

James A. Rushing, Jr. *Images of Adventure: Ywain in the Visual Arts.* 1995

James A. Schultz. *The Knowledge of Childhood in the German Middle Ages 1100–1350.* 1995

Pamela Sheingorn, ed. and trans. *The Book of Sainte Foy.* 1995

Robin Chapman Stacey. *The Road to Judgment: From Custom to Court in Medieval Ireland and Wales.* 1994

Sarah Stanbury. *Seeing the* Gawain-*Poet: Description and the Act of Perception.* 1992

Robert D. Stevick. *The Earliest Irish and English Bookarts: Visual and Poetic Forms Before A.D. 1000.* 1994

Thomas C. Stillinger. *The Song of Troilus: Lyric Authority in the Medieval Book.* 1992

Susan Mosher Stuard. *A State of Deference: Ragusa/Dubrovnik in the Medieval Centuries.* 1992

Susan Mosher Stuard, ed. *Women in Medieval History and Historiography.* 1987

Susan Mosher Stuard, ed. *Women in Medieval Society.* 1976

Jonathan Sumption. *The Hundred Years War: Trial by Battle.* 1992

Ronald E. Surtz. *Writing Women in Late Medieval and Early Modern Spain: The Mothers of Saint Teresa of Avila.* 1995

Del Sweeney, ed. *Agriculture in the Middle Ages: Technology, Practice, and Representation.* 1995

William H. TeBrake. *A Plague of Insurrection: Popular Politics and Peasant Revolt in Flanders, 1323–1328.* 1993

Patricia Terry, trans. *Poems of the Elder Edda.* 1990

Hugh M. Thomas. *Vassals, Heiresses, Crusaders, and Thugs: The Gentry of Angevin Yorkshire, 1154–1216.* 1993

Mary F. Wack. *Lovesickness in the Middle Ages: The* Viaticum *and Its Commentaries.* 1990

Benedicta Ward. *Miracles and the Medieval Mind: Theory, Record, and Event, 1000–1215.* 1982

Suzanne Fonay Wemple. *Women in Frankish Society: Marriage and the Cloister, 500–900.* 1981

Kenneth Baxter Wolf. *Making History: The Normans and Their Historians in Eleventh-Century Italy.* 1995

Jan M. Ziolkowski. *Talking Animals: Medieval Latin Beast Poetry, 750–1150.* 1993

This book has been set in Linotron Galliard. Galliard was designed for Mergenthaler in 1978 by Matthew Carter. Galliard retains many of the features of a sixteenth-century typeface cut by Robert Granjon but has some modifications that give it a more contemporary look.

Printed on acid-free paper.